MINORITY EDUCATION
AND CASTE

The American System
in Cross-Cultural Perspective

**Carnegie Council
on Children Publications**

Published by Academic Press

Child Care in the Family: A Review of Research and Some Propositions for Policy by Alison Clarke-Stewart (Fall, 1977)

Minority Education and Caste: The American System in Cross-Cultural Perspective by John U. Ogbu (Winter, 1978)

Handicapped Children in America (tentative title) by John Gliedman and William Roth (Fall, 1978)

Published by Harcourt Brace Jovanovich*

All Our Children: The American Family Under Pressure by Kenneth Keniston and the Carnegie Council on Children (Fall, 1977)

Small Futures: Inequality, Children and the Failure of Liberal Reform by Richard H. de Lone and the Carnegie Council on Children (Spring, 1978)

Growing Up American by Joan Costello, Phyllis LaFarge, and the Carnegie Council on Children (Fall, 1978)

*Harcourt Brace Jovanovich, Publishers
757 Third Avenue, New York, New York 10017

MINORITY EDUCATION AND CASTE

The American System in Cross-Cultural Perspective

JOHN U. OGBU

Department of Anthropology
University of California, Berkeley
Berkeley, California

ACADEMIC PRESS
New York   San Francisco   London
A Subsidiary of Harcourt Brace Jovanovich, Publishers

The writing of this book was made possible by
funds granted by Carnegie Corporation of New York
for the Carnegie Council on Children. The
statements made and views expressed are solely
the responsibility of the author.

ACADEMIC PRESS, INC.
111 Fifth Avenue, New York, New York 10003

United Kingdom Edition published by
ACADEMIC PRESS, INC. (LONDON) LTD.
24/28 Oval Road, London NW1

Library of Congress Cataloging in Publication Data

Ogbu, John U.
    Minority education and caste.

    Bibliography: p.
    Includes index.
    1. Minorities--Education--United States.
2. Intercultural education--United States.
I. Title.
LC3731.035   371.9'7   77-82419
ISBN 0-12-524250-6

PRINTED IN THE UNITED STATES OF AMERICA

Carnegie Council on Children

The Carnegie Council on Children was established in 1972 by the educational foundation known as Carnegie Corporation of New York to undertake a five-year investigation of what American society is doing to and for children, and what government, business, and individuals can do to protect and support family life. An independent study group, the Council is headed by Kenneth Keniston, the psychologist noted for his studies of dissenting youth and social change, and consists of individuals whose professional interests range from education and medicine to law and economics. *Minority Education and Caste* is one of several works done under the Council's sponsorship.

Members of the Carnegie Council on Children

To my wife, Ada,
a new immigrant minority

and

To all castelike minorities
in their struggle
to achieve complete
equality of opportunity

Contents

III   POLICY IMPLICATIONS

Foreword

In 1944, Gunnar Myrdal's *An American Dilemma* identified the gap between the creed of equality and the fact of racial inequality as the central contradiction in American life. Over the ensuing years, Myrdal's work shaped the thinking that led to the school desegregation decision of *Brown* v. *Board of Education,* and to the effort—still painfully far from complete—to move the United States toward its egalitarian ideal.

This book by John Ogbu is in the same tradition and deserves the same influence. Ogbu forces us to cast off the ideological blinders by which we rationalize the persistent inequities of our social system, and makes us confront the fact that ours remains in a real sense a caste society.

The evidence from which Ogbu starts is well known. Of all American children, blacks and certain other minorities live in conditions the most incompatible with our public ideals. By every standard of harm, these are the most endangered children in our society: the most likely to die at birth, to be malnourished thereafter, to suffer extreme material deprivation, to do poorly in school, and to end up in lowly positions as adults. Although our national creed insists that all children should have equal chances, from the start the deck is systematically stacked against some of them.

About 150 years ago, Americans began to place their faith in education as a great equalizer. Because we like to believe that adult position is determined by individual ability and skill, we have insisted that by schooling all children in the same skills, we can achieve our goal of equity. Yet more than a century of compulsory, free public education has not succeeded in erasing the contradiction between creed and reality. Black, native American, and Hispanic children continue not only to suffer the greatest harms as children, but to be the least successful in school and in our adult society.

The perspective from which we traditionally define the problem of subordinate minorities logically permits only two possible explanations for this lack of success: Either there is something wrong with our schools, or there is something wrong with minority children. The War on Poverty of the 1960s chose both explanations. The extraordinary deficiencies in the schooling offered minorities were rediscovered, with attendant efforts to "equalize inputs" for all children. At the same time, it was widely accepted that minority children themselves arrived in school with environmentally caused "deficits" stemming from their "cultural deprivation," "lack of verbal stimulation," and "inadequate home environments." Thus, the major thrusts of the War on Poverty concerning children were in areas like compensatory education, equalization of school resources, and preschool programs.

Yet these programs did not basically alter the facts they were designed to change. The performance of most nonwhite children in school and on IQ tests continues to lag behind that of white children. And the gap between the adult status of whites and subordinate minority group members has closed infinitesimally if at all. Many observers have drawn the conclusion that the true cause of this "failure" lies in even deeper flaws in the children or their family environments.

Starting from the apparently technical dispute over how much relative weight should be given to genetic and how much to environmental factors in explaining the lower IQ scores, Ogbu argues that both sides are wrong because both accept the entrenched view that nonwhite children's actual performance determines the adult position they will achieve. The real relationship, Ogbu shows, works in the opposite direction.

Furthermore, this situation is far from being merely an American problem. It characterizes many industrial societies like Japan, Israel, and New Zealand (three examples Ogbu analyzes at length) where castelike minorities, whatever their race, suffer the same kinds of problems in school as well as the same kinds of barriers to full functioning in adulthood. And in most of these countries, Ogbu finds, this contradiction is dealt with ideologically by the "American" tactic of finding the children of subordinate groups deficient in family background, heredity, or both. Thus, programs to help low-caste children usually aim at correcting deficits that are perceived to be in the children rather than at changing the caste system that ultimately causes both their inferior school performance and their inferior adult status.

Ogbu's argument is structural rather than psychological. He is as impatient with theories that blame only the psychological racism of whites for the exclusion of blacks as he is with theories that fault blacks for their "deficient" ego structure. Generations of teachers have encouraged black children to be "realistic" about their "place in society" not necessarily because these teachers are die-hard bigots, but because the school's explicit function is to prepare children for their adult roles.

Thus when Ogbu turns to proposals for change, he argues that only structural change can eliminate the caste system which, among its many effects, creates the discrepancy between groups in school performance. Improvement of educational opportunities, compensatory programs, and the like are necessary but not sufficient for dismantling caste structure. Equal educational opportunity will be effective only if there is comparable posteducational opportunity to compete for adult roles on equal terms. From de Tocqueville to Myrdal, the most perceptive views of American life have often come from non-Americans. John Ogbu, an anthropologist born and educated in Nigeria who has now spent over 15 years studying the United States, brings to his analysis of schooling and racial stratification this same sharp perspective. His work is more than a contribution to the heredity—environment controversy and more even than a study of caste and education: Above all, it reveals the flaws in the lens through which we view ourselves as Americans and thus helps us see ourselves as we are.

Kenneth Keniston
CHAIRMAN AND DIRECTOR,
CARNEGIE COUNCIL ON CHILDREN

Acknowledgments

This book was written while I was a staff member of the Carnegie Council on Children in New Haven, Connecticut, where I worked with others to evaluate the situation of children in America and to develop proposed policies for improving their lives.

I did some early work on the cross-cultural aspects of the work with the generous support of the Institute of International Studies of the University of California, Berkeley, which in 1972 funded an exploratory study of minority education in Great Britain, New Zealand, India, Israel, and Japan. A grant from the Institute of Race and Community Relations (now called the Institute for the Study of Social Change) of the University of California, Berkeley, supported my early efforts to compare the educational experiences of immigrant and nonimmigrant minorities in California. The University of California faculty research fund also helped, in particular by giving me a summer faculty fellowship in 1972 which enabled me to probe into the historical and structural forces affecting black education in the United States. Both the university administration and my colleagues in the Anthropology Department generously gave me a two-year leave of absence, from 1973 to

1975, to work on the book as a staff member of the Carnegie Council on Children.

I received assistance, inspiration, and criticism from many throughout the process of developing the book. Although I cannot acknowledge the help of everyone, I must mention a few to whom I am particularly grateful. I especially wish to thank my senior colleague at Berkeley and a member of the Carnegie Council, Laura Nader, who introduced me to the Council and who has inspired, encouraged, and assisted me through many phases of the work. I also wish to thank Kenneth Keniston, the director of the Council, and various Council members, especially Marian Wright Edelman and Faustina Solis, and my colleagues on the staff of the Council, for their valuable comments and encouragement. Valerie Estes of the University of California, Berkeley, and Christine Buckley, Debora Chernoff, Francesca Gobbo, and Georgia Goeters of the Carnegie Council on Children at Yale provided valuable research assistance. Invaluable editorial help came from Grace Buzaljko of the University of California, Berkeley, and from Laura Eby and Jill Kneerim of the Carnegie Council on Children. The typing was done by Margaret Jackewicz, Sheila Meyers, Sylvia Rifkin, and others of the Council's offices at Yale and in New York. Finally I wish to thank Leah E. Andersen, Ethel Himberg, and Sylvia Rifkin for their very special help and encouragement.

Quotation Credits

Introduction

Inequality exists in almost every society. Seldom, however, is it confined to inequality among individuals. Most often it is groups within a society that are regarded as unequal because they belong to different races or castes or different ethnic, language, or religious groups. In some traditional societies, group inequality is regarded as "natural," especially by the members of the dominant group. Often there are myths and legends that rationalize this inequality; sometimes there are also legal and moral sanctions to keep things the way they are.

Group inequality exists in modern industrial societies, although in only a few instances, as in South Africa, is it sanctioned by law. Most modern societies claim that they are committed to equality and freedom for all their citizens. The persisting inequality among different segments of modern societies in the face of an egalitarian and libertarian ideology is therefore a source of embarrassment, especially for the liberal elites of the dominant groups.

Most of these societies have introduced formal education as a means of eliminating inequality based on membership in the particular group into which one is born. Education is provided for all children so that they will learn similar skills for participation in adult life. In this

1

way, modern societies hope to transform inequality based on birth-ascribed status to inequality based on ability or lack of ability. For many groups, this transformation has not taken place, leading some to wonder about the real causes of inequality between groups.

Nowhere has this problem—the causes of group inequality—been more deeply probed and hotly debated than in the United States. Here the social and economic inequality or gap between blacks and whites persists, even though Americans espouse the principles of equality and freedom, and even though public education is believed to be a channel for individual self-improvement. The gap in education is just as wide as the gap in socioeconomic status, and equally persistent. In recent years, many Americans have come to perceive the educational gap as the cause of the socioeconomic gap. In recent years too, the question about the causes of black–white differences in school performance has become a significant and controversial issue because various educational programs introduced in the 1960s, especially compensatory education, have apparently failed to equalize the school performance of the two races.

It seems to me that certain assumptions which formed the basis of these programs are a major reason for their failure. The social scientists who have tried to explain why black children do not perform as well in school as white children, and upon whose theories many of these programs are based, appear to have reached the inadequate conclusion that there are three major factors which determine the way all children perform in school: home environment, school environment, and heredity. These scholars disagree among themselves about the relative weight of each of these factors, but their theories rarely take into account the most obvious and common-sense aspect of education, namely, that education (the attitudes, knowledge, and skills acquired by pupils in school) is directly related to typical adult roles in the contemporary postschool world. Consequently, these scholars have never seriously posed the question about how the different positions traditionally assigned to blacks and whites in American society might affect the school performance of each race. On the whole, the field of minority education, especially black education, is marred by theoretical confusion, barren methodology, politics, and lack of emotional detachment. It is not surprising that many policies and programs generated in this context are unsuccessful in reducing the school performance gap between blacks and whites.

The research for the present book was begun in 1970, specifically in response to Arthur R. Jensen's hypothesis (1969) that various remedial educational programs had failed to close the school performance gap between black and white children because the two groups differ in heredity. At that time I felt that Jensen was wrong, although not for the reasons given by his critics, who often sought to substitute simplistic environmental explanations for Jensen's genetic theory. It seemed to me that although the causes of the lower school performance of black children lay largely within the American caste system or system of racial stratification, many American social scientists had never examined the problem from that point of view. I wanted therefore to provide an alternative explanation of the problem by analyzing black education in the context of the American system of racial stratification both diachronically and synchronically. I also wanted to show that a school performance gap similar to that found between blacks and whites in America could be found in other societies with similar kinds of social stratification, based on birth-ascribed status rather than achievement criteria, irrespective of the racial affiliation of the groups involved.

For this purpose, I chose to study three societies where both the dominant and the minority groups belong to the same "race," namely: India (the high castes and the scheduled castes), Israel (the Ashkenazim and the Oriental Jews), and Japan (the Ippan and the Buraku outcastes); and three societies where the dominant and the minority groups belong to different "races," namely: Britain (the Anglo-British and the West Indians), New Zealand (the Pakeha and the Maori) and the United States (whites and black). Although the data available for such a study in a given country are only as good as the stage of development of the social sciences there, some generalizations are possible on the basis of available evidence.[1] First, the gap between the dominant and the minority groups in school performance is evident in each society, irrespective of its racial composition. Second, nearly all these societies are more or less stratified along birth-ascribed status, so that education does not necessarily serve the dominant and minority groups equally effectively as a vehicle of social mobility. Yet egalitarian ideology dominates, and often justifies, the education systems of these societies.

---

[1]The term *race* as used throughout this book does not denote its biological meaning of subspecies defined by gene frequencies (see Loehlin et al. 1975:13). It is, instead, used in the sense of the way a group of people defines itself or is defined by others as being different from other human groups because of some *assumed* innate and physical characteristics. More specifically, I am using the term *race* to correspond to the definition given to it by the societies included in this study. For example, the Israelis define all Jews in Israel as members of the "Jewish race," regardless of whether they come from England, Russia, Yemen, China, Japan, or Oceania. Therefore Oriental Jews in Israel are not classified by themselves or other Israelis as belonging to a separate race. In the United States, Mexican-Americans are classified as belonging to the Caucasian or white race, although the majority of them are mestizos or offspring of Indian and white mating, and many are offspring of Indian and black mating. On the other hand, all offsprings of black and white mating in the United States are classified as belonging to the black race (see van den Berghe 1967:9–10; Nava 1970).

This study is therefore an attempt to go beyond the present rhetoric in the United States in order to examine the way in which the position of blacks in the American system of caste or racial stratification contributes to their lower school performance. This book is also an effort to understand the myths and stereotypes that support the caste system and how they are translated into practices by school personnel. It further probes into the responses of the minority-group people themselves.

The evidence uncovered in the study strongly suggests that blacks and similarly placed minority groups often reject academic competition with members of the dominant groups. The reason they fail to work hard in school seems to be, in part, that such efforts have not traditionally benefited members of their group: In terms of ability and training, they have generally received lower social and occupational rewards when compared to members of the dominant group. In general, castelike societies and their schools, as well as the minorities themselves, all contribute to the lower school performance of minority-group children. Lower school performance and lower educational attainment are functionally adaptive to minorities' ascribed inferior social and occupational positions in adult life. As this study shows, blacks, for example, do not occupy inferior social and occupational positions in American society because they lack the educational qualifications for more desirable ones; rather, the exclusion of blacks from the more desirable social and occupational positions because of their castelike status is the major source of their academic retardation.

Another consequence of the traditional exclusion of blacks from the more desirable social and occupational positions in American society is only partially explored in the present study. Specifically, the question has to do with the consequence of generations of exclusion and segregation on the patterns of linguistic, cognitive, and motivational skills blacks have developed. A full and more systematic study of this problem is crucial to the final resolution of the debate concerning black–white differences in "intelligence." I do not think that differences between blacks and whites in cognitive and other skills can be explained in terms of black resistance to acculturation, the failure of black parents to train their children as white middle-class parents do, or to biological differences between the two races.

A more plausible but as yet unexplored hypothesis is that all these barriers have prevented blacks from developing the patterns of skills characteristic of the white group. What evidence there is suggests, for instance, that blacks would have developed their potentials for linguistic, cognitive, motivational, and other school-related skills to the same extent and in the same pattern (e.g., similar English dialects) if they had enjoyed the same opportunities as whites to be educated, to qualify for more desirable social and occupational positions, to occupy such positions when they qualified for them, to derive adequate financial and other rewards from their educations and jobs, to live where they desired and could afford, and to be evaluated as individuals on the basis of training and ability. There is a reciprocal relationship between the opportunities open to blacks (or to any other groups) in American society and the pattern of linguistic, cognitive, motivational, and other school-related skills they develop. Since American society has not provided blacks and whites with equal opportunities in adult life, an important problem for research is the consequence of generations of such inequality on the competence or skills characteristic of the two races. In my view, the efforts of American educational psychologists to explain black–white differences in terms of differences in genetic makeup or family socialization are quite misplaced.

The present study points to the need for studying the problems of minority education cross-culturally. One way to test many of the prevailing hypotheses, including Jensen's and those of his critics, is to compare both the school performance of majority and minority groups in different societies and the school performance of the same minority groups in different situations. There are some indications that minority groups which occupy positions similar to that of blacks in American society tend to do better in school outside their places of origin, in situations where they do not perceive their ascribed status as the basis for their social and occupational roles. Later in this study, I describe the contrasting experiences of the Buraku outcastes in Japan and the United States, and the West Indians in Britain (their "mother country") and the United States (Chapters 8 and 11).

The present study also suggests the need to redefine the concept of equality of educational opportunity as a first step toward developing sound policies and programs that will eliminate academic retardation among blacks and similarly situated minorities. As presently used, the concept refers only to equality of access to school resources and equality of school performance. I propose that the concept should be redefined to include equality of access to postschool rewards of formal education. The implication of this more complete definition is that efforts to improve black performance will undoubtedly go beyond prevailing approaches of individual rehabilitation and school reforms. Compensatory education, school integration, increased per-pupil expenditure, better trained school personnel, and allied reforms will probably reduce black academic retardation to some degree. But of greater significance in achieving this goal is the effort to remove all the barriers against black youths and adults in postschool society.

At the moment, there are parallel programs focusing on academic retardation and barriers in postschool society, but the link between the two areas is inadequately understood and much misrepresented. It is assumed, for instance, that improving black school performance and educational attainment is a prerequisite to increasing effectively their opportunities in society. The present study suggests that the reverse may be the case, so that there is a need to plan the policies and programs dealing with social and occupational barriers in terms of their possible effects on black school performance.

A word is necessary about the treatment in this book of such controversial issues as compensatory education and school integration. *This book does not conclude that compensatory education is irrelevant to any efforts to eliminate black academic retardation.* It does, however, reject the assumptions upon which current compensatory educational programs are based: that such programs are designed to "compensate" for the "deficits" in skills that black children take to school and that such "deficits" are the result of inadequate training at home or of cultural deprivation. Furthermore, the book is concerned primarily with the degree to which compensatory education programs have succeeded in achieving their central goal of raising the cognitive skills and scholastic performance of black children. It does not focus on other worthy goals of compensatory education. This is also true of its treatment of school integration. *I am concerned with the impact of school integration on black academic achievement and not with its social, constitutional, political, or ethical justifications.*

This is not a study of what is wrong with the American educational system in general. Although there surely are many things wrong with the system, my central concern is with why blacks are performing less well than whites. More specifically, the questions I attempt to answer throughout this book are these: Why do blacks perform less well than whites in school, whether they attend the same schools or different schools, either good or bad? And why do blacks often terminate their schooling earlier than whites?

Finally, this study has not dealt with the more general problem of social mobility of the lower class in the United States. The large body of literature on this subject suggests that upward social mobility is difficult for the lower classes of all racial and ethnic groups. The most common explanation of this relative lack of upward mobility is that lower-class children are socialized into norms and cognitive styles which impede their ability to achieve middle-class positions through formal education (see Perrucci 1967; Squibbs 1975; and Van Zeyl 1974 for extensive reviews of the literature). As Van Zeyl notes, however, there are some serious reservations about the assumed lack of upward mobility of the lower class and its explanation in terms of differential socialization of norms and cognitive styles. He points out for instance, that statistical studies of social mobility tend to show that "a large number of the incumbents of any particular class level were recruited from other levels" and says that many studies in industrialized countries generally show "consistent correlations of .4 to .5 between father's and son's occupations [Van Zeyl 1974:23]." This does not necessarily lead to the elimination of class boundaries because the system of unequal distribution of psychological, material, and social rewards persists in these societies. A large lower class may thus co-exist with a relatively high rate of social mobility, although this lower class is not necessarily composed of descendants of the same group of people from generation to generation (Van Zeyl 1974: 18–19). The inadequacy of the differential socialization hypothesis explanation of the lack of upward mobility of the lower class also stems from the fact that it does not attempt to explain how upwardly and downwardly mobile individuals acquire the norms and cognitive styles of different strata (Van Zeyl 1974:24).

My own reason for excluding from the present work a discussion of the general problem of upward social mobility of the lower class in the United States is based on a different theoretical reservation, namely, a suspicion that social mobility problems associated with class stratification are not necessarily the same as those associated with racial or other types of stratification. In this book *I am dealing with a system of social stratification which, unlike that of class stratification, is based on ascribed rather than achieved criteria.* In the United States racial stratification co-exists with class stratification and each is characterized by a distinct rate, pattern, and strategy of social mobility. Moreover, black and white social classes exist *within* stratified racial groups, so that their social mobility is influenced among other things by racial stratification and is not necessarily the same or equal.

In the first chapter of the book I describe the differences between class stratification and racial stratification. Here I note the following reasons for restricting the study to the problem of social mobility among blacks. First, unlike the more or less amorphous lower class in America, blacks are both a publicly recognized and clearly bounded group with a high degree of self-awareness. Second, upward social mobility has generally been more difficult for blacks, regardless of their social class background, than for the general population (see Duncan

1975; Ross, A. M. 1973; Siegel 1969; Thernstrom 1973; U.S. Commission on Civil Rights 1968). Third, the relative lack of upward mobility among blacks is largely due to their subordinate racial status, and not to their being socialized into different norms and cognitive styles; nor is it largely due to their lack of education (see Duncan 1975:180–181). As I show later in the book, differences between blacks and whites in occupation, income, and unemployment rates tend to increase with the increase in black educational attainment (see also Killingsworth 1969; Miller, H. P. 1971:183). Fourth, regardless of their class position, blacks tend to perceive their opportunities for social mobility as much more limited than is the case for the general population (see Rytina, Form, and Pease 1970). Fifth, the subordinate racial status of blacks, their collective identity and their perceptions of their opportunity structure have the combined effect of differentiating their strategies for social mobility in some significant ways from those strategies employed by the general population. Specifically, blacks tend to emphasize the importance of collective (e.g., protest, boycotts, and legislative and legal) actions over or in addition to individual strategies for achieving social mobility. For example, the increasing gap in upward mobility rates of the more educated blacks and whites is not attributed by blacks to individual failure and they do not see its remedy in terms of individual action. It is perceived as a collective problem requiring collective efforts to correct. Finally, class differences do not account for most of the observed differences in the school performance of black and white children (U.S. Senate Select Committee 1972:159–160). Class is an important explanatory variable when comparison is made between lower-class blacks and middle-class whites. But when the comparison is between blacks and whites of the same social class background it is no longer meaningful to explain the differences in school performance in terms of differential class socialization of norms and cognitive styles. The alternative explanation I propose in this book is based on the hypothesis that racial stratification, as distinct from class stratification, generates and sustains patterns of school performance compatible with the educational requirements of the social and occupational roles permitted to the component racial groups and the mode of social mobility characteristic of the system.

The Plan of the Book

The book is divided into three parts. Part I deals with black education in the United States. Conceptually, it deals with the relationship between caste and education and how this relationship functions in the United States. The first chapter outlines what I see as the role of education in preparing children for adult life in their society and how this role is modified in a society with a castelike system of social stratification. The chapter concludes with a thesis about the school performance of castelike minorities that underlies the rest of the book. The second chapter reviews other explanations of the lower school performance of black Americans; Chapter 3 deals with remedial programs based on these explanations. Chapters 4 and 5, respectively, examine the impact of the American system of racial castes on black access to education and to postschool rewards. In Chapter 6, I analyze black school performance as an adaptation. The last chapter of Part I, Chapter 7, briefly surveys the education of American Indians, Mexican-Americans, and mainland Puerto Ricans within the analytical framework of the book.

Part II presents case studies of castelike minority education in other societies. These case studies are intended to illustrate the thesis enunciated in Chapter 1: Chapters 8, 9, 10, 11, and 12 describe the education of castelike minorities in Great Britain, New Zealand, India, Japan, and Israel respectively.

Part II ends with a comparison of and some generalizations about the educational experiences of castelike minorities in the six societies, including the United States.

Part III, the final chapter of the book, considers the policy implications of the alternative explanation of black school performance developed throughout the book.

I

CASTE AND EDUCATION IN THE UNITED STATES

The decade of the 1960s will long be remembered as the era of important social reforms intended to improve the social and economic status of black Americans and other minorities. The War on Poverty was one such reform, and its particular significance for this study was the special role assigned to education. In order to wage a successful campaign against poverty, it was necessary first to explain why poverty existed. There subsequently evolved the theory of the poverty cycle in which inadequate education was seen as perhaps the most important causal link. It was asserted that people were poor because they lacked formal education or skills for better paying jobs than they currently could get. And it was further asserted that blacks were disproportionately represented among the poor because they were not as well educated as whites. Thus the strategy for reducing black poverty was to give blacks more and better education. But to do so also required an explanation of why blacks were less well educated and why black children performed less well in school than white children. The latter task resulted in a variety of theories, which then formed the bases of various compensatory and allied educational programs to boost the cognitive skills and academic achievements of black children. The

programs growing out of this venture have not been particularly successful in this central objective.

Chapter 1 outlines my view of the relationship between education
and adult roles and how this may relate to school learning as well as to
socialization in the family and community. I first describe the model
for a relatively homogeneous society and then show how it is modified
in a society stratified along caste lines. This chapter contains other
ideas essential for understanding the rest of the book. Thus I describe
different types of minority groups and show how they relate to formal
education in a given society. Job ceiling—a key concept throughout
this book—is next defined and its implications for the development of
school related skills examined. I then touch upon the question of education as an agent of status equalization and show how this functions
under two different principles of role-recruitment in changing caste or
castelike societies. Tying all these together, the chapter ends with the
central thesis of the book concerning the lower school performance of
castelike minorities such as black Americans.

Chapters 2 and 3 examine other theories of black school failure
and the programs developed to eliminate that failure. Chapter 2 describes and criticizes five main types of explanations of why blacks do
less well in school than whites. Chapter 3 describes and criticizes the
solutions arising from the theoretical assumptions dealt with in Chapter 2, focusing on school integration and compensatory education.

In Chapter 4, I present a historical survey of black education in the
United States and describe some of the subtle mechanisms through
which the public schools continue to reinforce black school failure. It
may seem pointless to some readers for me to document the fact that
blacks have traditionally been offered inferior education. The
documentation is important, however, for three reasons: First, to
readers who feel that it is well known that blacks have consistently
been provided with inferior education, I want to point out that various
theories purporting to explain why blacks do not perform as well as
whites in school have generally failed to consider the possible cumulative effects of generations of such inferior education on contemporary
black school performance. But more important, I want to emphasize
that it is the status of blacks in the social, political, and occupational
realms of American society, as seen by the dominant white caste,
which determines the kind of education offered to the former. Until
very recently, the motive of black education was not to equalize black
and white status but to prepare blacks for their traditional, though
changing, roles under the system of racial castes. A third and equally

important point of the chapter is to show that from emancipation to the present almost all changes in black education have been responses to changes or anticipated changes in the social, political, and occupational status of blacks. Recognizing this fact will cast serious doubts on the argument that blacks have been held back from achieving higher social and occupational positions because of a lack of (and sometimes inferior) education. This last point is made more pertinent in Chapter 5 where I examine how American society historically rewards blacks for their education. The major focus of Chapter 5 is the degree to which, under the job ceiling, education serves blacks as a bridge to good jobs, financial remuneration, and other benefits usually associated with education in terms of the white experience.

Up to this point, my examination of black school performance deals primarily with relatively objective data on black education, especially statistics and statements of social scientists and other observers. My examination of these data suggests that three factors contribute to lower black performance in school: the inferior education blacks have been given for generations; the subtle mechanisms or devices used in school to differentiate their training from that of whites and keep their education inferior; and the job ceiling. In Chapter 6, I turn to three other factors that also contribute to lower school performance. The first has to do with the possible effects of conscious and unconscious reactions by blacks to caste barriers against them. Basically, the questions to be answered are these: Do blacks perceive the job ceiling against them? Do they see their chances for future employment and other benefits of education as limited? How do blacks relate their perception of limited opportunities for future employment and other benefits of education to their perception of schooling? How are these perceptions transmitted to black children? And how, in turn, are these perceptions expressed in the children's work at school? Of course, the influence of limited future opportunity may exist even when blacks do not consciously perceive their opportunities as limited.

Following this, I examine two other important but less obvious ways in which the job ceiling influences black response to schooling: the influence of the job ceiling on black families and black status mobility and its influence on the development of black linguistic, cognitive, and motivational skills.

The final chapter of Part I, Chapter 7, first shows that some of America's other minorities—American Indians, Mexican-Americans, and mainland Puerto Ricans—also perform more poorly than whites both in school and on various measures of "intelligence." These groups *are also castelike minorities, although not to the same degree as blacks; and of course, they differ from blacks because many of their members speak a primary language other than English. This chapter includes a brief survey of their traditional inferior education, the job ceiling against them, and their perception of schooling in relation to the job ceiling.*

Caste and Education and How They Function in the United States

Education as a Bridge to Adult Status

Implicit and explicit models of American education which guide thinking about black–white differences in school performance are quite inadequate. In these models, it seems that American social scientists are more concerned with what education ought to be rather than with what it actually is. For example, in summarizing the psychological viewpoint, Andreas (1968:23) states that the ultimate goal of the education system is to produce "life-long learners," i.e., to develop the intellectual capacities of young Americans and turn them into lovers of learning. Although American education probably has this effect, this is not its traditional goal, but rather its by-product, at least from the standpoint of individuals and American society as a whole. Those who hold the view expressed by Andreas unfortunately often hold a companion assumption—that heredity and home experiences are the major determinants of differences in school learning. Other utopian models and assumptions about American education are summarized by Pounds and Bryner (1973: 528–529).

For my purpose, a more adequate model of American education, or any education for that matter, can be developed by studying its actual function in society—its function for individuals, for segments of the society, and for society as a whole. Although social science theories affect educational policies and practices, folk beliefs or theories about education and the behavioral concomitants of such beliefs seem to provide the main basis for anthropological inquiry. For example, what are the behavioral consequences for American education of the folk belief that formal education is the channel by which desirable adult roles are achieved in American society and that more education means higher social status, more self-esteem, better employment opportunities, better jobs, and better salaries? There are strong indications that this particular belief guides both individual behavior and social policies regarding education. There are also indications that this belief is not equally shared by all segments of American society and that it does not, therefore, influence the behavior of all groups to the same degree (see Berg 1969; Blair 1971). From the standpoint of social anthropology, an adequate model of education must incorporate not only folk beliefs and practices but also the factors that determine such beliefs and practices. It is from this perspective that I now suggest a way of looking at the relationship between education and social structure and the relevance of such a model to the study of black–white differences in school performance.

A useful way to look at the relationship between education and social structure is suggested by the work of a number of scholars in the field of socialization (Aberle and Naegele 1952; Aberle 1961; Y. A. Cohen 1971; Inkeles 1955; 1968b; Kohn 1969; LeVine 1967; LeVine *et al.* 1967; Miller and Swanson 1958). Implicit, and sometimes explicit, in the work of these scholars is the notion that socialization or child training is the preparation of the child for adult life as his or her society or segment of society conceives it. That is, socialization is the process by which individuals acquire the skills (cognitive, manual, etc.), motives, knowledge, and attitudes which will enable them to perform typical social and economic roles available to adult members of their society and be fully integrated into the society.

Child training, from this perspective, is future-oriented to a large degree since, for parents to prepare their children successfully for adult life, they must have ideas about the typical roles their children will occupy as adults and the skills required to fill such roles (Aberle and Naegele 1952). Moreover, in the absence of major social upheaval, socialization is adaptive: It prepares children to compete for and successfully perform the typical adult roles in their society by transmitting the necessary motivational, cognitive, and other skills required by such roles.

Major social and economic changes result in changes in the socialization practices of parents in order to train children who will live under changed conditions. This is illustrated by Miller and Swanson's study of entrepreneurial and bureaucratic middle-class families, which shows that changes in the technoeconomic structure of American society led to changes in childrearing practices (Miller and Swanson 1958). In general, the work of these scholars shows that the socialization pattern depends on other features of the wider society such as the technology, economy, political system, and social organization in which the group participates (Aberle 1961).

Variations in opportunity structure lead to variations not only in the ways parents raise their children but also in the ways children strive to attain available roles in adult society. Cultures differ both in the criteria prescribed for actual performance of specific roles and in the prescribed methods by which individuals come to occupy such roles. Of particular interest too is that among those societies that both rank social roles or status and permit upward mobility, there are differences in prevailing systems of status mobility. Both Turner (1961) and LeVine (1967) have described polar types of status mobility systems. Turner designates these as *contest mobility* and *sponsored mobility*: Upward mobility in the contest mobility system is won in open and fair competition based on individual efforts; whereas winners in a sponsored mobility system are preselected by the established elites or their agents on the basis of some criterion other than individual effort or strategy. LeVine uses no specific terms to designate his polar types, but his discussion of the determining influence of particular types of status mobility systems on the development of achievement behavior is more germane to the present work.

LeVine postulates two alternative hypotheses to explain ethnic differences in achievement motivation in contemporary Nigeria. The first hypothesis, which focuses on differences in traditional systems of status mobility, states that a given system of status mobility determines parents' ideas about successful individuals in their society, so that parents try to raise their children to develop those qualities that are relevant to successful social mobility. He summarizes the nature of such influence as follows:

> Each system of ranked status in which mobility is possible from one status to another constitutes in effect an allocation of social rewards for some types of behavior—those which make for upward movement. These rewarded types of behavior can be and are perceived as qualities of persons, the kind of persons who are

likely to rise in a given status mobility system. Thus each type of status mobility system generates an "ideal personality type"—that is, a normatively buttressed image of the successful man, which is widely held by the population or at least those segments of it for whom mobility is possible. This image is a part of the ideology of a status sytem, and insofar as the status system is actually legitimate— that is, accepted as the right order of things by the population—adults in that population will be imbued with that ideology. The status values inherent in the system will be their values, and the normative image of the successful man will serve as their catalogue of admirable qualities to foster in those who come under their tutelage. Insofar as such encouragement is successful, ... it will result in increasing the frequency in the population of those traits regarded as facilitating status mobility [1967:17].

Alternatively, LeVine hypothesizes that differences in achievement motive (or behavior, for that matter) may not necessarily be linked to child training. Instead, as children grow up they themselves may tend to develop accurate perceptions of their chances of rising socially and the types of behavior that lead to success in the status system (1967:89). The growing child receives information about opportunities for social mobility in his or her society from "various individuals and institutions, including older members of the family, school teachers, religious instructors, books, and mass media [p. 89]." With such information, children form increasingly accurate and stable images of the system of status mobility as they approach adolescence, and these images determine the type of achievement motivation or behavior they tend to manifest.

The theme common to both hypotheses is, of course, that achievement motivation and behavior are determined to a large extent by the prevailing system of social mobility. It seems best, therefore, to regard them as part of a broader hypothesis, namely, that a given system of status mobility determines both the kinds of persons parents strive to raise their children to be and the kinds of people children themselves strive to be when they grow up.[1]

This model of socialization (child training) can usefully be applied to formal education, for whatever else education may be, from the standpoint of society (parents, teachers, and pupils) it is a preparation of children for adult life as adults in their society conceive it. In simpler

[1] I do not mean to imply here that there is a tightly nested connection between social mobility, socialization, and children's behavior. The connection may be quite subtle and complex. However, existing literature on this particular issue is of little value in determining the degree to which the three variables are connected. Most studies begin with the socialization angle of the relationship and then proceed to explain variations in social mobility and children's behavior as the consequences of socialization. What we need to balance the perspective are studies which explicitly begin with analysis of the social mobility ideologies and patterns of a given society and then go on to examine how they affect parents' values, theories, and practices of child training as well as children's self-concepts and behavior.

societies, the family and kin are primarily responsible for training children to develop those personal attributes, qualities, or skills that will enable them to perform typical social and occupational roles competently when they become adults (Gore and Desai 1967; Y. A. Cohen 1971). In modern societies, schools have largely taken over this task, but in a given society, the curriculum and instructional techniques—in short, the education system—reflect the types of personal attributes or skills future adults are expected to acquire in the course of their training in order to be competent in their future roles. If competent performance of socially valued roles requires competitive skills, if it requires punctuality in time orientation, if it requires skills for long-range planning and organizational ability, the education system will foster these skills or qualities in the society's children. The type of education a society provides for its children is fundamentally related to the solution of what the adult members of that society perceive as the social, economic, and other problems posed by their macroenvironment (Castle 1964). Castle's review of education in ancient Sparta, Athens, and Rome, as well as the traditional Jewish education, shows that education was oriented toward the adult roles valued in each society. This is still true of education in modern societies like the Soviet Union and the United States.[2]

Formal education, like socialization, is future oriented. A given society may expect its schools, for instance, to train its children to become literate, informed citizens who can participate effectively in a democracy (citizenship goal), to prepare children for the labor market (certification function), and to keep children out of the labor market until they have attained a legally specified age. It may also, at least in principle, expect its schools to provide all children with equal opportunities to participate in adult life by equipping them with similar skills. Parents may send their children to school so that, among other things, they will acquire the skills and credentials with which to compete for desirable social and economic roles when they grow up. As children become older, they too learn to associate their school activities with future goals and opportunities in adult life. Teachers and other school personnel may see their job as essentially that of preparing

[2]To an impartial observer, it is quite obvious that American education is designed to fit people into future social and occupational slots. The role of various reports on the manpower needs of the nation and similar projections in shaping the curriculum and general orientation of American schools testifies to this. These projections may lead to a "talent search" and increasing emphasis on math and science teaching, to expansion of vocational education, or to a cutback in certain areas of graduate training. Furthermore, Wilson (1972) has pointed out that the trend toward increasing specialization of instruction, increasing amounts of time devoted to each subject, the probing of the potentials of students to see if they can begin their acquisition of specialized training at earlier ages, and other changes in the public schools in the past five decades can be seen as a response to the occupational specialization of the American industrial economy.

children so that when they grow up they will be able to compete for and successfully perform typical roles in adult society. Thus the values and ideas that shape teachers' behaviors and the practices of the schools, like those which shape the behaviors of parents in their childrearing practices, are derived from features of adult society. Neither teachers nor parents, for instance, will prepare those who come under their tutelage for the roles of vassals or lords in a society which does not include vassalage and lordship in its role repertoire.

Furthermore, like socialization, formal education is greatly influenced by the existing pattern of social mobility. Thus Turner (1961) hypothesizes not only that the American system of social mobility (contest mobility) differs from the traditional British system (sponsored mobility) but also that the two systems of social mobility lead to different types of education systems. In general, it appears that for a given population the prevailing pattern of social mobility influences both the ideology and the practices of educational agents and the achievement motive and behavior of the pupils and their parents and peers; that is, the structure of opportunities in adult society determines (a) the kinds of qualities schools seek to transmit to their pupils; and (b) the kinds of qualities the pupils themselves strive to possess by the time they move into the adult world.

Two points are suggested about the relationship between the preparation of children for adult life in the home (in the broadest sense) and their preparation at school. First, both are oriented toward preparing the children for typical roles in adult society.

At home, children may learn the type of relationship to authority that facilitates good rapport with their teachers. Ability to follow directions, long attention span, success in verbal comprehension, ability to grasp relationships between things, and ability to do schoolwork with diligence may also be influenced by home training. However, *families are likely to emphasize these things in their childrearing only if they lead to success in school and success in school leads to rewards in adult life in terms of jobs, income, prestige, and the like.* Similarly, the schools are likely to emphasize this training if those who are successful in learning the skills they teach are highly rewarded by society. Thus societal rewards reinforce the efforts of the schools, and these in turn are reinforced by the preparation children receive at home.[3] Second, both training at home and training in school are greatly influenced by existing patterns or status mobility.

[3]This can be illustrated with respect to caste differences in reading skills. See p. 212.

In some situations, however, this complementary relationship does not exist—for example, among recent immigrants to the United States and among many people in the developing nations of Africa and Asia to whom Western education has only recently been introduced. Among such people, families may continue to prepare children for traditional roles in their communities, whereas formal education tends to prepare them for nontraditional roles recently introduced or encountered from outside. This situation generates many educational problems, which have been well documented in several studies (Cole *et al.* 1971; Gay and Cole 1967; Grindal 1972).

For both recent immigrants and people in the developing nations of Africa and Asia, educational problems, which are primarily generated by culture contact and social change, may be only temporary. In these situations, the adaptive relationship between home training and roles in adult life is disturbed by the introduction of (*a*) some nontraditional roles which require a different kind of training from that provided by the family; and (*b*) a formal education not designed to train people for the available adult roles, which demands a kind of learning different from the kind people are accustomed to. But discontinuities created by these developments may be only temporary, so that children eventually come to acquire effectively what they have to learn through formal education. This transition is more likely to occur if the evolution of highly rewarding new roles continues and if *education is perceived and experienced as a major access to such highly rewarding roles.* When this is the case, a shift in family socialization will take place within a generation or two, so that parents come to stress in their childrearing those qualities they perceive as facilitating success in school learning. The transition is not always easy, but even before an overall transition has taken place many such people do learn more or less effectively.

In contrast, the educational problems associated with the position of nonimmigrant minorities in modern societies are different. They are generated by different structural and historical factors and they require different solutions. I show later how the model of education developed in this section is modified by the presence of caste minority groups in modern societies, but first we must distinguish among different types of minority groups.

Types of Minority Groups

One of the difficulties encountered in comparing black and white school performance lies in the use of the term *minority* group to refer to almost all nonwhites in the United States. A casual observation shows that some minority groups do as well as whites in school, leading some critics to point out that minority status per se cannot account for black–white differences (Jensen 1972a). What is needed, then, is to specify what kind of minority groups blacks represent in order to arrive at a more meaningful comparison. Minority groups may differ from one another just as much as they differ from the dominant group.

Few typologies of minority groups exist that provide an adequate basis for comparative studies of school performance. Yinger (1965), for instance, classifies minority groups in the United States according to their "long-range goals," such as assimilation, pluralism, secession, or domination. This classification is unsuitable for the purpose of this book because the goals of minority groups change under various conditions. Another typology is provided by Blauner (1972:53–57), who divides minority groups in the United States into *colonized* and *immigrant* minorities. He states that the former (primarily nonwhites) have been incorporated into American society against their will, whereas the latter (primarily whites) came to the United States by choice. But there are examples of nonwhite minorities who came to America by choice and for economic and other reasons similar to those that brought European immigrants to this country (see Kitano 1969; Kraus 1966; Sung 1971). Moreover, since Blauner's typology does not distinguish among various nonwhite groups, it is not helpful if one wants to explain why blacks are not doing as well in school as Chinese or Japanese Americans. Nor is this typology very useful in cross-cultural studies, where majority and minority groups do not necessarily belong to different races; for example, studies of the educational problems of Oriental Jews in Israel or the Burakumin of Japan.[4]

For my present purpose, I propose a typology which (a) indicates the distinct quality of majority–minority relations, (b) permits an analysis of historical changes in that relationship; and (c) has cross-cultural applicability. Applying these criteria, we can divide minority groups into three ideal types: *autonomous, caste (pariah),* and *immigrant* minorities.

Autonomous minorities tend to be numerically smaller than—but not totally subordinated economically or politically to—the dominant group. They often possess a distinct racial and ethnic, religious, linguistic, or cultural identity, which may be guaranteed by the national constitution or by tradition. Sometimes autonomous minorities occupy

[4]Leaving aside the issue of race, however, Blauner's categories of *colonized* versus *immigrant* minorities is a useful one. Immigrant minorities can emmigrate elsewhere, which colonized minorities cannot do. This option affects the attitudes of the immigrants toward the educational institutions of their host society.

distinct geographical domains, over which they exercise political control while participating in supralocal politics. They may be subject to some prejudice and discrimination, but their relationship with the dominant group is not characterized by rigid stratification. The ideology of innate inferiority may be completely absent in the majority–minority relationship.

Members of autonomous minorities do not necessarily regard the majority group as their reference group, nor do they necessarily want to be assimilated. The existence of autonomous minorities as separate groups is not based on any specialized economic, ritual, or political role they may fulfill; in fact, they are usually free to pursue most social and economic activities for which their training and abilities prepare them. Under various circumstances, the relationship between autonomous minorities and the dominant group may be characterized by competition, accommodation, or even a trend toward assimilation. Autonomous minorities are found in most developing nations of Africa and Asia; in the United States, the Jews and the Mormons probably best represent this type of minority group at the present.

Caste minorities are the polar opposite. The dominant group usually regards them as inherently inferior in all respects. Some caste minorities are more or less *pariah* groups. According to Berreman (1967a:293), pariahs are low-caste groups who are regarded as "intrinsically polluted and are stigmatized and excluded." Their economic, ritual, and political roles are often sharply defined. The kinds of work they do are usually "the necessary but dirty, demeaning, and unpleasant jobs for their superiors" [Berreman 1967a:292]. In general, caste minorities are not allowed to compete for the most desirable roles on the basis of their individual training and abilities. The least desirable roles they are forced to play are generally used to demonstrate that they are naturally suited for their low position in society. Thus their political subordination is reinforced by economic subordination.

Once these features have been firmly established, appropriate cultural features, including some overarching ideology, develop to support and rationalize the inferior position of caste minorities. Although caste minorities do not necessarily endorse the rationalizing ideology advocated by the dominant group (e.g., their biological or cultural inferiority), they are usually affected or influenced by it and the behaviors associated with it (Berreman 1967b:314; Plotnicoy and Tuden 1970). Blacks in the United States, the scheduled castes in India, and the Burakumin of Japan are examples of caste minorities.

Immigrant minorities fall between autonomous and caste minorities. These are people who have moved into a host society more or less voluntarily (Mabogunje 1972; Shibutani and Kwan 1965). As *strangers,* immigrant minorities can, if they live in groups, operate effectively outside the established definitions of social relations. They also tend to have instrumental attitudes toward their host society and its institutions. Such attitudes enable them to accept and even antici- pate prejudice and discrimination as the price of achieving their ulti- mate objectives. (This does not mean that immigrant minorities al- together eschew protest against maltreatment.)

Although immigrant minorities may initially occupy the lowest positions in the occupational structure of their host society and possess little political power or prestige, these do not necessarily define their true position in the local social hierarchy. Their hosts may regard the jobs held by immigrants as difficult and demeaning, but the latter may find such tasks relatively easy and the pay high in comparison with what they received at home; so they feel happy with their work and attempt to please their employers with enthusiasm and diligence (Shibutani and Kwan 1965:119).

A comparison of the attitudes of caste and immigrant minorities will show that the two groups tend to react to the same social situation differently. Unlike the caste groups, immigrant minorities operate out- side the beliefs of an established system of social hierarchy and are not deeply affected by the ideology of superiority and inferiority that sup- ports such a hierarchy. Furthermore, unlike the caste minorities, immi- grants have some options: They can usually leave their host society and return to their homeland or go to another society if their position be- comes particularly unbearable (unless they are political emigrés). In general, the goal of immigrant minorities is not necessarily to seek equality with the dominant group but to improve their economic condi- tion relative to the condition of people in their homeland. As Shibutani and Kwan (1965) point out "A substantial portion of the audience (ref- erence group) of many immigrants remains in the country whence they came [p. 517]." The Chinese and Japanese in the United States are examples of immigrant minorities.

Various forces, internal and external to the majority–minority rela- tionship, may later change the status of a given minority group. Auton- omous minorities may evolve into caste minorities and vice versa. Im- migrant minorities may develop into autonomous or caste minorities. Under appropriate conditions, minority groups may become assimi- lated into the dominant group, but incorporation or assimilation is not inevitable. Forces of urbanization, industrialization, and the egalitarian ideology in modern societies have all affected the status of caste minorities. In modern societies, the latter not only strive to be emanci- pated from their traditional roles but also seek equality with the domi-

nant groups (Berreman 1966a). Civil rights movements and achievements among blacks in the United States illustrate the aspirations of
castelike minorities in contemporary societies.

Caste Minority Status and Education

The problems associated with the education of caste minorities are
in some respects unique. However, the recognition of the unique features depends on the starting point of investigation. For example, one
may begin with classroom observations of the behaviors, motivations,
and achievements of children. Such observations will reveal differences not only among individual pupils but also between minority
and nonminority children. If an age cohort is observed longitudinally
from elementary school through high school and college into occupational and social roles of the adult world, the study will undoubtedly
show that fewer minority pupils complete high school or go to college
and that very few achieve high social and occupational roles. If the
investigator assumes, as is often the case with such studies, that the
major function of the school is that of manpower allocation, i.e., that
the school selects and trains pupils for various roles in adult life, two
hypotheses usually follow concerning differences in adult roles: (a)
that people (minority and nonminority alike) occupy different social
and occupational roles as adults because of differences in educational
attainment; and (b) that they differ in educational attainment because
they also differ in family backgrounds, individual abilities, genetic
makeup, and the like (Jensen 1969:78–79; Parsons 1968:69–73). The
sources of minority educational problems are therefore likely to be seen
as located in the individual and his or her family.

On the other hand, one may begin by studying the motives of
minority education, i.e., the way in which formal education is related
to the social and occupational status of adult members of the minority
group. The real motives for minority-group education are not to be
discovered in the rhetoric of school people, be they practitioners or
philosophers of education or educational psychologists. Such motives
are better discovered by studying the positions of adult members of the
minority group and comparing their positions with those of members
of the majority group. Such a study seeks to answer the following
questions: (a) To what extent is the present allocation of roles (social,
economic, etc.) among adult members of the minority group based on
formal education? (b) Is the relationship between formal education and
role allocation in the minority group the same as it is in the majority

group? In other words, are the motives of formal education the same for the minority and the majority groups?

Formal education, as stated previously, is future oriented. Therefore it is important to know what the motives of minority education are in order to understand more fully the behavior of parents and pupils, teachers, counselors, school administrators, and other school personnel, as well as the behavior of local school boards and other political groups that influence formal education. This second approach suggests additional and more pervasive sources of educational problems among caste minorities, namely, that they do not share the same motives for formal education with the majority and consequently the two groups are not necessarily participating in the same education system, even when they attend the same schools. This approach further suggests that the educational problems of caste minorities cannot be adequately understood except when analyzed in the context of a caste or racial stratification system which defines the status of the minority groups.

Since formal education is usually designed to equip children with personal qualities or attributes—attitudes, values, knowledge, and cognitive and other skills—which they will need as adults to perform adequately the social and economic roles characteristic of their group, the education of caste minorities and dominant groups are oriented toward producing different kinds of people. The education of caste minorities equips them with suitable qualities for their lower positions in society, while that of dominant groups equips them with qualities necessary for their superior roles. The dual nature of education in a caste-stratified society may be expressed in several ways: complete segregation, tracking within the same schools, classrooms, or courses; watered-down curriculums for caste minority groups, biased textbooks and learning materials; differences in educational identities—that is, stereotypes, treatment, and expectations; and different evaluations of and rewards for the same academic skills acquired by members of the two groups. In the United States, such differences between black and white education have been well documented (see Bond 1966; Harlan 1968; Leacock 1969; Sexton 1961; Stein 1971).

Schools which serve black or other castelike minorities often claim that their major goal is to enable their students to achieve the same social and occupational status as members of the dominant group by equipping them with similar skills, values, and motives. In the United States, this fits very well with the white belief system, which holds that public school education is established to provide equal opportunity for all who have the ability to achieve middle-class status. A myth which supports this belief states that in the past the public schools helped the children of poor immigrants to become middle-class professional and skilled workers. Some social scientists accept the myth as fact and proceed to suggest that blacks have been slower in achieving similar middle-class status through public school education because of genetic and other factors in their backgrounds (see Jensen 1969). That schools may not have been as successful as claimed in helping the children of immigrants has been probed by Greer (1971).

My major concern here is only the claim that formal education is intended to equalize black and white status. It becomes evident later (Chapter 5) that this claim arises from a lack of understanding of the real relationship among education, opportunity structures, and the systems of social mobility in the United States. Although an individual's level of education may enable him or her to raise his or her social status, it is the nature of opportunity for future adult roles and the noneducational factors in obtaining these roles that shape the education system (ideology and practices) to a large extent, not the other way around. Thus in a society with a dual system of social mobility, the same level of education does not necessarily possess equal value in both systems of social mobility.

The educational experiences of caste minorities contrast sharply with those of both autonomous minorities and immigrant minorities. Among autonomous minorities, children are prepared both at home and in school to compete successfully for, and perform adequately, typical adult roles in their society. Since members of autonomous minorities can and do compete with members of the dominant group for the same adult roles, the two groups tend to receive similar preparation in school.

The home and the schools do *not* seem to prepare caste minority children to compete effectively with members of the dominant group for the most desirable adult roles in their society. This happens because caste minorities are restricted to the least desirable social and occupational roles. The barriers against their competition for the more desirable roles generally influence the way their parents train them and the way schools prepare them for adult life.

Three factors influence the education of immigrant minorities, which differentiate them from caste minorities, even when both groups seem to occupy the same social and economic positions: (a) Immigrant minorities are outside the definitions of social relations in their host society, so that they are not too deeply influenced by conventional stereotypes in school and society; (b) they possess instrumental attitudes that lead them to view school as a means for acquiring the skills necessary for good jobs; and (c) they retain at least the symbolic option of returning to their ancestral homelands or moving to other host societies where they can benefit from their education if their present situation makes that necessary (Sung 1971). These forces motivate the children of immigrant minorities to maximize their school accomplishments. Thus even when immigrant minorities, as a group, have not experienced the social and economic benefits of formal education in their host society, they are strongly motivated by the anticipation that such rewards are possible either in their host society or elsewhere.[5] Unlike the caste minorities, the immigrants have the hope of escaping what may have been a long history of frustrated social mobility.[6]

Job Ceiling Against Castelike Minorities

Education is a bridge to adult status, but as already indicated in a castelike society all groups do not have equal access to the same types of adult roles. Although castelike minorities are generally restricted from participating in the more desirable social, political, and occupational positions, my primary focus is on their restricted participation in the economic sphere, for two reasons. First, most discussions about the education of caste minorities center on the influence of education on their economic status, especially on their ability to get better jobs and higher wages. It is generally assumed that improved economic conditions, creating more jobs and higher income levels, will result in their greater social and political participation. Second, economic restrictions have been the most studied and quantitatively documented.

Following Drake and Cayton (1962) and Frazier (1957), I will use the concept of *job ceiling* to describe the occupational experiences of

---

[5]Many immigrant groups in the United States originally came to escape from a long history of frustration in their desire for social mobility in their home countries: the Poles by the dominant Germans, Russians, and Austrians; the Irish by the English; the Scandinavians and the Chinese peasants by their landlords; Herzegovinians by the Serbs. For these immigrants, American society presented the kind of opportunity for social mobility they had never known but always yearned for. The caste minorities, on the other hand, have not escaped from the frustration in their desire for social mobility in their own country (Grace Buzaljko, personal communication).

[6]The usual argument against the ideas put forward here is that the higher achievement of immigrants is attributable to the fact that they are a select group. But this argument is defeated by the evidence about those who have been compelled by pogroms, wars, and other threats, to flee *en masse* yet have succeeded as a group—e.g., the flight of the Jews from Europe and of the Armenians from Turkey.

castelike minorities. The term means that (a) members of castelike minorities are not permitted to compete freely as individuals for any types of jobs to which they aspire and for which they are qualified; (b) castelike minorities are either excluded from the most desirable occupations or not permitted to obtain their proportionate share of such jobs, solely because of their caste status rather than because they lack the requisite training; and (c) as a result of these restrictions, castelike minorities are confined largely to the least desirable jobs. In castelike societies, occupations are thus divided into two broad categories: those above the job ceiling and those below it.

In the United States, occupations above the job ceiling are the four top occupational categories: (a) professionals and technicians; (b) managers, officials, and proprietors; (c) clerical, sales, and kindred workers; and (d) skilled craftsmen and foremen. In the American cultural idiom, these are the most desirable occupations in terms of financial remuneration, social prestige, and the like. But these are also the occupations from which castelike minorities like blacks have traditionally been excluded through various devices, even when they have obtained the qualifications required for such jobs. The occupations below the job ceiling include the following: (e) semiskilled workers; (f) personal and domestic service workers; (g) common laborers; and (h) farm laborers. These are the least desirable occupations in terms of pay, prestige, and other benefits, and they are the occupations to which blacks have traditionally been restricted and in which they are overrepresented. The occupational allocation of the American caste system distinguishes between these two broad occupational categories: those above the job ceiling, which may be properly called "white jobs," and those below the job ceiling, which may be called "black jobs." As is shown in Chapter 5, a survey of the history of black employment, in the South as well as the North, shows that this broad occupational division has existed since blacks became wage earners after slavery. Other societies have their own ways of classifying occupations within their own economies, but the operation of the job ceiling is the same: the most desirable jobs are reserved for the dominant caste and the less desirable ones for the caste minorities. The job ceiling and the general restriction of castelike minorities to low economic, political, and social roles have the consequence of stunting their development of linguistic, cognitive, motivational, and other skills that promote the type of school success enjoyed by the dominant group. The next section deals with the consequences of these restrictions on the development of cognitive skills among castelike minorities.

Social Structure and Intelligence:
The Implications of Caste Minority Status[7]

The interpretation of most behaviorist psychologists engaged in the debate over the influence of heredity and environment on IQ is based on the following assumptions: that IQ tests accurately measure intelligence; that hereditability can be inferred from IQ tests; and that the skills sampled by the IQ tests are more or less universal, i.e., that mental abilities can be found in all human populations with some variation according to genetic endowments. This is the ability theory of cognition (Cole et al. 1971) according to which intelligence is like a genealogical tree, with the generalized intelligence (the g-factor) at the base; above it are specialized types of abilities (such as verbal, numerical, spatial–perceptual, memorizing, reasoning, and mechanical (see Jensen 1969:11; Vernon, 1969:21). Some individuals and groups develop more or better intellectual skills than others in both the generalized and specialized areas. IQ tests are said to tap universal mental processes so that the way in which individuals and groups perform on such tests indicates their levels and types of mental abilities. The *ability theory* of cognition makes no allowance for the fact that IQ tests may evoke in subjects from different cultural backgrounds cognitive skills and strategies different from those intended by the testers (Cole et al. 1971:xii).

Cross-cultural evidence indicates that contrary to the ability theory different environments tend to generate different cultures and to encourage the development and use of different types of cognitive skills and strategies (see Cole et al. 1971; DeVos and Hippler 1969; LeVine 1970; Segall et al. 1966). The cognitive problems posed by the

[7]This section focuses on caste minorities rather than on all three types of minorities identified in the previous section. I assume that autonomous minorities have equal opportunity with the dominant group to develop their cognitive potentials, since there are few barriers to exclude them from full participation in the adult roles of their society. This does not necessarily mean that there are no differences between autonomous minorities and the dominant group in intelligence or cognitive skills. Such differences may be caused by genetic or cultural differences and, to my knowledge, are not the focus of current debate in America or other societies.

This section does not deal with immigrant minorities whose previous social and technoeconomic environment may well have encouraged the development of intelligence different from that required by the environment of their host society. However, it should be noted that it is the children of immigrant minorities who often grow up in the host society, who are likely to take intelligence tests, scholastic achievement tests, and so on. Unlike those of caste minorities, the cognitive and other skills of immigrant minorities are not necessarily adaptive to their new environment, so that immigrants are quite eager to acquire new skills required for adequate participation in their new environment. For this reason, motivation—which is certainly stronger in the immigrant than in the caste minority group—plays an important part both in the success of the former in the acquisition of new skills and in their demonstration of these skills in test and other situations.

technoeconomic environment of Western societies require cognitive skills and strategies that involve grasping relations and symbolic thinking; and these, according to Vernon (1969:10), have to some extent come to permeate all learning activities at school, at work, and in daily life. Other cultures require and stimulate the development and use of different cognitive skills for coping with their environments; i.e., the members of these cultures possess different intelligences. Vernon goes on to suggest that:

> We must try to discard the idea that intelligence is a kind of universal faculty, a trait which is the same (apart from variation in amount) in all cultural groups. Clearly, it develops differently in different physical and cultural environments. It should be regarded as a name for all the various cognitive skills which are developed in, and valued by, the group [p. 10].

Intelligence, as used by psychologists, may be a technical term (Jensen 1969:5), but since the term is used to determine the fate of virtually every child growing up in America, it must be defined within the context of various peoples' social and occupational realities.

While there is no general agreement among psychologists as to the meaning of *intelligence*, except that it can be measured and can predict scholastic performance, I suggest that Vernon's distinction among Intelligences A, B, and C is a good way to look at the relationship between intelligence and the cognitive skills characteristic of the members of a given culture (Vernon 1969:9–14).

Intelligences A and B correspond to the geneticist's distinction between the genotype and the phenotype. Intelligence A, the genotype, is the innate capacity children inherit from their ancestors through the genes which determines the limits of their mental or cognitive growth. Similarly, for members of a given population, Intelligence A represents their genetic potential for acquiring cognitive skills. But there is no way in which anyone can directly observe or measure Intelligence A (Vernon 1969:9).

Intelligence B, the phenotype, is a product of both nature (genetic equipment) and nurture (environmental pressures and forces). It refers to the everyday observed behavior of individuals and whether that behavior is considered intelligent or unintelligent by members of a given culture. Because Intelligence B is culturally defined, it differs from culture to culture in its attributes, even though the underlying processes may be the same. The kinds of behavior and the kinds of cognitive and perceptual skills which are, for example, included by middle-class Americans in their definition of intelligence will differ in some respects from those included by the Ibo or the Eskimo in their

definitions. But presumably all groups, while differing in their definitions, draw from the same pool of behavior and cognitive and perceptual skills available to the human species. Thus Intelligence B is not
simply a matter of cultural definition but also denotes the cognitive
skills and strategies selected by a given cultural group for adaptation to
its environment. As a matter of fact, we know almost nothing of the way
different cultures define intelligence or intelligent behavior, and we
have no ethnographic studies of cognition or intelligence.

We do know from a few cross-cultural studies, however, that the
cognitive skills demonstrated by members of different cultures usually
reflect their prior experiences. That is, the kinds of activities in which
members of a given culture are engaged tend to stimulate their development and expression of those cognitive and perceptual skills
necessary for competence in culturally valued activities. For example,
in a study in Mexico, Price-Williams, Gordon and Ramirez III (1969)
showed that experience with pottery making (and therefore manipulation of clay materials) results in the development of conservation skills.
Dennis' summary of scores on the Goodenough Draw-A-Man test given
to children from 40 different groups all over the world demonstrates
that there is a strong correlation between the involvement of a given
group with representational art and the test scores of its children (Dennis 1970:135). A third example comes from Dasen's (1973) study of
cognitive development in Australian aborigines and white Australian
children. He found that white Australian children (like their European
and American peers) develop logicomathematical concepts before they
develop spatial concepts but that among the aborigines the order was
reversed. Dasen's interpretation, which seems reasonable to me, is that
the aborigines develop spatial concepts more readily than logicomathematical concepts because the former are more important to their no-
madic hunting and gathering economy.

Nor is Intelligence B fixed; a person's cognitive capacity may
change as a result of some significant changes in his environment (e.g.,
a move from rural to urban residence or participation in new activities),
his education, or his personality. These changes may make him appear
more intelligent or less intelligent relative to his contemporaries. Similarly, the Intelligence B of a given cultural group may change after
significant changes in the group's environment or activities. Vernon
points out that in Western societies Intelligence B has probably increased in the past century as a result of industrialization and urbanization. The technological and other changes in Soviet Russia in the last
60 years have also probably resulted in an increase in its citizens'
Intelligence B. Under the impact of Western education, technology,

and urbanization, many cultural groups in the developing nations of Africa and Asia are probably experiencing changes in their Intelligence B. In particular, such people are to some degree acquiring the cognitive skills that characterize people in Western societies (Cole *et al.* 1971; LeVine 1970; Vernon 1969).[8]

Intelligence C, in Vernon's distinction, refers to those cognitive skills usually sampled by IQ tests. These are, of course, a part of the cognitive skills that make up Intelligence B. But Intelligence C differs from Intelligence B in that the skills sampled by IQ tests may be selected to serve a particular function—to predict scholastic perfor-mance or ability to perform other specific tasks. Thus IQ, or Intelli-gence C, may not correspond to what members of the society consider intelligent or unintelligent behavior or thinking.

In contemporary Western cultures, IQ tests are constructed to mea-sure certain aspects of Intelligence B vital for solving problems as-sociated with industrialization, bureaucracy, urbanism, and the like. The cognitive skills tapped by these tests are those which Western cultures emphasize in their formal education. Historical evidence indi-cates that the training in such cognitive skills was first institutionalized in formal education and later formed the basis upon which IQ tests were constructed to predict scholastic performance (Alland 1973; Brookover and Erickson 1965; Gartner and Riessman 1973). The pri-mary purpose of IQ tests, then, is to predict how well children in Western cultures learn the cognitive skills taught in Western schools and required for successful participation as adults in the occupational environment of Western societies. If peoples who live in the Arctic or in a tropical forest and had made different sociocultural and economic adaptations were to construct intelligence tests, they would probably include psychological tasks that measured those cognitive skills and strategies required for effective adaptation to their environments rather than tasks that tap the cognitive skills emphasized in contemporary Western tests of intelligence. In cross-cultural studies, contemporary Western tests tend to measure mainly those cognitive skills of indi-viduals and groups which would enable them to participate effectively in Western schools and in an industrial society—not the skills and strategies they have developed in order to adapt effectively to their own largely traditional environments (LeVine 1970).

[8]Empirical evidence is both growing and convincing that when non-Western peoples participate in Western-type schooling, their cognitive skills are significantly affected (see Cole and Scribner 1973; 1974; Greenfield 1966; Luria 1971). Cole and Scribner (1973:553) attribute this cognitive transforma-tion to the fact that school requires and promotes ways of thinking that are distinct from those required for indigenous activities.

To what extent is Intelligence C (IQ) an index of Intelligence A (genetic equipment)? That is, to what extent is IQ determined by heredity? There seems to be no empirical evidence for a precise answer to this queston. What is observed in everyday life (Intelligence B) and in IQ test scores (Intelligence C) is the phenotype, not the genotype (Vernon 1969:13). And no one has been able to show that particular genes determine particular cognitive skills. For, as Alland (1973) points out, "Divergent behavioral phenotypes could emerge from the same basic genotype through environmental shaping just as similar phenotypes could arise from different genotypes conditioned in different ways [p. 176]."

Behaviorist psychologists thus define intelligence too narrowly and attribute universality to certain Western cognitive skills sampled by psychological tests. They also believe that the skills sampled by IQ tests are genotypically based. Cross-cultural studies suggest, however, that intelligence, as defined in behavioral psychology, is not a universal faculty, that IQ is not synonymous with intelligence, and that there is at the moment no way of determining quantitatively the extent to which the repertoire of cognitive skills within a culture, let alone IQ, is influenced by genetic equipment.

Opposing sides in the heredity–environment debate generally agree that environment has some influence on intelligence, but they disagree as to the magnitude of that influence. Extreme hereditists may attribute as little as 20% influence to environment (Jensen 1969), while extreme environmentalists may attribute as much as 100% (expert consultants to UNESCO 1951, quoted in Vernon 1969:12). Both hereditists and environmentalists at least agree on the definition of environment. Both define environment in a very narrow sense, as consisting of prenatal factors, such as the mother's state of health and prenatal care and nutrition, as well as certain characteristics of individuals, families, and neighborhoods (see Denenberg 1970; Hunt 1969b; Jensen 1969; Kagan 1973; Vernon 1969). In general, the socioeconomic status of parents is considered a major environmental factor: It influences the quantity and quality of a child's interaction with parents and older siblings and determines the availability of material resources, both of which act to "stimulate" the child's cognitive development (Hunt 1964:207–208). From this perspective, some people develop more intelligence or better cognitive skills because they come from rich environments and receive more and better stimulation. This narrow conception of environment and its role in cognitive development derives primarily from laboratory studies in animal psychology (see Denenberg 1970; Hunt 1961, 1969a) and not from studies of children growing up in normal human societies. As a result, it fails to include other aspects of the environment which affect the development of cognitive skills.

As discussed earlier, the relationship between the cognitive skills characteristic of a group and the cognitive requirements of its culture suggests that the term *environment* should be defined more broadly to include not only prenatal and family conditions but also those features of the total society that generate the cognitive problems to be solved by the members of the society. I will designate the latter as *macroenvironment* and the former as *microenvironment*. The macroenvironment consists of those ecological, technological, social, and ideological or supernatural (a people's conception of or behavioral relationship to God or the unknown) features of society that generate the problems which must be solved by the group through the development of appropriate cognitive skills and strategies. It is thus the macroenvironment which determines the cognitive skills typical of a given group, although the microenvironment influences the acquisition of such skills and strategies by individuals in the group. These relationships are represented graphically in Figure 1.1.

Not all features of the macroenvironment exert equal force in generating the cognitive problems or tasks a given population must solve. It seems that the social, political, and occupational roles performed by the population would be primary in generating these cognitive problems. In order to adapt successfully to its physical environment, a population must develop an effective means of exploiting that environment. This task involves inventing not only appropriate tools and techniques of exploitation but also appropriate social structures or institutions, an appropriate ideology, and suitable individual behavior

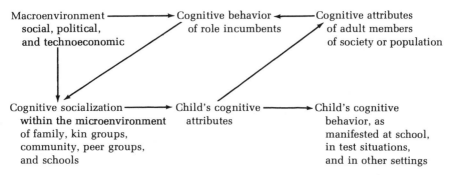

Figure 1.1. The relationship between the macroenvironment, the microenvironment, and the acquisition of cognitive skills. Adapted from Beatrice B. Whiting, ed. 1963. *Studies of Child Rearing.* New York: John Wiley and Sons, Inc., p. 5.

patterns (Goldschmidt 1971:5,13). Where two groups within the population, whether geographically separated from one another or within
the same physical boundary, follow different modes of exploitation
(e.g., herding and agriculture, white-collar and unskilled jobs), one
reasonably suspects that the two are faced with different cognitive
problems.

In modern industrial societies, the participation of minority groups
is often restricted to low and menial social and occupational roles.
Such positions require and stimulate the development of cognitive and
other skills different from those required and encouraged by the more
desirable social and occupational positions open to the members of the
dominant group. Thus a group with limited access or none at all to
professional or white-collar positions that is restricted largely to unskilled labor will have no opportunity to develop the ways of speaking,
conceptualizing, and thinking demanded by the professional and
white-collar occupations, and thus will be unable to transmit these
ways to its children. Instead, the group will develop ways of speaking,
conceptualizing, and thinking compatible with the demands of its menial and unskilled occupations. We can say that the group has made an
adaptation to the ecological niche open to it. The cognitive tasks posed
by the two sectors of the occupational system are different, and the
group restricted to one sector has therefore been denied the opportunity to develop its potential in relation to the skills required by the
other.

Barriers between caste minorities and the dominant group extend,
of course, to other areas of life, which also require that members of the
two groups develop appropriate ways of conceptualizing, thinking,
and behaving. Generally speaking, the two groups tend to differ in their
Intelligence B. However, the measurement of intelligence (IQ) in such
societies is usually done by sampling the Intelligence B of the dominant caste.[9] That is, the tests are constructed to tap primarily those
cognitive skills and strategies that are functional for the dominant caste

---

[9]Intelligence tests measure Intelligence C, and Intelligence C consists of skills and behavior
patterns from Intelligence B carefully selected for the purpose of predicting school performance or
other specific accomplishments. What is taught in school are skills and forms of behavior functionally
adaptive for members of a society. In a society where two or more groups make up the population,
schools tend to emphasize the skills and behavior patterns primarily functionally adaptive for each
group, but the skills and behavior patterns selected for measuring IQ and predicting school performance are usually chosen from the Intelligence B of the dominant group.

The Intelligence C measured by intelligence tests is derived from Intelligence B, which is culture
bound. Consequently, Intelligence C is also culture bound. The cultural context of Intelligence C is
well illustrated by the changes that have accompanied the adoption of the Binet Intelligence Test in
various countries. The test was first developed in France, where it measured relatively well the
Intelligence C of the French people. When the tests were brought to the United States, they proved

rather than those that are functional for the caste minorities, although there is some degree of overlap in the Intelligence B of the two groups. This overlap would, of course, be much greater if there were no social and occupational barriers. In terms of cognitive socialization, the microenvironment (the family, kin groups, neighborhood, peer group, and even the school) for each of the respective groups transmits mainly those cognitive skills that are functionally adaptive for the group.

Differences in the cognitive repertoires of the two groups and the fact that IQ tests primarily sample functional skills within the dominant caste partly explain the lower performance of caste minorities on such tests. But equally contributory to their lower performance is that doing well on these tests, like doing well on academic tasks generally, is not as rewarding for caste minorities as it is for the dominant group. Thus caste minority children often do not take such tests seriously enough to try for the best scores they can get. It is generally known among psychologists who test caste minority children that in nontest situations these children may be observed to communicate with their peers, solve problems, and use concepts in ways typical of children who have IQs of a Binet type 10 to 15 points higher than theirs.

Education and Social Change in Castelike Societies

Efforts to improve the school performance of castelike minorities as a way of improving their social and technoeconomic status are usually thwarted. Although education and socialization function essentially as complementary modes of preparing young people for future adult roles, caste and castelike societies possess one system of role recruitment for the dominant caste (i.e., recruitment based on training and ability) and another for the caste minorities (i.e., recruitment based on caste origin rather than training and ability). Under this dual system

---

inadequate for testing or measuring the Intelligence C of the American people. The French tests were therefore modified by the removal of certain standardized tasks unsuitable for American children and by the addition of other standardized tasks based on the experience of American children. This revision resulted in the Stanford-Binet Scale or the American Intelligence Scale. Similar revisions took place in Britain and Japan. Thus the French Binet scale, the British Binet scale, the American Stanford-Binet scale, and the Japanese Tanaka-Binet scale are not exactly interchangeable because the Intelligence C measured in each country is influenced by the culture of the respective country. The educational system of each country also influences the Intelligence C of its people and hence their IQ—the skills and behavior patterns taught by the education system of each country and those which are functionally adaptive. During the early years, all children learn a common curriculum—those common skills and behavior patterns. These are skills predicted by the IQ tests. The test samples well the kind of thinking of Western children in the school situation.

of recruitment to adult status, no amount of educational reform and no programs to rehabilitate members of the castelike minorities can bring about equal school performance by the two groups.

Let me illustrate this problem with two hypothetical caste societies which have introduced education as a means of preparing children from different castes for adult status. Suppose that a traditional caste society—in which children from different castes normally received different forms of education required by their positions in society—decided upon the idea of giving all children the same kind of education. Such a decision would at once raise some serious structural problems, reaching beyond the classroom and yet profoundly affecting education in the classroom. The most important would concern the basis upon which future graduates of the new universal education would be recruited for various social and occupational roles in adult life: Should it be on the basis of education and ability or on the basis of caste origin? How this particular problem is resolved will determine whether the new universal education will function as a unitary system or as a dual system of superior education for the dominant caste and inferior education for the caste minorities. But how the problem is resolved will also depend on the kind of society envisioned: a society stratified by caste status or one stratified by class status. The kind of society envisioned will therefore determine the basis of inducting the graduates of the universal education system into their adult roles.

The society may choose one of two modes of recruitment. One is to recruit school graduates to perform the roles traditionally performed by members of their castes, irrespective of individual training and ability. In this case the education system will eventually recognize—functionally if not ideologically—that it has to prepare children from different castes according to their different needs to perform their more or less prescribed roles in adult life. The education system may accomplish this by providing different schools or different curriculums for different castes "to meet their needs," or by tracking the students along caste lines. As a result of this principle of recruitment for adult roles, formal education will simply perpetuate the caste structure. The education system, although universal, is not intended to change the status quo (see Figure 1.2).

The other mode open to the society is to recruit school graduates for their adult roles on the basis of education and ability, irrespective of caste origin. Under this mode, schools are likely to stress a common training experience or preparation for all children. Tracking may occur as a result of individual differences in ability or interests. The long-range effect of this mode of role recruitment is to alter the traditional

	Role assignment based on caste origin or membership	Role assignment based on individual ability and training
Treatment roles	1. School prepares children from different castes "according to their needs"	1. Common preparation stressed for children from all castes by the schools
	2. Tracking along caste lines	2. Tracking by ability and interests
	3. Results in perpetuating the caste structure	3. Results in radical alteration of social structure. Society moves from castes to class-based stratification
Emergent roles	1. Common or different preparation for children from different castes	1. Common preparation for all children irrespective of their caste origin
	2. Tracking likely to be based on caste lines	2. Tracking based on individual ability and effort
	3. Caste structure reinforced	3. New sector of society based on class; possible eventual transformation of whole society to class-based stratification

Figure 1.2. Relationship between education and social change.

social structure, transforming the caste stratification into a class stratification. Education in this situation is certainly an important agent of social change.

Now, suppose that this traditional society is undergoing other changes, that its social and occupational roles are being changed under the impact of urbanization, industrialization, and bureaucratization. The major task of its universal education is certainly to prepare children for these emergent roles. Here again there will be the same two possible modes of recruitment for positions in adult society, each with its own implications for the education of children of various castes as well as for the structure of the society itself.

Just as the school training of children from various castes depends on what the schools perceive as the ultimate destination of these children, so also do other agencies of socialization depend on the same perception. Other agencies of socialization, particularly the family, also respond to the modes of role recruitment operating in society, and the response of the family is often complementary to that of the school. Moreover, as children grow older they tend to respond to their training at school and at home on the basis of how they perceive their future places in society as members of various castes. All these factors contribute to determine the nature of their school performance.

Castelike Minority School Failure: A New Perspective

The foregoing discussion bears directly on the school failure of castelike minorities. In all societies, education acts as a bridge to adult social and occupational status, but in castelike societies education prepares children of different castes for their different social and occupational positions in adult life. The schools in these latter societies are therefore not organized to train castelike minorities to achieve equal social and occupational status with members of the dominant caste. Thus it may be argued that in a castelike society like the United States, the "success" of the schools in regard to the dominant white caste is to be measured by the extent to which they equip white children with the knowledge and skills appropriate for high social and occupational roles in adult life, whereas their success in regard to blacks and other castelike minority groups is to be measured by the extent to which they equip the latter with knowledge and skills for their low social and occupational positions.[10] That schools are not organized to train castelike minorities to achieve equal status with the dominant caste is most evident when one studies historical changes in the education of castelike minorities. Almost always, changes in the education of caste-

[10]I first noted this relationship between changes in castelike minority education and other changes in their status when I began to investigate the developments in black education and other changes in black status since emancipation. This relationship is described more fully in chapter 5. Later, when I read Carter's study of Mexican-American education in the Southwest, I was impressed by the fact that he had come to a similar conclusion, namely, that the position occupied by a castelike minority group in society determines the type of education deemed appropriate for the group. Carter describes Mexican-American education in relation to their status in some local communities as follows:

The fact the school fails to Americanize or raise the group status of so many Mexican-Americans was evidence of its success. Local society functioned well with an easily controlled, politically impotent, and subordinate ethnic caste. School practices evolved that functioned to perpetuate the social and economic system by unconsciously encouraging the minority group to fail academically, drop out early, and enter society at the low status traditional for Mexican-Americans, thus producing the human types necessary to perpetuate the local society. Mexican-American failure to achieve well in school contributed to the Anglos' belief that they had innately inferior intelligence, that they were lazy, passive, fatalistic, and lacked initiative. This self-reinforcing circle of circumstances became well established in the Southwest and persists to the present [1970:204–205].

like minorities reflect changes that have already occurred or are expected to occur in their social and occupational status, not vice versa.

Complementing the organization of schools in producing minority academic failure are the effects of caste barriers on minority academic behavior. These are of two kinds. First, because caste minorities perceive their future chances for jobs and other benefits of education as limited, they are not so strongly motivated as the dominant-group members to persevere in their school work. The perception of schooling as it relates to limited future opportunities may be largely unconscious for many caste minority group members, but it is an important factor in their relative lack of serious attitudes and efforts in school. Second, caste barriers generate or promote the development of different types of school- and work-related skills among caste minorities, as compared to the skills characteristic of the members of the dominant group. I argue that the cognitive, linguistic, motivational, and other skills that dominant-group children take with them to school are intimately related to the types of such skills required and promoted by the social and occupational roles they will play as adult members of society. Furthermore, although these skills partially account for the academic success of dominant-group children, schooling does further improve these skills, making them more useful when the children eventually take up their roles in adult life. When we turn to caste minorities, we find that the situation is both different and the same. It is *different* because their ascribed social and occupational roles require and promote different types of linguistic, cognitive, and motivational skills and behavior. However, the situation is the *same* in the sense that caste minority children naturally acquire the linguistic, cognitive, motivational, and other skills or personal attributes adaptive to their adult roles. These skills may promote their failure in the dominant group's type of school success, but in that very way schooling improves their adaptability to the menial social and occupational roles they will play as adults. Whether the dominant-group parents and caste minority parents employ the same or different techniques to transmit their linguistic, cognitive, and motivational repertoires to their children is beside the point. But one may ask those who criticize black parents, for instance, for not using the techniques of childrearing characteristic of middle-class white parents: Why should black parents raise their children in the same way as white parents if they are going to transmit to them different linguistic, cognitive, and motivational skills so that they will be competent in their different social and occupational roles?

In Chapter 2, I review other explanations of why blacks do less well in school than whites. Chapter 3 is devoted to two principal strategies—school integration and compensatory education—used to attempt to close the black–white gap in school performance. Both strategies are based on some of the theories to be reviewed in Chapter 2. Then, after Chapter 3, I examine more closely the educational experiences of blacks in the light of the alternative thesis I have presented in this chapter.

2

Black–White Differences in
School Performance:
A Critique of Current
Explanations

There is no disagreement over the fact that in the United States, in classroom work and in standardized tests of cognitive skills (IQ) and scholastic achievement, black students generally do less well than white students. Nor is there any dispute about the fact that blacks tend to terminate their schooling earlier than whites. There is, however, disagreement about the reasons why these things happen. The purpose of this chapter is to review some of the major explanations being offered for these differences. I am particularly concerned with the biogenetic theory, which now seems to overshadow others in accounting for this problem.

Many of the views with which I disagree in the following pages have been expressed by those most deeply concerned with the welfare of black people in the United States. Because I do not question their intentions, it is important to point out from the outset a common fallacy in their assumptions which undermines their efforts to help black people. Their theories explicitly or implicitly assume that the socioeconomic inequality between blacks and whites is caused, at least in part, by differences in the school performance and educational attainment of the two races. They further assume that this socioeconomic inequality would largely disappear if only blacks would perform like whites in school.

These assumptions are fantasies from the era of the Great Society, during which mobilization for reform merely reinforced the ahistorical perspective of American social science in the field of race relations. Thus people with the best intentions began to put forward theories that took no account of the fact that socioeconomic inequality between blacks and whites has existed for centuries in the United States, even at those times and in those places where the two races had the same level and quality of education and achieved equally in school. Nor did they consider what the consequences of this historical situation might mean both in terms of the development of the cognitive skills required by the American occupational structure and measured by psychological instruments and in terms of black motivation to perform in the classroom. The fallacy of their perspective will become clear as the theories are reviewed in the following pages.

Cultural Deprivation

According to the cultural deprivation theory, children are culturally deprived when they come from home and neighborhood environments that do not provide them with adequately organized stimulation for normal development. Consequently they are retarded in linguistic, cognitive, and social development, which is why they fail in school (see Ausubel 1964; Bloom et al. 1965; M. Deutsch et al. 1967; Gottfried 1973; Hunt 1964). On the surface, the cultural deprivation theory purports to explain why lower-class children do not perform as well in school as middle-class children. A closer examination shows, however, that the theory is more deeply concerned with differences in school performance between blacks and whites. By the criteria used in the theory to sort out culturally deprived children, 75% of black children would be classified as lower-class or culturally deprived (Gottfried 1973).

The explanation of lower black school performance in terms of cultural deprivation and its developmental consequences was given weight by both the Chicago Conference on Compensatory Education for Cultural Deprivation in 1964 and Columbia University's Teachers College Work Conference on Curriculum and Teaching in Depressed Urban Areas in 1963. The Chicago conference, for instance, defined culturally deprived pupils as the students whose early experiences in the home, whose motivation for present school learning, and whose goals for the future are such as to handicap them in schoolwork. This group may also be defined as those who do not complete secondary education [Bloom et al. 1965:4].

As to why the children are culturally deprived, the conference report went on to say that

We will refer to this group as culturally disadvantaged or culturally deprived because we believe the roots of their problems may in large part be traced to their experiences in homes which do not transmit the cultural patterns necessary for the types of learnings characteristic of the schools and the larger society [Bloom et al. 1965:4; emphasis added].

The report cautioned that "cultural deprivation should not be equated with race [p. 5]." But it went on to observe that "It is true that a large number of Negro children, especially those from homes with functionally illiterate parents, are likely to be culturally deprived."

Since the second half of the 1960s, this theory of cultural deprivation has been very influential in generating compensatory education programs, including programs in early childhood education—Head Start, for example. The aim of such programs is often to change the culturally deprived child so that he or she will perform in school like the white middle-class child (Powledge 1967). Although questions have increasingly been raised as to the effectiveness of these programs to improve the cognitive skills (IQ) and academic achievement of black children (see Jensen 1969), the theory's proponents insist that although the theory is valid the programs have not been tried long enough, on a large enough scale, and with appropriate methods (Hunt 1969b).

A number of other scholars have subjected the cultural deprivation theory to scrutiny, pointing out many difficulties in its assumptions and methods (see Austin 1965a,b; Baratz and Baratz 1970; Gottfried 1973; Rosenham 1967; Spradley 1972; Stein 1971; Valentine 1971). Spradley, for instance, has made the following criticisms about the theory: First, it has a built-in bias in its method. It tells the investigator what to look for in school (e.g., test scores, school grades, evaluation by teachers, and failure to complete school), and in the process of data selection many positive attributes of the culturally deprived are ignored. Those who are culturally deprived but doing well and those who are not culturally deprived but doing poorly in school are not studied. Second, the criteria for measuring school performance and adequacy of cultural background are based on white middle-class cultural values: tests, grades, skills, and tasks of middle-class American schoolchildren. Spradley notes, "By these standards most of the world is culturally deprived, and in need of enrichment programs." Third, the theory embodies the assumption that children who are failing in school are to be blamed for their failure, not the school or society (Spradley 1972:17–18). Furthermore, the term *culture*, as used in cultural deprivation theory, is simply a misnomer. It is a list of traits which cultural deprivation theorists confuse with culture patterns (Valentine 1968:11).[1]

Finally, one central thesis of this theory is that lower-class parents (especially black parents) do not function adequately as teachers, for example, in teaching their children to acquire language skills (Bernstein 1961; Hess and Shipman 1967). But the theory does not explain the success of lower-class children in learning their own culture and language. Commenting on this point, Gottfried (1973) writes: "One wonders how lower-class children are able to acquire lower-class behaviors so well under such defective tutelage, and how, under the circumstances, they are able to resist the instruction of their well trained, middle-class teachers in school [p. 275]."

Cultural deprivation theory does not satisfactorily explain why black children do poorly in school. The theory erroneously labels many aspects of black childhood experiences as "pathological" and thus generates "remedial programs" dedicated to the elimination of the presumed pathologies. Although these programs have not generally proved successful in achieving their goals, they continue as the dominant approach to change in ghetto schools, sustained perhaps by the mythology that spawns them as well as by politics. These programs are examined more fully in Chapter 3.

Culture Conflict

Two variants of the culture conflict theory both argue that black children fail to do well in school because they grow up in a culture that

---

[1]In describing the poor and ethnic minorities' culture, which they assume to be the source of their difficulties in school, cultural deprivation theorists are often content to list indicators of poverty, such as lack of education, unemployment, and poor housing; aspects of social organization of these groups which differ from those of the middle class, such as high incidence of single-parent families and female-headed households; some behaviors of the poor and ethnic minorities which differ from those of the middle class, such as the fact that the entire family may not eat at the table together, that children are given responsibility in the family at an early age, or that parents supposedly do not read to their children or talk to them the way middle-class parents do. But the mere listing of these as traits or characteristics of the culturally deprived does not indicate an understanding of the culture of the poor and ethnic minorities or provide a sufficient guide to the source of their problems at school or indicate what can be done to help their children achieve white middle-class type of school success.

is different from the mainstream culture. Black children, the theory asserts, acquire values, attitudes, and learning styles within their culture that are different from and in conflict with those required for success in the public schools and in wider society.

One variant of the theory stresses the failure of black culture to equip black children with white middle-class skills necessary for school success. According to Inkeles (1968a:54–56), black families teach their children skills which, though perfectly adequate within the black community, are irrelevant to the demands of the school and American society. He illustrates this problem with respect to language skills, pointing out that the school "offers rewards to the middle-class child when he arrives at school *for what he already knows*, [while] it is likely to greet our Harlem Black boy with horror *for what he does not know and cannot do with language*. The result on his part, will be more avoidance of words and language" [Inkeles 1968a:60; emphasis added].

Inkeles' assertion that black pupils probably come to school with different language skills is supported by recent research (Labov 1972). Inkeles further suggests that American minority groups are like people in developing nations in that both are disadvantaged in "competence training." But this comparison is not quite appropriate. In the first place, the first generation urban residents and industrial workers in developing nations may successfully learn behaviors appropriate for the urban scene and work situations, as well as the norms associated with those behaviors, while they retain their traditional norms and behavioral patterns in other situations. They thus are able to switch back and forth between the old and the new, depending on the situation (Southall 1961). In the second place, the disadvantages suffered by first generation urban residents and industrial workers in developing nations are not necessarily passed on to their children.[2] Neither of these situations applies to black Americans, whose disadvantages have persisted for generations.

The other variant of the culture conflict theory stresses the failure of the schools to make full use of the unique black skills. This version asserts that the black child fails to perform in school precisely because the school fails to utilize what he *does* know and *can* do with language and other skills—i.e., his culture, attitudes, values, and language and learning styles. Empirical studies are used to show, for example, that black English has its own distinct logic, just like the standard American white middle-class English, and therefore can be used as a medium of

---

[2]There may be instances where such a transition does not occur, and this lack of occurrence requires an explanation.

instruction in public schools (see Baratz and Baratz 1970; Stewart 1970; Dillard 1972).

The proponents of this second view have made a good case for utilizing black English and culture in school; for one thing, in a pluralistic society like the United States, whites should become more aware of important features of black culture in order to promote interpersonal and intergroup relations. Furthermore, by recognizing as valid and respectable the language style and other cultural features of blacks, the schools will be helping to promote black pride and identity, which would undoubtedly have a positive influence on the schoolwork of black children. Finally, starting black children to learn to read in the dialect most familiar to them could facilitate their acquisition of reading skills more quickly perhaps than would otherwise be the case.

In the long run, what must be seriously considered is whether training black children in black English is sufficient for their training to function as adults in the wider society. There would, of course, be no serious problems if the social and economic roles in American society were adjusted to accommodate competence training in those skills that are uniquely black. Furthermore, granting that blacks and whites differ in their language dialects does not necessarily lead to the conclusion that the former cannot successfully learn to communicate competently in the white dialect—given adequate opportunities and incentives to do so.

In general, both variants of the culture conflict theory must be considered inadequate because they fail to explain why the conflict should exist at all. The existence of cultural differences does not automatically lead to conflict or to school failure. For example, children of some immigrant minorities (Arabs, Chinese, Filipinos, and Japanese, among others) do better than blacks in the public schools even though these groups have often retained aspects of their native cultures that differ radically from the white American middle-class culture.

Institutional Deficiency

Some people say that black children perform poorly in school because the public schools are organized to favor "middle class and upper class, non-minority children and to suppress the aspirations of children from disadvantaged groups [U.S. Senate, Select Committee 1972:129; see also Kohl 1969; Kozol 1966; Stein 1971]." The following methods are often cited as ways used by the educational system to promote academic failure among black children: assignment of pupils to separate and often inferior schools on the basis of their race; teacher attitudes, insensitivities, and low expectations; tracking and testing; and inadequate curriculum (see Chapter 4). Critics of the public schools say that while these mechanisms may not be deliberately used against black children, they nevertheless "operate to place [the black] child in an inferior status throughout his school career [U.S. Senate, Select Committee 1972:139]." These critics therefore suggest that the schools as presently organized cannot teach black children successfully.

School critics have pointed out many ways in which the public school systems may contribute to the academic problems of black children. They have, however, failed to see the deficiencies of the public schools in the context of the society that maintains them and therefore propose reforms that may be at odds with the economic and social reality of black Americans, or American society for that matter. Furthermore, I believe that many white middle-class reformers in the alternative schools movement not only misunderstand the basis of black academic problems but also have educational goals not regarded as a priority by blacks.

Middle-class white reformers are often motivated by three considerations: First, they think that the traditional school organization, curriculum, and teaching techniques have not been effective in dealing with the many handicaps which they believe black children bring with them to school; second, they believe that American society is changing so fast that it is no longer useful for children to learn the traditional skills taught by the schools—instead, they suggest schools should be reorganized to teach children the ability to adapt to the requirements of a fast-changing society of the year 2000; third, many white middle-class advocates of alternative schools or free schools see them as more conducive to the optimal development of children than is traditional school organization.

Blacks, especially lower-class blacks, see the problem differently. From their point of view, the main failure of the schools is that they do not equip or prepare black children effectively in those specific skills that enable middle-class whites today to have good jobs, good wages, and other benefits of education. Blacks are thus concerned that their children should learn such skills in schools; they are not primarily concerned with the requirements of the technocratic society of the year 2000. Moreover, blacks feel that if their children failed to learn as well as whites in the past it was probably because the schools attended by black children were inferior in the traditional organization, curriculum, and teaching techniques. Consequently, when blacks organize their own alternative schools, which they call "freedom" rather than "free" schools, they differ from the white school reformers as to what their schools should emphasize. Black freedom schools are usually more structured than the middle-class white "free schools" (Cooper 1971).

I do not know of any serious assessment of the alternative schools for blacks. My general impression is that white middle-class types of alternative schools will probably prove ineffective in solving the current problems of black school failures. I base my evaluation partly on the knowledge that in Britain the informal education approach has not provided solutions to similar problems among the racial minorities and the British lower class (see Bernstein 1970; Inner London Educational Authority 1967; Newson Report 1963). Furthermore, an educational reform that seeks to substitute an informal education for the present system constitutes a redefinition of the function of public school education. Such a redefinition must, however, be evaluated in the context of American social and economic reality. Noting a similar trend some decades ago, Kluckhohn pointed out that the progressive school movement was trying to remake the American personality without altering the larger culture: The progressive school movement was trying to produce a noncompetitive personality in a competitive society, a situation likely to create serious problems for the individual in adult life. Kluckhohn went on to say that

> No arbitrary change, divorced from the general emphasis of the culture, in methods of child rearing will suddenly alter adult personalities in a desired direction. This was the false assumption that underlay certain aspects of the progressive education movement. In these schools children were being prepared for a world that existed only in the dreams of certain educators. When the youngsters left the schools they either reverted naturally enough to the view of life they had absorbed in preschool days in their families or they dissipated their energies in impotent rebellion against the pattern of the larger society [Quoted in Kneller 1965:64].

More recently, Cohen (1971) has sounded a similar warning about the present trend in educational reforms in America, pointing out that "programs that advocate changes in modes of socialization and education must be congruent with the cultural realities for which the individuals are being prepared [p. 21]."

Critics of the school system, insofar as black school performance is concerned, confuse two distinct problems. The first has to do with the ability of public school education as it is presently organized to meet new needs, arising or likely to arise from a changing economy and technology. This problem affects the education of all children, whatever their racial, ethnic, or class background. The second problem has to do with the fact that blacks have not been and are not as successful as whites in learning the skills taught by these schools. This is a uniquely black problem which is not explained by the first; nor will the same remedy be sufficient. The two problems are distinct, requiring different analysis and different treatment, but some critics of the school system fail to differentiate between them.

In my view, black critics of the school system have a more realistic perception of their educational problem than do their white middle-class counterparts.[3] As I show in subsequent chapters, one of the main reasons why blacks do not perform as well as whites under the present system is that the schools have traditionally made less serious efforts to prepare them for the desirable adult roles for which they prepared white students. The reason for this differential treatment is that the schools are agents of a caste society that assigns blacks and whites different positions in adult life requiring different levels of education and skills. So long as the schools remain agents of the caste system, there is no guarantee that they will do better in educating black children under a reorganized, alternative education system.

Educational Equality

Some people argue that black children perform less well than white children in school because they do not have equal educational opportunity. Unlike those who support the institutional deficiency explanation, those who criticize educational opportunity do not question the suitability of traditional public schools.

Equal educational opportunity has been one of the main tenets of public school education. But according to Coleman (1969:18), the meaning of equality of educational opportunity has changed several times over the years, and by 1964 the concept had come to stand for two things: that all children in a given community have access to the same schools and the same curriculum free of charge and that the effects of schooling reflect this equality of educational opportunity.

However, the belief that every child should have equal educational opportunity coexists in American culture with the belief that every child has a fairly fixed intelligence, determined by heredity. The latter belief assumes that each individual has a limited ability to learn and that this ability is unaffected by external forces. It also assumes that

[3]There are, of course, some black critics of the school system whose views are similar to those of middle-class whites.

intelligence tests accurately measure the fixed ability of individuals; consequently one important aspect of the American education system is the identification and selection of people with various learning abilities or talents in order that they might be educated to the limits of their abilities (Brookover and Erickson 1965:3–18). Thus one fundamental assumption underlying American public school education is that there is an inherent (innate) inequality that makes children's educational experiences unequal.

Prior to 1964 it was known, of course, that all children did not benefit equally from the same curriculum open to them. For example, at the elementary school level, different groups of children attending the same schools achieved differently; and in the secondary schools, different groups of children took different types of courses and also varied in their successes. Furthermore, there was a good deal of evidence that inequality in student performance existed in terms of educational attainment (years of school completed) and other results of formal education. This inequality was particularly noted between minority and nonminority children.

But these differences in academic performance were not explained in terms of differences in fixed intelligence, as one might have expected. Instead, cultural deprivation (discussed at the beginning of the chapter) was invented as the causal explanation. Coleman (1966) investigated this problem and concluded that the home environments of lower-class and minority children are the principal sources of inequality of academic performance and that schools can do very little to bridge the gap between their achievements and those of white middle-class children (see Coleman 1966; Coleman *et al.* 1969; U.S. Senate Select Committee 1972). In testimony before the Senate Select Committee on Equality of Educational Opportunity, Coleman reiterated his previous conclusions, stating that

> The sources of inequality of educational opportunity appear to lie first in the home itself and the cultural differences immediately surrounding the home; then they lie in the school's ineffectiveness to free achievement from the impact of the home and in the school's cultural homogeneity which perpetuates the social influences of the home and its environs [U.S. Senate Select Committee 1972:167].

These conclusions have been challenged on several grounds, one of which is that school resources (e.g., instructional materials, the quality of the teaching staff, etc.) do indeed affect pupil performance. For example, James Guthrie and associates of the Urban Coalition reviewed the results of 17 previous studies dealing with the relationship between school resources and students' academic achievement; then they carried out an extensive study of the same problem in the state of Michigan. Their overall conclusion is that school resources can affect student achievement. Specifically, they state that the quality of school resources affects pupils' schoolwork: higher quality school services are associated with higher academic performance (see U.S. Senate Select Committee 1972:168; Guthrie *et al.* 1971).

Critics of the educational opportunity for blacks often point to the fact that black children are segregated into predominantly black schools and that the resources available in such schools are inferior to those found in predominantly white schools. Studies such as those of Guthrie (and even Colemen *et al.* 1966), as well as evidence presented in school desegregation suits, demonstrate clearly that blacks do not have equal access with whites to school resources (see Chapter 4).

Lack of access to adequate school resources is undoubtedly one of the main reasons for the lower school performance of black children, even though other factors like home environment also contribute to the problem. Indeed, the debate over the relative weights of home environment and school environment in influencing academic achievement is not particularly enlightening. It can be as protracted and as unresolvable as the debate over the roles of heredity and environment in influencing IQ. Some studies show that home environment, rather than school environment or resources, affects pupil performance; other studies show just the reverse. Still other studies may show that one or the other of the two environments affects the school performance of only some children. For other children, neither home nor school environment greatly affects school performance.

However, the educational opportunity explanation is not adequate, for a number of reasons. First, it cannot be shown that better school resources are always associated with higher pupil performance or that poorer resources are associated with lower performance. Other factors are also involved in determining pupil performance. Second, the concept of equality of educational opportunity is used in a very narrow sense. The concept as it is now used refers to equality of access to school resources and the use of these resources to enable children from non-middle-class and nonwhite backgrounds to perform like white middle-class children in school. This definition says nothing about the incentives society purports to offer American children to encourage maximum efforts in their schoolwork. Children do not succeed in school simply because they come from middle-class family backgrounds or attend well-equipped schools, nor do they perform well in school simply because they have high IQs or favorable attitudes. (Ohlin and Cloward 1960). An important determinant of school performance is what children and their parents or community expect to gain from their education in adult life. Such future expectations—*incentive motivation*—must be included in any full definition of the concept of equality of educational opportunity (see Hull 1943; Logan 1971). Third, the debate on equality of educational opportunity does not take into account the fact that people who have access to professional, technical, and other high-status occupations in modern industrial societies have better opportunities to develop their cognitive potentials than people for whom access to those roles has traditionally been denied.

Finally, current debates on the concept of equality of educational opportunity are ahistorical, which limits their usefulness. Many synchronic studies show that black children often attend schools with inferior resources and come from family backgrounds that differ from those of middle-class whites. The debates center on whether the lower school performance of black children is determined by inadequate school resources or inferior family backgrounds; but these synchronic studies—studies of present-day factors—do not show (a) that for nearly a century blacks have attended schools with inferior resources and that this background may have had a cumulative effect on their performance today; and (b) that for nearly a century education has not provided blacks and whites with equal access to jobs, wages, and other benefits which, according to Americans, depend on education. The cumulative effect of this lack of access may have depressed black school performance today. There are merits in the synchronic analysis of particular school features and particular family backgrounds; but a study of the historical experiences of black people in American education, together with such synchronic studies, is essential in determining to what extent a tradition of inequality of educational opportunity influences black school performance today.

Heredity: Jensen's Theory

There is overwhelming empirical evidence that in the United States blacks generally score lower than whites in intelligence (IQ) tests (Dreger 1973; Jensen 1969) and in academic performance (Jensen 1969, 1973; L'Abate et al. 1973). Some authorities attribute these differences between the two races to differences in environmental influence (Deutsch et al. 1967; Hunt 1969b; L'Abate et al. 1973). Many scholars who hold such views usually subscribe to the theory of cultural deprivation which was reviewed earlier and is not dealt with here. Instead, I focus on the explanation that black–white differences in IQ and school performance are attributable to innate differences (Garrett 1971; Ingle 1970; Jenson 1969, 1973).

According to the proponents of this view, blacks do not perform as well as whites in school because they have inferior genetic endowments for certain kinds of intellectual skills. This is an old theory, recently revived because of the apparent failure of compensatory education to raise the performance of black children on cognitive and academic tasks. The present debate on the effects of genetic endowment on black academic performance was triggered by the publication of Jensen's (1969) article in the *Harvard Educational Review*, "How Much Can We Boost IQ and Scholastic Achievement?" The response to Jensen's thesis has been enormous (Dreger 1973:194) but generally within the framework of the heredity–environment issue.

I focus my comments on Jensen's work because (a) unlike other hereditists (e.g., Herrnstein) Jensen deals directly with black–white differences; (b) Jensen has provided the most elaborate and systematic attempt to explain black–white differences in school performance in terms of innate racial differences; (c) his work contains many serious empirical distortions which both his critics and his supporters, enamored of his "methodological elegance," seem to have ignored; (d) the policy implication of Jensen's theory is likely to reinforce the very factors that cause black–white differences, factors largely ignored in his analysis; and (e) Jensen's work is being used by some whites to justify their opposition to school desegregation.

Jensen's Methodological Problems

Jensen calculates that about 80% of a person's IQ is inherited and about 20% is attributable to environment. He then suggests that not only are individual differences in IQ within a given population largely attributable to heredity, but so too are differences in IQ between two populations, such as blacks and whites in the United States. His position is succinctly stated in his testimony before the U.S. Senate Select Committee on Equal Educational Opportunity:

> A hypothesis that I believe comprehends more of the facts and is consistent with more of the converging lines of evidence than any other I know of, in its simplest terms, is the hypothesis that (a) the heritability of IQ is the same *within* the white and black population as *between* the populations, and (b) the genetic variance involved in IQ is about one-fifth less in the black than in the white population [1972:10].

Although he states that this is only an hypothesis, it is nevertheless the one he favors: "It is also, in my opinion, more consistent with all the evidence I have reviewed than any other hypothesis I have seen presented [by the environmentalists]." The major weakness of Jensen's argument is that the range of environmental variation within the general American population or within the black or within the white populations is of a different order from the range of environmental variation created by social differences between blacks and whites in American society (Sowell 1973). Hence the weight of environment influencing IQ within each population is much less than the weight of environment influencing IQ differences between the two populations. More important, a comparison of individuals within the black population or within the white population is a comparison of biological organisms, whereas a comparison between black and white populations is a comparison of sociologically rather than biologically defined groups. The two levels of comparison, the biological and the sociological, are not the same. As Alland (1973) points out, tests administered to individuals (within any given population) may validly demonstrate both hereditary and environmental factors in IQ because these are studies of "units that are biological in nature, i.e., individual organisms [pp. 181–183]." But studies of social groups such as blacks and whites in the United States, never include sufficient controls to distinguish biological differences from environmental (see also Crow 1969).

Jensen assumes that in the United States blacks belong to one genetic grouping and whites to another. Two factors, at least, suggest that this is not necessarily so. First, recent studies show that tribal groups in Africa belong to several distinct genetic groupings (Hiernaux 1968, quoted in Alland 1973). Thus the black Africans who initially entered the United States did not come from one genetic grouping. Alland (1973:190) cites a study by Pollitzer (1958) which shows that black slaves entering Charleston between 1733 and 1807 came from areas in Africa covering 1000 miles of coastland and extending some 600 miles inland. The range of genetic groupings from which those slaves were drawn was therefore extensive. In addition, within the United States there has always been a great deal of miscegenation between blacks and whites, the offspring of such relationships usually socially defined as black. It is doubtful that the black population of the United States constitutes a genetic group upon which a theory like Jensen's can be validly based. The extent to which the present white population in the United States constitutes a genetic group is similarly questionable.

Jensen's explanation of black–white differences in IQ in terms of heredity also suffers from what Bakan (1967) and LeVine (1970) have called *interpretive fallacy*. According to LeVine, this interpretive fallacy is commonly found in quantitative comparisons and, among some psychologists, "has assumed a certain legitimacy." The fallacy is the assumption that "the demonstration of a statistically significant difference in means between two groups necessarily supports the investigator's hypothesis concerning causes or symptoms of the difference" [LeVine 1970:571]. The investigator may pay scrupulous attention to those factors his hypothesis suggests to him are important while neglecting others that are equally significant or could suggest an alternative hypothesis. Several points in Jensen's explanation of black–white differences illustrate this fallacy.

He reports, for instance, that in his own study he has discovered that children from disadvantaged backgrounds score 8 to 10 points higher in IQ on a retest following a "play therapy" in which he and the children got better acquainted (Jensen 1969:100). But to support his thesis that black–white differences in IQ are attributable to genetic differences, Jensen uncritically cites evidence from previous studies, especially those reviewed by Shuey (1966), in which the researchers were not cautious about testing and retesting disadvantaged children.

A second example concerns the discussion of the hereditary basis of social class differences in IQ. Jensen (1969:75) cites Cyril Burt's (1963) contention that inheritance of intelligence conforms to a Mendelian polygenic model. But, as Alland (1973:195) points out, Jensen does not add that the reason why British class IQ has remained remarkably stable for nearly a century is that social mobility permits lower-class children with high IQs to move up, while middle- and upper-class children with low IQs move down in each generation. If social mobility were completely absent in Britain and the classes were static, the class means in IQ would disappear over a period of five generations. Alland further points out that this model cannot be applied to the study of class differences in IQ within the black population in the United States "because there is little real social mobility" for blacks. Most blacks are held in the lower class irrespective of their IQs.

Many scholars, including his critics, have given Jensen much credit for his careful scholarship, especially in amassing evidence to support his thesis. But few have taken pains to check Jensen's interpretations of these data against their original sources. Alland (1973:192–197) found many distortions in Jensen's representation: accepting uncritically those studies that appear to support his thesis (e.g., those contained in Shuey's review) and distorting others so that their results appear to conform to his general thesis. A few examples will illustrate these distortions.

1. Burt (1963), in his study of black IQ, indicated that there is a lack in the 70–90 IQ range, but Jensen (1969:23) quotes Burt as saying that there is an excess in the 70–90 IQ range among blacks.

2. Cooper and Zubek (1958) concluded that dull animals in their experimental study benefitted greatly from stimulation, but Jensen (1969:40–41) quotes them as saying the opposite.

3. Wheeler (1942) studied the effects of environmental improvement on IQ decline among Tennessee mountain children and found that in most years there was no decline in IQ. However, the chronological IQ of those children who were frequently held back (i.e., repeated grades), especially in the higher grades, dropped by as much as 10 points. The latter situation depressed the IQ scores of other children in a given grade.[4] Ignoring Wheeler's careful analysis, Jensen (1969:63) states that Wheeler's study showed a decline in IQ group, dropping from 103 to 80 points. In actual fact, the decline was from 102.76 to 101.00.

4. Heber and Dever (1969) studied a special group of mentally retarded children in a specific "problem" neighborhood in Milwaukee. This neighborhood, which contained 5% of the city's population, had about 33.3% of its mentally retarded children. The study was not about the relationship between race and intelligence; rather, it appeared to be an attempt to show that mental retardation is culturally, not genetically, determined. Yet Jensen (1969:83) interprets the authors' findings as estimating that IQs below 75 have a much higher incidence among black children than among white children at every level of socioeconomic status.

5. The final example concerns Jensen's attempt (1969:86–87) to demonstrate that blacks are intellectually inferior to whites because they are in the lower rung of the evolutionary ladder. According to Dreger (1973:199), underlying Jensen's view on the relative evolutionary positions of blacks and whites is the notion that members of a species on the lower scale of evolution tend to mature more quickly at birth. Jensen used the studies of intellectual and motor development of African children by Geber (1958) and Geber and Dean (1957) to show that blacks are on the lower rung of the evolutionary scale. To this end he cites Geber's statement that African children are superior to European children in motor development. (He does not mention Geber's finding that African children are also intellectually superior). But, as Alland notes (1973:197), what is the scientific basis upon which Jensen

---

[4]What is meant is that the overall effect of the low score of the repeaters was to lower the average score of the children of the same age group, although some of the children might be in higher grades.

can generalize from a single study of a single African community in Africa to behavioral and cognitive patterns among black Americans in the United States? Furthermore, one recent study (cited in Dreger 1973:199) has challenged the conclusions of Geber and Dean regarding the relative precocity of African infants.

It seems obvious from these and other distortions that Jensen's basic strategy is to manipulate available data to support his thesis that black–white differences in IQ and school performance are attributable to innate differences.

Theoretical Problems

There is some evidence that genetic factors account for differences in IQ among individuals (see Jensen 1969; Vandenberg 1971; Vernon 1969). This evidence comes from two types of research: One type is the study of similarity in IQ (a) of children and foster parents with children and biological parents, (b) of identical twins raised together and those raised apart, and (c) of identical and fraternal twins (Vandenberg 1971:184;198). The other type of research is the study of gene-controlled differences in individual intelligence, such as the effects of inbreeding, of mutant genes, and of chromosomal abnormalities on intelligence (Vandenberg 1971:198–212). It is doubtful, however, that the findings of these studies thus far are sufficient to warrant Jensen's generalization that 80% of a person's intelligence is inherited and 20% is attributable to environment. He rests this conclusion primarily on four separate studies of identical twins reared apart. He applies the same reasoning in explaining why blacks generally score lower on IQ tests than whites. He reports that the consensus among psychologists is that blacks are on the average 15 points lower than whites in IQ. This difference he says, may diminish but does not completely disappear when blacks and whites of the same income, occupation, and educational level are compared. He therefore concludes that black–white differences in IQ must be caused by heredity rather than the influence of environment.

As noted earlier, genetic factors that cause individual differences in cognitive skills or IQ within the black population are probably the same as those that cause individual differences within the white population; but the same factors do not necessarily cause black–white differences in cognitive skills. I do not mean by this that blacks and whites may not differ in their genetic equipment for cognitive development. Vandenberg (1971:203–204) reports, for instance, that one gene which causes mental deficiency, phenylketonuria (PKU), is known to occur more frequently in the white population than in the black. I only wish to point out that I have found no research which shows that specific genes linked to lower IQ are found in higher proportion among blacks than among whites. Nor have studies shown that specific genes that encourage conceptual and abstract thinking are found in higher proportion among whites than among blacks. In short, no studies have empirically demonstrated that gene-controlled deficiencies in mental abilities, such as inbreeding, mutant genes, or chromosomal abnormalities, are found in higher proportions among blacks than among whites.

Jensen distinguishes between two levels of intelligence (IQ), one of which is more evenly distributed among blacks and whites whereas the other is found in higher proportion among whites. According to Jensen, level I IQ is characterized by more concrete, nonabstracting thinking; level II, on the other hand, is characterized by conceptual and problem-solving skills, grasping relations, and symbolic thinking. The two levels, he says, are genotypically distinct. The children of all social classes, including both black and white children, possess type I IQ to about the same degree during the various stages of their development. They also possess type II IQ during the initial stages of their development, but type II IQ tends to develop more fully among higher social classes and whites with increasing age (Jensen 1969; see also Jensen 1972a:4):

> Level I abilities are seen as developing rapidly and as having about the same course of development and final level in both lower and middle SES [socioeconomic status] groups. Level II abilities, by contrast, develop slowly at first, attain prominence between four and six years of age, and show an increasing difference between the SES groups with increasing age. This formulation is consistent with the increasing SES differences in mental age on standard IQ tests, which tap mostly Level II ability [1969:115].

I prefer to designate Jensen's levels of intelligence (IQ) as types of cognitive skills. The qualitative difference in the cognitive skills of black and white children as sampled by IQ tests is not necessarily caused by differences in neural structures or heredity. I suggest, instead, that it may be caused by differences in the cognitive demands of their different social and occupational roles. White people, who traditionally occupy the professional and technical positions, have developed the second type of cognitive skills to a greater degree because it is required by their social roles. Blacks, who have traditionally been excluded from such positions, have not developed the second type of cognitive skills to the same degree. On the other hand, it is possible that blacks also possess the second type of cognitive skills to the same degree as whites, except that their skills are adapted to solving different problems which are not taken into account in the construction of the IQ tests. Just because the conceptual and problem-solving skills of a people are not directed primarily toward academic performance or the requirements of the social and occupational roles from which they have traditionally been excluded, it does not mean that they are deficient in intelligence.

Race, Sex, and Inequality

Jensen's "reasonable hypothesis" concerning the social and economic inequality between blacks and whites is the following. He first notes that there is a high correlation both between IQ and scholastic performance and between IQ and socioeconomic status. He then argues that socioeconomic status is determined primarily by IQ (Jensen 1969:76). He points out that people with high IQs are concentrated in the most desirable social and economic roles, whereas those with low IQs are concentrated in the least desirable social and economic roles. Blacks, he observes, are disproportionately represented in both the low IQ groups and the least desirable social and economic roles, whereas whites are heavily represented in both the high IQ groups and the most desirable social and economic roles. From these observations, he concludes that blacks occupy a lower social and economic position because they have low IQs which prevent them from doing well in school and thereby from moving into the more desirable social and economic roles (Jensen 1969:76–79).

Just as whites have more education, more desirable occupational roles, higher income, and higher IQs and scholastic achievement scores than blacks, so also black women rank higher than black men in most of these respects (Jensen 1971; see also Sowell 1973). Various studies among blacks of high IQ show females outnumbering males by ratios ranging from 2.7:1 to 5.5:1, whereas in the general population the distribution of high IQ between the sexes is about even (Sowell 1973:35). The differences between black men and black women, therefore, provide a good opportunity to test Jensen's hypothesis that black–white differences in the same areas are attributable to genetic differences.

Jensen has attempted to explain the sex differences in such matters among blacks. In a paper published in 1971, he posed the following question about the relationship between race, sex, and ability: "Are mental ability differences between the sexes greater among blacks than among whites?" He notes that this question is "suggested by a host of observations with great social, economic and educational implications [p. 107]." He presents data to show that when compared with members of their own sex in the general population, black women are superior to black men in the highest occupational categories (e.g., professional, managerial, and skilled workers), in income levels, educational attainment, classes for the gifted, college scholarships, and so forth. Furthermore, data from IQ and scholastic achievement tests show that black females are superior to black males by twice as much as white females are superior to white males in the same tests. Thus both forms of data show that "the socially observed sex differences among Blacks in areas in which mental ability and education are assumed to play an important role (e.g., most desirable occupational roles and the attendant monetary rewards) are quite in line with the sex differences measured by standard tests of mental ability and scholastic achievement [p. 155]."

Jensen then proceeds to explain the sex differences among blacks. He rejects various "cultural explanations" [1971:108], suggests the possibility of genetic or environmental explanation, but considers a statistical explanation more plausible. Briefly, Jensen says that more black women are found in the upper end of occupational and educational achievements than black men because black women have higher IQs than black men, while blacks as a group have a lower mean IQ than whites. As a result, in most selection situations the sex ratio is magnified more in favor of black females, since the selection cutoff is usually above the mean IQ of the black population (Jensen (1971:155–156).

But why is the mean IQ of black females higher than that of black males? Furthermore, would it not be just as well to explain black–white differences in terms of differences in mean IQ rather than heredity (i.e., to provide a statistical explanation rather than a genetic)? One can follow Jensen's logic and argue that whites are superior to blacks in college scholarships, gifted classes, skilled occupations, and the like because whites have a higher mean IQ than blacks, so that in most selection situations the race ratio is magnified in favor of whites over blacks.

An alternative interpretation I propose is applicable to both black–white differences and differences between black males and black females. It is actually suggested, but not explored, in Jensen's paper. He asks whether differences between the sexes in employment, income, and education, which "vary markedly within each racial group," could not be attributable entirely to cultural factors. For example, (a) differences in the roles black and white cultures assign to males and females may account for the observed differences; or (b) American society may discriminate against black males more than against black females in social and occupational roles (1971:108). I do not think that blacks prefer that their females have the most desirable occupations, earn more money, get more college education, and the like any more than whites do. The real explanation lies in the second alternative, which Jensen fails to explore, that American society, while it discriminates against blacks in general, gives preferential treatment to black females in education, occupation, and income (Clark 1967:142; Harrington 1967:250).

Although I have found no studies that systematically compare the social and occupational opportunities for black males and females within the caste system, I have discussed this matter with black Americans in different parts of the United States. Among them it appears to be generally believed that women have better opportunities than the men. Many of my informants themselves either come from or know families where the females are more educated than the males; in contrast, I have met fewer whites with similar backgrounds and knowledge. Among black married couples, there are proportionately far more instances in which the wife is more educated than the husband. The explanation blacks offer for this tendency is that black women have traditionally had greater opportunities to participate in more desirable positions in the caste system. It should be noted, too, that under slavery more black women tended to be house servants and more men field hands and that the whites had greater fear of the physical nearness of the black males. In any case, black families have responded to this differential opportunity by encouraging their daughters in their educational efforts more than their sons. As the former grow up, they become more aware of their opportunities and tend to develop better attitudes toward school and better work habits and therefore are able to do better in school. For this reason, I suggest that differential opportunity causes differences in IQ test scores and scholastic performance between blacks and whites and between black females and black males.

In conclusion, Jensen's biogenetic theory does not provide an adequate explanation of the black–white gap in academic performance—for both methodological and theoretical reasons. Those variables which adequately explain individual differences do not necessarily explain group differences; blacks and whites are sociologically defined races and cannot be treated as if they were precise genetic populations; some evidence presented to support the genetic theory distorts the findings of the original studies; and failure to consider an obvious alternative structural hypothesis does not lend strong support to the genetic theory.

Black School Failure: Jensen's Solution

Jensen explains black–white differences in school performance on the basis of his distinction between level I and level II intelligence, the learning abilities he says are distributed differently in black and white populations. He argues that blacks do less well than whites in their schoolwork because the traditional methods of classroom instruction rest on the assumption that all children possess level II intelligence, and hence teachers place great emphasis on cognitive and conceptual learning rather than associative learning. This puts blacks at a disadvantage, since they are not equipped for such cognitive and conceptual learning. Consequently, blacks fail to learn the basic skills of which they are capable.

The remedy Jensen proposes for boosting black scholastic achievement follows directly from his hypothesis regarding the genetic basis of black–white inequality. He says that the gap in intelligence or IQ between blacks and whites is not subject to closure, but he hypothesizes that the gap in formal education (and presumably social and economic status) can be bridged through a special technique of classroom instruction. To improve black academic performance the schools must adopt instructional techniques that make use of type I abilities, that is, techniques stressing memorization or rote learning, trial-and-error learning, and the like (Jensen 1969:112–113, 115–117).[5]

Jensen's solution is not satisfactory because differences in cognitive skills are not genetically based, as he supposes; they are probably adaptive responses to the different roles ascribed to blacks and whites in the American system of racial castes. Moreover, to adopt instructional techniques that emphasize associative learning is to accept Jensen's false assumption that blacks are capable only of those learning skills and styles forced upon them by their menial roles. This would mean perpetuating the very skills and styles which are dysfunctional for achieving and performing the more desirable roles in a modern industrial, bureaucratic, and urban society. On the contrary, a better solution to the present problem would be to expand the opportunity for blacks to participate in those more desirable social and occupa-

---

[5]Jensen illustrates this with the result of an experiment in which lower-class and middle-class children were both asked first to learn and recall 20 familiar objects (e.g., doll, toy car, comb, cap, etc.) and then to classify 20 familiar objects into categories (e.g., animals, furniture, clothing, or food). He states that both groups learned and recalled the objects just about the same. However, lower-class children were less able to classify the objects into categories according to attributes. That is, they were less able to treat the classification problem conceptually (Jensen 1969:112–113).

tional roles which facilitate the development and use of the conceptual and cognitive skills found not only among white middle-class Americans but also among the middle-class people of other societies.

Summary

The cultural deprivation theory assumes that black children fail in school because they are deficient in the cognitive, linguistic, and other skills that promote a white middle-class type of school success. The reason for their lack of such skills, according to this theory, is that black parents do not raise their children the way that white middle-class parents do. The cultural conflict theory, on the other hand, asserts that black children fail to achieve white middle-class type of school success because they possess different linguistic, cognitive, and other school-related skills that are not recognized by the schools for instructional purposes. The institutional deficiency theory maintains that the failure of black children is attributable to the fact that schools are organized to promote success among white middle-class children and failure among black children. Educational inequality theory blames black school failure on lack of sufficient remedial programs to counteract the negative educational influences of the home and community. Jensen's theory suggests that there may be a genetic or biological basis for the school failure.

None of these theories examines the nature of the American caste system and its possible influence on black school failure. Only the institutional deficiency theory comes close to doing so when it asserts that the schools are organized to promote failure among blacks and success among whites, but this theory does not explain why the schools are organized that way.

Jensen's proposed solution must be viewed with skepticism. No school district has, to my knowledge, taken his proposal seriously. However, the proposals of some other theorists reviewed earlier have been tried extensively. Chapter 3 focuses upon these efforts to close the academic gap between blacks and whites.

3

Closing the School
Performance Gap

An Overview of Earlier Reforms

Debates over the causes of differences in school performance between black and white students in the United States are at least as old as public school education for the two races. The debates became more pronounced in the North when many blacks from the rural South began to settle there after World War I (see Bond 1966; Klineberg 1935). While one theory after another was put forward to explain why blacks did not perform as well as whites in school, there were no public programs designed to reduce the achievement gap between the two races until the close of the 1940s.

The first major effect was the work of the National Association for the Advancement of Colored People (NAACP) in the areas of school equalization and desegregation (see Bullock 1970; Ovington 1911). The NAACP maintained that differences in the school resources provided to black and white children in the legally segregated schools of the South resulted in inferior education for blacks and therefore in lower black school performance. It sought to improve black school performance by eliminating such differences in resources through school desegregation, a point it won in the Supreme Court in 1954.

Other efforts to improve black school performance arose from national concern with manpower development to meet the scientific and professional needs of the United States after World War II. Because of the national concern with manpower development, these early programs were designed to meet the needs of the better-than-average or superior black students rather than to improve the school performance of black children in general. One of the earliest such programs was the National Scholarship Service Fund for Negro Students (NSSFNS), which was begun in 1949 and was in some ways similar to the Upward Bound Program of the 1960s which is discussed later in the chapter. The fund selected "superior" black students in high school and prepared them through counseling and in other ways for predominantly white colleges, where it supported them financially. By 1954, this program had placed some 2300 black students in interracial colleges at a cost of $450,000 in scholarship aid (Ferguson and Plaut 1954:137, 140). During the second half of the 1950s, programs designed to search out and develop talents were expanded in some school districts such as New York City to include more able students, who then received more intensive compensatory treatment. This was perhaps the beginning of modern compensatory education, although it addressed itself mainly to culturally deprived students who were also the academically superior students of their communities (Krugman 1965:241).

Programs for talent search and development among black students continued on a limited scale until the early part of the 1960s when a combination of factors led to their replacement by more comprehensive compensatory education programs. One of these factors was the need to deal with problems of urban juvenile delinquency; another was the developing goal of eliminating poverty in America. Both juvenile delinquency and poverty were causally linked to inadequate education. Eventually the target population of compensatory education changed from the academically able to the culturally deprived children in poverty areas in general. Since the early part of the 1960s, compensatory education has been the major strategy in efforts to improve black school performance. School integration, though not to the same extent, has also been an important strategy. These two strategies form the major focus of this chapter.

Other strategies which have emerged since the 1960s include attempts to control public schools by local (often ethnic) populations or neighborhood groups (community control strategy) and attempts to restructure children's education radically, either within or outside the existing school systems (alternative schools strategy). The demand for community control of public schools originated in the late 1960s as blacks and some other groups began to feel that public school systems had failed to change fast enough to meet their needs. In large cities like New York, advocates of the community control strategy sought to decentralize the school systems in order to vest various subcommunities with authority over local schools attended by their children and make these schools accountable to local parents rather than to remote central administrations. The community control strategy has not been effectively accomplished in any American city. In any case, there are as yet no studies showing its effectiveness in improving the school performance of black children or other children.

The alternative schools strategy also originated in the late 1960s because blacks and some other people felt that compensatory education was not likely to bring about the kind of change in the education system they desired. Alternative schools advocates also maintain that public school systems are either unresponsive to new needs or change too slowly for their liking. Some of these reformers have established alternative schools within the existing system of public schools; others have established alternative schools outside the public school system. Only a small number of such schools have been established primarily to meet the needs of black children, and only a few of these are operated by black people themselves. As I pointed out in Chapter 1, there are major differences between the alternative schools established to cater to the needs of white middle-class children and those established by blacks, since the latter perceive their educational needs to be essentially different from the needs of the former. As in the case of community control, black advocates of alternative schools for blacks want to demonstrate that black people can run their own schools just as successfully as white people do in the suburbs. They further want to show that the school performance of black children can be raised substantially in such schools. Alternative schools, like community controlled schools, probably succeed in enhancing black awareness. However, there are no adequate studies assessing their effectiveness in raising black school performance. For this reason, the present chapter does not discuss either the community control or the alternative school strategies further but focuses on school desegregation or integration and on compensatory education strategies, where sufficient studies have been carried out to assess their effectiveness in raising black school performance.

The School Integration Strategy

Why should integration improve black performance? Those who want to integrate the schools justify their position by saying that black children attending integrated schools do better than those attending segregated schools. But the reasons they give for the lower performance of those in segregated schools have changed. Before 1960, they argued that segregated black schools had inferior resources, which resulted in inferior education and hence in lower black school performance. As evidence of the disparity in school resources between black and white schools, they pointed to differences in school buildings (size, arrangement, and appearance); physical facilities (including toilets, laboratory capacity, textbooks, drinking fountains, basketball courts); the distance children had to travel to school; the number of courses offered in the curriculum; the length of school terms; the professional qualifications of the teachers; the system of grading and promoting pupils; and extracurricular activities (Ashmore 1954:109–110). Because school authorities were unwilling or unable to equalize resources in segregated schools, it was believed that school integration would eliminate the differences, provide blacks and whites with the same education, and thus raise the level of black school performance.

At the time the Supreme Court ordered the abolition of legally established separate school systems in the South, some southern states (e.g., Mississippi) began serious "equalization" programs which involved spending huge sums of money to bring black schools up to the standards of white schools (Bullock 1970:260). In the North, the urban school districts usually maintained that their local funds were apportioned equally to all schools, although it was not possible to show the exact amount spent on a specific school plant. However, several studies, especially those of Coleman *et al.* (1966), and the U.S. Commission on Civil Rights (1967), showed that segregated black schools throughout the country tended to have fewer resources and thereby provided inferior education relative to white schools.

The Supreme Court decision in 1954 has not resulted in a speedy dismantling of the dual school system in the South; nor has it prevented the continuation and further development of segregated schools in northern cities. Furthermore, it has not resulted in the elimination of the inequalities in school resources that existed between black and white schools. Thus, from the standpoint of the advocates of school integration, blacks continue to receive inferior education, which contributes to their lower school performance.

During the decade of the 1960s, advocates of school integration added a new dimension to the causal link between school segregation and lower black school performance. They argued that black students in segregated schools did not perform as well as white students, not only because of discriminatory policies and practices in the predominantly black schools but also because (a) black schools are stigmatized as inferior by the community; and (b) black schools do not provide black students with opportunities to interact with their white middle-class peers, who would provide them with models of success in both school and later life (U.S. Commission on Civil Rights 1967:106).

Integrationists further contended (U.S. Commission on Civil Rights 1967:105; see also U.S. Senate Select Committee 1972:220) that the environment of an integrated school offers "substantial support for high achievement and aspirations" for the following reasons:

> The majority of children in such schools do not have problems of self-confidence due to race and the schools are not stigmatized as inferior. The students are likely to assume that they will succeed in school and in their future careers, for the school often reflects the mainstream of American society. The environment in such schools is well endowed with models of academic and occupational success [p. 105].

This interactionist theory of the beneficial effects of school integration, rather than the concern for equality of resources between black and white schools, currently dominates the thinking of integrationists.

But the theory explains neither why black schools are stigmatized as inferior by their communities nor why black students have doubts about their ability to succeed in a predominantly white society. Because the theory provides only a superficial explanation of black school failure, it is therefore an inadequate basis for correcting the problem. The theory fails to see that the stigmatization of black schools by the white community is a part of the general white attitude toward blacks and their institutions (e.g., school, family, community). This attitude is often given substance through discriminatory policies and practices against predominantly black schools. The theory also fails to see the doubts of black students about their ability to succeed in adult life as a realistic appraisal of their chances in the American caste system. In fact, there is a kind of cultural deprivation assumption in this theory that might be translated as follows: Black children need to associate with middle-class white children who have been properly socialized because this association will compensate for the failure of black parents, peers, and communities to provide black students with adequate models of success. In general, the interactionist theory attempts to explain why black children do not perform as well as white children in school without reference to the operation of the caste system.

Not everyone, of course, accepts the theory that school integration will improve black school performance relative to white school performance. Many opponents of school desegregation point to the poorer school performance of black children as undeniable evidence that blacks are intellectually inferior to whites and therefore should be educated in separate schools. That is, they justify their opposition to school integration on the grounds that black school performance is lower than that of whites. To support their position that segregated schools should be maintained because whites are superior to blacks in intellectual functioning, several school districts in the South began to publish school test results of black and white students at about the time of the Supreme Court decision in 1954. In all cases, black school performance lagged behind that of whites. The opponents of school desegregation interpreted these differences in school performance not as results of differences in the qualities of education provided to blacks and whites but as evidence of inherent intellectual differences that justified maintaining separate schools for the two races (see Weinberg 1970:32–33; *Southern School News* 1956:2–3, 1957:13). Although not expressed in these terms, the opposition to school integration in the North, the flight of whites from the central cities to the suburbs, and the exclusion of blacks from the white suburbs arise partly from the belief that the gap between blacks and whites in school performance is attributable to lower black intellectual functioning rather than to discriminatory policies and practices against blacks in school and society.

The Extent of School Integration

Twenty years after the Supreme Court school desegregation order of 1954, most black children in the South as well as the North still attended schools that were predominantly black. In both regions, school integration had met with strong white opposition and political sabotage. A brief review of the course of events since 1954 will show some of the strategies used to slow down the rate of integration.

According to the U.S. Senate Select Committee's study (1972:192–215), school desegregation or integration has passed through three phases since the *Brown* v. *Board of Education* decision by the United States Supreme Court in 1954. The first phase, the period of *"all deliberate speed,"* lasted from 1954 to 1964, when all efforts were focused on desegregating the southern dual school system. Court orders permitted southern school districts a period of transition during which they were encouraged to eliminate officially sanctioned segregated schools "with all deliberate speed."

The response of southern whites varied from compliance to defiance. Compliance was easy in some school districts in the border states, where the changeover was less revolutionary or where blacks made up only a small percentage of the population, so that the economic benefits of a unified school district outweighed the breach with tradition (Bullock 1970:235). Some school districts (like those in St. Louis, San Antonio, and Louisville) developed well planned and successful desegregation programs. In others, like that of Baltimore, plans for desegregation were sabotaged by white opposition and violence. Still other desegregation plans were stalled by the intervention of higher political authorities like Governor Orval Faubus in Little Rock.

Except for Kentucky and West Virginia, various southern states generally resorted to legislative and administrative tactics to avoid complying with the desegregation order. Bullock lists a number of "resistance laws" passed by various southern legislatures, which he says were designed to achieve three things: (a) to force blacks to sue each school board or superintendent and thereby diffuse the impact of school desegregation through litigation; (b) to make it difficult for desegregated schools to exist for want of white students; and (c) to enable superintendents to exclude black students from all-white schools on spurious grounds which could not be proved to be in violation of the law. (Table 3.1 summarizes the resistance legislation passed between 1954 and 1957; other laws were adopted thereafter.)

Pupil placement laws, for example, authorized local school boards to assign pupils to schools on the basis of psychological aptitudes for certain kinds of teaching or on the basis of their effect on existing standards. Laws relating to public school funds either made it a felony for a school official to spend tax money on schools with pupils from both races or provided state funds for private schools. There was even a "readiness legislation," passed by the state of Mississippi, to abolish the public schools rather than comply with the desegregation order. Prince Edward County in Virginia closed its public schools in 1959 rather than desegregate them but was ordered to open the schools again in 1964 by the Supreme Court. Some states appropriated large sums of money to bring black schools up to the standards already enjoyed by white schools. The funds were used to increase the salaries of black teachers, construct new school buildings, and provide more varied courses in black schools. But these various tactics were usually declared unconstitutional by the courts (see Bullock 1970:250–262; Ladenburg and McFeeley 1969:101; U.S. Senate Select Committee

Table 3.1

Types of "Resistance Legislation" Adopted before 1957 by Southern States

Tactic authorized or required by legislation	Alabama	Arkansas	Florida	Georgia	Louisiana	Mississippi	North Carolina	South Carolina	Virginia
Abolition of schools by Legislation (L) Local option (O)				L		LO	O	L	O
Grants for private education				X			X		X
Sale or lease of school facilities	X			X		X		X	
Use of public funds for segregated schools only				X	X		X	X	X
Pupil assignment	X		X				X		X

Compulsory attendance
  Repeal (R)
  Modification (M)
	M			M	M	R	M

Extraordinary powers for governor		X				X	

Teacher employment law
  Abolition (A)
  Modification (M)
	M		M	M	M	A	A

Restrictions on or probe of NAACP	X		X	X	X	X	X
"Good character" college registration certificate				X			
Withdrawal of permission to sue				X			
Interposition, nullifi- cation, protest	X	X	X	X	X	X	X

SOURCE: *Southern School News* **3**(7):2.

1972). As of May 1965 (10 years after the desegregation order), 97% of all black children in the south were still attending all-black schools (Ladenburg and McFeeley 1969:101).

In the second phase, which lasted from 1964 to 1969, the federal government played a leading role in school desegregation, as a result of the Civil Rights Act of 1964. Several provisions of that act directly involved the federal government in desegregation issues. Title IV, for example, authorized the attorney general to file a desegregation suit against a school system "upon receiving citizen's complaint." It also authorized the U.S. Office of Education to provide technical and financial assistance to school districts attempting to desegregate their schools. The most important section of the act bearing on school desegregation was Title VI, which barred racial discrimination in any programs receiving federal financial assistance. In effect, Title VI compelled the Department of Health, Education, and Welfare to see "that school districts receiving Federal assistance operated their schools in compliance with the 14th Amendment standards [U.S. Senate Select Committee 1972:195]." On this basis, HEW provided a guideline which required most southern dual school systems to extend their "free choice" plan to all grades in the fall of 1965. The HEW guideline was later amended to require other means of desegregation (e.g., rezoning of school attendance areas) where free choice would not be adequate. The courts generally enforced the requirements of the guideline. As a result, the proportion of black students attending schools with whites in the Southern states increased from 2.25% in 1964–1965 to 13.9% in the 1967–1968 school year.

The Green decision in 1968 further accelerated the process of school desegregation in the South. In that case, the Supreme Court took a firm position about full school desegregation. The Court not only held that desegregation required more than a free-choice approach but also rejected its previous "all deliberate speed" formula. Instead, it held that "the burden of a school board today is to come forward with a plan which promises realistically to work and promises realistically to work *now*" [quoted in U.S. Senate Select Committee 1972:197]. On the basis of the *Green* decision, HEW drew up a new guideline which in effect ended the era of free choice. Among other things, the new guideline, enforced by the federal courts, encouraged such mechanisms as zoning, pairing of schools, grade reorganization, and the like as effective means of achieving desegregation where free choice had failed. School districts were asked to prepare to comply with the new law—to desegregate at the opening of the 1968–1969 school year or 1969–1970 at the latest (U.S. Senate Select Committee 1972:188). As a result, there was a

considerable increase in the number of black pupils attending integrated schools in the South at the end of this period (1972:112).

Efforts to integrate the schools during this period were not confined to the South. In the early part of the 1960s, civil rights groups
began more active campaigns to integrate the schools in northern cities,
partly because of growing inequalities in these schools and partly because they were encouraged by success in other areas of civil rights.
They filed suits in a number of cities to force local school boards to
integrate their schools. The position of the courts in such cases has been
that intentional segregation is unconstitutional. Also, in the early and
middle 1960s, a period of sensitivity to civil rights, a few northern
states—California, Massachusetts, New York, New Jersey, Wisconsin,
Connecticut, and Illinois—took some legislative and administrative
measures to correct racial imbalance in their public schools. These
states took the position that segregation in public schools had detrimental effects on the education of black children. At the end of this
period, however, most black children in the North were still attending
schools in which the majority or all the pupils were black (U.S. Senate
Select Committee 1972:112).

The third period began in 1969 with the start of the Nixon administration. It was a period marked by inconsistency and confusion in the
federal administration of school integration, a backlash in Congress,
and a decline in public support for school integration. The shift in
federal policy on school desegregation began in July 1969 with the
transfer of the responsibility for the enforcement of school desegregation from HEW to the Justice Department. HEW then requested delays
in court-ordered desegregation in Mississippi. In 1970, there was an
apparent resumption of the administration's commitment to enforcement of school desegregation.

Later, however, the administration proposed two bills—the national student transportation moratorium bill and the equal education
opportunity bill—which would have undermined desegregation efforts. These bills were not passed by the Ninety-second Congress, but
the U.S. Senate Select Committee (1972) suggested that

> with their focus on the misleading issues of "busing" and their misguided implica-
> tions that desegregation should be pursued more actively in later than in earlier
> grades, they have further distracted attention from the real and legitimate concerns
> of families and educators in 1,500 desegregated school districts [pp. 206–207].

Moreover, in the 1970–1971 school year, when "substantial numbers of school districts began to operate on a fully desegregated basis,"
lack of federal supervision resulted both in various forms of discrimina-

tion against black students and in the dismissal of black teachers and administrators. In the 1971–1972 school year alone, about 4207 black teachers and administrators were dismissed in North Carolina, South Carolina, Georgia, Alabama, Mississippi, and Louisiana (U.S. Senate Select Committee 1972:201).

The backlash in Congress manifested itself in the several amendments to the Emergency School Aid Act adopted in the fall of 1971 in the House of Representatives. These amendments prohibited federal funds from being used for transportation in desegregation; prohibited HEW and the Justice Department from requiring, supporting, or encouraging transportation to achieve desegregation; and limited the power of the federal courts to order desegregation that would involve transportation or school assignment other than by free choice before all other appeals had been exhausted. These amendments were rejected by the Senate early in 1972 (U.S. Senate Select Committee 1972:203–204). However, on July 24, 1974, the Senate approved "a compromise provision to limit the busing of children for school desegregation" when it passed the Education Act of 1974 (New York Times 1974:1).

During the same period, there was a significant decline in public support of busing to achieve school desegregation. In March 1971, the Harris poll of some 1600 families found that 47% were in favor of busing for the purpose of school integration; 41% were opposed to it. A year later, a similar poll found only 25% in favor of busing children for integration, a decline of 22%; 69% of the families polled were against it, an increase of 28%. The U.S. Senate Select Committee (1972) attributed the shift in public attitude toward integration "in large part to a lack of constructive national leadership in both the legislative and the executive branches of Government [p. 207]."

Public opposition to school integration is just as strong in the North as it is in the South, and segregation is a characteristic common to both regions. But because of the legal technicalities, desegregation is more difficult to accomplish in the North than in the South, where segregation was established by law and could be challenged on constitutional grounds. It is not always easy in the North to prove that segregation is the result of an official intention, nor has the federal government, even at the height of its leadership in desegregation cases, been active in encouraging or enforcing school integration in the North. This situation has resulted in increasing segregation in the North while the reverse has probably been true of the South. The ruling by the United States Supreme Court in 1974 against busing children across school district lines for the purpose of racial integration is likely to retard further the desegregation of the schools in northern metropolitan regions where black and white populations are almost totally segregated by school districts (see *New York Times* 1974:1).

The Results of Integration

A number of studies comparing the school performance of black students attending predominantly white schools and those attending predominantly black schools show that those in integrated schools tend to perform better than those in segregated schools (see Pettigrew 1969a,b; U.S. Civil Rights Commission 1967; U.S. Senate Select Committee 1972). These studies conclude that black students in integrated schools do better than those in segregated schools because they are in school together with white students and not merely because they are in schools with better resources. That is, the racial composition of the schools has a positive effect on black students' school performance in integrated schools, and a negative effect on their school performance in segregated schools. Does it then follow that the school performance of black students in segregated schools will improve when they are sent to integrated schools?

There has been no national assessment of the impact of school integration on the school performance of black students. This situation prompted the U.S. Senate Select Committee (1972) to remark that it is "deeply disturbed by the lack of well-organized, strategic research to more closely determine the educational effects of school integration and to explore the best educational techniques to use with integrated schools [p. 190]." Pettigrew (1969a:51–58) has noted some of the factors that inhibit systematic research on the educational effects of school integration. These include the political and ideological biases of researchers; attempts by interested parties to manage the research; lack of cooperation from different groups involved in such a politically sensitive issue as school integration; and the technical problem of designing research that would adequately account for all the variables involved.[1]

Research findings to date on the effects of school integration on school performance are mixed. Moreover, the findings tend to vary, although not systematically, "with level of education studied, the length of time in the desegregated situation, and the kinds of functions or abilities measured, the investigator, the section of the country, and so on [Roberts and Horton 1973:303]." Weinberg (1970) has reviewed several studies of the effects of school integration on the school perfor-

---

[1]Perhaps more foreign researchers should study the problems of minority education in the United States, since by virtue of their outside status they are less inhibited by these factors.

mance of black elementary and secondary school students. Eight of the ten studies reviewed dealing with the elementary school level were conducted between 1965 and 1969. The results are mixed: The studies show that when blacks and whites are matched according to socioeconomic status and IQ, the gap in school performance tends to be reduced substantially in both segregated and desegregated situations.[2] Generally, integration does not adversely affect the school performance of white students. Weinberg notes similar results in the 10 studies he reviews dealing with the secondary schools.

The U.S. Senate Select Committee study (1972:190–231) also noted similar mixed findings. The committee reviewed school integration programs in Hartford and Berkeley, as well as reports from Hoke County, North Carolina, Harrisburg, Pennsylvania, Riverside, California, and Nashville, Tennessee. The committee follows Pettigrew's crucial distinction between school desegregation and school integration. According to Pettigrew, desegregation may merely involve efforts to have black and white students in certain proportions that meet legal requirements, without any efforts to promote friendly relations in the school between the two races. Integration, on the other hand, is accompanied by such efforts (Pettigrew 1969a:74–75, 1969b:72–75). It is in the latter situation that black students are most likely to improve in school performance.

The U.S. Senate Select Committee (1972) further suggests that school integration is not necessarily a failure if it does not result in narrowing the gap in school performance between blacks and whites. Because black students tend to fall further and further behind as they get older, if integration or any other program simply holds the gap constant, it can be said to be "an impressive accomplishment [p. 225]."

The overall conclusion of the committee (and other advocates of integration) is that school integration leads to improved academic achievement for blacks if it begins in the early grades (1972:190; see also Pettigrew 1969a:72, 81–82); if it is combined with other efforts, such as strengthened curriculum, improved teaching techniques, better training of teachers, reductions in class size, and meaningful involvement of parents and members of the community (U.S. Senate Select Commitee 1972:217; see also Pettigrew 1969a:74–81); and if it involves interracial acceptance within the schools (U.S. Senate, Select Committee 1972:225; Pettigrew 1969a,b).

[2]These studies usually state that black and white students are matched according to socioeconomic status and abilities or IQ. In the context of this book, *abilities* and IQ do not refer to innate ability, because we argue that the IQs and schoolwork of black students are affected by their perceptions of their situation as a lower caste and by the nature of the skills required for performing the type of social and technoeconomic roles which American society permits them to occupy.

In spite of the lack of a systematic nationwide assessment of the impact of school integration on black school performance, available evidence suggests that the success of this strategy has been limited. This is partly because of the strong opposition to the strategy by the dominant white group, which has drastically limited the extent of integration. Furthermore, this opposition sometimes makes integration superficial, undermining whatever educational impact it is intended to have on black school performance. But a more important reason, perhaps, for this limited effect is the assumption upon which school integration is based—particularly the interactionist theory—which is not an adequate explanation of lower black school performance. Nevertheless, school integration is a desirable goal, for political, constitutional, social, and ethical reasons. Moreover, the integration movement of the past 20 years has probably prevented a further widening of the gap in school resources available to blacks and whites.

The Compensatory Education Strategy

Integrationists regard compensatory education as a necessary part of their program but not as an alternative strategy (Pettigrew 1969a:84–86; U.S. Civil Rights Commission 1967; U.S. Senate Select Committee 1972). They point out that while compensatory education is "politically expedient," there is no evidence that it can effectively improve the school performance of black children or close the gap between them and white children. Pettigrew (1969a) sums up the integrationists' view as follows:

> Compensatory education allows one to act and avoid controversy, especially if there are federal funds to pay the bill. There is only one difficulty with this "solution": there is no rigorous evidence that it works. Indeed, there is mounting evidence from throughout the nation that it resoundingly fails. This is not to say that those enthusiastically initiated programs do not improve for a time the tenor of many ghetto schools—not an unimportant achievement—... But it is to say that it remains to be demonstrated that these programs can lead to *lasting* and significant academic gains. So far, the record of programs is not encouraging [p. 85].

These comments are equally applicable to school integration strategy, but current thinking in the United States in both official and unofficial circles holds that compensatory education is a better strategy than integration.

Various compensatory education programs, based on cultural deprivation theory, are designed either to make up for the assumed deficits that cause black children to fail in school or to prevent such deficits

Table 3.2

Compensatory Education Projects in Various Communities and States before Title I and Head Start Compensatory Programs

State	Preventive compensatory projects				Remedial compensatory projects			
	Number of Communities	Before 1961	1962–1964	After 1964	Number of Communities	Before 1961	1962–1964	After 1964
Arizona	—	—	—	—	2	2	2	—
California	10	—	10	—	23	4	41	—
Colorado	1	—	—	—	1	—	2	—
Connecticut	1	—	1	—	2	1	7	2
Delaware	—	—	—	—	1	1	3	—
District of Columbia	1	—	1	—	1	3	1	—
Florida	1	—	—	1	4	—	5	—
Georgia	—	—	—	—	1	—	1	—
Illinois	1	—	1	1	2	9	11	4
Kansas	—	—	—	—	1	—	1	—
Kentucky	—	—	—	—	2	—	3	—
Maine	—	—	—	—	2	2	—	—
Maryland	2	1	1	—	3	3	11	—
Massachusetts	1	1	1		2			

Michigan	2	1	—	2	—	11	—
Minnesota	1	1	—	1	—	2	—
Missouri	2	2	—	2	2	4	—
New Jersey	1	1	—	2	—	2	—
New York	4	1	1	42+	32	34	12
New York City	1	1	1	New York	8	5	8+
North Carolina	1	1	—	2	—	3	—
North Dakota	1	—	1	—	—	—	—
Ohio	—	—	—	4	3	6	4
Oklahoma	—	—	—	1	1	2	—
Oregon	1	—	1	1	1	1	1
Pennsylvania	3	2	—	2	2	3	1
Rhode Island	1	1	—	1	—	3	—
South Carolina	1	1	—	—	—	—	—
Tennessee	1	1	—	—	—	—	—
Texas	2	1	—	2	2	3	—
Virginia	—	—	—	2	2	3	—
West Virginia	1	—	1	—	—	—	—
Wisconsin	—	—	—	2	1	6	1+

SOURCE: Edmund W. Gordon and Doxey A. Wilkerson: *Compensatory Education for the Disadvantaged: Programs and Practice: Preschool to College:* New York: College Entrance Examination Board, 1966, pp. 199–299.

[1] In a few communities and states, compensatory education programs were established exclusively or primarily to serve Native Americans, Mexican-Americans, or whites. These are communities in which the black population was relatively insignificant.

from developing in the first place. Thus the programs are either remedial or preventive. In general, compensatory education programs are
intended to rehabilitate or redeem the children from the influences of
their home environments by resocializing them to develop those skills
essential for success in the public schools: language or communication
skills, reasoning ability, motivation, pride in achievement, perceptual
skills, long attention span, and feeling of self-worth (Ogbu 1974a:209).

There were several remedial compensatory education programs
before the advent of the Title I ESEA Program of the same type in the
1960s (see Table 3.2). These programs may have differed in their
methods of operation, but they had three important features in common: First, they were all based on the notion of cultural deprivation (Riessman 1962:107); second, their principal objective was
educational—to raise the academic achievement of the children involved; third, all but one of the programs failed to improve the intellectual and school performance of black children as measured by the
standardized tests. The one exception—New York City's Demonstration Guidance Project—had a qualified success because the evaluation
study did not fully account for other factors that might have contributed to the improvement in school performance of the children in the
program.[3]

Preventive Strategy I: Before the Great Society Era

The failure of the remedial compensatory education programs did
not lead those using this strategy for improving black school perfor-

---

[3]The Demonstration Guidance Project began in 1956 with black and Puerto Rican junior high
school students who were academically above their peers from poverty areas but whose performance
on IQ and school work was poorer than that of their white middle-class peers. The program in the
project included curriculum modification, smaller classes, remedial instruction in reading, speech,
and mathematics. Special emphasis was placed on developing reading skills, so that teachers of every
subject also had to teach reading. Reading skills were further promoted through book fairs, circulating
paperback libraries, and the award of badges for reading improvements with the inscription: "Readers
are Leaders." Other aspects of the project included "cultural enrichment," clinical services, parent
meetings, and wall displays of the pictures of successful blacks and Puerto Ricans. A study of the
students who participated in the project and graduated from high school in 1960, 1961, and 1962
showed that they had lower dropout rates and obtained more academic diplomas than did black and
Puerto Rican students of the preproject period who graduated from the same high schools in 1957,
1958, and 1959; a higher proportion of the project students also continued their education beyond
high school. But a later reanalysis of the original study suggests that the apparent success of the
project was largely caused by two external events: One was subsequent inclusion in the project of
pupils from middle-class backgrounds as a result of a new housing project in the area; and the other
was the expansion of a junior college program in the area which opened up more opportunities for
post-high school education than were available to those who graduated from these high schools prior
to 1960 (U.S. Commission on Civil Rights 1967:124, footnote 31).

mance to question the theory of cultural deprivation. Instead they reinforced their theoretical assumption by stating that the harmful effects of cultural deprivation are established so early in the lives of black children that it is necessary to intervene during their preschool years to prevent the effects of cultural deprivation from taking place. As Kerber and Bommarito put it:

> Increasing evidence indicates that by the time the culturally disadvantaged child enters school *it is too late* to alter the course set toward academic failure. The cognitive set of the culturally disadvantaged child, that pattern of perception which handicaps him in learning tasks demanded by the school, is *irrevocably cast in preschool years* [1965b:345; emphasis added].

They go on to say that the preschool years constitute a period when "the basic set toward learning is developed. Later all that takes place is an addition of experience into the 'pre-ordained categories' [p. 346]." The home environments of culturally deprived children, they argue, do not provide them with opportunities to develop sufficiently during the preschool years. Consequently, the proposed solution to the educational problems of these children was "early intervention programs." The need for such programs was a major topic at both the Columbia University Work Conference on Curriculum and Teaching in Depressed Urban Areas in 1962 and the Chicago Conference on Compensatory Education of the Culturally Deprived (Bloom et al. 1965; Passow 1963).

In New York City, a pioneer program was started in 1962 by the Institute for Developmental Studies, in cooperation with the New York City Board of Education, under the leadership of Martin Deutsch. The program—the Early Childhood Project—was designed to extend from preschool through the third grade, and it involved a number of schools in Harlem. Each year some 120 to 200 children were recruited into the program. The children spent two years in preschool training before entering regular school, where they continued to receive services from the program until they finished the third grade. The children in the program and a control sample were tested for IQ and language skills at the start of the program. The curriculum stressed the development of linguistic, conceptual, and perceptual skills as well as "self-image." The children participated in a variety of activities designed to achieve these goals. A second testing given after the first two years indicated some improvement in the IQ test scores of the children in the program, whereas the scores of other children with similar backgrounds who had not participated tended to decline (Rees 1968:228). Still a third test, given much later, showed that the children who continued in the program did much better on standardized tests of various kinds than other children serving as a control group (Gottfried 1973:285–286; Little and Smith 1971:58; Rees 1968:222).

Another of the early preventive compensatory education programs was Baltimore's Early School Admissions Project, which also began in the fall of 1962, as a part of the Great Cities project. The goal of the Baltimore project was "to determine whether early admissions to schools can overcome any of the barriers to learning that environmental factors seem to impose [Rees 1968:215]." The children selected for the program were four- and five-year-olds. A progress report published in 1964 listed the following factors in the "home environment" as damaging to the normal development of children from a culturally deprived background: illness in the home; large number of siblings; death; separation; divorce; illegitimacy; poor family relationships; emotional disturbance; migration; limited education of parents; and limited social and economic circumstances (quoted in Rees 1968:215). In contrast, the school environment was seen as offering to culturally deprived preschool children "sensory-rich learning to arouse interest, stimulate thinking, and provoke questioning," as well as warmth and acceptance (p. 216). Four preschool centers were established in the city, each run by a staff of four: a senior teacher, an assistant teacher, a teacher aide, and a volunteer. Rees (1968:219) reported that there had been no objective evaluation of the program but that both teachers and parents said that the children in the program had made some progress in learning to understand and use language and in other areas important for doing well in school.

Philadelphia's Experimental Nursery School Program was established in the early 1960s for lower-class blacks, ranging in age from 3½ to 4½. It was intended to prevent the development of problems associated with language, auditory, and visual skills; to encourage concept building, self-esteem, ability to attend and listen, and good motor coordination. An evaluation study in the 1965–1966 school year found that the children who had completed the program gained 6 points on the Stanford-Binet IQ test, as contrasted to almost no gain by children from similar backgrounds who had not participated (Rees 1968:222).

Finally, there was the Early Training Project established for black preschool children in 1962 near Nashville, with the familiar goal of developing perceptual, conceptual, and linguistic aptitudes. The children, all four-year-olds, were divided into three groups. The first group attended a 10-week summer preschool for three years before entering the first grade in 1964. The second group attended two 10-week summer courses and then received monthly home visits for a period of nine months. The third group received no preschool training or home visits. Upon entering the public schools at the end of the three summers, the children were tested on Stanford-Binet intelligence tests. The first group had a mean gain of 9 IQ points from their starting scores, and the second group had a slightly higher gain. The third group, which had received no preschool training, had gained only 4 IQ points. Follow-up studies in 1966 and 1968 found that the children who completed the Early Training Project were still doing better than the children who had not, but that the differences between the two groups had been significantly reduced (Little and Smith 1971:56).

In the short run, the preschool programs were more successful than the remedial programs at the school level: Children who completed the preschool training generally scored higher on various standardized tests than they had when the programs began. They also performed better on these tests than other children of similar backgrounds who had not taken part in the preschool programs. But whether the "stimulated development" would really ensure their success in subsequent years of formal schooling was yet to be demonstrated.

By 1964, speculations about preschool programs preventing deficit development in blacks were beginning to be reinforced by early reports about successes of these programs in raising children's performance on IQ tests as well as helping them develop greater maturity in other areas and thus facilitating their adjustment to public schools (see Brazziel and Terrel 1962; Deutsch 1964; Gray and Klaus 1963; Similansky 1964; Weaver 1963). A number of theoretical works published between 1962 and 1964 further reinforced the belief that preschool programs would prevent the development of deficits among the poor and blacks and thus improve their later school performance (see Ausubel 1964; Bloom 1964; Deutsch 1963; Hunt 1964).

Preventive Strategy in the Great Society, 1965–1974

The War on Poverty, with its theory of the "poverty cycle," had much to do with the development of compensatory education in the period of the Great Society. According to the poverty-cycle theory, inadequate education, low income, limited job opportunities, poor housing, delinquency, and crime are both the causes and the consequences of poverty. Furthermore, these factors are interrelated in such a way as to make it extremely difficult for the poor to escape from poverty as adults. The poverty-cycle theory was, however, later reinterpreted to mean that it was possible to break the cycle of poverty at some point and thus prevent subsequent stages from developing (Little and Smith 1971:29; Marris and Rein 1967).

Two strategies of breaking the cycle were considered by the Johnson administration. One was a direct cash payment to the poor. This was rejected on the ground that it would neither motivate the poor nor provide them with opportunities to further improve their social and economic conditions. The second strategy, adopted by Congress in 1965, was to break the poverty cycle through education and training. Although it was understood that this approach to reducing poverty would produce neither dramatic nor immediate results, it was seen as a way to deal with poverty at its roots. It was considered a "one-generation up-and-out-from-poverty" strategy which, though more complex, would be more lasting than the "welfare approach" [Hughes and Hughes 1972:10].

The theory of a poverty cycle and the possibility of intervening at the level of education provided both the rationale and the strategy to secure federal legislation to fund public school education that would avoid constitutional obstacles of the past. The rationale was federal efforts to eliminate poverty, and the strategy was the "use of the poverty child as the unit of funding the educational system, public and non-public alike [Hughes and Hughes 1972:9]." Compensatory education was the specific method of fighting poverty with education.

The compensatory education programs generated by the War on Poverty fall into two groups: those administered through the Office of Economic Opportunity (OEO), such as Head Start, Follow Through, and Upward Bound; and various programs under Title I of the Elementary and Secondary Education Act (ESEA) of 1965, administered through the Office of Education.

The initial emphasis of the OEO programs was on youth training and the rehabilitation of youths 16–22 years of age. This was prompted by the exceptionally large number of draftees rejected by the armed forces for reasons believed to be associated with poverty. On the other hand, advocates of preschool education argued that preschool training would be more effective, for the same cost, in fighting poverty than the training of the 16 to 22-year-olds. Congressmen were told that if their legislation was to deal with the roots of poverty it meant "striking poverty where it hits first and most damagingly in the early childhood [Levitan 1969:135]." The Economic Opportunity Act was subsequently amended to provide funds for a preschool program which, in February 1965, was named *Head Start*. The Head Start program became so popular with the public, as well as with those in educational circles, that demands for the program during its first summer (1965) far exceeded expectation. A total of some 560,000 children participated that summer in some 2400 different communities. Federal and local financial support for the program was about $195 million. Participation in summer Head Start programs remained about the same in subsequent years while the number of children in full-year Head Start increased from 20,000 in 1965 to 215,000 in 1967 (Levitan 1969:139; Little and Smith 1971:50). Some of the projects were run by nonprofit community organizations; some were run by local school boards; and still others were small experimental or demonstration projects, often run as part of university research centers.

The Head Start program is essentially preventive compensatory education based on the same theory as that behind the preschool programs implemented before the War on Poverty (see Levitan 1969:133–134). The central objective of Head Start is therefore educational—to facilitate children's cognitive development so that they will later be able to do as well in school as their middle-class peers. But the program usually includes ancillary services as well, such as social services to children's families, health services, including medical diagnosis and treatment, clinical services, nutrition, and parent education through participation in the program.

Remedial Strategy in the Great Society, 1965–1974

Title I of the 1965 ESEA has become the single most important source of funding for remedial compensatory education. This legislation originated as part of the War on Poverty and was designed to bring federal money to the schools, using the children of the poor as the unit in the funding formula. The formula was particularly favorable to school systems in rural areas and cities. The inclusion of children from families on welfare insured that city school districts would get a significant share of the Title I money (Hughes and Hughes 1972:18).

It appears that the main purpose of Title I was at first in dispute within the Office of Education. The traditionalists, according to Hughes and Hughes, assumed that the purpose was "to assure that funds flowed as freely and as smoothly as possible into the coffers of the nation's school systems with the minimum number of strings attached [1972:32–40]." Such people regarded Title I more or less as a general federal aid to education. They claimed that the "child benefit theory" had been only a means of selling Title I to Congress; that it was not intended to serve a specifically targeted population of the poor as defined in the allocation formula in the act. That is, they said that Title

I was not intended as money to provide special educational programs to meet the special needs of the children of the poor.

On the other hand, there were others within and outside the Office of Education who saw the "child benefit theory" as the prime focus of the legislation and worked to restrict the use of the funds to the children of the poor. These advocates of the poor believed that Title I was a categorical aid program intended to serve only the special needs of the poverty target population as defined in the law. They eventually won, and Title I guidelines defined the target areas to be served as "places with 'higher than average' poor [Hughes and Hughes 1972:39–40]."[4] Furthermore, the supporters of this view within the Office of Education set out to ensure that this definition of the recipients of Title I was understood and that the programs would be so implemented at state and local levels throughout the country, an aim that was not easily accomplished. Only later in this clarification process (July 1966) was the term *compensatory education* adopted to describe the program funded under Title I.

The major objective of these compensatory education programs is educational: They are intended to improve the academic performance of disadvantaged children. Some of them have brought changes to the school systems themselves, such as modifications of curriculums and teaching techniques, introduction of specialist personnel, reduction in class size, and the like; but these are intended to facilitate improvements in the school performance of the children in the programs. Like the preschool programs, remedial programs under Title I are intended to narrow the gap in school performance between the poor and black on the one hand, and their white middle-class peers on the other (Hawkridge *et al.* 1968; Little and Smith 1971:31). Their theoretical assumptions are basically the same as those assumptions behind the remedial programs before the Great Society era.

The range of compensatory education programs under Title I is quite broad because Title I guidelines initially encouraged local school districts to submit for funding whatever special programs they believed would "meet the special educational needs of children in the attendance area having high concentrations of disadvantaged children [Miller 1967:104]." Even within one school district there are usually many and varied programs. A study of compensatory education programs in

---

[4]This does not mean that all children in a given poverty area qualified to participate in the program, but only those whose family incomes fell below a stipulated minimum. In Stockton, California, for instance, the welfare department was the principal agency certifying children for the program, and most of these children were from families subsisting on public assistance payments. The same was probably true of most other cities.

Cincinnati in 1967 showed that there were six main Title I program areas within which there were about 39 different specific projects "ranging from remedial provisions to summer camping expeditions, parent leadership training and community relations activities [Little and Smith 1971:69]." Some of the school districts eventually reduced the number of the programs they offered and designed better quality ones.

The Results

There are several ways to evaluate Head Start and the other compensatory education programs for the poor and blacks. First of all, one can assess the fiscal impact of compensatory education. A study of this kind is likely to reveal that unlike previous federal aid programs for education (such as those funded under the National Defense Education Act) compensatory education programs under Title I, through its formula of fund allocation, have funneled more money into the cities than into the suburbs. In so doing, they have helped to reduce the fiscal disparities between city and suburban school districts, thus enabling city schools to provide some of the educational services they could not previously afford. From this standpoint, compensatory education can be judged quite successful, even without measuring its actual effects on children's work in the classroom (see U.S. Civil Rights Commission 1967:25–31). Compensatory education programs can also be judged on the basis of their ancillary services in the areas of health, social, and psychological services to the families of children in the programs; parent education; parent and minority employment; and politicization. These services are important and their success is welcome, but they are only means to the ultimate goal of the compensatory education programs of the present era, which is to improve the school performance of the poor and black.

In the second annual report on Title I projects in 1967, HEW (cited in Little and Smith 1971:32) stated that the goal of the projects was to raise the level of school performance among disadvantaged students to that of their middle-class peers. The report presented a graph showing how far apart the two groups were in academic achievement and defined progress in compensatory education as convergence of the two levels. For these reasons, while I fully recognize the success of the ancillary services of Head Start and other compensatory education programs and the significance of this success, I am concerned here mainly with the educational objective of the programs: *To what extent have Head Start and other compensatory education programs increased the chances that black children will perform as well as their white middle-class peers in school?*

The first nationwide study of the educational impact of Head Start programs was undertaken in 1968 by the Westinghouse/Ohio University researchers. Before then, reports from various parts of the country had indicated that children who participated in the Head Start program scored higher on IQ tests than other children from similar backgrounds and of the same age and sex who had not participated in the program. However, these reports also indicated that when the two groups of children entered regular schools, the IQ differences tended to disappear. The Westinghouse study was planned as a systematic probe to determine how well those who had taken part in the Head Start projects were able to maintain their higher scores on IQ tests as well as their performance in other areas during the first three years of elementary school. The study focused on children who had completed the Head Start programs and were now in the grades 1, 2, or 3.

The study examined the effects of both the summer Head Start program and the full-year Head Start program. In general, it was found that the summer programs had no positive effects. According to White (1970), a consultant in the study, there were some suspicions that in tests of cognitive skills, the Head Start training might even have had a negative effect. He states that "with some regularity, there were slight differences favoring the control children registered on all three cognitive instruments and in all three grades [p. 174]." The children who had participated in full-year Head Start programs, on the other hand, did better than the control children: "In the first grade, the Head Start children were superior to the control children on the Metropolitan [Reading] Readiness Test. Otherwise, in the first and second grades, there was a pattern of scattered positive effects [1970:176]."

The effect of the full-year program, though statistically significant, was not enough "to make one believe that the child's academic prospects were much improved." The study also shows that blacks appeared to have benefited slightly more from both the summer and the full-year programs than, say, white lower-class children. But in general, even the full-year Head Start programs had not closed the gap in school performance between the advantaged and disadvantaged groups of students. For instance, children who had experienced a full year of Head Start training were about eight months behind the national norm on the Illinois Test of Psycholinguistic Abilities, and at about the forty-fourth percentile of the first grade Metropolitan Readiness Test. They were at the twentieth percentile on the second grade Stanford-Binet

Achievement Test (White 1970:175).[5] The national impact study thus confirmed the impressions from earlier reports of various school districts that the large IQ gains scored by children who participated in the preschool programs tended to fade out in the early years of their elementary school training (see also Goldberg 1971:79–81; Little and Smith 1971:52–53; Miller 1967:146; Passow 1971b:13–14; Wilkerson 1970:28).

The other experimental preschool programs are also marked by significant gains during the training period and fadeout of these gains in subsequent years. Among such projects are the Perry Preschool Project in Ypsilanti, Michigan; the Academic Preschool in Champaign, Illinois; the Early Childhood Project in New York City; the Early Education Program in North Carolina; the Learning to Learn Program in Jacksonville, Florida; the Marion Blank Individual Language Program in New York City; the Early Training Project near Nashville, Tennessee; the Infant Research Project in Washington, D.C.; the Merle Karnes Preschool Project at the University of Illinois; and the Syracuse Day Care Project. In almost every case, follow-up studies show that the gains in IQ scores the children made during their participation in the preschool projects faded out during the first few years of their careers in elementary school.

Children in the experimental preschool projects usually scored higher on IQ tests than children in ordinary Head Start preschool projects because the experimental projects are better financed and operated and have fewer children. For example, the Marion Blank Project had only 12 experimental and 10 control children, and the Early Training Project near Nashville had only 60 children divided into two experimental groups and one control group. Nevertheless, these experimental projects were no more successful in achieving their long-range educational goals than the relatively inexpensive preschool projects run by local schools and community organizations. Follow-up studies show that the gains in cognitive or intellectual functioning made during the training periods in both types of preschool training are not sustained beyond the third grade (see Gottfried 1973:278–286; Little and Smith 1971:53–77; Stanley 1973; U.S. Senate Select Committee 1972:83–87).

Thus the early intervention projects, both Head Start and the experimental preschool projects, have been partially successful in raising

[5] A percentile indicates the percentage of a distribution that is equal to or below that score; in other words, twentieth percentile indicates that 80% of the children tested nationwide scored better than children who had been in the Head Start Program.

performance on IQ tests, but they have not succeeded in enabling poor and black children to perform in elementary school at the same rate or level as their white middle-class peers. Even the most ardent advocates of early intervention programs now admit that the projects have not thus far succeeded in achieving this long-range goal, at least not beyond the third grade. The failure is significant because of the assumption underlying the intervention programs: that black children fail in school because they were not trained by their parents in the way that these projects undertook to train them at the preschool level (see Goldberg 1971;78–79; Stanley 1973:7–8).

Various evaluative reports on Title I remedial projects prepared by HEW, the Rand Corporation, and the American Institute for Research and Evaluation of Title I ESEA show that some projects have improved the school performance of disadvantaged children in the programs. Among these are some 14 projects that focused on raising IQ scores; 36 projects that focused on the development of language arts and reading skills; one project that focused on improved writing; and 15 projects that focused on basic skills in mathematics. According to the U.S. Senate, Select Committee (1972:311) these successful projects had the following features in common: clearly stated objectives and careful planning; modification of teaching techniques to fit the projects; individualized instructions or teaching in small groups; active parent involvement; and "intensive treatment," that is, concentration of resources on a limited number of students. To these projects may be added the Upward Bound program, started in the summer of 1965 by the Office of Economic Opportunity, which called it the "Head Start for Teenagers."[6]

But successful (remedial or preventive) programs are the exceptions rather than the rule. Although the results of compensatory educa-

---

[6]By 1967, about 50% of the children in the Upward Bound program were black. The program selects high school students who have high academic potential and gives them a 6- to 8-week intensive residential summer course on a college campus to make up for deficiencies in their public school training in such areas as English, mathematics, and science. (Upward Bound is essentially a college preparatory course for potential college students from the ghetto.) After the summer course, there is a follow-up session during the academic year to provide participants with academic support and encourage them to go on to college. Those who eventually do so receive some financial aid. A Syracuse University study of a sample of 10% of the students who had participated in the program in 1967 found that the program was quite successful in motivating participants to go to college.

An example of an Upward Bound type program which has been successful is New York City's College Bound program which operates in some 26 high schools (see Levitan 1969:165–174; Little and Smith 1971:77–78). The similarity between the Upward Bound program of the Great Society and New New York City's Demonstration Guidance Project (1950–1962), the one successful remedial program of the earlier period, should be noted. Both deal with the academically able, better-than-average ghetto student.

tion programs are not entirely negative, the overall picture is not encouraging. After several years of the remedial and preventive programs, the gap in school performance between black and white students still exists in every region and within every socioeconomic level (see Durham 1972:7; Farber and Lewis 1972:47–57; Goldberg 1971:78–79; Passow 1971b:19–20).

What Went Wrong?

One reason often given for the failure of the remedial programs is that Title I funds have been misused. In some communities, the money was used to provide services for children other than those for whom it was intended. In some southern dual school systems, Title I funds were used to make up for the unequal distribution of local school money. This kind of misuse was particularly serious in Mississippi, where it has been fully documented by a team of investigators from the U.S. Office of Education. The following gives some idea of the inequality in the Mississippi dual school system, which local school authorities attempted to remedy with Title I funds (Hughes and Hughes 1972):

> In 12 districts visited by the USOE investigators the expenditure in white schools was found to be 76 percent greater than in black schools; and the lowest average expenditure for white schools ($209.64) was found to be 12 percent more than the highest expenditure ($187.80) for the black schools in the 12 districts. When class sizes were compared in these 12 places it was found that black schools had 30 percent more pupils per teacher and 36 percent more pupils per class, than did the white schools [pp. 104–105].

A similar misuse of Title I funds—to make up for inequities in the distribution of local school money—probably occurs in many northern urban school districts, which often insist that their local school money is evenly distributed to all schools in their jursidction but that it is not possible to provide the exact figures for individual schools. However, in the earlier case of *Hobson* v. *Hansen* in Washington, D.C., it was revealed that in the 1963–1964 school year there were identifiable differences in school expenditure according to the racial composition of the schools, ranging from $292 per pupil in predominantly black schools to $392 per pupil in predominantly white schools. The situation did not change until 1970, when a federal judge ordered the Washington school board to implement a new distribution system of local money which would result in not more than 5% difference between the schools in per pupil expenditure (Hughes and Hughes 1972:106). Under such a circumstance, Title I funds in Washington and other cities have probably been used to provide the services that local money should have provided for the black schools rather than to provide additional services.

A third misuse of Title I money has been the purchase of school equipment which is at best inadequately utilized. The educational industry—the producers of textbooks, projectors, classroom furniture, teaching materials, and the like—have played a very important role in determining the course of compensatory education programs under Title I. Hughes and Hughes (1972) point out that "in a very real sense the educational industry has performed much of the 'thinking' for the schools in terms of educational programs [p. 98]."

These and other abuses of Title I money have been carefully documented in *Title I of ESEA: Is It Helping Poor Children?* prepared by the Washington [D.C.] Research Project and NAACP Legal Defense Fund (see also U.S. Senate Select Committee 1971).

Critics have also pointed out that Title I remedial compensatory education programs often lack clear goals and strategies for increasing the academic achievement of disadvantaged children (U.S. Senate Select Committee 1972:312), probably because school districts qualify to receive money on the basis of the number of "economically deprived children" in their populations, not for the soundness of their diagnoses of the educational problems of these children or of the proposals they have for solutions. There was no prior preparation of local school officials for a deeper understanding or analysis of the causes of school failures among disadvantaged children or for effective use of the kind of money that suddenly became available in the 1960s for preventing school failure among such children. Many of the programs were consequently hastily and poorly prepared, especially during the first few years of Title I.

This lack of clear goals and strategies is illustrated by both the soft focus and the multiplicity of the compensatory education programs that may be found within a given school district. The same children are often participating in several programs, so that it is difficult to ascertain which program is responsible for the findings in a given study (Little and Smith 1971:69). The U.S. Civil Rights Commission states that the programs have not been successful in reaching their educational objectives because they are treating educational problems of black children who are in the same environment that generated the problems in the first place, racially segregated schools.

The above explanations are not generally applicable to the preschool programs, especially the experimental programs which, as we have seen, have also been unsuccessful when judged on a long-range basis. Since the experimental programs are usually carefully planned and controlled, expensively run, and small in size, what went wrong? Why do the gains children make during their preschool training fade out when they enter regular schools? Four types of explanations are currently being offered to account for it. The first argues that intervention at the age of five, four, or three comes too late, that the influence of the home establishes itself at a much earlier period, and that intervention should begin at birth or earlier. The second explanation contends that the preschool programs are not strong enough to counteract the influence of the home, which reasserts itself when the preschool programs are over, nor are they strong enough to counteract the influence of peers, which begins to assert itself when the children begin school. Those who hold this view suggest that the intervention program should be made into an all-day program, a boarding school, or a kibbutz-like situation. According to Little and Smith (1971), some educators now believe "that only complete institutional care will bring disadvantaged children to a normal level of development and maintain them at this point [p. 66]." The total institutionalization approach is already being tried at the Frank Porter Graham Child Development Center in North Carolina (see also Goldberg 1971:81; Little and Smith 1971:65; Stanley 1973:8; White 1970:183).

The third explanation maintains that there is something basically wrong with the programs and organization of the public school system and that until these are changed they will continue to neutralize the gains made in preschool training. Proponents of this view argue for the extension of the preschool programs into the elementary school in the form of the Follow-Through program (see Deutsch 1971; Goldberg 1971:81; Levitan 1969:162–163; Little and Smith 1971:72–73; White 1970:183).

Finally, there are some who raised questions about the presumed causes of the poorer school performance of black children. Goldberg (1971) has pointed out that the "deficit theory was derived from correlational studies which did not necessarily establish or prove a causal relationship between the observed phenomena [p. 80]." She points out further that some of the assumptions based on the deficit theory need to be reexamined. For instance, she asks whether the learning in preschool training can really make up for the absence of earlier learning in the home? Can home learning be reproduced in school? Are observed deficits causes or symptoms of school failure? Can preschool training, whether a summer training or a full-year training, "cure" the child, or does he or she require continuing help during the regular school years?

There is, of course, a good deal of polarization over the issue of the effectiveness of compensatory education. At one end are those who say that assessing the accomplishments of the compensatory education program of the Great Society is premature because it has not been tried long enough, or had sufficient resources to deal with the educational problems caused by cultural deprivation (Hunt 1969a). At the other extreme are those who argue that compensatory education cannot succeed in closing the gaps between blacks and whites in IQ test scores and in scholastic achievement because the differences between the two races are innate. Compensatory education cannot, therefore, according to Jensen (1969), boost the IQs and scholastic achievements of black children.

In some localities, compensatory education programs may have failed for some of the above reasons, especially the misuse of Title I money and the poorly designed and poorly managed preschool and remedial programs. But these factors cannot account for the general ineffectiveness of compensatory education in improving the academic achievement of disadvantaged students. It should be remembered that most of the remedial programs instituted before the advent of Title I programs, such as the Higher Horizons program, were carefully planned and managed, and yet they also failed to produce any encouraging results.[7]

I reject these explanations and contend that compensatory education programs, both preventive and remedial, fail to produce significant improvement in the school performance of black children because the theoretical assumptions upon which they are based are wrong. Although lower-class blacks (who form the majority of the black population) probably come to school with preschool training and cognitive and other skills that differ from those of their white middle-class peers, the difference does not arise from the fact that there is some deficit in black development because of cultural deprivation. It arises from the respective positions of blacks and whites in the American caste system which require that the two races develop different patterns of child training and different types of cognitive and motivational skills. These differences were, until recently, reinforced by the education system itself.

[7]The Higher Horizon project began in New York City in 1959. Its programs were similar to those of the Demonstration Guidance project which preceded it. But it differed from the latter in some important respects. For instance, the Higher Horizon project was open to all disadvantaged pupils in the project schools and not just the superior pupils; it involved more pupils (64,000 in 52 elementary and junior high schools by 1962, contrasted with fewer than 1000 pupils in the Demonstration Guidance project); the administration of the Higher Horizon project was decentralized, and the cost per pupil was smaller. Although studies of the Higher Horizon project did not find it particularly successful, it subsequently became the model of remedial education projects adopted by school systems of several large American cities prior to 1965.

The programs reviewed in this chapter and their supportive theories reviewed in Chapter 2 point to two broad views of Americans on the causes of black school failure. On the one hand are those who see black children's background as the source of the problem and therefore see its solution in the rehabilitation of these children from the influences of that background. On the other hand are those who attribute the problem of black school failure to the inadequacy of the school systems and point to school reform as the answer to the problem. There are, of course, overlaps in the views of the two groups and in the solutions they propose.

Overall evidence suggests that the rehabilitation approach with its compensatory education programs has not been particularly effective because of the inadequacy of the underlying explanation of the problem. The rehabilitation programs see the roots of the problem in the preschool training of black children and the continuing influence of their families, peer groups, and communities; these programs regard any negative influences of the school and society at large, especially the caste system, as merely reinforcing the pattern of deficits already established before the children begin their school careers. Perhaps some rehabilitationists recognize the influence of social and occupational forces on black education, but they probably assume that regardless of these external forces black children can transcend them and succeed in school through personal transformation. The assumption that the roots of the problem lie in the biography of each individual black child is associated with the naive expectation that a short-term treatment lasting one summer or one full academic year will lead to immediate, dramatic, and permanent improvement in the pupil's IQ test score and school performance.

The failure of the rehabilitation strategy or approach is attributable to two misconceptions. The first—which has already been discussed— involves looking for the origins of black academic retardation in the biography of each black child without showing how that biography is shaped by historical and structural experiences of blacks as a group. The theory upon which the rehabilitation approach is based takes no account of the way the caste system determines the pattern of attitudes, self-conceptions, learning habits, and linguistic, cognitive, and motivational skills developed by blacks. The second misconception has to do with the theory of human development that underlies the rehabilitation approach. Cognitive, motivational, and other skills characteristic of a given society or any one of its segments are functionally adaptive. That is, these skills become a part of the personality system of the group because they are required to meet the demands of the group's social and technoeconomic environment, not merely because children growing up in the group are "stimulated" by their parents, family surroundings, or preschool programs.

Uncertainty over the ability of the rehabilitation strategy to produce significant and general improvement in black school performance has resulted in increasing demands and proposals for school reforms. The reforms already attempted—school integration, community control of the schools, and alternative or free schools—are neither extensive nor particularly encouraging in their effects on black school performance. While more school reformers than rehabilitationists are aware of the influence of caste barriers on black school performance, the former nevertheless tend to assume that black children can improve their school performance in spite of the caste system if only the schools are organized and run in some way that would exclude the influences of the caste system (see Clark 1972:14).

There are two problems ignored by the reformists. First, the school is an agent of society, and it is doubtful that it can altogether abandon its exclusionary policies and practices unless changes in the larger society force it to do so. In other words, it is not certain that schools can be effectively reformed so that they will result in a general improvement in black school performance without a simultaneous or even a prior elimination of caste barriers in adult life. Second, it is not at all certain that school reforms will lead to general improvement in black school performance so long as blacks continue to live in blighted communities from which they perceive their opportunities in postschool society as limited for no other reason than because they are black and so long as the forces producing these conditions remain effective.

These criticisms do not mean that compensatory education, school integration, and other reforms are not needed; they are. But they are based on a partial explanation of the problem and represent only part of the solution. An adequate explanation of black school failure must take into account the influence of the caste system. To do this requires an adequate conception of what education is and does in a given society, as outlined in Chapter 1. In Chapter 4, I demonstrate its relevance to the school failure by examining the structural and historical forces which have affected black access to formal education and postschool roles and rewards and the consequences of the latter on black development of school-related skills, black perception of schooling, and black academic efforts.

4

Black Access to Education

Black Americans as a Caste Minority Group

A number of scholars have suggested that black–white stratification in the United States is organized along the principle of caste (Berreman 1960, 1967a,b; Davis *et al.* 1965; Dollard 1957; Lyman 1973; Mack 1968; Warner 1965, 1970). Black–white stratification satisfies Berreman's definition of a caste system as a *hierarchy* of endogamous groups whose membership is *determined permanently at birth* (Berreman 1967a:279). The basis of ranking the white caste as superior and the black caste as inferior is skin color, socially defined race.

Other scholars have raised objections to this approach, arguing that the phenomenon of caste is probably unique to India (Cox 1945; Dumont 1961; Johnson 1966).[1] Most Americans prefer to think of American racial stratification in terms of its behavioral manifestations. For example, social scientists focus their analyses on so-called issues,

[1] In these citations, the date for Cox's paper is earlier than those of the caste proponents listed in the preceding paragraph. It should be pointed out that the latter citations do not represent the original publication dates of the works in question.

such as restrictions on sex relations, marriage, and housing; job and other economic discriminations; segregation in public schools, public facilities, and social clubs; and the like. Instead of recognizing these practices as expressions of a common structural principle, they often prefer to explain them in terms of *racial prejudice*, a psychodynamic phenomenon characteristic of individuals rather than social structure; racial prejudice is in turn explained as a result of errors in socialization and faulty personality development (Lyman 1973:91). The implication of this mode of thinking for the study of black education is that black–white differences in school performance are rarely analyzed as a consequence of *racial stratification*, a concept which does not even appear in most of the influential literature on this problem (Coleman *et al.* 1966; Jencks 1972; Jensen 1969, 1972b, 1973; Mosteller and Moynihan 1972). The dominant orientation emphasizes the social class basis of educational differences.

There seem to be two sources of resistance to the analysis of American racial stratification in terms of caste. One is the extension of the experiences of certain European immigrant groups as a universally applicable variable. Thus proponents of the theory of the "race-relations cycle" argue that every group in the United States, including blacks, will eventually be assimilated into the dominant white group. It is acknowledged, of course, that black assimilation may be somewhat slower than most (Shibutani and Kwan 1965). The second source of resistance is the pervading egalitarian ideology (based mainly on white experience) and mythology of individualism. Such mythology and ideology, Maquet (1971) correctly observes, form a screen that prevents its wearers from seeing the system that underlies their own behavior in conforming to superior and inferior roles.

For my present purpose, it is more useful to analyze black–white stratification in terms of caste. Berreman (1967a:295–304) has clearly demonstrated that the features often said to make caste unique to India are also found elsewhere, including the United States. Particularly important for the present analysis is that blacks not only rank lower than whites in the caste system but also constitute a pariah caste. Pariahs, as indicated in Chapter 1, are a denigrated group excluded from major institutions of the social structure, although they are required to perform important social and economic functions for society (Berreman 1967a:292–295; Bohannon 1963:183–184, 205). According to Bohannon, the evolution of black status as a pariah group began even before their emancipation from slavery but became more rigid at the end of the Reconstruction period. To prevent free and equal competition between blacks and whites for the scarce goods of society, the freed slaves and all others who could be recognized as black came to be clearly defined as pariahs. In the South, their pariah status was established by law and custom, and outside the South by extralegal mechanisms (van den Berghe 1967). As a pariah caste, blacks are comparable to the scheduled castes of India and the Eta of Japan (Berreman 1966a).

Caste stratification differs from class stratification in many important ways germane to the study of black–white differences in school performance (see Berreman 1972:398–399). Both systems of social stratification coexist in the United States and elsewhere, but they are governed by two different principles with different implications for the education of future adult members of the society. The differences between caste stratification and class stratification are succinctly summarized by Berreman (1972):

> Class is a matter of acquired status rather than of birth-ascription, and is in this respect distinct from race, caste, and ethnic stratification, with different social consequences. In a class system, one is ranked in accord with his behavior and attributes (income, occupation, education, life style, etc.). In a birth-ascribed system, by contrast, one behaves and exhibits attributes in accord with his rank. In a class system, individual mobility is legitimate albeit often difficult, while in ascribed stratification it is explicitly forbidden. Systems of acquired rank—class system—prescribe the means to social mobility; systems of ascribed rank proscribe them. As a consequence, a class system is a continuum; there are individuals who are intergrades, there are individuals in the process of movement, there are individuals who have experienced more than one rank. . . . A birth-ascribed system is comprised of discrete ranks on the pattern of echelon organization, without legitimate mobility, without intergrades; the strata are named, publicly recognized, [and] clearly bounded [pp. 398–399].

Where caste and class systems coexist, as in the United States, the basic principle of social structure is the caste system. Class is secondary to the named black and white castes, which are publicly recognized and clearly bounded groups. Each caste has its own classes, but the two class systems are not equal because members of the two castes have unequal access to education, occupation, income, and other attributes that determine social class membership for a given individual. Figure 4.1 illustrates the unequal contiguous class systems of black and white castes.

In class attributes, a large portion of the middle class in the white caste ranks above the entire upper class in the black caste, while a good portion of the middle class in the black caste ranks at the same level as the lower class in the white caste. Members of both castes have, of course, advanced their class status as a result of the general social and economic progress of the nation since blacks were emancipated from slavery over a century ago. But blacks have improved their class status at a much slower rate than whites because, by virtue of their caste

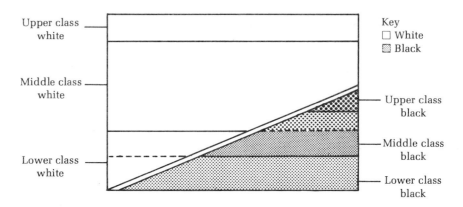

Figure 4.1. Contiguous systems of the black and white castes in the United States. (Note that this illustration is not drawn according to scale.)

membership, they have been restricted from competing for the most desirable adult roles in society on the basis of their individual training and ability (Drake and Cayton 1970).

The educational implications of caste status for blacks and whites differ from the implications of their class status. Differences in academic performance within the black caste as well as within the white caste may be largely caused by class differences. For example, middle-class pupils tend to do better than lower-class pupils in both the black caste and the white caste. But class status cannot explain why blacks as a group do not perform as well as whites, especially where the two groups have comparable class attributes. The structural variable responsible for the differences in performance between blacks and whites is related to their caste status.

The caste organization of black–white stratification leads to divergent development in the education of the two groups. As caste groups, blacks and whites have tended to occupy two different worlds which require different attitudes, values, personalities, skills, and behavioral patterns. In order to produce the kinds of people who will adapt to such different worlds, the caste system requires different modes of training the young members of both groups, including the institutionalization of differences in their formal education.

Unequal Access to Education: A Reflection of Caste Minority Status

Examining black education from an historical point of view brings out two important points which are hardly discussed in current debates about the causes of black school failure. First, for many generations American society has provided blacks with inferior education because blacks have been defined as inferior to whites and thus not in need of the same kind of education. Specifically, until perhaps the 1960s, American society never seriously intended that blacks should achieve equal social and occupational status with whites through education. The kind of education considered adequate for blacks in various historical periods depended on the way their position in society was defined relative to that of whites—as inferior, equal, or superior. This changing relationship between black social and technoeconomic status, as defined by society, and the kind of education offered to blacks are presented in the pages that follow.

The second point, discussed later, concerns the cumulative effect on their present school performance of providing blacks with inferior educations for generations. These two points should be kept in mind as we review black education historically, in both the North and the South. Racial stratification in the South evolved somewhat differently from that in the North, so that the pattern of development of black education is not identical in the two regions. But black education in the South as well as the North has many features in common.

The South

Exclusion: Before 1861

Public education for whites in the South began to be of great interest around 1835. However, formal education for blacks before and after 1835 was never considered necessary. There seem to be three main reasons why blacks were excluded from any official consideration for formal education prior to 1861. First, most white people believed that blacks were inferior to whites in intelligence and were therefore not as capable as benefiting from formal education (Bond 1969; Bullock 1970; Johnson 1930:224; Pierce et al. 1955:30). Second, it was argued that formal education would make blacks less useful as workers. Third, it was widely believed that formal education of blacks was a threat to the social order because it would encourage discontent and rebellion. This belief was particularly reinforced after a series of slave rebellions occurred between 1790 and 1830. In addition to the popular white sentiments against the formal education of blacks, legislative prohibitions were enacted in all the slave states between 1740 and 1847 against formal instruction of blacks (Bond 1969; Bullock 1970; Johnson 1930:225; Pierce et al. 1955:34).

In spite of these exclusionary measures, some blacks—both free and slave—received some formal education during the period. Free blacks were generally forbidden to send their children to public schools, but some enjoyed special status which favored formal education among them. Some other free blacks in the antebellum South received formal education from missionary societies, especially the Quakers. Some slaves received formal education, though this was illegal, because (a) as the plantations grew larger, tending to become self-sufficient, some slaves became skilled artisans and record keepers who required some formal education; (b) slave children associating with their masters' children were taught by the latter, and their education was sometimes taken seriously by the adult members of their masters' households; and (c) some planters and southern churches believed that slavery would be saved if the slaves learned to read the Bible. These whites believed that it would make the slaves more obedient and faithful, and so some slaves were given formal instruction in Sunday schools (see Bond 1969:19; Bullock 1970:11).

Thus some blacks received formal education prior to 1861, but it was a different kind of education from that received by whites of the same period. Black education was largely determined by what the dominant white caste perceived as required by the blacks' inferior position in the social order. It was not an education intended to prepare blacks for the same social and occupational positions open to whites in adult life. It merely prepared blacks for their inferior positions in life.

Education for Full Citizenship: 1861–1877

Although blacks were emancipated from slavery by the proclamation of 1863, their status as free citizens equal with whites was not universally established before 1865. The proclamation freed them from involuntary servitude, but this did not necessarily mean that they were free to follow social and economic pursuits open to whites. After the Civil War, some states accepted the emancipation but refused to recognize blacks as full citizens of equal status with whites. The provisional assemblies of these states proceeded to reenact the "black codes," defining the status of "all persons of color" as less than full citizenship.[2] These codes limited the rights of blacks in the courts of law, restricted their rights to ownership and use of the land, and prohibited them from marrying white persons.

The ambiguous status of blacks during this period affected their education, which was being offered mainly by missionaries from the

---

[2]Provisional assemblies were those which replaced the Confederate assemblies before the Southern states were again granted full statehood.

North. The latter could not offer blacks a classical education, which would have prepared them for the same roles as those performed by whites in adult life, partly because they were not sure that blacks would have access to such roles and partly because they feared southern whites, who were opposed to such education for blacks. The missionaries therefore took a neutral course, emphasizing religious and moral training. But this did not allay the fears of the dominant whites, who suspected that the missionaries were teaching blacks about social equality and who also feared that education would make blacks unwilling to work. Some therefore refused to let the blacks on their plantations go to school. More important, the black codes attempted to restrict black education. Some governors (e.g., North Carolina, 1862) ordered black schools closed; some states (e.g., Florida, 1865; Texas, 1866) passed laws requiring black schools to be supported only with taxes collected from blacks, a group that at this time had little property of tax value. In still other states, local whites were encouraged to replace the northern teachers whose ideas were suspected as revolutionary (Bullock 1970:39–40).

The passage of the Fourteenth Amendment to the United States Constitution (1866) significantly changed both the conception of black status in the social order of the South and the type of education considered adequate for them. The Fourteenth Amendment guaranteed blacks full privileges of citizenship, including the franchise (Pierce *et al.* 1955:40). The southern whites from the former slaveholding class (one fourth of the whites) who dominated the provisional assemblies and refused to accept the Fourteenth Amendment were removed from power through congressional action (Bond 1966; Bullock 1970; Pierce *et al.* 1955). Their places were taken by an alliance of three groups which ruled the region from 1867 to 1875, namely, northerners newly come to the South (the carpetbaggers); native white southerners who supported the Republican party (the scalawags); and the newly enfranchised blacks. This alliance endorsed the new social order, which anticipated the incorporation of blacks and whites into one socioeconomic hierarchy based on training and ability.

The passage of the Fourteenth Amendment ushered in three new developments in black education. The first was a change in the educational goals and methods of the northern missionaries; the second was the cooperation between the Freedmen's Bureau and the northern missionaries in developing a school system for blacks throughout the South; and the third was the creation of public school systems for whites and blacks by the state legislatures.

With the passage of the Fourteenth Amendment, the northern missionaries and other benevolent societies broadened their educational objectives beyond moral and religious instruction to include New England standard textbooks and extracurricular activities in which black pupils were taught the art of politics, including campaigning, voting, and the like (Bond 1966:115). The general orientation of black education turned toward enabling blacks to attain equal status with whites in the social, economic, and political realms.

The Freedmen's Bureau was created by Congress in 1865 and, in cooperation with various benevolent societies already providing education for blacks, it soon embarked upon establishing schools for blacks throughout the South. According to Bullock (1975), "the Freedmen's school curriculum was designed to give Negro children the same kind of education given to the White. It was classical in purpose, like the schools of New England [p. 30]." In addition, the bureau and the benevolent societies cooperated to establish institutions of higher education to train black teachers and other professionals. But the institutionalization of black education under the bureau was mostly outside the public school system.

The inclusion of blacks in public school systems was accomplished by the reconstruction legislatures. Between 1867 and 1874 the constitutional conventions and legislatures of various southern states established tax-supported public school systems and placed the education of black and white children on an equal basis. The issue of mixed schools was not entirely resolved, so that some states included provisions for separate schools for blacks and whites in their laws and constitutions (Bond 1966:47). But during this period and for a few years following, the education of the two races was maintained on a more or less equal basis in terms of average monthly salaries for teachers, teacher–pupil ratios, and length of school term (Bond 1966:80). In districts with heavy black populations (the "black counties"), there was even a tendency for black schools to have longer school terms and for their teachers to be slightly better paid.

Although the alliance which established tax-supported public schools for blacks and whites included some native whites, the inclusion of blacks on an equal basis with whites did not reflect the sentiments of most white southerners, especially the former slaveholding class, the conservative Democratic leaders. Nevertheless, before the end of the period, even the conservatives gradually began to accept the education of blacks in the public schools. Bond (1966:32–35) suggests that this acceptance was based on pragmatic considerations, namely, to prevent outsiders (northerners) from teaching blacks; to provide jobs for the widows of Confederate veterans and for soldiers of the Confederate Army disabled in the war; and to maintain the labor supply, since the black population tended to be more stable where schools were provided for their children. In fact, concern for labor supply led some planters to establish schools on their plantations. But these prominent white southerners generally favored giving blacks primarily moral and religious education, not the classical education intended for whites.

The Transition: 1878–1900

By 1877, control of the legislatures of the various states in the South had passed from the alliance of carpetbaggers, scalawags, and blacks to the conservative Democratic leaders, who set out to reestablish blacks as a pariah caste.

First, between 1876 and 1901 constitutional conventions and the legislatures of various states established new state constitutions and laws which curtailed the rights of blacks as full citizens, including restrictions on black voting rights, segregation in public facilities such as transportation, bans on interracial marriage, and restrictions on blacks from engaging in certain skilled occupations. Second, a series of decisions by the United States Supreme Court between 1873 and 1898 sanctioned the pariah status of blacks. These decisions made it difficult for blacks to enjoy the full privileges of civil rights which the Fourteenth Amendment had guaranteed them. A few examples will illustrate this point. In 1873, the Court's decision in the *Slaughterhouse* case constituted, in effect, a distinction between federal citizenship and citizenship in a particular state. The Court's decision in several cases in 1876 legalized discrimination by individuals as long as they were not acting as agents of the state. And in the *Plessy* v. *Ferguson* case in 1896 the Court permitted segregation in state statutes (see Bullock 1970; Bond 1966; Konvitz 1961; Wise 1972).

Developments in southern agriculture and industry constituted the third factor in the reemergence of caste-minority status for blacks. The particular development in southern agriculture which profoundly affected black status was the tenant farm system, in which "the laborer agreed with the owner to work a crop in the course of a year, the hire of the laborer to be paid from the anticipated returns on the crops when sold [Bond 1969:120]." The system was initiated after the Civil War when the former planters had no money to pay wages to emancipated blacks and poor whites now working as "free" laborers. It was approved by the Freedmen's Bureau with the expectation that it would benefit both planters and laborers. However, it soon developed into a hierarchy of credit systems, with the tenant and sharecropper at the bottom. With the support of political and judicial authorities, the tenant farmers became little more than peons, a status from which it was difficult to escape.

The other economic factor in the recrystallization of black caste minority status was the position of blacks in the industrializing South. First, blacks were excluded from working in the growing textile industries, which were often established with local capital as humanitarian services to provide jobs for poor whites. In industries to which blacks were admitted, they were used primarily as common laborers, i.e., they were placed at the bottom of the labor hierarchy. Furthermore, they were generally paid lower wages than whites and often used as strikebreakers.

Thus by 1900 blacks and whites were no longer participating in a single system of social class stratification based on individual ability and achievement. Rather, they formed two distinct components of a caste system based on color. The redefinition of black status in this transitional period was accompanied by two significant changes in black education. One was a redefinition of what type of education was appropriate for blacks, and the other was the termination of equal funding and related services for black and white schools.

As was pointed out previously, the sentiments of the majority of white southerners, especially the former slaveholding class which regained power during this period, who had never really accepted that blacks and whites were intellectual equals, remained the same. Between 1877 and 1900 they promoted the idea that blacks needed only industrial or manual training, not academic education, which they argued should be for whites only. This new conception of black education was, of course, in accord with the status of blacks as peons in the tenant system of southern agriculture. The ruling white elites clearly recognized that the tenant system would break down if black children, as future laborers, received the same kind of education as whites, since such education would encourage them to question the high rates of interest and the exploitative methods of account keeping used by the planters in dealing with their illiterate tenants. Thus the planter class developed a general dissatisfaction with academic education for blacks. They regarded the educated younger blacks as getting out of hand and preferred the older and uneducated ones who knew "their place" [Bond 1969:142]. The social and economic status of blacks in the tenant system dictated that blacks and whites should be provided with different educations and that education for blacks should not train them to aspire beyond their fixed status as plowhands. The emphasis was also on manual education for blacks in the urban areas where they occupied the lowest position in the industrial labor.

The other change in black education was the increasing disparity in funding and other services between black and white schoolchildren.

Funds were reduced for black education but increased for white education, on the grounds that it cost less to educate blacks than to educate
whites, given the type of education considered appropriate for blacks.
But the immediate cause was the inability of the various southern states
to support adequately two separate educational systems for the two
races.

First, local officials illegally diverted funds from black children to
white children with the connivance of state school officials. Second,
state legislatures passed laws (clearly unconstitutional) permitting
local school officials to divert educational funds for black children to
support the education of white children. One such law, for example,
empowered local school officials to apportion education money "as
nearly practicably equal as possible" (Bond 1966). This enabled school
officials to meet the federal constitutional requirement of "equal educational opportunity" by providing for equal school terms but not for
equally trained teachers for black and white schools. Another example
is the "Certificate Laws," (such as that passed in Mississippi in 1885)
which usually established a system of uniform examinations for
teachers. Salary scales were based upon the certificate obtained in the
examination (Bond 1966:93). The diversion of funds from black children to white resulting from the Certificate Laws worked as follows:
Examination officers would grant lower certificates to black teachers,
or local school boards would pay different salaries, within the limits of a
given scale for the same certificate, to black and white teachers. Thus if
the salary range for a first grade teacher was $25 to $55 a month, a black
teacher would be paid $25 while a white teacher received $55. The
situation in Mississippi well illustrates the effect of the Certificate Law
on the salary gap. The average monthly salaries of white and black
teachers were equal ($29.19 in 1877 and $28.74 in 1885) until the
Certificate Law was passed in 1886. That same year the gap between
white and black salaries began to widen: $31.37 for whites and $27.40
for blacks in 1886, to $33.04 for whites and $21.46 for blacks in 1895.
Furthermore, by permitting local school authorities to maintain a
teacher–pupil ratio of 1:100 in black schools as opposed to a ratio of
3:100 in white schools, the Certificate Law satisfied the constitutional
requirement of providing equal education for the two races (Bond
1966:97). The diversion of funds from black children's education to
that of white children was made possible within both the letter and the
spirit of the state constitutional amendments (Bond 1966:98, 1969:132).

But these laws did not entirely solve the financial problems of the
public schools, particularly in those counties or school districts where
the black population was small (the "white counties"). In such coun-

ties, the funds diverted from black children were so small that they could not solve the financial problems of white children's education.

Thus at the close of this period, black caste minority status in the racial stratification of the South had become firmly crystallized. Black education had also come to be defined as different from white education. It was intended to train blacks for a fixed place in the social, economic, and political systems. This differentiation between black and white education was partly accomplished through unequal financial support which, by the end of this transitional period, had achieved both a constitutional and a legal basis.

Caste Minority Status and "Special Education": 1900–1930

By 1900, various southern states had disenfranchised blacks. By 1915, various southern legislatures had passed laws requiring the separation of the black and white races in areas of social and economic life. These laws reinforced the caste minority status of blacks so that during this period "it became quite evident that whites and blacks were destined to live in two separate worlds for many years to come [see Bullock 1970:72–74]."

The changes that occurred in southern agriculture during this period made it practically impossible for black tenants to improve their position within the agricultural system. Southern cotton encountered both increasing foreign competition and destruction by the boll weevil between 1912 and 1917, which led to a general economic deterioration in the cotton belt, where most blacks lived at this time. More and more blacks became sharecropper tenants and laborers instead of cash tenants or farm owners (Myrdal 1944:236–237). Blacks were not represented in state or local government and therefore had no political position from which to express their grievances or defend themselves against white oppression (Bond 1966:196). The only option open to them for improving their economic status was to migrate to urbanized and industrial areas of the South or to northern cities.

Changes in southern industry during the same period offered a few blacks slightly better opportunities to improve their economic status. With the availability of more northern capital, local southern industries expanded and were reorganized into larger enterprises with national affiliations. They created labor demands that attracted black and white migrants from the deteriorating agricultural areas. Some factories began to employ blacks in skilled and semiskilled jobs previously reserved for whites, as an insurance against labor troubles in their northern branches. In case of strikes by the white unions, the plants would use blacks as strikebreakers or to keep the southern plants in operation.

Except for those few blacks employed in semiskilled and skilled jobs in the industries, the social and economic changes which took place between 1900 and 1930 generally reinforced the caste status which had been established at the end of the preceding period. Likewise, these developments did not alter the course of black education which had emerged at the end of the last period. They merely accelerated the process toward rigid separation and inferior schools for blacks.

Black education in the agricultural South during this period was tailored to produce a black person who adapted well to the tenant system, who was "neither too illiterate to take advantage of his surrounding, nor more educated than is demanded by his dependent economic situation [Bond 1969:245]." Expenditure per pupil in average daily attendance in the black schools was far below that in the white schools. In 1930, the amount of money spent on black public school education represented only 37% of their proportionate share of the school funds. The remaining 63% of the funds for black schools was diverted to support white education (Bond 1966:225–226).

The schools of the two races were provided with teachers varying in professional preparation, workload (teacher–pupil ratio), and salary ranges. More black teachers than white had not graduated from high school.[3] Teacher–pupil ratios in black schools were reported to be much higher than those in white schools and considerably higher than normal for the period. According to Bond (1966:264–265), the ratio was 1:67 in 1912, 1:50 in 1921, and 1:47 in 1928–1929. In the city of Nashville, the ratio between expenditures for enrollments in black and white schools was 1:1.95 in 1899–1900 and 1:1.58 in 1930–1931 (Bond 1966:157–159). The average annual salaries of black teachers were far below those of white teachers. For example, in the four seaboard states of Virginia, North Carolina, South Carolina, and Georgia, it was $287.29 for whites and $127.88 for blacks in 1911–1913 (Harlan 1968:257).

The differences in the average annual salaries were not simply the result of differential educational attainments of black and white teachers. Although a study of the black teaching force in 15 states in

---

[3]After the emancipation, black schools were first staffed with white missionaries from the North, northern blacks, and a few educated southern blacks. Widows of Confederate soldiers and disabled Confederate veterans displaced the missionaries at the end of the Reconstruction. But at the same time, black normal schools, which by then existed throughout the South, and later the county training schools, became the main source of supply of black teachers for the black schools.

1930 showed that one-third of the teachers had less than a high school education, and 58% had fewer than two years of college training, white state officials were partly responsible for the preponderance of less educated teachers in black schools. School officials generally tended to favor hiring blacks with less education because it meant saving money from their salaries. Furthermore, these school officials paid black college graduates inferior salaries compared with those paid to white college graduates because they knew that black college graduates faced many occupational restrictions outside the teaching profession (Bond 1966:269).

In addition to inadequate funding and an inadequate teaching force, black schools had shorter terms than white schools. Since the average length of a school term is the length of time that children actually engage in educational pursuits, Pierce *et al.* (1955:234) have pointed out that it can be used to measure the educational opportunities of children. Bullock notes that in a 12-year period of elementary and high school education, the system allocated 65.6 months of classroom study to white children but only 57.6 months to black children—nearly one school year less.

Blacks who moved to urban and industrial centers attended schools superior to those found in the rural areas. The cities had more money to support better schools than the agricultural belts had. Some industries built better schools for blacks in their company towns. But even in these urban and industrial centers, the education offered to blacks was inferior to and different from that offered to whites. Black education generally emphasized manual rather than academic training.

Having neither legal nor political means to influence these developments, blacks had to rely on white patronage—the goodwill of influential whites—to effect any improvements in their education. But the efforts of these white patrons, especially from the North, were made within the caste system. Although these patrons helped to expand black education, they reinforced the already existing southern system of separate and unequal education for blacks and whites.

One of these northern patrons was General S. C. Armstrong, whose ideas of black education were instrumental in establishing black education in the South as industrial or manual education. Armstrong believed that manual education was more suitable for blacks because their "mental processes" were different from those of whites, and he put these ideas into practice at Hampton Institute in Virginia which he headed. Hampton eventually became a model of black higher education acceptable to southern whites because it meant training blacks for their already ascribed roles in southern agriculture, domestic and personal service, common labor, and the like, and not a training for social equality or competition for white jobs.

When northern philanthropists came to the aid of black education in the South at the beginning of this century, they also accepted Armstrong's philosophy of black education, which he recommended to them in 1890 (Bullock 1970:77).[4] Northern philanthropists became more actively involved in southern public education during the first decade of the twentieth century because of the increasingly adverse consequences of the white supremacy movement, which was at its height at this time. The movement had made the caste system so rigid that blacks were forced into almost total submission to all the barriers against them, including barriers to education. The philanthropists, who were primarily concerned with preserving interracial harmony in the South, thought that the causes of white prejudice against blacks were ignorance and fear of economic competition. They therefore reasoned that both could be eliminated through education in two ways. If an adequate education were provided for whites, the latter would acquire skills for better economic opportunities and at the same time learn racial tolerance. Improved economic opportunities and racial tolerance would eventually neutralize the white supremacy movement.

The philanthropists also sought to improve social and economic conditions of blacks, but they were not concerned with improving general civil rights for blacks. They accepted the caste system, thinking that black education could be improved within it. In their plan, whites and blacks would receive different types of education: white education would prepare them for the more desirable social and technoeconomic positions in society, while black education would prepare them for the more menial ones. Black education would be "industrial." Although the philanthropists acknowledged that blacks were capable of acquiring higher education, they felt that higher education for blacks should be directed mainly to train black professionals, such as teachers, preachers, doctors, and lawyers, to serve the black community. The masses of black people should receive industrial education (Bullock 1970:93–98; Harlan 1968:76–80).

By 1920, the philanthropists had helped to establish universal public school education for blacks and whites. They expanded high school education for blacks and established several colleges for them. But their work was dominated by the ideology of industrial education for blacks.

[4]The following funds have been some of the principal sources of money for the philanthropic work in black education: Peabody, Slater, Jean, General Education Board, and Rosenwald. Their representatives were generally influential in determining the course of black education.

They encouraged the establishment of industrial departments in black public schools in the form of farms, shops, and kitchens. In the course of time, most of their money for the support of black education was earmarked for the support of such programs rather than for academic training.

Thus during the period from 1900 to 1930, black status as a caste minority group became even more firmly entrenched, as did the educational system of rigid separate and inferior schools for blacks. Northern philanthropists who came to the aid of blacks accepted the existing caste system, and their efforts merely reinforced the system of separate and unequal education.

Special Education in Transition: 1931–1953

In the period of 1931–1953, black status in the South did not undergo any radical change, but a number of factors led to a nationwide dispersal of the black population. For one, the collapse of cotton agriculture brought about by the Great Depression and the falling off of the foreign market resulted eventually in many blacks being forced out. The Agricultural Adjustment Administration (AAA), set up by the federal government to raise and stabilize farm income, initiated farm consolidation, which forced the small farmers out of work and gave too much power over local programs to landlords, providing them with strong economic incentives to reduce their cotton acreage as well as their tenant labor force, mostly black. Blacks who were forced out of agriculture could not get on relief in the South and began to migrate to the North (Myrdal 1944:197).

Black migration to the North during the depression was further increased by the white invasion of traditional black jobs in southern cities, for whites began to displace blacks as waiters, porters, elevator operators, railroad laborers, and so on. A combined effort of employers, unions, and lawmakers restricted black job opportunities in the cities. For example, Ross (1967) reports that southern municipal authorities began to revive "licensing ordinances in order to drive blacks out of barbering, plumbing, and other new occupations [they] had entered during recent years [pp. 14–15]."

Migrating blacks were attracted to the urban centers of the North where there were relatively fewer racial barriers in the relief programs once the new arrivals met the residence requirements. World War II (1941–1945) and the Korean War (1950–1953) further stimulated waves of migration from southern agriculture and generally from the South to the North. Many blacks were able to enter some semiskilled and skilled jobs in the war industries because of the efforts of civil rights organizations and presidential orders. Black employment opportunities outside agriculture reached their peak during the Korean War. Many blacks also went into military service in both wars (see C. S. Johnson 1943:104–105; Myrdal 1944; Ross 1967:17).

Despite the social and economic changes brought about by the depression and the two wars, the conception of blacks as a caste minority persisted. These changes merely provided opportunities for blacks to escape from the South, especially southern agriculture, into the urban centers of the North, but they did not escape their lower-caste status.

As the nation's industrial development demanded more and more workers trained in industrial skills and as industrial education became a nationwide movement with financial backing from the federal and state governments, the participation of blacks in it became progressively restricted. The curriculums of black schools began to emphasize classical or academic rather than industrial training, while white schools began to emphasize industrial education, thus reversing the emphasis prevailing during the previous periods. Myrdal observes that while southern whites, in theory, believed that blacks should receive industrial education, they could not provide blacks with such education if it meant preparing them for effective competition with whites for skilled and economically rewarding jobs (1944:897–89; see also Bond 1966:404; Frazier 1957:439).

In 18 southern and border states in 1935, for every $1.00 spent on vocational education of a white child, only $0.58 was spent on a black child. Blacks made up 21% of the population of these states but constituted only 16% of the enrollment in the vocational education programs that received federal funds. And they received only 10% of the federal funds. White enrollment in the programs was evenly distributed in the three major categories: agriculture (36%), home economics (34%), and trades and industries (30%). Black enrollment, on the other hand, was heavily concentrated in agriculture (55%) and home economics (29%) with only 16% in trades and industries. Distributive (sales) occupations, which became a part of the vocational education program after the passage of the George–Dean Act (1929), were hardly extended to blacks. This situation persisted until the end of the period (Pierce et al. 1955:262, 268).

The reversal of the policy of emphasizing industrial education for blacks in this period points to the fact that education for blacks, industrial or academic, was not seriously intended to elevate blacks above their current status. For blacks to have received industrial education to the same level as whites would not only have prepared them to compete effectively with whites in the occupational world but also have enabled them to raise their economic status above the expectations of southern whites.

The depression had caused a reduction in school expenditure, and as it became increasingly difficult for the southern states to maintain two separate school systems, more money was diverted from black children to support the education of white children (Bond 1966:169–171, 1969:259; Pierce *et al.* 1955:202–203). Since the constitutions of these states provided for *separate but equal education,* the inequality was clearly unconstitutional and could be (and was) legally challenged on that ground. The large differences between the salaries paid to white and black teachers provided a common grievance for blacks. Bullock (1970:216) estimates that this discrimination was costing black teachers some $10 million annually. In 1900, black teachers had averaged 65% of the salaries of white teachers, and this figure had dropped to 47% by 1930. But by the 1930s blacks had developed an organizational support for collective action—the National Association for the Advancement of Colored People.

The NAACP began a legal campaign to equalize teachers' salaries in border states, as in Maryland in 1936. By 1941, it had filed and won suits in eight southern states; by 1948, of the 38 cases filed, 27 had been won. Five other states in the South initiated policies of salary equalization on their own. By 1952, the gap in salaries had largely disappeared. In fact, in 1952 black teachers had average annual salaries above those of white teachers in North Carolina, Oklahoma, Tennessee, and Virginia, where they also had higher levels of educational attainment (Pierce *et al.* 1955:207). The NAACP also successfully challenged inequality in higher education, especially in professional training, where it was very difficult to practice the doctrine of separate but equal education in a realistic way.

These successful legal challenges against the practice of the separate but equal doctrine had a ripple effect, so that equalization began to show up in other aspects of public school education for blacks. For example, by 1953 the exclusion of blacks from the public school administration hierarchy had been relaxed in some states, so that a few black professional educators were working in the state offices of black education. Whereas up to 1940 no blacks were members of school boards in the South except in Oklahoma, by 1952 blacks were on local school boards in Kentucky and North Carolina (Pierce *et al.* 1955:80). The difference in the expenditure per pupil in average daily attendance for instructional purposes in white and black schools had also become smaller by the end of the period. For example, in nine states for which data are available, it was $41.99 for whites and $16.29 for blacks in the 1939–1940 school year; by 1951–1952 it was $132.38 for whites and $90.30 for blacks.

Although at the end of this period there was a greater trend toward equalization than ever before since 1900, large gaps remained in such areas as school consolidation, transportation, libraries, and school lunch services. The average length of the school term had become nearly equal for both races (177 days for whites and 176 days for blacks in 1952). Blacks had more one-teacher schools than whites—32.9% of all black schools as compared with 14.0% of all white public schools in 1952. In 1940, transportation services were provided almost exclusively for whites; in 1952 these services had been extended to blacks, so that about 31.6% of black pupils were being transported (as compared with 45.5% of white pupils). The percentage ratio of books per black pupil to books per white pupil rose from 24% in 1940 to 47% in 1952; and the percentage ratio of library expenditure per black pupil to that per white pupil rose from 31% in 1940 to 77% in 1952 (see Pierce et al. 1955:235, 227, 232, 252, 255). But in spite of their relatively improved economic condition, black participation in the federally aided school lunch program in 1950 and 1952 remained considerably below that of whites. In 10 southern states with separate records for the two races, white participation was 478 per 1000 pupils in 1950 and 526 per 1000 pupils in 1952. Black participation, on the other hand, was 226 per 1000 pupils in 1950 and 228 per 1000 pupils in 1952. The percentage ratio of black participation to white participation per 1000 pupils in average daily attendance was 47% in 1950 but dropped to 43% in 1952 (Pierce et al. 1955:275–281).

Thus the changes in the education given blacks were consistent with the definition of their status during this period. The reversal of the policy of industrial education for blacks occurred when training in industrial skills became important for effective participation in the national economy and competition from blacks was feared. A trend toward equalization in some aspects of black and white public school education was achieved through legal action, not through a new conception of black status in the South.

Changes in Educational Opportunity: 1954 to 1974

In the previous periods, changes in black education usually occurred *after* changes in the social and technoeconomic status of blacks. In this way, the changes in their education were used to prepare them for whatever positions they were assigned in the caste system. However, since 1954, the order of change has been somewhat reversed, so that changes in black education began to occur *before* there were significant changes in their social and technoeconomic position in society. The period began with the United States Supreme Court's desegregation ruling of 1954 in *Brown* v. *Board of Education,* Topeka, Kansas, which meant in effect that blacks and whites legally had to be given the same kind of education within a single school system. The response of southern whites to the desegregation ruling and the extent to which desegregation has taken place to date are described in Chapter 2.

An equally important factor in bringing about other changes in black education during this period has been the compensatory education program, which began in the 1960s. The formula for allocating the funds used in compensatory education favored both inner-city and rural schools, where the majority of black pupils are to be found. The availability of compensatory education funds has enabled black schools to purchase educational services that they previously could not afford. Furthermore, the requirements of some compensatory education programs, such as the stipulation that parents must participate in decisions about how the programs should be run, have increased the control of blacks over their education.

The Supreme Court ruling on school desegregation in 1954 was a legal victory that encouraged blacks and civil rights groups to initiate legal action, and later political pressures and civil protests, to demolish the formal structure of the caste system in other areas. Subsequent changes in the political, social, and technoeconomic status of blacks further reinforced the improvements in their education. Efforts to improve black political status began in 1957 with the passage of a voting rights bill, the first passed by Congress since Reconstruction. The bill outlawed discrimination against voters in state and federal elections by state officials or private citizens. It authorized the attorney general to file suits against violators of the law but did not permit him to inspect voter registration records to prove the existence of discrimination. This weakness was remedied by the Civil Rights Acts of 1960 and 1961, although not completely, as later developments in the Selma, Alabama case have shown. It took 19 months before the court reached a decision in a suit filed by the Department of Justice against the voter registrar of Selma, who had systematically discriminated against blacks. But a lower court decided that it could not order the registrar to register blacks because discrimination had stopped in Selma. When the Department of Justice appealed the decision and obtained an order against discrimination, the Selma registrar raised the registration requirements for both blacks and whites. In addition, the Alabama state legislature passed a law applying the more difficult registration tests throughout the state (Ladenburg and McFeeley 1969). The official barriers to black enfranchisement in the South were finally removed by the Voting Rights Act of 1965. This act suspended automatically the literacy tests and other qualifying devices in several states. It was followed by a voter registration drive organized by civil rights workers, mostly from the North. The result has been some significant changes in black political status: Some blacks are now elected to local offices as sheriffs, city council members, and mayors; some are elected to state legislatures; the Democratic party in some states (e.g., Alabama) dropped its white supremacy label; and some white politicians now pay more attention to their black constituents (see Ladenburg and McFeeley 1969:112-119).

Some of the barriers to employment encountered by blacks were formally eliminated by the Civil Rights Act of 1964, which prohibited racial discrimination in employment. This act established the Equal Opportunities Commission to assist individuals discriminated against through mediation and conciliation. The commission could also recommend to the attorney general a civil suit against an employer. The Equal Employment Opportunity Act has resulted in some changes in the occupational status of blacks in the South. In 1972, the act was expanded to cover employment in state and local governments in addition to governmental agencies (see Ladenburg and McFeeley 1969:120-124; Ross 1973).

Formal barriers in public accommodations also broke down during this period. Segregation had been enforced by both law and custom in such areas as workplaces (separate rest rooms, separate doors); grocery and other stores (separate rest rooms, drinking fountains, and lunch counters); public transportation (separate sections in trains and buses, separate taxis, separate waiting rooms and ticket booths); courts (separate Bibles for oath taking; blacks occupied back seats in the courtrooms and could not serve on juries; and amusement places (blacks were barred from theaters, movie houses, parks, swimming pools, pool halls, bowling alleys, zoos, etc.). Where once separate restaurants, hotels, motels, soda fountains, lunch counters, haberdashers, barbershops, beauty parlors, and so forth were designated to serve either blacks or whites, the barriers in these facilities have broken down, partly because blacks revolted against them (e.g., the boycott of Montgomery, Alabama buses in 1956; the students' sit-in protests in Jackson, Mississippi; and Greensboro, North Carolina; "freedom riding" in interstate buses, and so on); and partly because of the passage of the Public Accommodations Act of 1964. The act has made it illegal to prevent blacks from using public facilities because of their race or color (Ladenburg and McFeeley 1969:104–111). The role of blacks in breaking down racial barriers in these situations has had some important psychological consequences for both blacks and whites. It has not only generated new pride and self-confidence for blacks but also forced many whites to see blacks with less patronizing attitudes than before (Bullock 1970:274).

The changes in black education as well as in their political, social, and technoeconomic status since 1954 are not the result of changed conceptions of blacks by southern whites. Rather they have been imposed on the South by outside forces (the Congress, the Supreme Court, the federal administration) in support of black demands. They are in the first instance legally required changes, which it is hoped will in the course of time lead to changes in attitudes and conceptions of black status on the part of southern whites.

The North

Although the evolution of racial stratification in the North has followed a different course from that pursued in the South, the pattern of stratification that emerged has generally been the same. In both regions, blacks have occupied a subordinate position at any given period, but for various reasons they have generally enjoyed more privileges in the North than in the South. Reddick (1947:290) gives the following reasons for the higher status enjoyed by northern blacks: *the law*—which is on the side of blacks in their fight for equal rights; *the ballot*—blacks are not disenfranchised; *tradition*—northern whites do not have a tradition of proslavery, a "lost cause," and the "terrible Reconstruction days"; *"cultural liberalism"*—the North has a higher social and intellectual development, and presumably a more enlightened citizenry; and *general humanitarian movement*—the struggle of blacks for equality in the North is a part of the general struggle for equality by labor, women, and the foreign born. The influence of these factors on black status in the North has varied between different periods, as has the influence of black status on black education.

An historical overview of the relationship between black status and black education in the North is complicated by the absence of reliable data (the 31 states which make up the North do not usually keep records by race, since they have no constitutional or legal bases for operating separate schools for blacks and whites); the absence of "regional problems" in black education (up to 1910 only about 10.4%

of the total black population in the United States lived in the North; their small numerical strength did not make them visible as a regional problem until much later, and consequently their education was treated on a local basis); liberal ideology (black problems in the South were more visible to northerners, who therefore devoted time and resources to studying or remedying black education in the South, and in so doing probably thought conditions to be much better in the North and so neglected to study the actual situation at hand; developments in social science (at the time blacks from the South began to migrate to northern cities in large numbers, northern social scientists had had a history of studying urban immigrant settlements and tended to see the problems of southern blacks in northern cities as similar to those of foreign immigrants, whose problems they perceived in terms of personal and social disorganization). Consequently, when social scientists turned their attention to northern blacks, they failed to study them in the context of racial stratification, as was done in southern studies. Nevertheless, a general outline of the developments in black education in the North is presented here in order to show that in each period black education has generally reflected the conception of black status by the dominant white caste.

Marginal Participation: Before 1861

Racial stratification in the North prior to 1861 was initially based on the institution of chattel slavery, with blacks in a position similar to that they occupied in the South: The relatively free black population formed an intermediate stratum between the slave population at the bottom and the white population at the top. The free black population was mostly disenfranchised and restricted in its economic activities and social privileges.

The abolition of slavery did not necessarily enhance the status of blacks in the region: The entire black population remained restricted in its economic activities and social privileges and was almost totally disenfranchised at a time when the North was extending universal suffrage to all white males.[5] The constitutions of several northern states specifically limited suffrage to white males (Frazier 1957:79, 521; Myrdal 1944:438). Blacks who had escaped from slavery in the South, according to Frazier (1957) "found themselves isolated, disenfranchised,

[5]The abolition of slavery in northern states occurred after the Revolutionary War, but it was a very gradual process. Pennsylvania, for example, passed a gradual abolition law in 1780. By this law, the children of slaves had to serve their masters until the age of 28. In 1790, there were still over 800 slaves in Pennsylvania, though this number dropped to 70 by 1820 (Buck and Buck 1939:279–280).

and denied employment in the white communities of the North [p. 80]." This marginal status in northern society prior to 1861 was instrumental in shaping their education.

In the early phase of the period, blacks received their educations from religious groups, especially from the Quakers. Frazier (1957:418) reports that in New England some masters considered it an obligation of religion to educate their slaves (e.g., Bond 1966:358). After the War of Independence, various religious groups and white philanthropists, as well as many black volunteer organizations, opened more schools for black children.

In general, before 1861 blacks attended mainly private and separate "pauper institutions" and, according to Bond (1966), they were advised by white friends to support their own schools to avoid being "accused of being a charge upon the public [p. 370]." Yet even these separate private schools for blacks faced opposition from the white communities. A black schoolhouse was burned in Canaan, New Hampshire; after mob violence, the authorities in Canterbury, Connecticut jailed a white teacher who had opened her previously white school to blacks; and in New York, black pupils were confronted with mob violence. Thus, although individual abolitionists and philanthropists and some white religious groups favored some kind of formal education for blacks, the general sentiment of the northern white population was against it, even when blacks supported such schools themselves.

The opposition to the admission of blacks into the public schools was even stronger. New England abolitionists like Horace Mann and Thaddeus Stevens, who were also public school advocates, favored the education of blacks in these schools, but others wanted the public school system for white children only. Opposition to the inclusion of blacks lessened only after a public school system had been firmly established for whites. Beginning in Boston in 1820, blacks gradually gained admission into the public schools of various northern cities such as Philadelphia and New York (Frazier 1957:420; DuBois 1967).

Both before and after the general abolition of slavery, education was not intended as a means of equalizing black and white status or of integrating blacks into the white communities of the region. In many northern states, separate public schools were established for blacks, although some decades later the statutes establishing them were repealed on constitutional grounds. The history of public school education for blacks in the following states illustrates this sequence of events (the dates for the enactment and repeal of separate school laws are given in each case): Massachusetts (1820, 1857), Connecticut (1846, 1868), New York (1841, 1900), Pennsylvania (1822, 1881), New Jersey (by tradition), Ohio (1820, 1887), Indiana (1837, 1879), and Illinois (1847, 1874) (see Bond 1966:374–384; Pierce *et al.* 1955:35–36). The sources I have consulted do not say to what extent blacks and whites received the same kind of education in the public schools of the period; but they are firm in pointing out that blacks were not being educated for full citizenship because educated blacks were disenfranchised along with uneducated blacks until the passage of the Fourteenth and Fifteenth amendments, and their economic activities and social privileges were restricted even after that.[6]

Liberalism: 1861–1910

At the time America achieved her independence, free blacks were granted suffrage in all the original states except South Carolina and Georgia; but after the northern states emancipated their slaves, they tended to disenfranchise their black populations, so that by the beginning of the Civil War blacks could vote only in the New England states. They could also vote in New York if they met the property test, which was required only of blacks. The Civil War and the subsequent Fourteenth and Fifteenth amendments to the Constitution forced northern states to enfranchise blacks. One northern state after another initially defeated the proposal; they finally accepted and ratified the amendments, partly to bolster the Republican party in the South and partly as a part of the Reconstruction program. According to Myrdal (1944), "If the North had not been so bent upon reforming the South, it is doubtful whether and when some of the Northern states would have reformed themselves [p. 439]." He adds, however, that once the northern states enfranchised blacks, the change became permanent, for it was immediately "solidified into the traditionally rooted order of things." After that, northern blacks enjoyed "unfringed, the right to vote as other American citizens [1944:439; 429–430]."

But in such areas as employment and housing black status did not improve very much; northern blacks actually lost some of their former advantages as southern blacks began to migrate to the North in increasing numbers. For example, black neighborhoods became ghettos from which even the upper-class northern blacks were unable to escape. The population of blacks in the North (and West) increased from 5.1% of the total black population in the United States in 1860, to 10.4% in 1910.

[6]The Fifteenth Amendment to the United States Constitution granted the rights of franchise to United States citizens. It states: "The rights of citizens of the United States to vote shall not be denied or abridged by the United States or by any state on account of race, color, or previous condition of servitude." This was principally in reference to blacks after their emancipation.

Most of the immigrant blacks went to the big cities; the percentage of northern blacks who lived in cities grew from 64.3% in 1860 to 79.3% in 1910.

The economic status of blacks in the North was more precarious than it was in the South. There were no traditional "Negro jobs" as in the South, and blacks in northern cities had to compete with white workers at every level. Although this was a period of industrial expansion which created immense employment opportunities, blacks were successfully kept out of industrial labor by immigrant competition, white unions, and a lack of training in skilled crafts. On the other hand, blacks sometimes made temporary gains in employment when employers wanted to prevent the formation of labor unions or used black workers as strikebreakers. But black workers in such situations usually lost their jobs as soon as the labor crisis was over. Most black workers during this period were to be found in domestic and other service jobs (Frazier 1957:166, 596–597; Myrdal 1944:191–192; Spear 1967:29, see also DuBois 1967; Katzman 1973; Ovington 1911; Thernstrom 1973).

These changes in black status in the North from 1861 to 1910 are reflected in black education during the period, an initial attempt to educate blacks and whites in the same schools followed by segregated and inferior schools for blacks. Before 1861, blacks were educated in private schools; they were also educated in separate public schools until about 1870. The passage of the Fourteenth and Fifteenth amendments led to the eventual abolition of separate schools for blacks in various northern states. By 1910, the northern states, at least in theory, had passed laws which forbade school boards or school committees to maintain separate schools for blacks and whites. Illinois required its school boards to establish mixed schools in 1874. In 1877, Indiana gave its school boards the discretion of establishing either mixed or separate schools, but two years later discontinued separate schools. In 1881, New Jersey made it unlawful to exclude any pupil from any school because of race. Pennsylvania in 1884, Ohio in 1887, and New York in 1900 repealed their separate school laws. The laws eliminating the separate schools sometimes contained penalty clauses against their violation and in the case of Massachusetts gave the injured party the right to claim damages if he could prove that there had been discrimination (Bond 1966:375).

Since separate schools were rarely equal in reality, it could be assumed that their abolition meant that blacks were now to have access to better school facilities and therefore to better education. But separate schools continued to exist after their legal basis had been eliminated, partly because of the opposition of local whites, which forced school boards to adopt various devices to keep blacks and whites from attending the same schools. For example, the school board in Philadelphia retained separate schools for blacks and whites through district gerrymandering. In East Orange, New Jersey, black and white children attended the same schools but not the same classes; in cities in southern New Jersey, where the two groups went to the same schools, they had different classes and playgrounds. Some New Jersey cities openly maintained separate schools for blacks and whites. In Cincinnati, 50% of the black children went to separate schools and the other 50% attended mixed schools. And in Upper Alton, Illinois, black children were assigned to separate schools in 1886, 1899, and 1907, but each time black parents brought suit against the school board and the board's action was declared unconstitutional (Bond 1966:375–382).

There are, of course, no statistics by which it can be determined whether funding for the education of the two races was equal where there were separate schools. But studies of the specific cities already mentioned suggest that the schools blacks attended were generally inferior to those attended by whites during this period. Local school boards often refused to appoint black teachers to white schools, and the need to retain black teachers already working in a district became the rationale for maintaining separate schools for blacks (see Dubois 1967:89; Ovington 1911:17–18).

Thus although blacks were granted the privileges of citizenship during this period, their status in employment and housing decreased, particularly toward the end of the period. Although the separate public school statutes were repealed and better public school facilities for blacks were then provided for a time, separate and inferior schools reappeared in the latter part of the period.

Northward Migration and Ghettoization: 1910–1960

Between 1910 and 1960, the black population in the North increased at phenomenal rates. Only one out of ten blacks in the United States lived in the North in 1910, but by 1960 the figure had risen to four out of ten. Because most black newcomers from the South were poorly educated and unsophisticated, they tended to reinforce the stereotypes in white minds of blacks as ignorant, lazy, and undesirable. The social status of blacks in general—both the indigenous and the newcomers—fell because most blacks were now of low status (Forman 1971:9). The result was increased segregation and discrimination.

One of the ways in which the new, rigid racial stratification was expressed was the formation of black ghettos in northern cities, residential sections of a city set apart primarily on racial or ethnic, rather than economic, status. A ghetto is not necessarily a slum, although it can deteriorate into one. Its unique feature is that the residents are for the most part involuntarily restricted to live within it because of their racial or ethnic status. Thus a ghetto contains some well-to-do members of the racial or ethnic group who would prefer to live elsewhere if there were no external barriers to doing so. Such black ghettos developed in most northern cities to which blacks migrated between 1910 and 1960. These ghettos often assumed specific names, such as the Black Belt in Chicago or Black Harlem in New York City. They were created and maintained by deliberate attempts on the part of whites to confine the black population to certain areas of the cities. Their evolution appears to have followed a similar pattern in major northern cities: First, blacks immigrating from the South tended to occupy some poorer section of the city, and as their number increased this section came to be regarded as the black community.

Second, various devices were used to prevent blacks from expanding their residence beyond designated areas. Among the mechanisms for achieving this, according to Forman (1971:43–102), were local government ordinances; restrictive covenants (legally binding agreements among property owners not to convey or lease their properties to blacks or other undesirable groups); the refusal of real estate brokers to sell property to blacks in white areas and vice versa; and the refusal of lending institutions to finance homes for blacks or whites in certain areas. Even federal housing programs, such as the Federal Housing Administration (FHA) supported restrictive covenants until 1947, and federal public housing projects tended to be either predominantly black or predominantly white.

There were also other and more subtle means of creating and maintaining ghettos, including informal pressures on either blacks or whites, often accompanied by sanctions involving social disapproval or physical violence. By 1940, black ghettos had become firmly established, and little progress has been made since then in efforts to eliminate them (see Frazier 1957:260–261; McEntire 1960:83; Myrdal 1944:622; Taeuber and Taeuber 1965; U.S. Civil Rights Commission 1967; Weaver 1948).

The type of racial stratification which developed in the North between 1910 and 1960 also shaped black economic status. Southern blacks migrated to the North primarily to improve their economic status, and to some extent they succeeded in doing so. They fared better than they had in the South, but they did not necessarily improve their economic status to the extent that it was comparable to white economic status in the North.

The political status blacks had acquired during the preceding period grew in significance between 1910 and 1960. Blacks learned to use their voting potential and organized pressure groups to bargain for social, economic, and other benefits they might not have otherwise been able to get (Drake and Cayton 1970). However, black voting strength was reduced by the lack of political sophistication among the newcomers from the South and the practice of gerrymandering. In the latter case, whites often set the boundaries of election districts so that black votes would be split and overwhelmed by white majority votes (Myrdal 1944:492).

Residential segregation, predetermined menial technoeconomic roles, and political status which could easily be manipulated had considerable influence on black education in the period from 1910 to 1960. Official ideology for education in the North asserts that all children, black as well as white, should have equal access to educational resources; that blacks should be educated to become good and equal citizens in the American democracy; and that all schools in the same community should have equal standards, irrespective of their racial or ethnic composition (see Myrdal 1944:338, 893). This official egalitarian principle, which was formulated in the period following the Civil War, continued to be enunciated throughout the period, but it often failed to be translated into educational policies and practices at the local level, where white folk beliefs about blacks as an inferior racial group determined educational practices. As Myrdal (2944) observes, "probably most White people in the North (like the White people in the South) believe the Negroes to be inferior and, anyhow, do not care so much for their potentialities and possibilities as for those of Whites [p. 893]."

A survey of school laws in 28 northern states in 1947 revealed that only 12 had legislation prohibiting segregation against blacks, but studies of the local urban school districts showed that the existence of segregated schools was not determined by the presence or absence of state legislation prohibiting or permitting segregation (Frazier 1957:442; see also Jackson 1947; 302–310; Reddick 1947:290–300). The prevalence of separate or segregated schools where they were forbidden by an official egalitarian principle was an inevitable outcome of the involuntary confinement of blacks to ghetto residence. Both white chilren and black were required to attend specific schools designated by local school board regulations, or schools within their attendance areas or neighborhoods. Consequently, black children who lived in ghetto neighborhoods attended schools located there. Because whites did not live in the ghetto, the schools were inevitably segregated. School segregation was (and still is), in part at least, the result of involuntary residential segregation.

Even though northern school officials did not keep records by race, it was generally recognized by 1960 (and, indeed, during most of the period) that the education offered to black children in ghetto schools was inferior to that offered to white children who lived outside the ghettos, a situation reflecting the inferior status of the former.

Rehabilitation and Integration:
Changes from 1960 to 1974

In the early 1960s, a number of legal and other changes which raised the status of blacks relative to that of whites led to attempts to change black education so it could prepare blacks for their new status. The major legal change was the civil rights legislation. Much of it (e.g., the Voting Rights Act of 1965) was specifically aimed at raising the status of blacks living in the South, but it also enhanced the status of blacks throughout the nation. Other civil rights legislation, such as the equal employment opportunities section of the Civil Rights Act of 1964 (Title VII), which barred racial discrimination in employment, directly raised the status of blacks in the North. This legislation, in theory at least, aimed at increasing the social and technoeconomic participation of blacks to an equal footing with whites, but since it was believed that existing black education had neither prepared blacks to take advantage of their new status nor was capable of doing so, it became necessary to redesign education for its new function. The relationship between the new black status and black education was clearly emphasized by President Johnson in his letter to the chairman of the Civil Rights Commission in 1965. The president (U.S. Civil Rights Commission 1967) wrote:

> Because millions of Negroes were deprived of quality education and training in basic skills, because they were given to believe that they could aspire only to the most menial and insecure places in our society, *they are seriously handicapped in taking advantage of opportunities afforded by new laws, new attitudes and expanding economy. We can no longer tolerate such waste of human resources* [p. ix; emphasis added].

Two principal methods used to redesign education during this period were school integration and compensatory education. In reality, both approaches were aimed not so much at changing the education provided to blacks as at changing blacks themselves so that they would perform like middle-class whites within the existing education system (see Chapter 3). In the case of school integration, this was to be accomplished through the interaction of blacks with white students who would provide them with models of success in school and society. In the case of compensatory education, the goal was to be accomplished through some form of rehabilitation or resocialization. The point to be stressed here, however, is that school integration and massive compensatory education in the North have been necessitated by the changes in the social, economic, and political status of blacks in the 1960s which were initiated through legislative and executive actions.

In conclusion, black education in the North has always been superior to that in the South, but inferior to white education in both regions. The relative superiority of black education in the North is partly attributable to the higher political status of blacks in that region, which in turn is the result of northern egalitarian principles and pragmatic politics. But the egalitarian principles of the North provided no reasonable guide to local educational policies and practices. This is one of the major differences between the North and the South, because in the South the regional principle of inequality permeated educational policies and practices at all levels.

The inescapable conclusion from the data presented here is that blacks have never had equal access with whites to educational resources in either the South or the North. In both regions, blacks have occupied the status of a lower caste, filling the menial social and technoeconomic roles, and this status has greatly influenced the kind of education considered adequate for them. In various periods, their education has tended to be designed to prepare them to fill these inferior social and technoeconomic roles rather than to compete effectively with whites for the more desirable roles in society.

Subtle Mechanisms of Inferior Education

Gross mechanisms like segregation or inadequate funding, facilities, and staffing for black schools may be deliberately employed by the dominant group to keep black education inferior. The responsibility for these mechanisms lies with those having power in the state or local community and outside the school walls. But these techniques do not exhaust the devices employed to keep black education inferior. If they did, their removal would significantly increase black school performance, which is not often the case. Moreover, blacks who attend the same schools as whites presumably share equal facilities, funding, and staffing with the latter, but they still do not perform as well. The reason for lower black performance lies partly in the way that schools and their classrooms operate, which involves many subtle devices to differentiate black training from white in such a way that the former is inferior whether or not it is given in the same schools and classrooms.

The historical analysis of black education presented in the preceding sections tells us *why* black education is different from and infeior to white education, namely, to fit blacks' lower-caste status. An analysis of the subtle devices embodied in the policies and practices within the schools (like the analysis of segregation, inadequate funding, and the like) shows *how* the schools and their personnel contribute to keep black training inferior and thus support the caste system. Through these devices, the schools unconsciously encourage black students to fail academically, to drop out of school earlier than white students, and to enter postschool society with just so much education as the dominant group considers appropriate for their traditional social and technoeconomic roles. By repeating this process generation after generation, the schools help to maintain and rationalize the job ceiling and other caste barriers against blacks.

These subtle devices have existed throughout the history of black education, in both the North and the South, and were probably more prevalent and forceful before the 1960s, when debates about the causes of black academic retardation led to their publicization through systematic studies of specific schools and classrooms (see Kozol 1966; Leacock 1969; Moore 1964; Rist 1972; Stein 1971). The findings of these and other studies have led some people to place most of the responsibility for black school failure on schools and their personnel, some to recommend starting alternative schools, and others to advocate abolishing the schools altogether. But critics miss the essential point in that they fail to see the connection between the educational processes in the schools and the level of academic skills the caste system requires of blacks, which can force not only "good schools" but also well-intentioned black or white school personnel to apply the same subtle devices against black children. Studying how the schools and their classrooms operate shows us *how* academic failure or low school performance of black children is promoted by the schools; but it does not tell us *why* the schools do this. To understand the reason behind this probably unconscious use of these devices against black children, we have to examine the educational requirements of their social and technoeconomic roles in the wider society. Unfortunately, critics have long confused the *how* aspects of the problem with the why aspects, and as a result they mistakenly believe that school reforms will largely solve the problem. They are baffled when this does not happen. They do not realize that so long as the job ceiling and other caste barriers remain, the schools will continue to produce blacks whose academic skills are just compatible with their status under the caste system.

In the following description of the devices by which schools encourage black children to fail, I draw from my research experience in Stockton, California for illustration; but I must add that Stockton is in no way unique in these matters. Other works cited in this section show their prevalence elsewhere. I use the Stockton materials as I do only because it is a situation with which I am most familiar.

Teacher attitudes and expectations are now generally recognized as a crucial factor influencing children's performance in school. Children who sense that their teachers think them capable of doing well and expect them to do well are usually successful, whereas children who believe the opposite tend to fail. Teacher attitudes and expectations toward black children are influenced by caste ideologies and barriers. Many teachers regard blacks as intellectually inferior and do not expect them to do as well as whites. Their subsequent failure usually reinforces the teachers' expectations and in turn contributes to more failure (see Hobbs 1975; Knowles and Prewitt 1969; U.S. Senate, Select Committee 1972).

My research in Stockton reveals two other aspects of the problem connected with teacher attitudes and expectations. The first has to do with the kind of relationship between teachers and parents that prevents a mutual understanding of children's academic problems and what to do about them; the second has to do with teachers' evaluations of children's classroom performance which, among other things, prevents children from learning how their efforts are related to rewards in the form of marks and consequently prevents them from acquiring the good study or work habits necessary for maximizing both efforts and rewards.

The physical and social distances between blacks and teachers in Stockton generate stereotypes, attitudes, and expectations on both sides; and this contributes to the problem of school failure. Most teachers not only live outside black neighborhoods but also confine their contacts with blacks to the school setting. As members of the dominant caste, teachers bring to these contacts the latter's expectations concerning blacks; blacks, too, bring to the contacts their own prior stereotypes. Because of these, parent–teacher contacts do not usually result in a better understanding of why the children have problems at school or what can be done to improve their performance. Because teachers do not think that parents have enough "expertise" to understand such matters, they are often reluctant to accept the parents' diagnoses of their children's problems and therefore tend to reject the parents' suggestions of what to do about them. Black parents also frequently reject teachers' explanations of their children's problems because they do not like to hear teachers emphasize "the home background" as the major source of their children's failure.

Many instances of such failures in communication were recounted to me during interviews with some families. In one family, for example, I was told that the oldest son ceased to be "smart" because he was bored with courses that were too easy for him. When his parents went to discuss the matter with his teacher and the principal, their explanation and request for extra work for their son was rejected. Their son's work continued to deteriorate, and at the time of my study he was receiving Ds and Fs in his twelfth-grade courses. The lack of mutual understanding may also be illustrated with the parent–teacher conferences which are held at the end of each quarter. Parents invited to these conferences are often those whose children are failing. These parents say that teachers are really the ones to be blamed for their children's failures and that teachers wrongly attribute it to the children's home situations. Privately they reject the teachers' explanations of their children's failures, but they have no power to insist otherwise; moreover, they go to the conferences feeling that they must comply with the teachers to avoid being labeled uncooperative and thus compromising their children's chances of future success at school. Under these circumstances, the parents' defense against accusations of personal responsibility for a child's failure is to behave according to the teacher's expectations. That is, the parents pretend to agree with the teachers' explanations that home and neighborhood situations cause children in the area to fail in school. the parents' behavior thus confirms the teachers' beliefs about the negative effects of black families and neighborhoods on children's education. But the conference itself has provided no real basis for teachers and parents to understand children's problems or to do something to improve their performance.

The way in which teachers evaluate children's classroom work also contributes to the well-known phenomenon of decline in school marks as black students move from elementary to junior and senior high schools. Black students frequently start elementary school with ratings of C or D, which are locally known as average grades. Thereafter, teachers are remarkably consistent in giving the same average grades to the same students year after year regardless of their actual performance. This may be illustrated by my study of 17 pupils (blacks and Mexican-Americans) who received the average mark of C in the 1964–1965 school year. Over a four-year period, and under four or more teachers, all the children except one—94.2%—where given the same rating of C. The one exception received a rating of C+ to B− one year. When I examined the teachers' comments about individual children in the group over the same period, there was no correspondence between the written assessments and the letter grades. A child who received a C rating in grade one continues to receive the same rating in subsequent years, although the teacher at each grade level writes that she is "delighted" at his "progress." By giving the child the same rating he had the year before, the teacher fails to reward the child for his efforts or progress. One possible consequence of the failure of the teachers to reward black elementary school children is that these children do not learn to associate efforts or hard work with higher marks or rewards. They receive the same average marks whether or not they work hard. The more serious effect of this begins to show up later, when the children enter junior and senior high schools where teachers do not have access to their previous marks and probably evaluate them more accurately for their performance in subject areas. Under these circumstances, black children begin to do worse and worse, partly because they have not been trained to associate hard work with making higher marks, and partly because even those who realize that they have to work hard in order to get higher marks have not acquired the self-discipline and study habits that would maximize their efforts and their marks (Ogbu 1974a:164–169).

Testing, Misclassification, and Ability Grouping

The use of IQ testing and related techniques to exclude black children from high-quality education intensified after the Supreme Court order of 1954 to desegregate schools. Blacks consistently score lower than whites of similar socioeconomic status in such tests because the tests are culturally biased (i.e., they usually reflect the values, lifestyles, and needs of the white middle class rather than those of blacks) and because caste barriers do not provide black children with the same incentives to maximize their performance on these tests. The results of the tests are nevertheless used to rank children in ability groups for the purpose of teaching basic skills. The results also reinforce the conception of blacks as mentally inferior to whites. IQ tests thus form a rational and superficially legitimate basis for denying blacks the same quality of education provided to their white peers.

Misclassification is based on the standardized tests, especially the IQ tests. Children are classified and labeled as mentally superior, average, below average, retarded but educable, or retarded and uneducable on the basis of test results. The kinds of education that various categories of children receive are decided on the basis of such classification and labeling, and all these work to prevent black children in disproportionate numbers from receiving high-quality educations. The classification itself is based on a statistical model that falsely assumes that all children fit into one normal curve, a curve that more accurately reflects the behavior of the dominant white group. Black children from the ghetto whose behaviors (including test scores) are different are then classified as deficient and channeled into special education classes where they learn very little. Their misclassification and disproportionate representation in special education classes throughout the country are well documented. For example, a recent survey for HEW (Hobbs 1975) found that in San Francisco black children made up only 27.8% of the school enrollment in 1973 but constituted 47.4% of all children in educationally handicapped classes and 53.3% of all children in the educable mentally retarded classes. In Riverside, California, according to the same survey, black and Mexican-American students were overrepresented in the mentally retarded groups by more than 50% and 300%, respectively, than would be expected from their representation in the community. The same study also stated that white children in the school district were overrepresented by about 60%.

A study of Chicago public schools by the Civil Rights Commission (1974) found that in the 1970–1971 school year blacks and other minority-group children were proportionately represented in classes for the physically handicapped but disproportionately represented in classes for the mentally subnormal, the latter being based on standardized tests. Whereas about 75% of the students labeled physically handicapped were white, more than 80% of those labeled mentally retarded or pupils with learning disabilities were minorities: blacks, Mexican-Americans, or Puerto Ricans. The report points out that:

> This [disproportionate representation] seems to indicate evidence of systematic discrimination by race and national origin in the referral and/or testing, classifica-

tion, and placement of students in special education classes. A non-discriminatory special education program should have a significantly lower minority enrollment, especially in the category of non-physical impairment [p. 35].

A study by the Children's Defense Fund also found widespread racial discrimination in the classification system. The study analyzed data submitted to the Office of Civil Rights by 505 school districts in Arkansas, Mississippi, Georgia, and South Carolina and found that in the 1973–1974 school year over 80% of the students in the educable mentally retarded classes were black, whereas blacks constituted less than 40% of the total school population in these school districts (Children's Defense Fund 1974:101–114). Misclassification and special education thus combine to form an effective technique by which the schools legitimately contribute to lower black performance.

Tracking or ability grouping based on standardized tests contributes in its own way to black academic retardation. Because they generally score lower than whites on IQ and aptitude tests, blacks are highly underrepresented in the top tracks, which have superior curriculums and college preparatory programs; conversely, they are overrepresented in the bottom tracks, which get watered down curriculums and dead-end courses. Black students who are channeled into such low tracks know that they are labeled as stupid by their teachers, counselors, and schools; and this labeling reinforces their own low opinions of their ability to succeed in school and their negative attitudes toward school. One of the major consequences of tracking is that the schools end up preparing the white children who monopolize the top tracks for the more desirable roles in society, while they prepare the black children who dominate the bottom tracks for the low and menial roles. Ability grouping is thus an effective method of encouraging black academic retardation and perpetuating low and menial positions for blacks in adult life (see Children's Defense Fund 1974; Findley 1973; Knowles and Prewitt 1969; U.S. Senate, Select Committee 1972).

The Stockton study sheds further light on these problems. The failure of black students to associate effort with the marks they receive manifests itself in their performance in the standardized tests given by the school district. Let me illustrate this with one incident. A boy who scored 115 on a group IQ test was sent up to take an individual test for possible classification as an exceptional student, but he did so poorly on the individual test that the person who tested him wondered why he was sent to take the test. My informant explained that "the boy did not do well on the individual test—because the consequences of that test did not matter a hell of a lot to [him]. He didn't know the importance of the one-to-one testing and he didn't show his ability at all [Ogbu 1974a:169]."

Some Stockton teachers and principals agree that their pupils' true abilities are not reflected in test results. Annual reports of elementary and junior and senior high school principals of the schools serving the neighborhood I studied frequently noted that these tests do not tap their pupils' real abilities. In 1967, the elementary school principal reported to the central administration that there was a discrepancy between the tested IQs of his sixth-grade students and their scores in reading and math tests: Some of the good students had very low scores and the top students had mediocre scores on the Stanford Achievement Tests. This, he said, did not reflect what he and the teachers knew of the students. He pointed out that in checking the daily work, grouping, and tests given by the teacher he had found that the students had made more progress than sixth-grade students of previous years. He also said that in 1966 there was a discrepancy between the ability levels of this particular group of students and their scores on the Stanford Achievement Tests: In the 1966 reading test, they were above their expected achievement level on the basis of their IQ test scores [Stockton Unified School District (SUSD) 1967:8–9].[7]

The junior high school principal wrote in 1969 that there was a need to reevaluate the way his students were selected for compensatory education programs because conventional tests did not provide a reliable guide for selection of those who needed the program. He went on to say:

> And, of course, I can't help wishing that we had tests that were less fragrantly "stacked" against the cultural background of disadvantaged and/or minority-group students. If one were to take our I.Q. distribution at face value, one would conclude that we have a lot of pretty dumb kids; but the more I work with them the more acute is my realization that this simply is not the case [SUSD 1969:2].

A year earlier, the senior high school principal had pointed out in his annual report that while the test results were used to assign his students to various classes, their actual performance in those classes was determined primarily by their willingness and determination to do their classwork (SUSD 1968a:3).

[7]At the elementary school, the students are given the Lorge-Thorndike Intelligence Tests; at the junior high they are given both the Otis Beta Quick Scoring Battery Test and the Iowa Test of Basic Skills. The same tests are used at the senior high school along with some additional tests for specific purposes.

In spite of these internal criticisms (and external ones discussed later), the school district continued extensive testing for "levels of intelligence" or "levels of ability" at all grades of its schools. Testing is done in both majority and minority schools, but more tests are given in the latter schools because of several state and federal programs requiring testing for the selection of participating students and for evaluation.

The results of the tests are usually tabulated on a 9-point scale (the Stanine Scale), with 7, 8, and 9 indicating high scores; 4, 5, and 6 middle scores; and 1, 2, and 3 low scores. Pupils with high scores form the X ability group and those with middle scores the Y group; the Z group is made up of students with low scores. The majority of the black students belong to the Z group.

Ability grouping determines what the students study in two important ways. First, it affects the level at which they participate in a given course. For example, all children in the same grade in the elementary school study reading and arithmetic, but on the basis of the ability grouping, children in the same grade begin their reading and arithmetic at different levels and cover different amounts and types of material. In the elementary school I studied, there were some arrangements whereby teachers at different grades exchange students of different ability groups for reading and math. Thus some third-grade students are sent to join second-graders for reading or math, though only rarely is the reverse practice employed. Further developments in tracking take place at the junior high level where the ability group for each course becomes a separate class with a different teacher who must adapt his materials and techniques to the abilities of his students. For example, an eighth-grade history course was divided into 4 tracks on the ground that the four groups of students differed in their ability to read and understand the standard textbook (SUSD 1969:2).

The second impact of tracking on students' courses is most visible at the senior high school, but it begins toward the end of the junior high: This is the division of the courses into major curriculum areas in which participation is primarily determined by the ability grouping and the school personnel's conception of what the students will do after high school graduation. The four major curriculum areas are college preparatory, business, vocational, and general education. The official ideology of the schools is that a student's participation in any of these four areas should be determined by his or her interest, needs, and ability. In practice, however, few students of the Y group participate in the college preparatory courses, and as for the Z students, the exclusion is a settled matter because they are not considered "college material" (Ogbu 1974a:200).

External criticisms were more effective than the complaints in the principals' reports in bringing about some changes in the testing and tracking practices in Stockton. In 1968, the Black Unity Council, a coalition of local civil rights organizations, demanded that all tracking should be eliminated during the 1968–1969 school year (MUSD, Minutes, Board of Education 1968b:4251). The school superintendent responded by admitting at a meeting of the board of education that although the district had long practiced tracking, tracking probably had a detrimental effect on children's education because a child placed in the Z group rarely emerged into Y or X group. He further acknowledged that the intelligence tests that determined the classification of the students into the X, Y, or Z groups did not measure their real abilities; and he added that the curriculum designed for each group often reinforced the assumed differences between the groups. The superintendent summed up the "tragedy" of testing, classification, and tracking in his schools as follows:

> The tragedy of tracking is simply this—once [a student is] measured as "slow" or "low-achieving" the curriculum is designed to agree with his slowness or low-achieving status. There is little opportunity to overcome the language or curriculum disadvantage. Since the prime instrument of measurement is based on language, those children with language handicaps are incorrectly assumed to be of lesser intelligence. Obviously, any measure of language and culture is going to find the children of the poor deficient. This embraces a significant portion of the minority community. It is an insidious means of segregation. There is a validity in the request to eliminate tracking [SUSD, Minutes, Board of Education, 1968b:4252].

Under pressure from blacks and other minorities, Stockton schools began to dismantle their tracking system in the 1968–1969 school year, starting with the high school. The high school principal and his staff were asked to eliminate tracking, and the teachers were given in-service training to prepare them for the change. Nearly two years later, I interviewed one of the high school counselors who reported that the Z groups (mainly black and Mexican-American students) were allowed to take college preparatory courses, higher math and algebra, chemistry, physics, and senior biology, and that they were not failing these courses. The counselor concluded by saying that he had come to realize that he and other counselors were previously tracking the minority students into low-ability courses whereas there was actually a need to give them something more challenging (Ogbu 1974a:199–200).

So far, the discussion of testing, classification, and tracking has concerned normal students. There are others who on the basis of these tests are classified as "retarded." The retarded group (called educable mentally retarded, EMR, or trainable mentally retarded, TMR) consists of those students whose test scores are so poor that they could not qualify for even the low-ability Z group. They are sent to a special school which has contracts with the Goodwill Industries and other local agencies with training programs for "handicapped people." As the TMR students get older, they graduate from their special school into these job training programs to prepare themselves for their place in the adult world. I do not have the exact figures as to the proportion of black or minority students in the TMR group, but some informants during the fieldwork said that blacks and Mexican-Americans were overrepresented in it.

Biased textbooks and curriculums are also used by the schools to encourage academic retardation among blacks. These biases may take the form of omission—a refusal to acknowledge the positive role and accomplishments of blacks and other minorities in American history and society. More significant, the biases are intentional and unintentional slurs, suggestions as to what blacks are and are not capable of doing, character representations which reflect only their ascribed low and menial social and techneconomic roles, and unscientific representations of the issue of race. Consciously and unconsciously, the textbooks and curriculums teach black and white children their respective places in American society (see Carnegie Quarterly 1974; Kane 1970; Knowles and Prewitt 1969; U.S. Senate, Select Committee 1972).

Data from Stockton also illustrate the problem of biased textbooks and curriculums. Before 1967, the Stockton public school curriculum and textbooks either ignored blacks and other minorities as an important segment of society or referred to them in terms of popular stereotypes. These forms of bias were most evident in the history and literature courses. At the time of my research, there were occasional protests about such biases by minority individuals and organizations. For example, one black woman told the board of education in 1968 that blacks were unhappy about the use of such books as *Little Black Sambo*, *Uncle Tom's Cabin*, and *Tom Sawyer* in local schools. She cited instances in which the use of *Little Black Sambo* had caused embarrassment to black children (SUSD, Minutes, Board of Education, 1968a:4211–4213).

Some previous protests had also occurred which led the school district in 1967 to conduct an in-service training for some 80 teachers to "familiarize them with the significant contributions of minorities to the history, culture, and economy of the United States," and to identify some materials suitable for classroom use for teaching about minorities. Later the district appointed four teachers to develop an eleventh-grade course on United States history which would include a substantial amount of material on the minorities. But blacks and other minorities did not consider this adequate, and in 1968 the Black Unity Council complained that the district's history textbooks still diminished, ignored, or stereotyped black American accomplishments. The council then demanded "that measures be implemented at once to include Black American history in the school curriculum in its proper context, a natural part of history, and not an addendum to it [SUSD, Minutes, Board of Education 1968b:4241–4255]." This and subsequent demands by Mexican-Americans led to further changes in the curriculum.[8] These changes included both the elimination of parts of the curriculum that blacks and Mexican Americans considered damaging to their self-images and introduction of new courses that intended to improve their self-image. Among the new courses introduced in 1969 were *The Negro in Literature* (grades 11–12), *History of Mexico* (grades 11–12), *United States as History: Ideas in Conflict* (grade 11), *Black Studies* (grades 10–12), and *Mexican-American Studies* (grades 10–12) (SUSD 1969b:4497).

A clinical definition of black academic problems arises from school personnel's belief that the nature of black families and neighborhoods is responsible for many black problems in school. Especially at the junior and senior high schools, they see students' problems mainly as those of social and psychological adjustments to the school; consequently they tend to substitute group counseling for academic and vocational counseling (Ogbu 1973:120).

It is believed by many Stockton school personnel, for instance, that black children come from homes where they have no models for academic success and the types of middle-class jobs for which, they say, the schools are preparing black children. On the basis of these assumptions, one would have expected that a major function of the counseling service would be to show the children how to succeed in school and the connection between the kind of education they receive and their chances for white middle-class type employment in the fu-

[8]Demands to correct biased textbooks and curriculum were made by Mexican-American organizations such as Mexican-Americans United for Action (SUSD, Minutes, Board of Education 1968c:4422 and 1968d:4428–4430) and Council for the Spanish Speaking People (SUSD, Minutes, Board of Education 1969b:4623).

ture. On the contrary, the counseling service does not do this—for several reasons. First, there are not enough counselors: In the junior high school, only the head counselor was full time, but she was preoccupied with administrative matters and did no counseling; others were teaching counselors, devoting 1½ to 2½ hours a day to counseling 300 to 360 students each. At the senior high school, all the counselors were full time, but they had 307 to 358 students each. In addition to the large number of students, the counselors spent much of their time on such noncounseling matters as programming course changes. Still another reason for the inadequate academic counseling was that the counselors were faced with role conflicts which arose from the fact that they act as buffers between different groups: parents, teachers, and local and central office administrators.

Interviews with parents and students showed that students went to see their counselors (a) for course changes and other administrative matters; (b) when teachers sent them because of classroom misconduct; and (c) if, in rare cases, the counselor suspected that the student had a high potential (as indicated by his IQ test score) but was not doing well in his classwork. That few students went to their counselors for academic guidance is indicated by a survey of 96 students in grades 7 through 12 in one neighborhood. Of these, only 9.39% said that they went to their counselors when they had academic problems; these were mainly twelfth-grade students concerned with meeting the requirements for graduation.

Interviews with counselors showed that they realized they could not reach all the students who needed academic guidance because they had too many students or were part-time counselors. And they complained that they were also expected by teachers and others to perform other, noncounseling functions. Faced with these limitations, some counselors redefined their work with students in terms of therapy intended to eliminate problems of school adjustment which, as they believed, arose from the students' family backgrounds and interfered with classroom learning. One counselor summarized the effects of the home environment on children's motivation in the classroom as follows:

> Perhaps the most serious problem is that of motivation. Often we are working with youngsters from an environment where the people are suspicious of education and see no future beyond day-to-day existence; or those who find among their peers the reinforcement of success, acceptance, and mutuality of interests which they do not find among adults with whom they associate. These "adult models" with whom they are familiar are persons who have rejected them—often their parents, or, perhaps, teachers who have considered them failures and below normal or average

individuals or adults who have part-time, unskilled and semi-skilled jobs and are
dependent upon welfare agencies [Ogbu 1974a:196].

Some counselors therefore believe that the way to help the children
learn better in school is to help them solve their psychological and
social adjustment problems. The way some counselors go about this is
what they term "group counseling," described by one counselor as:

the students [will] work through their feelings and hopefully [come] to understand
why they feel the way they do, so they can do something positive about it. It also
can help them better understand their peers, their parents, and other authority
figures in their lives [Ogbu 1974:197].

Thus, having defined the problem as a matter of social and
psychological adjustment to the school, the counselors encourage the
students to talk about their problems and work out their solutions.
They see the solution of adjustment problems as a prerequisite for
classroom success. Unfortunately, not many students are able to solve
their adjustment problem in group counseling; they are therefore rarely
able to get to the point where they can deal with their academic problems.

Classroom Dynamics in Status Reinforcement

The public school system reinforces inferior education for blacks
and superior education for whites in a still more subtle way. This is the
mechanism by which it socializes blacks to develop personal qualities
such as dependence, compliance, and manipulation while it socializes
whites to develop the personal qualities of independence, initiative,
industriousness, and individualistic competitiveness. These contrasting qualities, of course, are related to the contrasting patterns of status
mobility available to the two groups under the caste system. The black
pattern is described more fully in Chapter 6. Here I deal only with the
way black education reinforces the black pattern.

The role of the education system in reinforcing the traditional
black approach to self-improvement has not been adequately studied.
One study which does examine this issue is that of Leacock (1969). She
studied four schools, attended primarily by middle-class whites,
lower-class whites, middle-class blacks, and lower-class blacks, respectively, and found that the schools tended to prepare each group for its
respective place in adult life: White schools stressed initiative and
decision-making skills, while black schools stressed poise and cultiva-
tion of behavior patterns acceptable to the dominant whites.

Specifically, Leacock studied how a committee of fifth-grade pupils in each school was organized and run. She found that the committee composed of white middle-class pupils emphasized the skills necessary for carrying out responsible and leadership roles in adult life; the committee of lower-class black pupils emphasized skills for menial roles and dependent status; and the committee of middle-class black pupils emphasized skills which made them adaptable to the restricted and lower level "competitive niche" occupied by middle-class blacks in American society. For example, in real life there are few channels open to blacks for full leadership, and those who attain such positions are often made to feel that they owe their achievement to white sponsorship. Leacock's study shows that this dilemma of black leadership was reflected in teacher–pupil relationships in the student organization, where "leadership is formally assigned but devoid of real responsibility [1969:167]." In contrast, in the white middle-class school, the leadership role assigned to the pupils involved real responsibility, "coupled with a fine sense of when it is appropriate to defer to authority, [and this] parallels the pattern of relations on professional and administrative levels of organization [1969:166]."

The emphasis on socialization over the teaching of curriculum content begins quite early in black schools. For example, in another study kindergarten teachers were asked to list in order of importance the things children should learn to prepare them for first grade, and most of the teachers of minority children chose "socialization goals" over "educational goals" (Stein 1971):

> In the black and Puerto Rican kindergartens all the teachers listed socialization goals first; in a mixed school, educational goals were primary. In fact, in a list of six or seven goals, several teachers in the minority-group kindergarten forgot to mention any educational goals at all [pp. 166–167].

Educators consciously or unconsciously inculcate black children with qualities compatible with their dependence on white patronage rather than skills for direct and open competition with whites for desirable status. This observation probably explains why fewer blacks believe that they can achieve material and social rewards in American society through their own efforts, including, of course, their efforts in school (see Katz 1969; Coleman et al. 1966).

In this and the preceding chapters I argue that American society has generally provided blacks with inferior education because it defines blacks as an inferior caste minority. The educational policies and practices of the American public school system toward blacks cannot be fully understood without considering the way in which society, especially the dominant white caste, views black status. The stereotypes about blacks held by the white caste influence the way the public school systems perceive and treat them. White school personnel— teachers, counselors, administrators, school board members—generally subscribe to the white assumption that blacks are inherently less intelligent than whites (Conant 1961) or that blacks are incapable of being trained to perform certain roles dominated by whites. Such conceptions partly determine the curriculum content of black education. When black children's behavior conforms to these stereotypes, such behavior reinforces the beliefs about the inferiority of blacks.

Furthermore, school authorities often realistically assess the socioeconomic opportunities available to blacks in their local communities. On the basis of such assessments, they decide what skills black children need to acquire in school in order to take their "proper place" in these communities at the completion of their formal education. This usually results in equipping blacks with skills for inferior adult roles, i.e., inferior education. The actions of the schools, like those of society at large, simply reinforce the pariah status of blacks. The fact that black schools in the South were, until recently, staffed almost entirely by blacks does not necessarily change the role of the schools in the educational adaptation. Black school personnel in the South (and even in the North) do not have the power to make policy decisions affecting black education. They mainly carry out policies determined by their white superiors.

Summary

The history of black education in the South as well as in the North is one of exclusion from the high-quality education received by whites. The exclusion was based on the fact that whites forced blacks to occupy social and technoeconomic positions that required less education than their own social and technoeconomic positions. In the South, laws were used to keep black education separate and inferior, although such laws were unconstitutional; in the North, the same effect was achieved through extralegal means. Furthermore, throughout the history of black education, the policies and practices of the schools themselves have included many conscious and unconscious devices which made the education of blacks even more inferior. Generations of inferior education no doubt contribute to the lower school performance of black children in comparison with the performance of white children with a history of superior education; the ongoing subtle devices of exclusion within the schools also contribute to the lower performance of blacks. A third factor is the job ceiling, the fact that American society does not sufficiently reward blacks for their efforts in school, especially in terms of jobs. How the job ceiling operates against blacks is described in the next chapter. The effects of the job ceiling on school performance are taken up in Chapter 6, where I consider how it influences the way blacks perceive their schooling, the devices developed by blacks to improve their positions in life, the nature of the black family, and the development of school-related skills among blacks.

5

The Job Ceiling
and Other Barriers
to Rewards of Education

The lower-caste status of black Americans is reflected not only in the use of inferior education to prepare them for adult life but also in the kinds of opportunities available to them in society after they have finished school. The purpose of this chapter is to show how job opportunities for blacks have been based on their lower-caste status.[1] I first show the development of the job ceiling against blacks because of their lower-caste status and how this determined the kinds of jobs available to them in various periods in both the South and the North. Then I probe the reasons for the disparity between blacks and whites in occupational status.

The Job Ceiling in the South

Black occupational history in the region is best seen in five phases determined by changes in the job ceiling.

[1]Quantitative data on black participation at various levels of the labor force during the earlier periods are not available. However, the data for the more recent periods, 1940 to 1970, for the South, North, and United States as a whole, are shown in Tables 5.1, 5.2, and 5.3.

149

Table 5.1

Nonwhite as a Percentage of All Employed Persons in the South, 1940, 1950, 1960, and 1970, and Index of Nonwhite Participation

	Percentage nonwhite				Index of nonwhite participation			
	1940	1950	1960	1970	1940	1950	1960	1970
Professional, technical, and kindred workers	11.3	9.8	8.9	3.9	66.5	45.2	46.8	23.4
Farmers and farm managers	25.8	24.3	17.6	0.7	151.8	12.0	92.6	4.2
Managers and administrators, except farm	3.1	3.8	2.9	2.1	18.2	17.6	15.3	12.6
Clerical, sales, and kindred workers	2.4	3.8	4.1	7.6	14.1	17.5	21.6	45.5
Craftsmen, foremen, and kindred workers	8.0	7.8	8.0	4.5	47.1	35.9	42.1	27.0
Job ceiling								
Operatives and kindred workers	15.5	18.5	17.6	20.8	91.2	65.3	92.6	129.6
Domestic service	60.5	84.6	79.7	30.0	355.9	389.9	419.5	179.6
Service, except domestic	—	40.0	37.3	11.6	—	184.3	196.3	69.5
Farm laborers and foremen	47.2	41.3	46.0	2.9	277.7	190.3	246.8	17.4
Laborers, except farm	50.2	49.7	47.4	11.3	295.3	229.0	249.5	67.7
Total, all persons employed	17.0	21.7	19.0	16.7				

Source: Compiled from data contained in U.S. census reports, *Characteristics of the population,* for 1940, 1950, 1960, and 1970.

Table 5.2

Nonwhite as Percentage of All Employed Persons in the North, 1940, 1950, 1960, and 1970, and Index of Nonwhite Participation

	Percentage nonwhite				Index of nonwhite participation			
	1940	1950	1960	1970	1940	1950	1960	1970
Professional, technical, and kindred workers	1.4	1.6	2.3	3.9	41.2	35.6	41.1	59.1
Farmers and farm managers	0.3	0.3	0.2	0.7	8.8	6.7	3.6	10.6
Managers and administrators, except farm	0.9	1.2	1.3	2.1	26.5	26.7	23.2	31.8
Clerical, sales, and kindred workers	0.8	1.8	2.9	5.6	23.5	40.0	51.8	84.9
Craftsmen, foremen, and kindred workers	1.4	2.2	3.0	4.5	41.2	48.9	53.6	68.2
Job ceiling								
Operatives and kindred workers	2.8	5.7	7.1	9.4	82.4	126.7	126.8	142.4
Domestic service		33.9	29.3	30.0		753.3	523.2	454.6
Service, except domestic	15.3	11.6	12.0	11.6	460.0	257.8	214.3	175.8
Farm laborers and foremen	1.4	1.6	2.2	2.9	41.2	35.6	39.3	43.9
Laborers, except farm	8.6	12.9	13.2	11.3	252.9	264.4	235.7	171.2
Total, all persons employed	3.4	4.5	5.6	6.6				

SOURCE: Compiled from data contained in U.S. census reports, *Characteristics of the population,* for 1940, 1950, 1960, and 1970.

Table 5.3

Nonwhite as Percentage of Total Civilian Labor Force, United States, 1940, 1950, 1960, and 1970, and Index of Nonwhite Participation

	Percentage nonwhite				Index of nonwhite participation			
	1940	1950	1960	1970	1940	1950	1960	1970
Professional and kindred workers	3.6	3.6	4.9	5.0	36.4	37.5	47.6	52.1
Farmers and farm managers	12.9	11.5	7.7	3.4	130.3	119.8	74.8	35.4
Managers and administrators except farm	1.3	1.9	2.3	2.7	13.1	19.8	22.3	28.1
Clerical, sales, and kindred workers	1.1	2.3	3.8	6.3	11.1	24.0	36.9	65.6
Craftsmen, foremen, and kindred workers	2.7	3.7	4.9	6.5	27.3	38.5	47.6	67.7
Job ceiling								
Operators and kindred workers	5.7	9.1	10.7	13.2	57.5	94.8	103.9	137.5
Domestic service	47.1	57.6	53.9	52.5	475.8	600.0	523.3	546.9
Service, except domestic	15.6	19.0	20.1	17.0	157.6	197.9	195.2	177.1
Farm laborers and formen	24.8	20.8	25.0	19.0	250.5	216.7	242.7	197.9
Laborers, except farm	20.4	26.0	25.8	20.5	206.1	260.4	250.5	213.5
Total, all persons employed	9.9	9.6	10.3	9.6				

SOURCE: Compiled from data contained in U.S. census reports, *Characteristics of the population*, for 1940, 1950, 1960, and 1970.

Protected Occupations: Before 1861

Up to the Civil War, black slaves were engaged in two principal occupations: agriculture and domestic and personal service. On the plantations, most slaves were agricultural laborers, but some were skilled laborers working as blacksmiths, carpenters, masons, bricklayers, painters, shoemakers, harnessmakers, and so forth. The plantation was, to some extent, "a protoindustrial school," where some slaves were formally trained not only to work for their masters but also to be hired out to private employers or public agencies. Some were even permitted to work for themselves in return for a certain percentage of their earnings. In the field of skilled crafts and trades, blacks had competitive advantages over white workers because they had the backing of the planter class who had a vested interest in their skills. Some writers (Ross 1967:8) estimate that toward the end of this period there were about five black mechanics to every white mechanic in the South. The occupational census of Charleston, South Carolina, in 1848, proved that blacks in that city, both slave and free, were trained and employed as craftsmen at least to the same degree as whites. Blacks also were involved in the mining and manufacturing industries of the South: quarrying, coal mining, iron milling, foundry works, textile milling, tobacco manufacturing, and so on. Their activities in these industries ranged from unskilled to skilled labor.

There were rarely any professionals among blacks except for a few teachers and preachers, nor was their formal education directed toward training them for white-collar jobs. But their formal training in skilled crafts was fully utilized both on the plantation and in the city (see Bullock 1970; Greene and Woodson 1930; Johnson 1943:81; Myrdal 1944; Strauss and Ingerman 1968).

Evolution of "Negro Jobs": 1861–1900

After the Civil War, most blacks in the South continued to work in agriculture and in domestic and personal service, although now as wage earners, but they were prevented from making further advances in the skilled crafts; in fact, they gradually lost most of what they had gained in these fields through a combination of factors, including the enactment of the "black codes" (statutes governing black behavior), vagrancy laws, lawsuits for breach of contract, and the activities of the Ku Klux Klan. Blacks became restricted to unskilled and unpleasant jobs repugnant to the whites.

The displacement of blacks from skilled jobs in the mines, textile and other factories, railroads, and the building trades appears to have followed a definite pattern. First, white workers gradually invaded the skilled jobs traditionally held by blacks; second, the white craft unions and apprentice system which arose between 1865 and 1885 excluded blacks from membership and participation, thus allowing whites to consolidate their positions; third, as blacks were unable to obtain further training, their skills gradually became obsolete with the changing demands of the work conditions; fourth, where technological changes made a particular type of work done by blacks easier or cleaner, making it less strenuous and dirty, the work was redefined as "white man's work."

The final step in the displacement of black skilled workers was the entry of southern white women into industrial work. This provided a new source of competition for some of the work done by blacks, especially black women. But more important, the southern code dictated that white women and black men could not work together. Consequently, the southern states passed legislation, especially during the economic depression of the 1890s, that drew the color line in occupations even more sharply. According to Marshall (1968), by 1900 the South had evolved a complete segregation in jobs: "Employment was ... segregated and Negores generally were frozen out of occupations they had formerly held and were relegated to "Negro jobs" in urban occupations. The jobs set aside for Negroes were usually the most disagreeable ones that Whites would not take [p. 35]."

By 1900, most blacks were to be found in three occupations: agriculture, domestic and personal service, and unskilled common labor. Very few were in skilled labor. But there was also another development of significance in black occupational status: this was the emergence of a small professional and white-color class of workers (which in 1900 constituted barely 1.1% of the total black workers serving the segregated black community and the public institutions that primarily served blacks. The existence of a separate black community and segregated public institutions provided the only opportunity for occupational differentiation among blacks on the basis of training and abilities. That is, the job ceiling was somewhat higher here than in the general southern economy controlled by the dominant white caste. The job ceiling in the wider society acted to keep blacks in the lower class. However, black middle and upper classes gradually developed as a result of white-collar and professional positions open to blacks in such segregated institutions as hospitals, schools, and churches. The opportunity for some entrepreneurial activities within the black community also contributed to the class differentiation (Frazier 1957; Greene and Woodson 1930:19–32; Johnson 1943:82–83; Marshall 1968:28–52; Ross 1967:10–11).

Biracial Economy I: 1900–1940

The primary fields of black employment during this period were still agriculture and domestic and personal service. Southern industries were divided into three categories with differential black participation: those from which blacks were totally excluded; those in which they participated only marginally; and those which were "Negro jobs," that is, those in which most of the workers were black. But this distinction was somewhat arbitrary, since blacks worked in all three types, although they always occupied menial positions. According to Myrdal: "When Negroes do compete with White workers in 'non-Negro jobs,' there is usually some concentration of Negroes in certain specific occupations. Even industries excluding Negroes may use Negroes exclusively for work carrying social stigma (e.g. charwoman, toilet attendant) [1944:1079]."

The principal groups of Negro jobs in southern industries included domestic service; home laundering; certain other types of service occupations; home sewing; lumber milling; turpentine farming and distilling; fertilizer manufacturing; unskilled work in building construction; maintenance-of-way work on railroads; longshore work; delivery and messenger work; work as helpers in stores; unskilled work in blast furnaces and steel rolling mills; tobacco rehandling and other unskilled work in tobacco factories; unskilled work in buildings, repairing, and maintenance of roads, streets, and sewers; and work as teamsters, truck drivers, and so forth (Myrdal 1944:1080). Myrdal adds that when any of these became "motorized" (i.e., mechanized) it became attractive to white labor, leading to black displacement.

Those industries categorized as Negro jobs had certain common features which made them unacceptable to whites: Most of them were associated with social stigma, low wages, a high degree of intermittency in employment, and a high degree of "physical and psychological disutility [Myrdal 1944:1081]."

The displacement of blacks from skilled occupations and their subsequent restriction to the Negro jobs was accompanied by an evolution of "defense beliefs" among whites which rationalized black occupational status. These rationalizations tended to be strongly held, even when realities, past and present, contradicted them. According to Myrdal (1944):

Defensive beliefs were constantly growing among the Whites in the South that the Negro was inefficient, unreliable, and incompetent to work with machines. Conditions varied in different localities, and these beliefs were not consistent. To justify their exclusion from the textile mills, it is said that of course Negroes are unable to do skilled tasks. Yet in the next town one hears that they have greater manual dexterity than Whites, and therefore hold many of the skilled jobs in the handling of tobacco. Oddly enough, in the textile villages, their lack of competence is given as a proof of their inferiority, while in the tobacco communities the fact they have manual skill is equally regarded as evidence of low mentality, since it is well known that superior races are not clever with their hands! In the iron and steel mills, since Negroes have been given work about the furnaces, there has grown up a tradition that they are best adapted to work in the presence of great heat. Yet formerly it was held to be foolhardy to try colored laborers in such jobs, because they would not stand up under trying conditions of blast furnaces [p. 283].

Thus the job ceiling for black wage earners in southern industries was not based on an objective evaluation of their training and abilities. Blacks were assigned to menial, unskilled occupations on the basis of their pariah status. The same was true of their peon status in southern agriculture, a position from which they were unable to advance after 1900. No significant changes occurred in black wage earning status between 1900 and 1940 except that the expansion of the nonagricultural industries during World War I increased the number of Negro jobs. Subsequent technological innovations and the economic depression, however, caused them to lose some of the Negro jobs. Many black wage earners migrated to the North, especially during World War I and after (see Frazier 1957; Greene and Woodson 1930:344ff; Henderson 1967; Marshall 1968:38ff; Myrdal 1944:280–297, 1079–1086; Ross 1967).

In occupations above the level of skilled labor in the general, white-dominated economy, there was not so much a job ceiling as total exclusion of blacks from participation. Myrdal (1944) writes that "in the occupations traditionally associated with upper and middle-class status the exclusion policy [was] much more complete and 'settled.' This is because it was fortified by 'social' considerations, as well as by economic ones [p. 304]." Hence, the development of the black business, professional, and white-collar class continued to depend almost solely on the needs of the segregated black community and the public institutions such as schools and hospitals set up exclusively for blacks, and a few areas in the federal civil service. This limited the number of blacks who could achieve middle- and upper-class status and retarded the growth of this class of workers. The development was also retarded because white businessmen, professionals, and other white-collar workers extended their services to both the black community and segregated public institutions and thus reduced the number of their potential black competitors. In the federal civil service, where participation was based on examination, various devices were used to limit the number and advancement of blacks (Greene and Woodson 1930).

This situation skewed black occupational distribution: While it encouraged growth in the number of preachers and teachers (who made up two-thirds of black professionals), it provided no place for black architects, civil engineers, managers of industry, and the like who would have had to work in the general economy, where blacks were not wanted. In his study of black occupational status in southern cities, Frazier states that by 1940 the situation had not changed (1957:241). Only in such cities as Atlanta and New Orleans (where there were black colleges), were black clerical and white-collar workers to be found in significant numbers. In other cities, where blacks depended "almost entirely on Black business and fraternal organizations for employment in white-collar occupations," their number was considerably smaller.

The exclusion of blacks from occupations above the level of skilled labor in the white-dominated economy was not based on lack of formal training and abilities. The slow growth of a black business, professional, and white-collar class within the segregated community and its institutions was further caused by restrictions in opportunities there. Studies in the 1930s showed that this situation forced almost one-half of the black doctors and lawyers to migrate to the North, although only 23% of the black population lived there. (Callis 1935; Houston 1935; see also Frazier 1957; 240–241; Greene and Woodson 1930:116–121; Myrdal 1944: 304–239).

Biracial Economy II: 1940–1960

During this period, two national emergencies created labor shortages: World War II and the Korean War. Partly because of the general labor shortage and partly because of external pressures (e.g., President Roosevelt's executive order regarding fair employment practices in war-related industries), blacks made some occupational gains, especially in semiskilled and skilled labor. By the end of the period, a few had been admitted to the skilled labor and higher occupations in the general white-dominated economy. Nevertheless, the practice of classsifying jobs as Negro jobs and white jobs continued to be the basis of the labor market in the South. Thus Henderson (1967) reports that during this period, "whether on the assembly line or elsewhere in the plant or business, Blacks did not work side by side with Whites, especially in jobs with advantages in income, responsibility, potential upgrading, and cleanliness [p. 78]." She further reports that black skills or training and abilities continued to be underutilized because these were not the bases of their occupational status: "Opportunities for [blacks] to apply themselves to tasks commensurate with their skills and abilities [were] overwhelmingly confined to segregated areas of the economy that provided services to other [blacks] [p. 18]."

Henderson found that clerical and supervisory jobs in both the public and private sectors were generally reserved for whites, and this was prescribed "by tradition in race relations [p. 78]." In both agricultural and nonagricultural industires, blacks continued to occupy their traditional positions in unskilled labor until displaced by technological improvement when such jobs were redefined as white jobs.

Three separate studies conducted by Henderson help to illustrate the ascribed occupational status of blacks during this period: (a) a study in four states of 372 firms holding contracts with the federal government; (b) a study of Tennessee state government employment practices; and (c) a study of black employment in Nashville.

The 372 firms with federal government contracts were located in Kentucky (63 firms), Tennessee (107), North Carolina (149), and South Carolina (53). Henderson, who made her study in 1960, found that 27% of the firms did not employ any black workers: the rates were 40% in Kentucky, 32% in Tennessee, and 20% in North and South Carolina. In Tennessee, 3% of the firms with black employees had 4 or fewer black workers; in South Carolina 37% of the firms had fewer than 10 black workers; the North Carolina firms had on the average 20 black workers, although the average number of employees for the firms studied in all four states was 363. There were few opportunities for black female employees; all the Kentucky firms had a total of only 14 black females; only 3.5% of the North Carolina firms had one or more black female employees, although 76% of the firms had white female workers. In South Carolina, 80% of the firms had white female workers, whereas 17% had black ones. In qualitative terms, Henderson found that black employees were heavily concentrated in the unskilled and service jobs. Very few were in jobs classified as skilled, technical, or professional. Furthermore, most black employees had not been "upgraded in recent experience" (Henderson 1967:98–99).

The Tennessee state government employment study made in 1960, covered 17,295 positions or 85% of the total state work force outside the educational institutions.[2] The study showed that blacks had access to only 115 or 9.5% of the 1216 classified jobs, 90.5% being closed to

[2]In 1960, Tennessee had a total experienced civilian labor force of 1,286,495 of whom 201,770 or 15.7% were black.

them. Within a given department, the range of occupational choice was very limited for blacks. For example, the Highway Department had only 55 blacks among its 6000 employees, and blacks had access to only 8 or 3.4% of the 288 occupational classes. Only in segregated public services such as the Department of Public Welfare and Health Services did blacks have better opportunities. For example, in the Department of Mental Health, blacks held 797 (65%) of the jobs and had access to 17 (73%) of the 22 occupational classes. Henderson (1967) concludes that over half the blacks employed by the state worked in such unskilled positions as maids, janitors, porters, and messengers, and only 19.7% were in white-collar jobs. For the total state employees, the figures for white-collar workers were 10% and 65%, respectively. Only 1.5% of the black workers, but 20% of all state employees, were in clerical jobs. The number of black professionals was 132, or 11.3% of the black total; in contrast, 35% of all state employees were at the professional level.

Henderson's Nashville study (described by Marshall 1968:40–41) was done in 1960. It showed that 80% of the black employees in the city were in menial, unskilled occupations. Furthermore, those employed in higher level occupations were found only in the segregated black community and in the segregated public institutions such as schools and hospitals. The dominant white caste used the schools to reinforce this division of labor into black and white jobs. The two castes attended separate schools, and the vocational training in their respective schools reflected their traditional jobs. The white children studied elctronics, business machines, refrigeration, air conditioning, drafting, radio, and television. Black children, on the other hand, studied tailoring, bricklaying, cabinetmaking, cooking, maid and maintenance services, and dietetics.

Marshall (1968:40–41) also mentions studies in other southern cities such as Birmingham and Chattanooga, as well as studies of specific industrial plants (e.g., International Harvester), which found the same pattern of restricting blacks to the menial and least-paying jobs. A report by the U.S. Civil Rights Commission in 1961 concluded that blacks had not made much occupational progress over the previous 20 year because of the job ceiling (Marshall 1968:40–41).

Between 1940 and 1960, the exclusion of blacks from the more desirable occupations in the South, outside the segregated black community and public institution for blacks, was based on their caste minority status. Furthermore, as the Nashville study shows, black schools were geared to train black children only for the occupations open to blacks in adult life. Thus the kind of education which the dominant white caste designed for blacks was an important instrument in the process of excluding blacks from the more desirable occupations. If blacks did not qualify for such occupations, it was because their education was designed to disqualify them, rather than because they were incapable of qualifying for the jobs.

The End of the Job Ceiling? 1961–1974

Some studies of black employment in the South in the middle 1960s indicated that the job ceiling remained unbroken, although slightly raised. For example, Henderson (1967) reports a restudy of the Tennessee state employment situation in 1964 which showed that 20 blacks were employed in some agencies and departments in the traditional white job categories. Her follow-up study of Tennessee firms with federal government contracts showed that only two firms still had no black employees in 1964. In general, a few more black workers had been placed in clerical, technical, and professional positions; and some were working in traditional white jobs, on the production line, for example, "where they worked side by side with White workers." But five of the firms had no black workers above the janitor rank, and 19 had made no significant changes in their employment policies. She noted further that a chemical plant not previously studied had made some significant changes. Although it had no black employees in 1961, it had 20 black female workers in 1964 (out of 1500 employees) working side by side with white workers. Studies by the Southern Regional Council indicate that in Atlanta, Miami, and Houston the basic pattern of the job ceiling remained (Marshall 1968:41).

Since the second half of the 1960s, blacks have made further inroads into the skilled and higher occupations in both the private and public sectors of the general southern technoeconomic system. This is partly attributable to the influence of Title VII of the Civil Rights Act of 1964, which prohibits racial discrimination in employment and established the Equal Employment Opportunity Commission to investigate and rectify instances of discrimination. The potential influence of Title VII in raising the job ceiling would be enormous were it fully implemented, but more recent studies show that it is not, so that its influence is uneven. That Title VII has not significantly raised the job ceiling is revealed by studies of black employment in the South funded by the Manpower Administration of the Department of Labor. These studies (cited in Marshall 1968) cover employment patterns in specific communities such as Memphis and Houston, and in the state and local governments. In most cases, the job ceiling for black wage earners and those in higher occupations remains relatively unchanged. Ross's study (1973) of the employment patterns of local and state governments will serve as an illustration.

Ross found three types of changes in black employment during the previous decade. First, token integration, in which employing some blacks in occupations above the job ceiling represents less a desire on the part of the local white power elites to achieve equal employment opportunities for blacks and whites than an attempt to comply with pressures from the press, the federal government, local white liberals, and the black community. Another kind of change exists in those communities where blacks have achieved a voting majority and have been able to gain control of the machinery of government. In such communities, blacks are employed in high occupations previously above the job ceiling.

The third type of change in Ross's findings has taken place in the traditional black jobs—both (a) those which are menial and unpleasant, and (b) those which are higher occupations in segregated public institutions. Actually, there has been no change in the former: Blacks still do most of the menial, unpleasant jobs, including manual labor on the public roads, garbage collecting, and the like.[3] But in the higher occupational classes in the public institutions (e.g., in social work, public welfare, supplementary services administration, counseling, neighborhood police protection, etc.), especially those involving federal funds, more blacks are now employed to serve other blacks. But the employment statistics of several southern states show that the job ceiling operates as effectively here as in skilled labor to prevent blacks from achieving their proportionate share of the jobs.

Ross's study provides detailed tables of black representation at various levels of state employment in many southern states. These tables appear to indicate that some states have taken steps toward employing blacks in the more desirable jobs from which they were previously excluded. However, a careful agency-by-agency analysis of the table for a given state shows that the appearance is deceptive. For example, Ross found that in North Carolina, about 50% of the black state employees in white-collar jobs were in segregated schools and medical facilities, and even there they held only a small proportion (9 out of 37) of the top-level jobs of supervisors, administrators, and directors. In many other southern states covered by the study, the job ceiling is even lower (see Table 5.1).

By 1900, the pattern had evolved wherein blacks were restricted to menial jobs through the job ceiling and inferior education. This pattern

---

[3]These menial jobs are, of course, generally those with the lowest wages.

has continued with modifications in periods of national emergencies and labor shortages and as a result of federal legislation against discrimination in employment and protests and boycotts by blacks against white businesses in southern cities in the 1960s. The overall result of the historical development of the job ceiling is that the evolution of occupational differentiation among blacks in the South has not been determined by formal training and abilities.

The Job Ceiling in the North

Black occupational history in the North is also centered around the phenomenon of the job ceiling, although there are many variations on the theme.[4] The job ceiling in the North differs from that in the South in a number of ways: It began much earlier; the development of a black business and professional class was slower because the number of blacks living in the North in the earlier period was smaller and because blacks were not totally segregated; its impact is more severe—blacks have access to higher formal education but less opportunity to use it in acquiring jobs commensurate with their education; and, on the other hand, since the turn of the century the job ceiling has been more susceptible to change because of various national emergencies, fair employment laws, and black political pressures. The five phases presented here do not necessarily correspond with those in the South.

Evolution of The Job Ceiling: Before 1861

The number of blacks in the North before 1861 was small, and almost all were engaged in two principal occupations: agriculture and, particularly, domestic and personal service. Others were skilled craftsmen—blacksmiths, anchormakers, bricklayers, brickmakers, carpenters, distillers, hammermen, refiners, shoemakers, tailors, and tanners (Greene and Woodson 1930:5), but opportunities for skilled trade or labor were more limited in the North because of competition with white workers who were often preferred by employers. The displacement of black wage earners from skilled labor was escalated after the Irish and German immigrations began in 1846 and 1848 respectively. As a result, black wage earners became more restricted to domestic and personal service. The job ceiling which thus evolved affected men more

---

[4]See Table 5.2 for the quantitative data on black participation in the labor force in the North since 1940.

severely because the domestic and personal service jobs available to blacks were usually those suitable for women. Surveys of black employment in Cincinnati in 1835 and in Philadelphia in 1849 showed that most gainfully employed blacks were women, engaged primarily as washerwomen. (Greene and Woodson 1930:4; see also Ross 1967:9; New York State Commission 1960:29).

The Absence of Negro Jobs: 1861–1910

By 1861, the job ceiling for black wage earners in the North had evolved. The perpetuation and the lowering of the job ceiling were made easier because no tradition of Negro jobs existed in the North at that time. Slavery had been abolished two generations earlier, so that no white group had a vested interest in preserving certain occupations for blacks. Blacks therefore had to compete with whites in every sector of the labor force. As a result, there were frequent race riots before the Civil War. Moreover, blacks generally lost to whites in the competition for jobs, even in those areas that had previously been their domain (Myrdal 1944:292). Thus during this period blacks were displaced as stevedores and longshoremen by European immigrants in Cleveland, Detroit, Chicago, Boston, New York, and elsewhere. The rise in craft unions and the apprenticeship system also resulted in the exclusion of blacks from training and participation in the skilled trades. In New York City, a race riot in 1863 was partly caused by white opposition to emancipation on the grounds that skilled black laborers from the South would flood the job market by moving north. Following this riot, the black population of the city decreased by 20% within a few years; by 1905, only 5% of the gainfully employed blacks in the city were members of the skilled crafts unions affiliated with the AFL (Myrdal 1944:291; New York State Commission 1960:29, 35; Ovington 1911).

Before World War I, the black male labor force in the North had increased to about 160,000, but they were virtually restricted to menial employment, engaging primarily in four occupational groups: service occupations, general labor, jacks-of-all-trades, and unspecified "others" like farm labor and building and "hand trades" (Myrdal 1944:293). One evidence of the more drastic effect of the job ceiling in the North at the turn of the century was that more black men were in domestic and personal service than women, whereas in the South more women were in such occupations. The reason for this, according to Greene and Woodson (1930) was that "there was a greater diversity of employment for Black males in the South than in the North [pp. 77–78]." But even in domestic and personal service, blacks were beginning to face serious competition from immigrants who had begun to displace them as house servants, waiters, porters, and bellboys.

In the North, blacks were generally excluded from business, the professions, and white-collar occupations in the general society. And the absence of large segregated black communities and segregated public institutions retarded the growth of this class of workers among the blacks more severely in the North than in the South during the period.

National Emergencies I: 1910–1940

World War I, the industrial boom of the 1920s, and the restriction of immigrant labor resulted in labor shortages in the North. They increased the employment opportunities for blacks so that the black male labor force in the North rose from 160,000 in 1910 to 480,000 in 1930. The occupational niche into which blacks were permitted to move was in unskilled, manual labor, jobs not desired by whites, such as those in steel mills, auto plants, foundries, packing houses, highway construction, railroad maintenance, laundries, food industries, coal mines, and domestic and service work.

A fairly large number of northern manufacturing industries continued to proscribe the employment of blacks. These included textile factories, sawmills, electric machinery and supply factories, shoe factories, bakeries, furniture factories, utility companies. Although blacks gained a first foothold in some northern manufacturing industries during this period, they did so in the niche that would have been considered traditional Negro jobs in the South. While black males concentrated in unskilled manual labor, black females found their niche as domestic servants in northern cities. In sum, the job ceiling in the North almost equaled that in the South although it was not nearly as rigid. In both regions, black workers were concentrated at the bottom of the occupational ladder.

During the depression, many black wage earners lost their jobs. Myrdal reports that blacks actually fared better in the South than in the North during the depression because "many labor unions [in the North] discriminated against the Negro workers. So did many employers, especially when it came to skilled work [1944:296]."

The white-dominated technoeconomic organization of the North almost totally excluded black participation above the level of skilled labor. The exception was, of course, in some state governments and in the federal government, where employment was based on civil service examinations. Beginning about 1929, however, blacks began to organize boycotts of white businesses to force them to hire blacks in white-collar positions. They were fairly successful in New York City, Newark, Washington, D.C., Chicago, and Philadelphia. The hiring of black teachers was also the result of pressures from the black community. A study of the employment of black school personnel in several northern cities in 1939–1940 showed that many cities did not hire black teachers; that where black teachers were hired their number tended to vary with the political strength of the black population; and that blacks were rarely placed in administrative or supervisory positions except in segregated black schools (Jackson 1947). One other factor which added to the numbers in the black technical and professional class was the Work Projects Administration. Some blacks working on relief programs were given opportunities to acquire and utilize technical and professional skills.

It was mainly the emergence of northern black ghettos that encouraged the development of a black business, professional, and white-collar class. As early as 1920, blacks began to establish stores and organize banks and insurance companies in their ghettos. Furthermore, many professionals from the South—preachers, doctors, lawyers, and teachers—came to the North with the migrating wage earners. And these, together with their clerical assistants, formed the core of the black higher occupational class.

Developments in black occupational status between 1910 and 1940 show that although the job ceiling in the North was somewhat less rigid than it was in the South, increases in black occupational status generally depended largely on such factors as war and depression (see Callis 1935; Frazier 1957; Greene and Woodson 1930; Houston 1935; Jackson 1947; Johnson 1935; Myrdal 1944; Ross 1967).

National Emergencies II: 1940–1960

Initially blacks were virtually excluded from skilled jobs in the war-related industries, not because they lacked the skills but because they were blacks. Employers contended that they had to honor the "customs" of the communities where their plants were located. That is, they would not hire even qualified blacks if the community did not want them or if white workers did not want to work with blacks. (Segregation was, of course, not confined to the civilian labor force; the United States Army was segregated until after World War II). Other blacks were excluded from government-sponsored training programs because it would have been difficult to place them in war-related industries. Thus up to 1943, in spite of the nationwide labor shortage, many blacks were forced to remain on relief or continue in domestic and personal service. Some found unskilled jobs in consumer and service industries or in the construction of airports, military bases, arsenals, and other military projects, some were hired in their traditional jobs in the iron and steel and meatpacking industries.

It took enormous pressures from blacks and civil rights groups to open up employment opportunities for black wage earners in war industries. First, in September 1940, at the urging of black leaders and civil rights groups, the National Defense Advisory Commission put out a weak statement against job discrimination on the basis of "age, race, sex, or color." Further pressures led President Roosevelt to issue Executive Order 8902 in 1941, which required future contracts in defense-related industries to carry nondiscriminatory clauses and directed that more blacks should be allowed to participate in vocational training programs. It also established the Committee on Fair Employment Practices to study and redress complaints of discrimination (Ross 1967:17). With mounting publicity and pressures, the war-related industries then began to employ blacks in semiskilled and skilled positions.

Advances above the level of skilled labor during the 1940s were more limited, according to Ross. There seemed to be only two areas in which blacks made some significant gains in the wider society: teaching and public administration or government service. Advances in clerical, sales, professional, proprietory, and managerial positions were negligible. The relatively small gain in these positions was partly the outcome of the growth of the ghettos, where blacks had the best opportunities to fill such positions.

The Korean War (1950–1953) provided another opportunity for occupational advances among black wage earners. This period is often regarded as "the apex" of black prosperity, relative to whites.

The End of the Job Ceiling? 1961–1974

It is difficult to present a clear picture of the job ceiling in the North between 1961 and 1974, partly because there have been so many occurrences which bear on the job ceiling whose effects have not been properly studied and partly because there are few systematic studies of black occupational status in the North. Good descriptive studies of black employment status in specific communities, in firms, and in local, state, and federal governments in the South abound; but such studies are rare in the North. But a comparison of Table 5.1 with Table 5.2 shows that the job ceiling in the North remains, although it is higher than the ceiling in the South (see also Harrison 1972; Hill 1968; Kain 1969; Marshall 1967; Marshall and Briggs 1966; Means 1968; Ross 1967; Thernstorn 1973). The job ceiling in the North would probably not have risen as high as it did during this period had it not been for the enforcement of various state and federal laws against discrimination.

Recent Nationwide Efforts to Raise the Job Ceiling

Since 1961, a combination of forces tending to raise the job ceiling nationwide has largely been responsible for raising it in the North. Among these are presidential executive orders, (such as President Kennedy's Committee on Equal Employment Opportunity, 1961), legislative actions at the federal and state levels (Title VII of the Civil Rights Act of 1964, the War on Poverty, etc.), and pressures from civil rights organizations (such as the NAACP, the National Urban League, etc.). Some institutions (e.g., the public schools and the universities) have been forced to respond to these forces by recruiting blacks to positions on their staffs from which they were previously excluded or in which they had only token representation. The private sector of the economy is also making similar efforts for the same reason, and firms that hold federal contracts are required by law to increase their minority representation in the higher-level jobs. Some business firms and various institutions are also recruiting blacks to higher-level jobs because since the later part of the 1960s it has become a good public relations device to have one or more blacks or representatives of other minorities among their ranking personnel.

Because of these developments, many blacks have now been able to enter high-level occupations from which they were previously excluded or in which they had only token representation. Brimmer (1974:160) reports that between 1960 and 1970 the number of blacks in the top two occupational categories nearly doubled. In the top category, the professional and technical occupations, the increase was about 128% for blacks although the increase for the general population in these occupations was only 49%. Black representation in this top occupational category rose from 4.4% of the total in 1960 to 6.8% in 1971. In the second highest paying occupational category—managers, officials, and proprietors—the number of blacks increased by almost 100% although the increase for all individuals in this category was only 23%. The Manpower Administration Study (A. R. Ross 1973:1) reports that gains were particularly sharp in large companies; between 1966 and 1970 the proportion of black professionals, technical, and managerial workers almost doubled in companies with 100 or more employees.

The Job Ceiling and Education: Conventional Explanations

Given the cultural emphasis that education is a training in marketable skills and given the fact that an individual's job is so important for both his or her life and those of his or her children, it is surprising that until recently social scientists expended little effort to study the ways in which American society uses black academic skills and rewards blacks for educational accomplishment. One reason for this, already mentioned, is the widely held belief among middle-class white Americans, including politicians, businessmen, economists, social scientists, and educators, that individual members of American society achieve desirable social and economic status through formal education. It is said that more education means higher social status, more self-esteem, more employment opportunities, better jobs, and better wages and salaries (see Berg 1969; Blair 1971; Harrison 1972; Parsons 1968). Usually these generalizations are extended to blacks and whites alike.

Jensen (1969:78–79) insists, for example, that American society applies the same criteria in selecting both blacks and whites for various social and occupational roles and that the disproportionate representation of blacks in the least desirable of these roles must be attributable to other causes, particularly to differences in the genetic makeup of the two castes. It is necessary to quote Jensen's perspective on the sources of the disparities in social and occupational roles between blacks and whites, at some length, partly because his false assumptions here are an important part of his heredity theory and partly because he views himself as not just a scientist, but a humanitarian scientist honestly seeking to provide the best explanation for and the best solution to an important social problem. Jensen states that:

> The question of *race* differences in intelligence comes up not when we deal with individuals as individuals, but when certain identifiable groups or sub-cultures within the society are brought into comparison with one another *as groups or populations*. It is only when the groups are disproportionately represented in what are commonly perceived as the most desirable and the least desirable social and occupational roles in a society that the question arises concerning average differences among groups. Since much current thinking behind civil rights, fair employment, and equality of educational opportunity appeals to the fact that there is a

disproportionate representation of different racial groups in the various levels of the educational, occupational and socioeconomic hierarchy, we are forced to examine all possible reasons for this inequality among racial groups in the attainments and rewards generally valued by all groups within our society. To what extent can such inequalities be attributed to unfairness of society's multiple selection processes? ("Unfair" meaning that selection is influenced by intrinsically irrelevant criteria, such as skin color, racial or national origin, etc.) And to what extent are these inequalities attributed to really relevant selection criteria which apply equally to all individuals but at the same time select disproportionately between some racial groups because there exists, in fact, real average differences among the groups—differences in the population distributions of those characteristics which are indisputably relevant to educational and occupational performances? This is certainly one of the most important questions confronting our nation today. The answer, which can be found only through unfettered research, has enormous consequences for the welfare of all, particularly of minorities whose plight is now in the foreground of public attention [1969:78–79].

The trouble with Jensen's approach—and a major basis for evaluating his central thesis that social and occupational inequality is attributable to racial differences in intelligence—is that *he has studied only one of American society's multiple selection processes: that of standardized testing.* There is no evidence in any of Jensen's works that he has studied the hiring policies and practices of American employers, the policies and practices of American real estate agents, or even the hiring policies and practices of the school districts within which he carried out his studies of the "intelligence differences" of the racial groups (see Jensen 1969, 1971, 1972a, 1973).

The application of human capital theory to explain the overrepresentation of blacks in low-status jobs is another reason why social scientists long neglected to study the way American society uses black academic skills and rewards blacks for their educational accomplishments. The human capital theory had much influence on the social policies of the 1960s. It asserts that people who are engaged in low-paying jobs are in them because they lack the skills, especially formal education or training, for higher-paying jobs. Furthermore, the productive worth of those who work in menial jobs can be increased by giving them more training, i.e., making a substantial investment in their education.

From the standpoint of this theory, blacks are disproportionately represented in the least desirable, low-paying jobs precisely because these are the jobs for which the job market finds them best qualified. Like Jensen's heredity theory, the human capital theory almost assumes that the job market operates fairly and impartially without regard to race, color, sex, or creed (Harrison 1972:4). The solution to the problem of black overrepresentation in menial, low-paying jobs proposed in this theory is more education and training, through which blacks will be able to "command higher quality jobs, higher wages," etc. That is, blacks' educational credentials will be translated into higher-quality employment and will be proportionately rewarded by society through the labor market.

Finally, both the folk belief about the relationship between education and self-improvement and the economic theory of human capital combine to give rise to yet another assumption, that lack of equal education (in quantity and quality) is primarily responsible for the inequality between blacks and whites in social and economic status. This assumption underlies current explanations by some economists of the high rate of unemployment among blacks. Available data show that the unemployment rate is twice as high among blacks; that blacks disproportionately experience long-term unemployment; and that black–white differences in unemployment rates increase as the level of education increases. Killingsworth, for example, rejects the idea that these differences could be caused by racial discrimination. Instead, he says that they are caused by the fact that blacks have inferior education; that better educated blacks are younger than better educated whites; and that better educated blacks are not as well groomed by their families for white-collar jobs in terms of manner of speech, mode of dress, deportment, and the like as their white peers (Killingsworth 1967:63–72, 1969). Available evidence suggests, however, that this may not be an accurate picture of black occupational experience.

It is evident from the survey of black occupational history presented earlier in the chapter that these theories do not accurately represent the black experience. Indeed, the advances made by blacks in the field of employment above the job ceiling since 1961, particularly since 1966, actually refute these theories. These advances have been made neither as the result of changes in the genetic makeup of blacks nor as the result of changes in their culture, family organization, and child-rearing practices. The dramatic rise in black representation above the job ceiling since 1961 was brought about by external pressures against caste barriers in employment. In general, it can be concluded that the advances made by blacks in this period support Myrdal's earlier observations (1944:293) that the occupational advances of blacks, are not the result of a normal development and that it would be more accurate to describe them as a series of unique happenings.

The lack of normality in black occupational advances still exists and can be seen in the folklore associated with black occupational advances since 1966. This folklore is described in a study by the Manpower Administration (A. R. Ross 1973):

> At the same time that medium and large firms were stepping up their recruitment of Black college graduates, stories were being circulated about tokenism. Instances were cited of men given high-sounding titles and high visibility but few and vaguely defined duties—something to do with public relations or community relations—or in those firms with black blue-collar workers—industrial relations. Cases were also related of graduates of Black colleges hired as accountants with the salaries of accountants but assigned to what were essentially clerical duties. There were many other variations on the theme, but the motif was always the same. Black college graduates were hired for window-dressing—to demonstrate to the Civil Rights Commission or to a Federal Contract Compliant Officer that the firm was an "equal opportunity employer" [p. 1].

The Manpower Administration study investigated what happened to black male college graduates who have gained entry into white business firms. It found that the above folklore was not entirely either true or false. Moreover, the study revealed that although blacks have gained entry into occupations above the job ceiling in these firms, they do not necessarily have opportunities for advancement equal to those of whites. Most black professionals interviewed in the study felt that within their firms there was a low ceiling beyond which they, as blacks, could not advance. The few white managers and supervisors who were also interviewed tended to support this. To quote from the summary and conclusions of the study:

> Slightly more than half of the men were satisfied with their career's progress. And, in comparing their progress with Whites in their department of similar background, about half thought they had advanced as well and about one-fifth felt they had done better, whereas over nine-tenths felt at least as well qualified. . . .
>
> Nevertheless, 3 out of 5 of the surveyed men felt that they, as black business professionals, did not have the same opportunities as whites in their firm. Their comments indicated that the basis for this view was expectations concerning the future. The men felt that *there was a ceiling on how far they could go, and that the ceiling was rather low. The fact that so few of the surveyed group had attained supervisory or managerial positions and that average salaries did not increase beyond the ninth year of service, though some of the men had worked for the same firm more than 25 years, suggests that the respondents' evaluation of their situation was based on observation and experiences. If the future were to mirror the past their attitudes were realistic.*
>
> Another possible indicator of the realism of the black men's appraisal is found in the reports concerning equality of opportunity of those white supervisors who agreed to be interviewed. . . .
>
> Slightly half of them reported that their firm did not offer equal opportunities to blacks. Considered separately, the opinions of so select a group as these white

managers would not be a reliable piece of evidence, but considered in conjunction with the reports of the large group of blacks, they carry weight. They reinforce the blacks' pessimism concerning the future. As one of the managers pointed out, management tends to be reluctant to accept members of minority groups [p. 2; emphasis added].

These findings are not confined to blacks in business firms. A similar study of those employed in other areas (e.g., public institutions) would probably reveal the same situation: Black employees are not given responsibilities commensurate with their training and abilities, and they have less opportunity for advancement than their white peers. The job ceiling has been raised significantly since 1961, but the new black representation in the high-status jobs is not yet accompanied by an equal share of the responsibilities that go with such jobs.

The Job Ceiling and Educational Attainment

How is this pattern of black occupational advances related to the pattern of black educational attainment? In other words, is it not possible that black occupational advances are determined primarily by black educational progress rather than by a raised job ceiling? To answer this question reasonably well would require a survey of black educational attainment for various periods in which occupational status was surveyed for each region. It would be particularly appropriate to compare the proportion of blacks possessing the educational credentials required by the occupations above the job ceiling in the periods surveyed. This problem has not been studied systematically enough to permit the kind of answer posed by the question. On the other hand, at least four kinds of evidence strongly suggest that black occupational progress does not depend on black educational progress in the same way that white occupational progress depends on white educational attainment.[5]

The first kind of evidence comes from comparing the rates of progress made by blacks in both education and occupational status in the

[5]Chapter 4 showed that blacks have generally received inferior education, and it may not be logically consistent in this chapter to say that they have been denied access to the same kinds of jobs available to whites with superior education. But the point of this chapter is not that blacks with inferior education should have access to the same kinds of jobs available to whites with superior education. Rather, the point is that American society uses two different criteria in assigning whites and blacks to adult roles. Whites are judged qualified for jobs on the basis of education and ability, whereas the jobs available to blacks are predetermined on the basis of the ascriptive criterion of caste status or skin color. Inferior education is the first step in excluding blacks from obtaining the more

Table 5.4

Percentage Distribution of Years of School Completed by Persons 25 Years of Age and Older, United States

	1940		1960		1970	
	White	Nonwhite	White	Nonwhite	White	Nonwhite
College						
4 or more years	4.9	1.3	8.1	3.5	11.3	4.4
1 to 3 years	5.9	1.9	9.3	4.4	11.1	5.9
High school						
4 years	15.3	4.5	25.7	13.4	32.2	21.2
1 to 3 years	15.8	8.7	19.3	18.8	16.6	24.8
Elementary school						
8 years	29.9	11.9	18.1	12.8	13.0	16.5
5 to 7 years	17.3	29.9	12.8	23.6	9.1	18.7
1 to 4 years	7.8	31.3	4.8	18.0	3.1	11.3
None	3.1	10.5	1.9	5.5	3.5	2.7

Sources: Computed from the following: U.S. Bureau of the Census, U.S. Census of Population, 1960, *General social and economic characteristics, U.S. summary, Final report* PC(1)-1C, Table 76, Alaska and Hawaii excluded; U.S. Bureau of the Census, U.S. Census of Population, 1970, *General social and economic characteristics, U.S. summary, Final report*, Tables 197, 198, and 199.

past four decades. This approach suggested by Norgren and Hill (1964:83–84) would compare the indexes of black participation in the four upper-level occupational categories: professional–technical, managers-proprietors, clerical–sales, and craftsmen–foremen (i.e., occupational categories above the job ceiling), against the proportions of blacks completing the top four educational attainment levels: four or more years of college, one to three years of college, four years of high school, and one to three years of high school (see Table 5.4). The four upper level educational attainments may be taken to approximate the credentials required to fill the jobs in the top four occupational categories. By comparison (see Tables 5.1, 5.2, and 5.3), it is evident that the occupational gap between blacks and whites is much wider

desirable jobs open to whites. Then those blacks who manage to achieve the same kind of quality education as whites are still not judged eligible for the more desirable jobs on the basis of education and ability. For this reason, the rate of improvement in black occupational status does not follow the rate of improvement in their education the same way that the rate of occupational improvement among whites follows their rate of improvement in education. Improvements in black occupational status occur primarily as a result of national crises and labor shortages.

than the educational gap. More important, the educational gap is closing at a much faster pace than the occupational gap.

The distribution of blacks with high school and college educations in various occupational categories provides another kind of evidence. Blacks and whites with equivalent levels of education are not distributed in equivalent occupational levels. For example, Kahn's study (1968:21) shows that among males only 5% of black college graduates become proprietors, managers, or officials, compared with 22% of white college graduates. Blacks with some college training work in service and laborer occupations "in numbers five times greater than Whites with similar training." And 10% of black women who finish college end up as domestic workers. Kahn concludes from his study that "such a distribution cannot be explained in terms of lack of training." In their study of the effectiveness of various examples of fair employment practices legislation, Norgren and Hill (1964:84) note that large numbers of black high school and college graduates are unable to find jobs commensurate with their educational qualifications. We also saw earlier that differences in unemployment rates between blacks and whites are greatest among those with four or more years of college education, the difference being 3.31, whereas among those with the lowest level of education (zero to four years of schooling), the difference was only 0.74 in 1964. These discrepancies in the relationship between education and occupational and employment status for the two racial castes lead one to conclude that blacks and whites are not selected for their occupations on the basis of the same objective criteria.

A third approach might be to compare the incomes of blacks and whites of a given age cohort who have completed equivalent levels of schooling. The human capital theory reviewed earlier in this chapter posits that the earnings of individuals will vary according to their marketable skills or education. But when we compare the financial returns for equivalent levels of education for blacks and whites we find, as shown in Table 5.5, not merely an income gap, but an increasing income gap as we move up the educational ladder. More education means more income for members of both castes, but the additional income resulting from additional education is lower for blacks. For instance, in both 1959 and 1969, the average black man with four years of high school was earning less than the average white man with only an elementary school education. This difference in earnings, which is an expression of the difference in occupational opportunity, is nationwide and a traditional pattern (see Becker 1957; Harrison 1972; Michelson 1972; Reich 1972).

Table 5.5

Median Income in 1959 and 1969 by Years of School Completed, Males 25–54 Years Old

	1959 (in 1969 dollars)			1969		
	Total	Black	White	Total	Black	White
Median income	$6408	$3570	$6637	$8465	$5222	$8795
Ratio to median education	1.00	.56	1.04	1.00	.62	1.04
Elementary school: total	.75	.47	.82	.70	.49	.75
Less than 8 years	.63	.44	.71	.61	.46	.65
8 years	.87	.58	.90	.80	.53	.83
High school: total	1.03	.66	1.05	.98	.69	1.01
1–3 years	.98	.64	1.01	.88	.63	.92
4 years	1.06	.70	1.08	1.02	.73	1.04
College: total	1.32	.82	1.35	1.28	.94	1.30
1–3 years	1.19	.78	1.22	1.14	.88	1.16
4 years	1.48	.88	1.50	1.44	1.02	1.46

SOURCE: Andrew F. Brimmer 1974. Economic development in the black community. In *The great society: Lessons for the future*, edited by Eli Ginzberg and Robert M. Solow. New York: Basic Books. Table 2, p. 152.

Fourth, the lack of fit between the educational progress of blacks and their occupational progress is clearly demonstrated by their occupational achievements in the decade of the 1960s, which far outpaced their educational achievements during the same period. The reason for this was precisely that their occupational advances in the 1960s were determined by such noneducational forces as the Vietnam War and the social reforms of the Kennedy and Johnson administrations, especially the implementation of Title VII of the Civil Rights Act of 1964 which prohibited employment discrimination based on race. This point is underscored by the fact that most of the gains made by blacks in the top four occupational categories (i.e., those above the job ceiling) occurred after Title VII became effective in 1966. These reforms were themselves precipitated by national crises, so that the gains were a continuation of the pattern I have described for the previous periods: Blacks have achieved their occupational advances not by virtue of their progress in the field of education and training but in times of national crises and labor shortages, i.e., in periods when their occupational gains do not conflict with the interests of the white workers, such as the period of economic growth of 1900–1908; World War I; the period of economic growth of 1922–1929 (the latter was also the period of the restriction of immigrant and foreign labor supply); World War II; the Korean War; the Vietnam War; and the current legal attempts to equalize opportunities without regard to caste status. Nevertheless, advances in these periods have not been achieved without additional push in terms of executive orders, legislative action, and political pressures.

Because American society treats blacks as a caste minority, black education does not serve as a bridge to the same adult roles as those available to whites on the basis of education. The inferior education offered to blacks is the first step in channeling them away from the more desirable roles open to whites in adult life. But even when blacks receive equal education, the job ceiling has denied them equal access to jobs commensurate with their training and abilities. It is thus the caste status which determines access to both education and jobs for blacks.

6

The Consequences: Black School Performance as an Adaptation

In Chapter 4 I argued that black Americans have historically been provided with inferior education as a means of fitting them for their lower caste status. Over the past 100 years, some significant changes have occurred in their education in response to changes in the caste system. In Chapter 5, I showed how the caste system has operated a job ceiling against blacks, forcing them to take inferior jobs not merely because of their inferior education but because black education is just one of the mechanisms, although a very powerful one, by which the job ceiling is sustained. Thus from the standpoint of the system, there is a reciprocal relationship between black access to inferior jobs (the job ceiling) and black access to inferior education. But this appears to be only one-half the relationship between the job ceiling and black education, for it tells us nothing of the way this relationship affects the behavior of blacks in the field of education. This is the aspect of the problem I deal with in this chapter.

The usual orientation among those who study the relationship between education and jobs is to examine the influence of educational attainment on job status. Education is perceived as a bridge, the far end of which is connected to many roads or levels of occupations. Indi-

viduals as well as groups take different roads according to their credentials or educational qualifications. We have seen, however, that the
road taken by blacks is not determined primarily by their educational
credentials. Instead, their road or occupational status appears to be
foreordained, regardless of their levels of educational attainment. For
this reason, I shall reverse the usual orientation and examine the way in
which the ascribed occupational status of blacks (the job ceiling) affects
their educational efforts. Specifically, what effects does the job ceiling
have on black educational efforts?

How Blacks Perceive the Job Ceiling

We have already demonstrated that a job ceiling operates against
blacks. We now focus on the way in which blacks perceive the job
ceiling and how they feel about their experiences with it. Most researchers have been content to use official and unofficial statistical
records to show that blacks and whites occupy unequal occupational
status or that blacks do not have employment opportunities equal to
those of whites. They have been far less concerned with how blacks feel
about these matters.[1] For this reason, the data on how blacks feel about
the job ceiling are neither as plentiful nor as direct as we would have
liked. But there is enough evidence to support our contention that
blacks are bitter and frustrated and preoccupied with their limited opportunities for employment under the caste system. This evidence
comes from a few ethnographic and semiethnographic studies of black
communities and from studies of the strategies blacks employ to break
down the job ceiling or achieve a higher social and economic status.

Ethnographic Studies. Classic ethnographic studies dealing with
how blacks feel about the job ceiling are few, most of them from the
South, especially Mississippi, and not too recent. But their paucity,
regional concentration, and age do not make them irrelevant because
more recent information from other sources confirms these earlier findings.

Powdermaker's *After Freedom* (1968) is one of the earliest ethnographic studies dealing with black perceptions of the job ceiling. It is
based on her field work in Mississippi carried out from 1932 to 1934.

---

[1]It is ironic that we may have very little information on how blacks think or feel about the job
ceiling, even though we have tons of information on the job ceiling itself, some of which must have
come from black informants. The views in the literature seem to be those coming from the top
downwards. This particular point has been remarked upon by Ferman *et al.* (1968:355) in his comment on black experiences in the labor market.

This study shows that the job ceiling was very low and very pervasive (p. 304) and that blacks felt they were unable to improve their economic and social status because of it (pp. 92–94, 322). Under this circumstance, blacks—especially the educated and younger ones—were critical of the caste system and generally felt helpless in dealing with the problem. Consider, for example, the case of a black college graduate "from one of the better colleges in the South." Faced with the job ceiling, wage ceiling, and lack of a vote, he was bitter about the caste system; and Powdermaker tells us, he shared this feeling with his contemporaries:

> He says, as many of his contemporaries say and feel, that he sometimes wonders how he can bear it any longer. He sees the futility of fighting, since he thinks there is no chance of winning now—At times the underlying bitterness finds vent in words. For the most part, it accumulates, unexpressed [1968:322].

John Dollard's *Caste and Class in a Southern Town* (1957), based on field work in the same community from 1935 to 1936, confirms Powdermaker's earlier findings. Blacks perceived and resented the job ceiling in the late 1930s and early 1940s; they also found that the job (1965) describe the prevalence of the job ceiling in another Mississippi community they studied between 1933 and 1935 (pp. 251–252 footnote). Educated blacks in this community were bitter or disillusioned and tended to outmigrate (pp. 250–252). In their study of Chicago, Drake and Cayton (1970:246,300) documented the prevalence of the job ceiling in the late 1930s and early 1940s; they also found that the job ceiling generated both bitterness and self-doubt among blacks. This is how they described the frustrations of black high school graduates who were forced by the job celing to do domestic work in Chicago: "Colored girls are often bitter in their comments about a society which condemns them to 'the white folk's kitchen.' Girls who have high school training, especially, look upon domestic service as the most undesirable form of unemployment [p. 246]." Frazier's study of black youths in Washington, D.C. and Louisville, Kentucky (1940) provides one of the best direct clues as to how blacks, especially young blacks, feel about the job ceiling. It is important to note, too, that Frazier did not specifically ask his informants about the job ceiling. What he asked about was the changes they desired to see in race relations, but nearly every one of those questioned mentioned first the chance for equal employment as the number one change he would like to see (p. 134).

The 1960s editions of some of these early studies contain additional materials on changes in the job ceiling since the initial studies. In each case, the job ceiling had been raised slightly; but blacks still perceived it as the major barrier to the improvement of their social and technoeconomic status. Few of the more recent ethnographic studies that probed how blacks feel about the job ceiling generally show that they are frustrated and disillusioned. In *Coming Up Black* (1969) Schulz found that both adolescent and adult blacks in St. Louis are concerned about the job ceiling (pp. 161–162) and frustrated by their experiences in being unable to get decent jobs. He reports that "despite what, from a middle-class perspective, might be perceived as a foolish, stubborn, or lazy attitude toward work, the young men are in fact faced with great difficulties in finding jobs, given who they are." And considering all things stacked against them, "they perceive themselves effectively cut off from the American dream [p. 165]." My findings on the problem of the job ceiling in Stockton, California have been partially reported in *The Next Generation* (Ogbu 1974a). Blacks and Mexican-Americans in Stockton feel that they do not have equal opportunities with whites in matters of employment and promotion, and they are very unhappy because, as they put it, they have to be "twice qualified" in order to get a job or promotion when they compete directly with whites (pp. 98–101).

Evidence from Black Strategies against the Job Ceiling. Various strategies blacks use to evade or break the job ceiling indicate that they view it as a serious impediment to their well-being and progress in American society. These strategies include playing Uncle Tom or "tomming," collective protests, organized boycotts and threats of boycotts, riots, legal actions, and the use of complaint channels or government agencies for redressing discrimination.

At the level of individual efforts, blacks traditionally avoid direct competition with whites for fear of reprisals. Nearly all the ethnographic studies cited thus far document this point. Powdermaker (1968:107) found that blacks attempting to improve their economic status in the community she studied were careful to show that they "knew their place," to play the Uncle Tom, to be diplomatic and manipulative in dealing with whites (pp. 107, 112, 330). Successful blacks in the same community were those who employed diplomatic and manipulative skills to secure loans and obtain titles to their land. They generally behaved in such a way that whites could point to them and say, "Even though he acquired property, he was always humble and knew his place." Both Shack (1970) and Farmer (1968) also report the use of "uncle tomming" or manipulation as prevalent among blacks generally.

Uncle tomming and other manipulative skills enable a few individuals to improve their jobs and economic status, but they do not raise or break the job ceiling for the group. To raise the job ceiling, blacks resort to other strategies involving collective efforts. Many such strategies used today by blacks were documented by Drake and Cayton (1970:743) in their study of the campaigns against the job ceiling in Chicago between 1929 and 1944. These early campaigns were directed against specific targets such as white business establishments in black neighborhoods, labor unions, and the like. And political pressures, picketing, threats of boycotts, boycotts, demonstrations, and violence were among the major strategies effectively employed in these campaigns. Some were particularly successful in piercing the job ceiling. For example, the boycotts and picketing in the 1929 campaign of "Spend-Your-Money-Where-You-Can-Work" resulted in the hiring of 2000 blacks in white businesses. Blacks in other cities conducted similar campaigns in the 1930s with similar results. And they also successfully employed the same campaign strategies in the 1960s in their continuing efforts to break the job ceiling. Thus Schermer reports (1965:88) that blacks in Philadelphia used boycotts to win more and better jobs in local business establishments like the publishers of a Philadelphia daily newspaper, the *Bulletin*; the Sun Oil Company; and the A & P Supermarket chain. In Stockton, blacks boycotted several white business establishments in 1967, forcing the latter to hire them and other minorities, especially in jobs above the job ceiling. The threat of another boycott was issued in 1969 by the Ebony Young Men of Action, a local black civil rights organization, and resulted in the hiring of nearly 400 members of minority groups within two years, some in jobs above the job ceiling.

These campaigns and techniques are indicative of how blacks see their employment opportunities. Drake and Cayton (1970:287) found a widespread belief among blacks in Chicago in the late 1930s that further progress for blacks depended on breaking the job ceiling. This was true of blacks in other cities at the time; and that it is true of blacks today throughout the nation is borne out by studies of the strategies blacks employed against the job ceiling in the 1960s. According to the report of the U.S. National Advisory Commission on Civil Disorders (1968:81), blacks' complaints about the job ceiling ranked second only to their grievances against the police (42 points compared to 54½ points) and was present in all 20 cities studied by the commission. The commission compared the intensity of the grievance generated by the job ceiling with those generated by other factors and found that

Grievance in the employment areas were ranked first in three cities, second in seven cities, third in four cities, and fourth in three cities. In only three cities was such a grievance present but not mentioned among the first four highest levels of intensity (1968:81; see also *The Keesing Research Report*, No. 4, 1970:80).

The activities of civil rights organizations provide yet another source of insights about the way blacks and their sympathizers view the job ceiling. Major civil rights organizations, such as the National Association for The Advancement of Colored People (NAACP), the National Urban League, and so on, have from their inception regarded breaking the job ceiling as one of their prime goals. The NAACP has approached the problem both through legal action (Bullock 1970; Huff 1974) and through research studies; the latter publicize the false assumptions behind the job ceiling and its operation and thus provide a factual basis for remedial action.

Quantitative evidence that blacks regard the job ceiling as a serious barrier to their progress is found in the extensive use they make of the Fair Employment Practices Commissions (FEPC) and the Equal Employment Opportunities Commission (EEOC), the two federal agencies for handling complaints against employment discrimination. The FEPC was established at the federal level, as well as in some states, to deal with job discrimination based on race, color, religion, sex, and national origin; but the greatest proportion of the complaints it receives are based on race and brought by blacks against white employers, labor unions, employment agencies, and so on. Table 6.1, which shows only the number of cases satisfactorily adjusted by the commissions in the northeastern states from 1945 to 1961, indicates both the magnitude of the problem of discrimination and the extensive use of this agency by blacks (Norgren and Hill 1964:116) to combat it.

The EEOC was set up to handle complaints of job discrimination prohibited by Title VII of the Civil Rights Act of 1964 and the Equal

Table 6.1

Cases of Job Discrimination Satisfactorily Adjusted by the FEPC in Five Northeastern States from 1945 to 1961.

Commission	Total number of cases	Period covered
New York	3262	1945–1960
New Jersey	701	1945–1960
Massachusetts	793	1946–1961
Connecticut	506	1946–1961
Pennsylvania	523	1947–1961

SOURCE: Paul H. Norgren and Samuel E. Hill 1964. *Toward fair employment.* New York: Columbia University Press. P. 116.

Employment Opportunity Act of 1972. These laws made it illegal for an employer to use tests and other devices to discriminate against employees or prospective employees on the basis of race, color, religion, sex, and national origin. A study covering a three-year period from 1968 to 1970 indicates that about 60% of the employment complaints brought to the EEOC involved racial discrimination, as can be seen in Table 6.2.

Differences between Black and White Perceptions of the Job Ceiling. Blacks and whites perceive the job ceiling differently as evidenced by their disagreement regarding the reasons for limited black participation in the occupations above the job ceiling. Whites often contend that blacks are not more represented in these jobs because they are not qualified, by which they mean that blacks do not have the education or other formal training required for such positions. Blacks, on the other hand, claim that many white business establishments and public institutions controlled by whites do not hire them even if they are qualified. A number of court decisions in cases involving job discrimination tend to support the black position (see Huff 1974). I illustrate the divergent views of blacks and whites on the issue of black qualification for jobs above the job ceiling in order to show further how blacks perceive the problem.

Throughout my research in Stockton, the issue of qualification was paramount in every discussion of black employment status. My data on the subject were collected over a five-year period from many varied sources: black and white informants of diverse backgrounds; panel discussions involving both black and white employment experts attached to various public and private agencies; interviews with individuals in such agencies who specialized in minority employment; organizations such as the local NAACP and the Black Unity Council, which have been involved in the issue of black employment; studies of local employment problems and practices; reports of the "Workshop on Equality"; a special committee appointed by the city council to study the problem of hiring discrimination in city hall; and the report of the affirmative action survey conducted by the California State Fair Employment Practices Commission (1972). There were also local disputes over the use of standardized tests in hiring employees, an issue to be discussed shortly. The minority-group spokesmen alleged that this was a mechanism to exclude them from good jobs; the employers and the dominant white community generally maintained that the tests were an objective way to hire qualified workers for available jobs. Data from these sources strongly suggest that in the past, especially before the 1960s, most high-status occupations above the job ceiling were closed to blacks in both the public and private sectors of the local economy.

Table 6.2

Distribution of Discrimination Charges by Type of Respondents and Basis of Discrimination, Fiscal Years 1968–1970

Respondent	1970			1969			1968		
	Total	Black	Percentage	Total	Black	Percentage	Total	Black	Percentage
All	17,780	11,806	66	14,471	9,562	66	11,172	6,650	60
Employers	15,395	10,118	66	12,456	8,107	65	9,339	5,349	57
Unions	1,849	1,244	67	1,495	1,122	68	1,535	1,039	70
Employment agencies	139	87	63	140	90	64	159	112	70
Other	397	357	90	380	343	90	139	110	79

SOURCE: Avril V. Adams 1972. *Toward fair employment and the EEOC: A study of compliance procedures under Title VII of the Civil Rights Act of 1964: Final report.* Washington, D.C.: U.S. Government Printing Office. P. 8.

In the late 1960s, when public agencies and local white business establishments began to open up employment opportunities for blacks, the blacks often did not have the necessary qualifications for these positions. Because such positions had traditionally not been open to blacks, they had never prepared themselves through academic, professional, or vocational training. It was therefore logical that the sudden opening of these positions to blacks in the second half of the 1960s found them without the necessary qualifications. The time lag involved between the sudden opening up of these new opportunities and the acquisition of the necessary skills or qualifications was not generally recognized in Stockton. Consequently there was a tendency for members of the dominant white caste, including those responsible for assisting blacks to obtain better jobs, to rationalize the job ceiling by saying that the major employment problem for blacks was their lack of qualification.

The different views of blacks and whites on the use of civil service tests to select local government employees further shows how far apart the two groups are on the issue of black qualification and hence on the job ceiling. Between 1968 and 1969, representatives of black and other minority groups said at several public meetings that they were excluded from local (city and county) employment because of discrimination. They specifically mentioned the requirement of these local government bodies that prospective employees or candidates for promotion pass standardized examinations and further stated that the examinations were used to keep the number of minority employees to a minimum. They also pointed out that out of 886 people employed by the city as of March 1969, only 30 were black, most of whom held jobs below the job ceiling. Following repeated demands for changes by the minority spokesmen, in 1969 the city council set up a committee called the Workshop in Equality to study the problem.

The city requirement that recruitment and promotion be by examination engaged much of the committee's attention. The examination required was included in the city charter of 1935, which provided that it could be written or oral, but it appeared that a written examination had become the accepted practice. At the time of my research, administration of the examination was entrusted to the Curnfeenhagen-Kroeger firm of San Francisco and the Cooperative Personnel Service of the State Personnel Board. According to the city charter, candidates should be tested for physical or mental abilities or both, but they should also be tested for relative ability to perform only the duties for which they are being hired. The charter originally suggested that candidates should have attained a given level of formal education in order to be eligible to take the examination; that they should obtain a minimum of 95 to 110 on IQ tests, and that tests comparable to the revised edition of the written Alpha test, developed by the army to test recruits, be used in examination. Some of these requirements had been modified by 1969 when the city hiring practices were being studied. For example, the army Alpha tests were no longer in use; candidates were required only to obtain a score of 70% in each part of the examination and an average of 70% to get on the list of prospective employees. There was a further modification for war veterans, who needed only a score of 65% (or 60% if they had suffered disabilities during their military service). The list was rank-ordered according to the test scores.

Stockton city authorities justified the test requirements on the grounds that the test provided a universal and objective criterion for selecting city workers, that it eliminated politics from civil service jobs, and that it ensured a high standard of civil service by selecting the most able people available for employment. The chairman of the Workshop in Equality suggested that if minority-group members were failing the test, the fault was not with the test but with the minority groups. The remedy he suggested was to discover the weaknesses of the minority-group candidates and develop programs to help them overcome their so-called handicaps. Minority representatives, on the other hand, argued that the tests were culturally biased against them, that minority-group members who failed the civil service tests and were rejected for the city and county employment were able to get similar jobs with private business establishments (truck drivers whom the city would not employ got jobs with private companies) and perform well on those jobs, and that city and county authorities were using prisoners (who had not taken the civil service tests) to do the same minor jobs that were denied ordinary citizens because they had not passed the written test.

Public agencies receiving state and federal funds generally found "qualified" minority personnel in their attempts to comply with the affirmative action policy under local and extralocal state and federal pressures. They did so in various ways: First, some of them trained or upgraded blacks already on their staffs; second, they recruited and trained "promising" local blacks; and third, they actively went outside the city, particularly to the southern states, to recruit black professionals and technicians. The issue of qualification was also partially met through local branches of various national recruitment and training programs such as the Job Opportunities in the Business Sector (JOBS), Manpower Development and Training Act Program (MDTA), and the Work Incentive Program (WIN).

But most important, as already indicated, the issue of qualification was challenged by active protest in the form of boycotts or threats of boycotts by blacks. I have already cited the boycott of business establishments in 1967. In the same year, the Black Unity Council organized a boycott of the local public schools, and the following year the school authorities appointed the first black principal in the district.

Until the latter half of the 1960s, blacks were fully aware that the more desirable jobs in Stockton and in the nation were closed to them because of their lower-caste status, and they often saw various employment criteria, such as tests and interviews, as devices to exclude them from good jobs. Consequently, blacks did not always prepare themselves for jobs above the job ceiling; those who achieved the required educational qualification for such jobs often got less satisfactory jobs, wages, and promotions and were generally disappointed. When legal machinery was developed at the state and federal levels to raise the job ceiling (e.g., FEPC, and EEOC), blacks found that these agencies were not sufficient to change the attitudes of the dominant white caste toward black labor, which means that often blacks still have to resort to their traditional strategies. They admit that the job ceiling is rising but still consider it essential to apply pressure. Moreover, the attitudes and habits formed in the past about preparing themselves for future employment still persist to some extent and constitute a barrier to their taking full advantage of new opportunities. Finally, the loss of jobs in the recent recession by a disproportionate number of blacks because they were the last hired has probably reinforced the beliefs about and frustrations over the job ceiling. The next question is whether and how their perception of the job ceiling affects their perception of schooling.

Influence of the Job Ceiling on Perception of Schooling

On the surface, two factors appear to contradict any assertion that the perception of the job ceiling by blacks adversely affects the way they perceive their schooling. The first is the high educational aspirations commonly found among blacks and the second is their well-documented fight for equal education with whites.

The literature is replete with references to the high educational aspirations of black people (Davis, et al. 1965:251; Dollard 1957:200; Drake and Cayton 1970:246; Frazier 1940; Johnson 1966:114ff; Ogbu 1974a:70–80; Pettigrew 1964:84; Powdermaker 1968:292–304; Schulz

1969:160; Weinberg 1970:89–92). Like other Americans, blacks want good educations to give their children better chances in life than they enjoyed themselves—in particular, chances at better jobs (Drake and Cayton 1970:246; Johnson 1966:116ff; Powdermaker 1968:215). The children, too, desire education so that they will not have to do the menial jobs done by their parents.[2]

While individual blacks desire education for themselves or for their children as a means of self-improvement, blacks as a group desire education as a means of improving their status in the caste system. That is, they use education as an instrument with which to break the caste barriers in jobs, housing, and the like and eventually achieve equality with white people. Consequently, blacks have carried out a collective struggle for more and better education for many generations: They established and supported private schools for their children; they played important roles in the establishment of the public school systems in several states in the South during the Reconstruction; and they have fought incessantly against school segregation and other discriminatory practices.

These aspirations and events do not, however, contradict the assertion that their perception of the job ceiling adversely affects their schooling. For although blacks say they desire education and although they try in many ways to change the education system so that their children will receive better education, black students neither make sufficient efforts in their studies nor match their aspirations with accomplishments. The lack of serious effort has developed partly because they see their future opportunities for employment limited by the job ceiling. They compare themselves with whites whom they see as having more job opportunities for no other reason than their color. Because of their own limited future employment opportunities and the preferential treatment of whites in the job market, black students often become disillusioned about the future and doubtful about the value of schooling. Of course, blacks also react in other ways to this wide discrepancy between expectations or promise and reality. I have already discussed their attempts to break or raise the job ceiling as a means of realizing greater benefits from education. Here I will focus on their

[2]Some social scientists accuse blacks of having instrumental attitudes toward school for this reason, i.e., they say that blacks desire education in order to get jobs and not for its own sake (see Hippler 1974:151–155). These writers, however, present no evidence to show that white Americans do not desire education for the same reason. My own impression is that Americans, be they white or black, have instrumental attitudes toward schooling. Witness the shift toward professional and vocational training attributable to changes in the job market since equal employment opportunity legislation became effective in 1966.

feelings of frustration, disillusionment, and a phenomenon that Carter has termed "mental withdrawal" (1970:136). In the following survey, I deal with the reactions of black college graduates, black youths in school, and young black children.

The College Graduates. Powdermaker (1968:321) describes the case of a college graduate from "one of the better colleges in the South" which she says is "typical of the educated young [blacks] whose number is rapidly increasing." This young man supported himself through college partly through part-time jobs and partly through loans. Upon completion of this education, he was not able to find a job commensurate with his training and abilities; nor was he paid the same wage as his white counterpart in the same job. Powdermaker (1968) sums up the reaction of this young man and others like him as follows:

> Now, having received his education and paid off his debts, he asks himself what use he can make of this thing he has struggled to obtain. He feels himself debarred from enjoying and profiting from the fruits of his labor. For this young man, and the group he represents, the new faith [in education] has not come up to expectations. Education has brought them advantages denied to their parents; but it has also brought them difficulties, perplexities, wounds, and it has not yet offered the anticipated solution to their problems. The development of their abilities has not been matched by growth of their opportunities or improvement in their position. Accordingly, those who have acquired a college degree for the most part lost the hope and confidence which made them work so hard to attain it. For these few, the new faith is already outworn. So far they have found no substitute [p. 34; see also Dollard 1957:202].

Although Powdermaker's study is the only one I have found describing how black college graduates feel about their education in view of their lack of occupational and economic opportunities, black college graduates in other communities are faced with the same problems and no doubt feel the same way. Opportunities and rewards for black professionals such as physicians (Johnson 1935), lawyers (Callis 1935), and teachers (Caliver 1935; Bond 1966) were very limited. Drake and Cayton (1970:239) report that the job ceiling in Chicago forced black college graduates to become sleeping-car porters or red caps. They were informed by an official of one local union that 72 of the 90 black members of the local union were college graduates, including two practicing physicians, and that none had less than a high school diploma. Black college graduates were until recently (and to some extent still are) fully aware that the job ceiling denied them adequate outlets for the middle-class skills they acquired in college. As Dollard (19570 sums up their dilemma, "Education dresses them up and they have no, or little professional place to go [p. 202]."

The Youth in School. Education also dresses up the black high school students and graduates who have really no place to go. Davis *et al.* (1965:251–252) describe the difficulties facing high school graduates in obtaining jobs commensurate with their training and abilities in the community they studied. Because of the job ceiling, even black teachers who previously stressed the importance of education to black parents became disillusioned. These authors quote a black teacher who told black parents that he no longer thought it a good thing to educate their children because they were being denied jobs commensurate with their training and abilities. In Chicago, Drake and Cayton (1962:255, 287) found that a wide discrepancy existed between the dominant white caste theory of equal job opportunities as expounded in the schools and the actual experiences of blacks; that this made educated blacks bitter. The discrepancy also made black youths reluctant to take technical training in both public and private schools; they felt that they would be wasting their time, since local industries did not employ blacks for technical jobs.

Frazier's study of black youths in Washington, D.C. and Louisville, Kentucky (1940) has already been cited. The youths he interviewed not only worried about their future employment prospects because of the job ceiling, but also "expressed misgivings concerning the value of education for [blacks], since many avenues of employment were closed to them" [p. 134]. Conant (1965:170–171), among others, provides some interesting and impressive statistical information about the proportion of black high school graduates and dropouts who were "out of school and out of work" in northern cities at the beginning of the 1960s. In one study he cited, 48% of the high school graduates and 64% of the dropouts were out of school and out of work. In another study, 70% of the ghetto youth ages 16 to 21 were neither in school nor employed. Unfortunately, Conant cites no information as to how these youths felt about their joblessness and their schooling. More recently, however, Schulz (1969:159) found that black youths in St. Louis were frustrated by the gap between their expectations and their actual experiences under the job ceiling. They believed that education did not lead them to good jobs and the good things in life as it did the white middle class. They "rarely had the occupational or financial incentive to work hard in school and get more education ... they could generally earn more illegitimately without an education" if they wanted [p. 160].

Elementary School Children. The influence of the job ceiling on the perception of schooling is also found at the elementary school level. Parents who have themselves not experienced the full benefit of their education because of the job ceiling do not often encourage their children to do well in school. In Johnson's study (1966:18–19), parents who had become disillusioned about the material rewards of education under the caste system did not stress it for their children. Johnson's interpretation of these parents' statements differs, however, from the one presented here: He labels them as rationalizations of their inability to promote academic achievement in their children. But his own accounts of the impact of the job ceiling on the occupational opportunities for blacks clearly show that these parents' statements were a realistic assessment of the role of education in their social and technoeconomic advancement.

Class and Sex Differences. Members of all social classes within the black caste are aware of the job ceiling, and their perception of schooling is colored by this awareness. There is some evidence in Frazier's (1940) study that the job ceiling probably affects lower-class blacks more in their perception of schooling than it affects the middle- and upper-class blacks. He reports that lower-class youth "in almost every case placed the wish for an equal chance for employment first" among the changes they desired to see in the caste system (p. 134). But he also points out that all the three classes "are in essential agreement" about the lack of equal employment opportunities with whites. The following statements from Frazier's young informants will illustrate how they viewed the job ceiling, especially in relation to their education. The first statement is that of a 20-year-old lower-class high school graduate; the second is from an 18-year-old middle-class youth; and the third comes from an upper-class 17-year-old:

> Our chances aren't as good by any means as the white man's and never will be unless the white man's attitude changes and [blacks] make adjustment in their training and study. It's a situation like that [which] makes fellows like me not want to waste years of studying to do what? I know that there's no difference between the white man and me, but I can't help feeling he is better than I am when he is trained to do his work and then has all the chance of doing it [p. 136–137].
>
> I don't believe a [black] has a good chance to get anything as white people have! They see to it that our chances are always few and far between. They ought to have more opportunities than they have now and even if in time they can get them [blacks'] chances will not be equal to the whites'. Manhood, ability, and education come in all colors—white to black, and a [black] is never considered equal to a white man no matter how good a man he is or what his ability and training is [p. 154].
>
> I used to feel if I knew my work and could do it better than white or black, my chances would be as good. From observation, I've noted that no matter how good I am, my chances with whites are never as good. It is quite obvious in Washington that [blacks] do not have the chances for the jobs that whites have. That should not be, of course, and there should be hundreds of jobs available for trained [blacks]. There certainly isn't much inducement to work or study knowing that in competi-

tion with a white fellow your chances are slim. It's enough to discourage the best of us [p. 159].

Frazier's comment about the upper-class youth quoted here is worth noting. He says that the upper-class youth is often protected "from the cruder forms of prejudice" and kept ignorant of discrimination. Some of them grow up believing that blacks and whites alike are evaluated for jobs and social positions as individuals on the basis of competence and efficiency. Some of the upper-class youth, however, like this 17-year-old, do eventually learn about the job ceiling and other forms of caste barriers and become disillusioned (p. 159).

Neither Frazier nor any of the other authors cited in this section gives information concerning sex differences in the way blacks perceive the job ceiling and schooling. There probably are some, judging from sex differences in school performance. Black females, as indicated in Chapter 2, perform better than black males at every socioeconomic level and at all ages, but especially among the older groups. There differences are probably attributable to the fact that although American society discriminates against all blacks, it tends to give preferential treatment to black females in matters of jobs, income, and other material and social rewards as well as in stereotypes. Black males and females eventually learn to perceive the job ceiling and their schooling somewhat differently and respond differently to their somewhat different opportunities: Females, for example, tend to develop higher expectations, better work or study habits, and more competitive and persistent efforts toward their school work.[3]

---

[3]Jackson (1973:215–250) states that black females are judged as more academically successful than black males in the elementary and secondary schools and that they are also judged as scholastically superior to the males when both groups participate in academic programs at "the very highest levels of education." But her interpretation of these observations differs from the one I present here. She says that the superiority of black females over black males in the elementary and secondary schools may be due to the "artifact of the school environment" or because "the females are intellectually superior to the males with whom they have to compete." The superiority of black females at higher levels of education, she says, is "largely because admitting procedures include a wider latitude of scholastic competence for the males" [pp. 229–230]. Jackson does not think that black females do better in school because black parents prefer to educate their daughters over their sons and therefore stress education more for their daughters than for their sons. If such preferences existed in the past, she says, it was probably because black parents saw mainly low options open to their daughters in terms of future occupations: teaching or domestic service. Since most of them did not want their daughters to go into domestic service, they tended to stress education to enable them to go into teaching. At present, however, there is no evidence that any systematic parental preference to educate daughters over sons exists among blacks.

With regard to the overall educational differences between the sexes, Jackson says that from 1920 to 1970 black females surpassed black males in median years of schooling completed. Among those completing high school or more education in the age bracket of 25 to 29, the females surpassed the males .5 years in 1960 and .9 years in 1966 but fell below the males by two years in 1969 and

Recognizing, then, that some differences exist within the black caste and that some recent changes in American society in the area of job opportunities (some trend toward raising the job ceiling) may have affected the way blacks evaluate their schooling, I think that their perception of the job ceiling is still a major factor that colors their attitudes toward schooling as well as their school performance. The job ceiling continues to generate ambivalent attitudes toward schooling which result in a lack of serious efforts to maximize achievement. This is one of the ways in which the job ceiling contributes to black educational adaptation to their lower-caste status.

Generational Differences. The impact of the job ceiling on the black view of schooling varies by generation. The older generations of relatively uneducated parents and grandparents did not, and in some places still do not, perceive the discrepancy between the job ceiling and schooling because their own occupational and educational aspirations and expectations were well within the range of opportunities available to blacks under the caste system (see Powdermaker 1968:215). But if uneducated parents are satisfied with the jobs available to their more educated children under the job ceiling (e.g., becoming teachers, nurses, band players, instead of domestic workers, washerwomen, porters, or janitors like their parents), their children are not (Powdermaker 1968:320).

The younger generation, educated blacks and black students in general, perceive the gap between the job ceiling and schooling much more sharply. The influence of formal education itself is largely responsible for this generational difference. Education, as Dollard (1957:201:see also Powdermaker 1968:321) pointed out long ago, teaches blacks to reject the caste principles upon which the job ceiling

---

then surpassed them again by .6 years in 1970. Of those completing four years of college or more in the age group of 25 to 34, black females surpassed black males between 1940 and 1970, although the gap between the sexes was not constant. Jackson says that the superiority of the females over the males in the college educated group is due to changes in educational requirements of public school teaching [in the South] traditionally dominated by women. Specifically, since the 1940s public school teaching has required more than normal school certification, with the result that many female teachers have stayed in school longer to meet the teaching requirements. Those with more than four years of college pursued primarily the masters degree in education to qualify as elementary school principals.

Thus Jackson would not attribute the educational superiority of black females to greater availability of occupational opportunities for the females or what she calls "the utilitarian theory of Black female education" [p. 222]. She argues that black females have had greater access only to jobs at the lower end of the more desirable occupations above the job ceiling, namely, public school teaching, social work, nursing, and librarianship. Females have been far less represented in the higher categories—among physicians, dentists, lawyers, and the like. On the whole, her data (Table 7.6, pp. 236–238 and Table 7.7, p. 241) show that from 1800 to 1969 black females have had a higher representation among professional and semiprofessional workers than black males.

is based. In both the South and the North, curriculums and textbooks teach both black and white students the American ideal that social rewards and status should be distributed on the basis of training and ability rather than on caste membership. Dollard (1957) sums up the influence of education in the perception of the caste system and job ceiling as follows:

> Education for [blacks] tends to break down the uncompromising adjustment to caste status; acceptance of inferior position seems more natural and tolerable as long as cultural differences (like lack of education) can be cited to make caste seem reasonable. Educated [blacks] became more fully aware of their formal rights and the gains of the white middle class; as they increase their social efficiency by education they compare themselves with White people and perceive that their lower status is categorical and not based on a factual inferiority [p. 201].

This increases both the expectations of black students and their demands. The question then is whether their opportunities keep pace with their rising expectations. Thus, education itself provides the ideological framework through which blacks relate their perception of the job ceiling to schooling. The gap between job status and education is perceived much more sharply and rejected more uncompromisingly by educated blacks than by their parents or more by the less educated.

How Black Children Acquire Perceptions about the Job Ceiling and Schooling. Young black children learn about the job ceiling and later learn to relate it to their schooling, but not necessarily from deliberate instruction by parents and other adults. They learn by observing the job experiences of their parents, older siblings, other relatives, family friends, and neighbors. They learn, too, to evaluate education in terms of the job ceiling by assimilating the reactions to the job ceiling and schooling of older people around them. As the children grow older, they acquire increasing knowledge of these matters far beyond the experiences of those around them and begin to see the situation as a problem facing *all* black Americans. Furthermore, until recently the type of career counseling black students received in school, which tended to channel them into traditional black jobs, also increased their awareness of the job ceiling and its relation to their education. School officials often discouraged blacks from taking courses that would prepare them for white colleges or for occupations other than those the white community considered appropriate for blacks. Logan (1933, quoted in Weinberg, 1970) reports, for example, that in one school in Boston in the 1930s, "a separate assembly of colored students was ordered for the purpose of extolling to them the virtues of manual training, and of colored schools [p. 90]." In my field work in Stockton, both the school personnel and members of the black and white castes repeatedly said that limited occupational opportunities for blacks before the 1960s influenced blacks' choice of schooling and the types of courses recommended by their teachers and counselors. Finally, as black youth themselves begin to think about future employment or actually look for some part-time work, their symbolic or actual experience of job discrimination increases their disillustionment and further depresses their school performance.

I suggested in Chapter 1 that what motivates Americans to maximize their achievement efforts in school is their belief that the more education one has the better are one's chances for a better job, higher wages, higher social status, and more self-esteem. Employment opportunities are, in particular, a very powerful influence on the American perception of schooling. Because of increasing scarcity of good jobs with good pay for people with college degrees in the humanities and general curriculum fields, students in recent years have taken up professional and technical training in disproportionate numbers. Furthermore, there has been a trend toward job-oriented training which began in the early 1960s, causing the enrollment in vocational education to rise from 2.1 million to 8.6 million (*Los Angeles Times* August 16, 1976). This too has been a response to changing employment opportunities. If employment opportunities and other anticipated rewards are such a powerful influence on the way Americans, especially the white middle class, perceive their schooling, is there any reason to think that blacks would not be influenced by the same factors? In other words, is it logical to expect that blacks and whites would exert the same energy and perform alike in school when the caste system, through the job ceiling, consistently underutilizes black training and ability and underrewards blacks for their education?

Historical Development of the Problem. We can only hazard a guess about the historical origin of this pattern of response to schooling. At the end of slavery, blacks responded to formal education enthusiastically, hoping that their social and technoeconomic status would improve and eventually equal that of whites (Bond 1966, 1969; Bullock 1970; Pierce *et al.* 1955). But they soon faced two parallel developments as American society began to redefine their caste status more rigidly at the end of Reconstruction. First, their education became progressively separate from and inferior to white education. Second, they became more and more aware that American society valued their educational credentials less than those of the whites. For blacks, this situation constituted a dilemma: On the one hand, they were asked to compete with whites in acquiring academic skills, and presumably in preparing themselves for similar roles in adult life; on the other, they were offered inferior education and inferior training for adult life, and more important, when they succeeded in achieving qualifications similar to those of whites, they were denied equal rewards in terms of occupations, wages, and the like.

The persistence of such a frustrating experience over generations led to the evolution of the belief that education does not help blacks to achieve the same degree of self-improvement as whites. Blacks came to believe that in the areas of jobs, promotions, wages, and social position in the community, they are judged not as individuals, on the basis of education and ability, but as blacks. They responded to this situation by repudiating the rhetorically and explicitly expressed educational expectations of the schools and society. The repudiation took various forms, such as truancy, lack of serious efforts in and attitudes toward school, refusal to do classwork or assignments, delinquency, and even early withdrawal from school altogether. As these attitudes and habits developed, they complemented the policies and practices of black schools. And just as such policies and practices were determined partly by the schools' assessment of the opportunities available to blacks in adult life, so also blacks responded to schooling in terms of their own perceptions of the job ceiling and future expectations.

Up to this point, I have argued that the lower school performance among blacks is an adaptation maintained by two processes: First, blacks are forced by the caste system to occupy social and occupational positions that do not require high educational credentials; second, a job ceiling and other caste barriers generate doubts in blacks about the value of education and of working hard to succeed in school when they do not expect to get jobs and wages commensurate with their training and abilities in comparison with whites. These two processes do not, however, fully account for the adaptation. They do not, for example, explain why some blacks, who do not consciously evaluate their schooling in terms of the job ceiling, still do poorly in school. Nor do they account for the inadequate performance of young black children who are not old enough to understand the meaning of the job ceiling. A fuller explanation lies in the impact of the job ceiling on such black institutions as the family and the status mobility system, as well as on the nature of the skills or personal attributes required for competence in the social and occupational positions to which blacks have traditionally been restricted.

Caste Barriers, Divergent Cultural Elements, and School Performance

In this section, I consider two examples of how the caste system shapes black indigenous institutions, status mobility and family patterns, and how these in turn influence black school performance.

The evolution of some black cultural elements that diverge from those emphasized by the public schools is attributable to the physical and social segregation of blacks in the ghettos, a process begun during slavery. After emancipation, the slave quarters in the old southern towns became restricted black residential areas. In the newer southern towns and in the North, residential segregation is more nearly complete, resulting in larger ghettos (Drake 1968:112). Various mechanisms by which the ghettos are created and maintained are described in Chapter 4.

Caste barriers generated many sociocultural and economic features within the ghettos that further differentiate them from white residential areas. For example, although a ghetto is not a slum, a large part of a black ghetto usually has many features of a slum—poor-quality housing, overcrowding, high rents, and so on—all of which converge to undermine the physical well-being of its residents (Forman 1971). Another distinguishing feature is that a ghetto has two sets of institutions: caretaker institutions (e.g., welfare and economic, legal, communication, education, and political institutions) controlled by members of the dominant caste; and indigenous institutions (e.g., family and kinship, social class, religious, and voluntary associations) which have developed because its residents have been excluded from participating in similar institutions among the dominant caste. Ghetto culture also develops its own forms of folklore, literature, music, dialect, and self-image. Since the dominant caste controls the caretaker institutions, blacks participate in such institutions mostly in the role of clients; they do not easily establish parallel institutions in these areas because they lack the power and other resources to do so.

How the caste system shapes indigenous black institutions can be illustrated with two examples, both of which are relevant to black school performance: the black status mobility system and the family. Earlier, while discussing the differential impact of class and caste systems on education, I pointed out that although social classes exist within the two castes, these two systems of social class are not equal because blacks have less access to the resources for class mobility. Here I describe the way in which the caste system affects the social mobility of blacks, i.e., their status mobility system, and its implications for black school performance.

Caste Barriers and the Black Status Mobility System. In addition to retarding the development of the middle-class sector of the black community, the American caste system has fostered different patterns of social mobility for blacks and whites. Basically, the same criteria for self-betterment or social mobility are found within the class systems of the two castes. These are good education, good jobs, income, housing, and the like. Traditionally, however, members of the two castes have been required by the caste system to use different approaches to achieve these goals. Among whites, the approved method emphasizes individual efforts in more or less open and fair competition. Their status mobility system thus encourages the development of such personal qualities as independence, foresight, initiative, industriousness, and individualistic competitiveness. For blacks, on the other hand, achieving a good education, desirable occupations, good incomes, adequate housing, and the like has traditionally required more than individual efforts. Blacks desiring self-betterment have had to depend on members of the dominant white group who, as individuals or organized groups, controlled the access to such things. Furthermore, because the amount of these resources available to blacks is proportionately more limited than the amount available to whites, blacks cannot obtain them on the basis of ability in open competition. The more limited opportunities for status mobility among blacks call for stiffer competition than occurs among whites. This situation has resulted in a commonly held belief among blacks that if blacks and whites are found holding equivalent jobs, especially if they are high status jobs, the blacks are probably twice as qualified as the whites; when black live in a predominantly white neighborhood, they are probably twice as wealthy or twice as good as their white neighbors, and so on. The point of the present discussion is that the stiffness of the competition for such limited resources has forced blacks to develop three types of responses to the situation: withdrawal from the competition altogether; reliance on the patronage of individual whites or white organizations; or reliance on cooperative efforts of organized groups (e.g., civil rights organizations). Black experience over many generations showed that reliance on white patronage was the most effective approach to self-betterment, though reliance on organized civil rights efforts is becoming increasingly important.

The reliance on white patronage has encouraged such personal qualities as dependency, compliance, and manipulation, which are quite different from the qualities of initiative, competitiveness, and perseverance which the white approach to self-betterment encourages them to develop. The influence of caste barriers on the evolution of some black qualities is suggested in the following description by Shack (1970):

> Real and potential coercive force at the disposal of the Whites summarily denied Black parents and by extension their children also, opportunities for engaging in the kinds of positive social [and techno-economic] experiences which give rise to that focal value which underlies the conception of a mechanistic, controllable universe. A substantive norm evolved for Black people which stressed the manipulation of persons and things, actually and symbolically, through verbal and nonverbal forms of behavior. Traditionally, manipulative behavior has been stereotypically expressed in the story book caricatures of Uncle Tom and Brer Rabbits, or say, the humble, grinning Pullman Porter. On the current scene [1970s], some forms of Black militancy with the threatening virtuperative rhetoric of ritually condemning the White world represents a variation on the traditional stereotypical theme. For neither Uncle Tom, the grinning porter, nor the black militant ever gain *control* over the situation at hand; it is rather that they *manipulate* Whites whom they confront to avoid thrashing, to gain a gratuity, or to gain public exposure which might result in a token reward. These institutionalized cultural mechanisms serve the function of enabling temporary adjustment to situations over which Blacks are, or believe themselves to be, powerless to control [pp. 24–25].

Shack goes on to point out that this adjustive behavior spills over into the school setting:

> In the school situation, the flight from learning involves employment of similar verbal and behavioral manipulative techniques to which Black children resort in adjusting to their day-to-day relation with teachers [who represent the dominant caste to them]. It is an extension of the adult cultural pattern of manipulating uncontrollable situations; it is a part of a much wider cultural pattern which historically started off in a particular direction of development and the momentum derived from the Black experience has carried it on [p. 25].

But black children's school behavior is not just a spillover of adult adjustive behavior; *it is a part of the training of black children for their survival in the American caste system.* Since blacks achieve high status by renouncing those behaviors which are functional for whites (e.g., academic competition), black children must learn this captive behavior in school as they also learn it in their families and peer groups. This is not, however, to say that blacks are not competitive; they are. The point is that the American caste system which encourages one mode of status mobility for whites and another for blacks forces blacks to channel their competitiveness into areas not regarded as the domain of white competitiveness, such as sports or physical and verbal dueling. This diversion of black competitiveness into nonacademic realms is what Clark (1972:43) has called *compensatory competition.*

Caste Barriers and the Black Family. In American society, the traditional orientation of the family is basically patriarchal; that is, the father is accorded the role of titular head and is expected to be responsible for the family's subsistence and protection. The woman is responsible for childbearing and caring for the young children during their early years.[4] Among blacks, marginal participation in the economic system, especially the marginal participation of black men, has resulted in a different form of family adaptation: a tendency for the woman to be the dominant person in the household. The development of this pattern began during slavery, when black men had no independent economic status. The black woman, on the other hand, partly because of her procreative value and partly because she was sometimes taken as a concubine by the white master, acquired higher social and economic advantages that made her the head of the household in which her children were born and raised. The dominant position of the female in the household remained after emancipation because caste barriers prevented the men from advancing beyond their marginal position in the economic system. The evidence supporting this point of view comes from the fact that the incidence of female-headed households tends to be highest in the poorest sections of the ghetto, that is, among those who are economically worst off. The economic insecurity of the black male reinforces the dominant position of the black female in the family. The economic system of American society thus functions differently with respect to white and black families: it strengthens the authority of white men and emasculates black men.

The influence of caste barriers in shaping the ghetto system of status mobility, family structure, and other indigenous institutions directly contributes to educational adaptation. The restriction of black parents largely to low-level and menial social and occupational roles and their traditional lack of opportunity to advance above these positions through their own abilities, education, or other efforts probably prevents them from training their children effectively to develop competitive attitudes and persistent efforts toward schoolwork. The social

---

[4] I am fully aware of the vast changes in sex roles now taking place among white Americans. While these changes may substantially reduce the dominance of the white male in the family, they do not invalidate my claim here that the caste system has functioned to create a black family pattern in which the female has tended to be the more dominant. Nor am I concerned with the political aspect of changing sex roles, such as whether the family should be male dominated, female dominated, or egalitarian.

and economic emasculation of the black male ensures both that a large number of black children grow up in households without the full benefit of the role models provided by two-parent families and that they will grow up in poverty with all its consequences for school learning.

The Job Ceiling and the Development of School-Related Skills

It is well known that black and white children differ in the linguistic, cognitive, and motivational skills they possess when they first come to school. This difference has been used to explain why black children do less well in school than white children (see Chapter 2). It has also been said that black children differ from white middle-class children in these skills because black parents do not socialize their children in the same way as white middle-class parents. This explanation, which I shall call the *failure-of-socialization hypothesis,* had an enormous influence on the compensatory education and other programs begun in the 1960s to help black children do better in school. The relative inability of these programs to eliminate the assumed black "deficits" in linguistic, cognitive, and motivational skills is discussed in Chapter 3.

The problem with the failure-of-socialization hypothesis and with various studies of black socialization is that they focus almost exclusively on the *process* of socialization and pay little attention to the *objective* of socialization, why a particular form of the skill being studied should be transmitted. They rarely ask: Why should black parents transmit to their children *the same* linguistic, cognitive, and motivational skills as white parents, using *the same* techniques, when as adults black and white children are destined to occupy different status positions? A more adequate study of socialization will have to take into account the fact that socialization is also immensely influenced by the needs of the wider society; it does not depend simply on the ability and capability of individual parents to raise their children.

Job Ceiling, Competence, and Personal Attributes. Alex Inkeles's writings on the role of socialization in producing competent people in society suggest how we can begin to understand the consequences of the job ceiling and other caste barriers on the types of skills or personal attributes that black parents as agents of socialization transmit to their children. According to Inkeles (1968b:85), each society has its role repertoire which determines the pattern of behavior expected of typical status incumbents. The role repertoire, therefore, determines the qualities the incumbents must have. These qualities are "what the individuals in the culture must learn and be if they are to meet the role demands" set for them by their society and they are acquired through the process of socialization. Hence, for Inkeles as for myself, there are two important tasks of socialization study: first, *to identify the qualities* demanded for effective role performance in the society of its segment under study, and then *to study how these qualities are transmitted* to the younger generation. Inkeles introduces the concept of *competence* as the linkage between socialization and the status positions in society. Competence—the end product of socialization—is defined by him as "the ability to attain and perform valued social roles (1968a:52)." Socialization, on the other hand, is the formative process of competence, its objective being to produce competent people. Both competence and socialization vary from culture to culture according to variation in role repertoire.

According to Inkeles (1968a:65), American society defines competence as

> the ability to work at gainful and reasonable remunerative employment, to meet the competition of those who would undo us while yet observing the rules for such competition as set down by society, and to manage one's own affairs, to achieve some significant and effective participation in community and political life, and to establish and maintain a reasonably stable home and family life.

It is evident from what has been said so far in this book that this type of competence described by Inkeles does not fit the status position of blacks in American society. It is the competence associated with the status position of white middle-class people, which requires certain kinds of personal qualities transmitted to white middle-class children in their socialization. Among these qualities, Inkeles tells us (1968a:66), are the ability to tell and manage time, a certain kind of language skill, level of information, motive, and cognitive modes.

If American society unevenly distributes socially valued status positions between two castes, does it seem logical for society to expect the two to possess the same kinds of competence and hence the same types of personal qualities or attributes? We should not expect blacks and whites to have the same socialization practices and experiences, because they are not being prepared for roles requiring the same kinds of competence. My guess is that given different forms of competence requiring different personal attributes or qualities, the socialization processes of the two castes probably differ, although they may be equally valid. It makes no sense to judge black socialization in terms of white socialization without first establishing that both are directed toward producing the same kind of competence. With this background, next focus on language, motivation, and cognition for illustrative purposes. I argue that when blacks differ from whites in these or other skills it is probably because their status positions require variant forms of the skills in question, not because black parents have failed in their socialization duty.

Command of Language. Until recently, it was not generally known that black children had difficulty learning to read in school because they possessed a separate English dialect which interferes with their attempts to read standard English. This phenomenon was not recognized until lately because social scientists tended to study black speech behavior as a deviation from the speech behavior of the white middle class rather than as a system in its own right and a phenomenon related to black lower-caste status. Baratz and Baratz (1970) pointed out that under prevailing American sociopolitical ideology, social scientists tend to confuse legal equality with sameness and therefore judge black behavior by white middle-class standards:

> The application of this misinterpretation of egalitarian principle to social science data has often left the investigator with the unwelcome task of describing [black] behavior not as it is, but rather as it deviates from the normative system defined by the White middle class [pp. 113–114].

Thus social scientists, particularly educational psychologists, generally labeled black students as "verbally deprived" (see Bereiter 1965; Bereiter et al. 1966; Bereiter and Engelman 1966; C. Deutsch 1964; M. Deutsch et al. 1967; Jensen 1968; Whiteman and Deutsch 1968). Many of the efforts in the 1960s to explain why black children were failing in school, especially in reading skills, and what solutions were needed to prevent that failure were based on the notion of verbal deprivation. The myth of verbal deprivation is described by Labov (1972) as follows:

> Black children from the ghetto area are said to receive little verbal stimulation, to hear very little well-formed language, and as a result are impoverished in their means of verbal expression. They cannot speak complete sentences, do not know the names of common objects, cannot form concepts or convey logical thoughts [p. 201].

The same educational psychologists blamed the phenomenon of verbal deprivation on black parents and their methods of language training for their children. It was said that these parents did not provide their children with the same kind and amount of verbal stimulation as did their white counterparts in the suburbs.

Field studies by linguists and anthropologists have now provided sufficient evidence for rejecting the concept of verbal deprivation on the grounds that it is inapplicable to black children in the ghetto. These scholars have conducted careful studies of the structure and function of everyday conversations (vernacular speech) of black ghetto residents in various cities, such as Chicago, Detroit, and New York, and have come to the following conclusions: that blacks possess a separate English dialect which is a normal and well-formed language system like the standard English dialect of the white middle-class; that black children acquire this black English dialect in a normal way, much as white children acquire the white English dialect; and that black children are not verbally deprived. Summarizing the present position of linguists and anthropologists on the matter, Labov (1972) states that:

> The most careful statement of the situation as it actually exists might read as follows: Many features of pronunciation, grammar, and lexicon are closely associated with black speakers—so closely as to identify the great majority of black people in the Northern cities (as well as in the South generally) by their speech alone [p. 7].

This identification of blacks with a particular speech pattern is the basis of the social reality of their language skills. These studies show that black children, far from being verbally deprived, receive a good deal of verbal stimulation. Labov (1972) points out that

> the concept of verbal deprivation has no basis in social reality. In fact, black children in the urban ghettos receive a great deal of verbal stimulation, hear more well-formed sentences than middle-class children, and participate fully in a highly verbal culture. They have the same basic vocabulary, possess the same capacity for conceptual learning, and use the same logic as anyone else who learns to speak and understand English [p. 201].

But the English dialect ghetto children learn and use is different from that learned and used by their white middle-class peers (Stewart 1970:367).

Linguists have also gone on to explain why a separate English dialect exists, in spite of opposition to the idea from teachers, principals, and civil rights leaders (Labov 1972:7). Partly to forestall any possible misuse of the concept for "a racist" cause, Stewart (1970) warns linguists that "quite objective and innocently made statements about dialect differences between whites and [blacks] might be interpreted by white racists as evidence of [black] cultural backwardness or mental inferiority, or even seized upon by black racists as evidence of some sort of mythical Negro 'soul' [p. 356]." Consequently, Stewart and others have tried to trace the origins of the black English dialect from the eighteenth-century West African pidgin English dialect, through the evolution of the latter into the Creole English dialect of the plantation

South and the process of decreolization following emancipation, leading finally to the present-day form (Stewart 1968, 1970; see also Dillard
1972). Labov (1972:66) acknowledges the validity of some aspects of
the Creole hypothesis of Stewart and other historical dialectologists but
emphasizes the fusion of southern and northern Black English dialects
in the evolution of the present-day ghetto dialect.

These and other accounts of the evolution of the ghetto dialect may
be sufficient to dispel potential opposition to and misuse of the concept; but they hardly touch upon the influence of caste barriers in
creating and perpetuating the separate dialect. Moreover, the Creole
hypothesis almost overstresses the persistence of the grammatical
structure of West African pidgin English so as to suggest that its resistance to change is responsible for the present-day dialect. The evidence
offered by Stewart and others, however, strongly suggests the need to
explore the influence of caste barriers in the evolution and perpetuation of this dialect. This evidence indicates that during slavery the
Creole dialect came into being because caste barriers limited contacts
between black speakers of pidgin English and white speakers of standard English. The same forces limited the process of decreolization
after emanicpation. The influence of racial isolation on black language
patterns during slavery is well described by Stewart when he points out
that house slaves quickly acquired a "more standard variety of English
than the Creole of the field hands," as did the educated blacks of the
period (1970:360). Labov (1972) describes an interesting case of four-
teen present-day black and white individuals whose racial identities
could not be established on the basis of their speech patterns. These
individuals were

> blacks raised without any black friends in solidly white areas; whites raised in areas
> dominated by black cultural values; white Southerners in Gullah-speaking territory;
> blacks from small northern communities untouched by recent migration; college-
> educated blacks who reject the northern ghetto and the South alike [p. 10].

It seems likely that if blacks had not been isolated from whites during
slavery they would have given up their dialect to acquire standard
English just as the Chinese gave up their own pidgin English and
learned standard English. The Creole dialect evolved on the plantations
because of racial isolation, not because the grammatical structure of
West African pidgin English resisted change. Caste barriers resulting in
racial isolation also account for the incompleteness of decreolization
after emancipation. If social mobility in American society requires
standard English, as Stewart (1970:361) suggests, then the caste barriers which have traditionally limited social mobility among blacks

have also limited their opportunities to acquire standard English. A more complete account of the evolution and persistence of present-day black English must examine the problem in the context of the American caste system.

These findings—the existence of a separate black dialect and its acquisition in a normal way by ghetto children—have led linguists and anthropologists working in the field to suggest that the failure of black children to learn to read at the same pace and with the same ease as their white middle-class peers is caused by interference from their own dialect when they are trying to use standard English. Baratz (1970), for instance, writes that

> When the middle-class child starts the process of learning to read, his problem is primarily one of decoding the graphic representations of a language he already speaks. The disadvantaged black child must also "translate" them into his own language. This presents him with an almost insurmountable obstacle since the written words frequently do not go together in any pattern that is familiar or meaningful to him [p. 20].

The more difficult task of ghetto children in learning to read is compounded by the fact that neither their teachers nor their schools recognize that they come to school with an essentially *different* English dialect, different both structurally and functionally from the standard English they have to learn to read. In fact, teachers and other school personnel are likely to label black English as pathological, lazy, disordered, or sloppy (Baratz 1970; Labov 1972; Stewart 1970).

Cognitive Skills. Cognitive function refers to both the forms and styles of thinking characteristic of individuals (Inkeles 1968a:61). Thinking may be concrete, abstract, or both as Bruner, Piaget, Vernon, and others have indicated. Cognitive modes of functioning are an important quality for effective participation in any society; and contemporary technological societies emphasize the abstract and related forms more than the concrete. The dominant social sciences' view of the past two decades has been that children acquire their cognitive skills and styles in the course of interacting with their environment, the latter being narrowly defined to mean parental, familial, and neighborhood factors. I have already pointed out the inadequacy of this concept and suggested another way of looking at environment that would include such features of the wider society as economic systems, sociopolitical organization, and the like. Ultimately, it is these broader features—the macroenvironment—which determine cognitive skills and styles required for competence by role incumbents. The family, the peer groups, and even the schools—the microenvironments—are only channels or instruments through which the adaptive cognitive repertoire of a society or a segment of it is transmitted in each generation.

Blacks and whites have been shown to differ in their cognitive skills as measured by intelligence tests (Baugham 1971; Dreger 1973; Jensen 1969). The lower performance of blacks is usually explained in terms of the failure-of-socialization hypothesis. But as shown in Chapter 3, efforts to resocialize black children to develop white middle-class forms of cognitive skills have not proved successful. These efforts failed primarily because the hypothesis upon which they were based assumed that blacks and whites ought to have *the same* cognitive skills acquired in *the same* way, despite the fact that the status positions of the two castes are *different* and probably require *different* cognitive adaptations.

I suggest that the cognitive differences between blacks and whites are attributable primarily to the fact that the two groups have traditionally occupied different and unequal positions in both the occupational and sociopolitical structures of American society. As I argued in Chapter 3, the low and menial roles to which blacks have been restricted require and stimulate the development of cognitive and other skills different from those associated with the more desirable positions open to whites. The fact that blacks have had only limited access to white-collar, technical, managerial, and professional positions and have been confined to unskilled and menial labor for generations has probably meant that they have not had the same opportunities as whites to develop those ways of conceptualizing, thinking, and speaking demanded by the former positions. Scientific analysis, control, and exploitation of the physical environment, large-scale and long-range planning and execution require the type of thinking characteristic of the Western middle class. But this class did not always possess those cognitive skills, at least not to the same degree. Participation in these activities not only requires them but also stimulates their development. In the case of blacks, we find that their initial and arbitrary exclusion from these activities was based on their lower-caste status, not their lack of the requisite mental capacities and processes. The menial social positions to which they have been confined required and stimulated different forms of cognitive skills, which black parents as agents of socialization under the caste system, transmit to their children.

Cognitive Styles. Studies of cultural differences in cognitive styles are becoming popular. Group differences in cognitive styles are sometimes explained in terms of genetic differences (Jensen 1969), but most often they are explained in terms of differences in socialization styles (Berry 1966; Cohen 1969; Ramirez and Castaneda 1974; Witkin *et al.*

1954, 1962) and occasionally in terms of differences in ecological factors (Berry 1971; Dawson 1967). I dealt with the genetic hypothesis in Chapter 2 and focus here on the socialization hypothesis as it applies to black Americans.

Witkin, who initiated the study of cognitive styles during World War II, distinguished between two polar styles of thinking—the global and the articulated. People with the articulated style of thinking are able to differentiate and organize features of their environments and approach tasks more objectively than those with the global style. According to Witkin *et al.* (1962), the two types of cognitive styles arise from differences in socialization styles: articulated or field-independent people are raised by parents who use child-rearing practices typical of well-educated white middle- and upper-middle-class parents; global or field-dependent people are raised by parents who do not use such childrearing techniques.[5]

In her Pittsburgh study, Cohen (1969) also identifies two polar cognitive styles, which she calls analytical and relational. People with analytical cognitive styles function well in formal organizational settings such as schools and use the analytic approach in abstracting information from a stimulus situation, whereas those characterized by a relational style are more descriptive in their approach to a stimulus, tend to relate mainly to the global features of the situation, and are more self-centered in their orientation to reality. Cohen's analytic and relational styles are, in fact, equivalent to Witkin's articulated (field-independent) and global (field-dependent) styles. Like Witkin, Cohen suggests that her polar types originate from difference in socialization styles. People with analytic cognitive styles are raised in more formally organized family and peer settings, while those with relational styles are raised in "shared-function" primary groups. Careful reading of Cohen's presentation suggests that formally organized group socialization characterizes the white middle class while the shared-function primary group socialization is typical of the lower class and disadvantaged minorities.

Ramirez and Castañeda (1974) argue that Anglo-Americans and Mexican-Americans of Texas have different cognitive styles: Anglo-Americans are field independent; Mexican-Americans are field dependent. Like Witkin and Cohen, they trace the differences in cognitive styles to differences in socialization styles: "Socialization styles, including teaching approaches, the nature of rewards, and characteristics

[5]Most cross-cultural studies use the terms *field-independence* and *field-dependence* to represent the two polar types of cognitive style identified by Witkin, although *field-independence* and *field-dependence* refer primarily to perceptual styles (see Cole and Scribner 1974:82).

of the relationship between 'teacher' and learner, which children experience at home, differ from culture to culture. Values and socialization styles determine or affect development of cognitive styles in children [p. 60]."

None of these studies of differences in cognitive styles in the United States has attempted to examine the way in which groups' positions in the wider society affect their characteristic cognitive styles. But we find that those reported to be global, field dependent, relational, and concrete in their cognitive styles are found primarily in subordinate groups, such as women (Witkin *et al.* 1962), members of shared-function primary groups (i.e., lower class) (Cohen 1969), Mexican-Americans (Ramirez and Castañeda 1974), blacks (Jensen 1969), and Jewish boys from mother-dominated, father-emasculated families (Castello and Peyton 1973). In other words, the socialization pattern that produces global, field-dependent, relational, and concrete thinking is associated with subordinate status. The competence associated with the different (and usually unequal) power and technoeconomic positions occupied by different groups based on sex, class, and caste status requires different types of cognitive styles. Differences in socialization styles are determined by the need to transmit cognitive styles adaptive to the different positions. Socialization processes show us *how* the adaptive cognitive styles are acquired or transmitted, not why they exist in the population.

I do not deny that there are group differences in cognitive styles. My contention, however, is that the explanations of why they occur are inadequate. Studies of cognitive styles, though becoming popular, are as yet few, poorly conceptualized, and culture bound. Many of their conclusions are premature and unwarranted.[6]

---

[6]There is a curious but dangerous parallel in the policy implications of Jensen's theory and the theories of some of his opponents. Referring to the work of Jensen (advocate of genetic basis of cognitive differences) and of Ramirez (advocate of the cultural basis of cognitive differences), De Avila and Havassy (1975) note this parallel:

> While the Jensen and Ramirez positions imply very differnt causal explanations, functionally speaking their arguments run the risk of being reduced to the same position regarding the educational approach to be taken with Mexican-American children. That is, Ramirez's position that Mexican-American children are field-sensitive [i.e., field-dependent, global, relational, etc.] and consequently not receptive to learning abstract problem-solving strategies is much the same, at the practical level, as Jensen's position—that the intellectual capabilities of Mexican-American [and blacks] are limited to Level 1 [i.e., the level of concrete, nonanalytical thinking] because of genetic endowment. Both arguments suggest a curriculum for Mexican-American students which eliminates or minimizes tasks requiring the abstract manipulations of impersonal data [p. 250].

Ramirez bases his research partly on Witkin and partly on the work of Lesser, Fifer, and Clark (see Stodolsky and Lesser 1971). The latter found that there are ethnic differences in the mean scores for verbal, reasoning, numerical, and spatial portions of the intelligence test they administered to

Achievement Motivation. Research on achievement motivation among blacks reveals an interesting paradox. Black children do not have a lower interest in education than white children (Katz 1967; Mingione 1965; Rosen 1959). At the same time, they do not perform as well as whites in the intellectual tasks of the classroom (Katz 1967:144). Why is there a lack of motivation to perform in the classroom among black children? Almost all explanations point to the failure of black socialization as the ultimate cause. Here I discuss two variants of the failure-of-socialization hypothesis because they are directly related to the issue of competence in a caste society.

Inkles (1968a), Riessman (1962), and Cloward and Jones (1963) attribute the lack of motivation to perform in the classroom to culture conflict. They argue that the competence goals of the schools are probably different from the competence goals to which black families have socialized their children. They suggest that to eliminate the conflict and increase black motivation to perform in the classroom, the goals of education should be modified to make them more compatible with the values, goals, and learning styles of black children. But they do not say exactly what they consider these values, goals, and learning styles to be. Their main point is that since black parents are not able to socialize their children to acquire the white middle-class attributes that fit successful learning in the schools, the schools should modify their approach to fit the qualities or skills possessed by black children. One wonders, however, how this modification would prepare black children to participate competently as adults in a technological society requiring white middle-class qualities and competence.

In my view, Katz (1967) identifies the problem more correctly as *the lack of the will to learn,* but I think that he incorrectly explains it in terms of the failure-of-socialization hypothesis. He states:

Chinese, Jewish, black, and Puerto Rican children in New York and Boston. Although they disclaimed any attempt to relate their finds on ethnic cognitive styles to school ability or learning styles, their findings have been used to argue the case against school integration (see Weinberg 1970:375). Potential misuse of the findings on ethnic differences in cognitive styles is as likely by well-meaning school personnel as by racist "expert" psychologists. I think that the potential for this misuse is most likely to occur when no adequate explanation for the differences is provided, as in the case of Lesser and his associates. In none of their writings on this particular study have they examined the possible influence of historical and social structural forces on the test performance of their groups. The fact that Jewish children did best on tasks of verbal ability but not on tasks of space conceptualization, while for Chinese children the reverse was true might be due to several factors not mentioned in their interpretation. For example, (a) Jewish literary background, their relative fluency in English—the language in which the test was given—and the relative absence of architectural (and constructional) investment in Jewish ghettos during the Diaspora; and (b) the difference between the Chinese and English languages and the relative lack of fluency in English among some Chinese children, which partly accounts for the tendency among Chinese-Americans as a group to go into fields of science where there is less need for English usage than other skills (e.g., those involving space conceptualization).

I think that the crux of the matter is the differential capacity of children from different social backgrounds for vigorous and sustained efforts on tasks that are not consistently interesting and attractive and which offer no immediate payoff, either positive or negative. In this view, effective scholastic motivation is largely reducible to self-control—*an outcome of socialization processes involving the internalization of standards of excellence and of affect-mediating evaluation response to one's own performance* [p. 140; emphasis added].

He then suggests a new experimental approach to the study of the socialization of motivational competence. The results of the experiment show that children who perform the experimental task correctly and have good academic records are less self-critical than those who also perform the experimental task correctly but have poor academic records. The results of the experiment show that ghetto children who fail in school may come from homes with high achievement standards but that their standards are so stringent and rigid as to be utterly dysfunctional [p. 161]. Self-criticism is an effective mechanism for self-discouragement, which, according to Katz, the children have internalized in the course of their socialization.

In explaining why black students usually express about the same scholastic interests and aspirations as white students but perform less well in school, Katz argues that the majority of black parents teach their children to aspire to high educational goals and lay down verbal rules and regulations about classroom behavior, the transgression of which they punish severely. However, they do not teach their children the instrumental behavior necessary for achieving their educational goals (1967:174).

As in other instances, the failure-of-socialization hypothesis confuses the process of transmitting a given skill or personal quality that exists or is emphasized in a society or group with the reason why a particular form of the skill exists at all. We know from studies cited by Katz (1967) and others that the quality noticeably absent from black students is seriousness and perseverance in their schoolwork. At the same time, there are reports that these students are very skilled at manipulating the system. It is reasonable to infer that in the course of their socialization black children learn manipulative skills but do not learn skills that enable them to be serious and persevering in schoolwork. The reason for this failure to learn lies partly in the effect of the job ceiling on their perceptions of schooling and partly in the form of status mobility or paths for self-improvement the caste system fosters among them.

Both of these phenomena force blacks to rely on white patronage to achieve jobs and other necessities of life. And competence in winning their objectives through patronage requires the skills of dependence, compliance, and manipulation. Thus the caste system requires blacks to renounce such white motivational skills as autonomy, independence, initiative, and competitiveness in order to "make it" in the wider society. Under the caste system, black parents perform their socialization task competently by transmitting to their children the motivational skills adaptive to their status positions as dictated by both the job ceiling and their status mobility.

The failure-of-socialization hypothesis leads to a gross misconception of the development of personal qualities or attributes. It fails to separate the reason *why* a particular skill or attribute or its variant form is characteristic of a society or its segment from a different question, the question of *how* the skill is transmitted to each generation. Skills or personal qualities dominant in a given population are functionally adaptive for its members. Conversely, skills only marginally present or entirely absent are not functionally adaptive. Socialization is the process by which an already existent skill or its variant is transmitted to the younger generation; socialization does not by itself generate the skills thus transmitted. This assertion is well illustrated by reference to differences between blacks and whites in reading skills.

The fact that American society rewards blacks and whites differently for reading and language proficiency, for example, contributes to the difference between the two groups in their reading performance. Although both blacks and whites are required to learn reading and other associated skills, for whites, proficiency in these skills is a passport to professional and white-collar jobs, financial rewards, and social prestige; for blacks, it is not—at least not to the same extent. The higher proficiency of whites in reading and associated skills does not result merely from the fact that white parents do more to encourage their children to read than black parents. White parents encourage their children more because in their own experience *as a group*, proficiency in reading leads to good jobs and other rewards in adult life. In other words, proficiency in reading is functionally adaptive for whites. This is a strong incentive for white parents to encourage their children and for the children to strive to acquire good reading habits and skills as well as to demonstrate their proficiency in test situations as they begin to perceive the importance of reading to their future roles in adult life. The situation is quite different for black parents and children, to whom society offers less incentive to acquire and express proficiency in reading. This analysis can be extended to other skills, such as mathematical skills, which are taught and measured in the schools.

Summary

The hypothesis presented in this book is that lower school performance on the part of blacks is an adaptation to their lower social and occupational positions in adult life, which do not require high educational qualifications. On the one hand, the dominant white caste maintains the adaptation by providing blacks with inferior educations and then channeling them mainly to inferior jobs after they finish school. On the other hand, the adaptation is also maintained by certain structural and cultural features of the black environment which have evolved under the caste system. Caste barriers are thus able to encourage lower school performance through indirect and less obvious influence on black attitudes, institutions, and skills. It is the various forms of the indirect influence of caste barriers on black school performance that I have tried to explore in this chapter. I have tried to show that the preoccupation of blacks with the effects of the job ceiling on their chances for future employment adversely affects their attitudes toward schooling and their academic efforts. The effects of the job ceiling and other caste barriers, moreover, are not limited to the conscious and unconscious reactions of blacks to their lack of future opportunities or limited future opportunities. I have suggested how these barriers might affect black institutions like the family and status mobility system, which in turn affect the ability of black children to achieve white middle-class type of school success. Finally, the job ceiling and other caste barriers influence the course of the linguistic, cognitive, and motivational development of black children. This comes about because the type of competence demanded by the generally low social and technoeconomic positions occupied by blacks in adult life is associated with linguistic, cognitive, and motivational attributes or forms different from those associated with the higher social and technoeconomic position of the white middle-class. Thus the personal attributes transmitted to black children in the course of their socialization may be perfectly normal skills required by their position in the caste system, although they are not the types of skills that encourage the white middle-class type of school success.

The hypothesis presented here—that black school performance is an adaptation—does not, of course, deal with the question of why one black child does better than another. It is not the purpose of this study to explore individual differences within the black caste. The study is principally concerned with the general differences in school performance of the two racial castes. Nor does the hypothesis deal with the actual process of education in the classroom. These microlevel studies—why some children perform better than others, and what actually goes on in the learning situation of the classroom—have been fully explored in other works. Such studies often suggest intervention programs directed at changing the situation in the home or the school, or at changing the child himself. Important as these intervention programs are, I have argued that they deal primarily with the symptoms rather than with the cause of black school problems. They often fail to explore how the broader features of American society may have created the conditions in the home, the school, and the child which are the cause of black school failure.

My study is an attempt to show how the features of the wider society, particularly American caste stratification, affect black school performance. The literature strongly suggests that the way black status is defined in that stratification system at any point in history influences both the way the schools treat black children and the way blacks respond to education. It therefore seems to me that the school and the home are not the ultimate source of influence on school performance. Both are the media through which the influences of the caste system are transmitted to the black child. And these influences, to a large extent, condition the child's behavior in school. When I state, for example, that the education of blacks is affected by their low position in the technoeconomic organization of society, I do not mean simply that black education is affected by poverty. What does affect black education is the fact that American society, through its political, economic, administrative, and other institutions, restricts blacks to menial social and occupational roles, low income, and poor residential status. These devices perpetuate their poverty.

Historical evidence suggests that the schools are not indifferent to black status. Because educational activities of the schools cannot be divorced from the goal of preparation for adult life, the schools have traditionally tended to prepare blacks for the status society assigns to them. Black families, consciously or unconsciously, have also reinforced the situation because they too must raise their children to survive in the system.

In Chapter 3, I examined the two principal strategies currently being used to improve black school performance—compensatory education, with its emphasis on improving black school performance within ghetto schools, and school integration, which seeks to educate black and white children in the same schools. These two strategies are based on the assumptions that lower black school performance is caused either by the student's home environments or by their school environments or by both, and that lower school performance and educational attainment by blacks are hindering them from achieving equality with whites in terms of jobs, wages, housing, and social and political roles in American society. However, as I have argued, evidence suggests that lack of education is not in itself responsible for the confinement of blacks to menial jobs, low wages, poor housing, and low social and political roles—although inferior education has certainly been used to accomplish these things. These conditions, together with inferior education, are concomitants of structured inequality in the American caste system. The hypothesis presented here suggests that the elimination of caste barriers will eventually change the educational attitudes and work habits of blacks and increase their competitive efforts in academic work. The schools themselves will also change the attitudes toward and conceptions of blacks they have built up in the past and begin to equip black children with the same sets of skills they presently provide to white students. What is needed, I strongly believe, is implementation of the second half of the concept of equality of educational opportunity, i.e., equality of postschool opportunity. In Chapter 14, I take up the implications for social policy of the alternative hypothesis I have presented in this chapter. Meanwhile I wish to examine the extent to which some other nonimmigrant minorities in the United States share the educational experiences of black Americans.

7

America's Other Castelike Minorities: American Indians, Mexican-Americans, and Puerto Ricans

Patterns of Performance

Low school performance is also found among other castelike minorities in the United States, including American Indians, Mexican-Americans, and Puerto Ricans. In the area of tested IQ, these groups generally score lower than Anglo-Americans. Coleman's study (1966) provides a partial comparison of these minorities with Anglo-Americans.[1] On both verbal and nonverbal tests, Indians, Mexican-Americans, blacks, and Puerto Ricans score below Anglo-Americans and Orientals. Other studies comparing castelike minorities with Anglo-Americans also show that the former score lower.

American Indians. Early studies such as that of Garth (1931) and more recent studies like that of Parmee (1973) show that Indians score much lower than Anglos (see also Brophy and Aberle 1966:139–141). Parmee administered the Lorge-Thorndike Intelligence Test to Apache and non-Apache students and found that the non-Apaches "tended to

---

[1]In this chapter, the dominant white caste is referred to as Anglo-American to distinguish them from Mexican-Americans and Puerto Ricans who are also officially classified as whites.

score somewhat near the national norms on the verbal tests and slightly above norms on the non-verbal tests." He goes on to say that "The Apache students, however, tended to score below the national norms on both tests, to level approximately 25 points on the verbal section and 10–15 points lower on the non-verbal section [1973:56–57]." Parmee attributes the differences in the Apache scores between the verbal and nonverbal sections of the test to language handicaps (the differences between the two scores were statistically significant). In one type of IQ test, the Goodenough Draw-A-Man Test, Indians, especially those from the southwestern states, generally score above the national norms. But scores on this particular type of test have been shown in cross-cultural studies to correlate highly with art experience. The Indians of the Southwest have highly developed arts and therefore do well on this test (see Fuchs and Havighurst 1973; Dennis 1970).

Mexican-Americans. Various studies since the early 1920s show that Mexican-Americans score substantially lower than Anglo-Americans on IQ tests (see Blackman 1939; Coers 1935; Cook and Arthur 1955; Garrett 1928; Garth and Johnson 1934; Hill 1936—all cited in Jensen 1961). Their lower scores have continued, as shown in recent studies (see Jensen 1961; Mercer 1973; Padilla and Ruiz 1973; De Avila and Havassy 1975). Mercer (1973) describes the differences between the test scores of preschool to adult Mexican-Americans and those of Anglo-Americans in Riverside, California as follows:

> We found that over half of the children 7 months through 15 years of age who had low IQs, regardless of the criterion cutoff used, were of Mexican American heritage, while only 7.1 to 11.4 percent of those passing the intelligence tests were from this group. Similarly, over 25 percent of the children receiving failing scores were Black, while only 8.1 percent of the children in the passing population were Black. Although 79.6 percent of the children in the study were Anglos, only 12.5 percent of those with an IQ below 85 were Anglo. The correlation between ethnic group and IQ was not significant for pre-school children—but was significant for school-age children.
>
>   The correlation was even greater for adults. . . . Seventy percent of the adults with an IQ below 70 were of Mexican heritage. The disproportion is not so large when the IQ cutoff is 84, but even then, 53.1 percent were Mexican Americans, a figure four and one half times higher than would be expected from their percentage in the general population. Black adults are also slightly overrepresented in the low-scoring category [pp. 167–168].

The low score of the Mexican-Americans in IQ tests subsequently leads to their overrepresentation in low ability groups in classrooms [see U.S. Commission on Civil Rights (USCCR) 1974b:23, table 8].

Puerto Ricans. Data on Puerto Rican scores on IQ tests date from the 1930s (Armstrong *et al.* 1935; Dunklin 1935; Porteus 1939—all cited in Anastasi and Cordova 1972). In Dunklin's study, Puerto Ricans scored at the national norms in some but not all of the tests. In the study by Armstrong, Achilles, and Sacks, Puerto Ricans scored below the Anglo-American control group from Manhattan and Westchester County. Porteus found that the Puerto Ricans had the lowest scores of all national groups he tested in Hawaii on the Stanford-Binet Test and the Porteus Maze. In a study on some 108 Puerto Rican children in grades 6, 7, and 8 in New York City in 1953, Anastasi and Cordova found that their IQ averaged about 80 or 81, that is, about 20 points below the national norm. They concluded that bilingualism was not responsible for the low scores since the children did about the same whether the tests were given in English or in Spanish (Anastasi and Cordova 1972:376). Stodolsky and Lesser (1971) also report relatively low scores for Puerto Ricans when they administered IQ tests to a number of ethnic groups in New York and Boston. Loehlin *et al.* (1975:139) report a study in Hawaii in which Puerto Ricans scored lowest in an IQ test given to 12 ethnic and semiethnic groups. According to Sexton (1972:391), the IQ test scores of Puerto Rican children tend to decline as they get older and move into higher grades. For example, in New York City the average IQ score of Puerto Rican pupils in grade 3 was 91.2, compared with 98 for the city; however, by grade 8 it averaged only 83.2, compared with 103.4 for the city. In general, Puerto Ricans score lower than Anglo-Americans in IQ tests whether they were born and educated in Puerto Rico or on the mainland (New York City, Board of Education, 1972:180). The use of IQ test scores for placing children in academic programs usually results in a disproportionate number of Puerto Rican children in low-ability or mentally retarded groups (see U.S. Commission on Civil Rights 1974a:32–39).

Scholastic Achievement Lag

Coleman's study (1966) also provides some data for comparing the achievement of Indians, Mexican-Americans, and Puerto Ricans in such vital subject areas as reading and math. This comparison is shown in Table 7.1 for grades 6, 9, and 12. These groups are behind Anglo-Americans by more than one grade level at the sixth grade, and the gap between them widens in subsequent years. Studies of individual minority groups also show a similar gap.

American Indians. One extensive and representative study of Indian scholastic achievement was conducted by Coombs and his as-

America's Other Castelike Minorities

Table 7.1

Test Scores of Blacks, American Indians, Mexican-Americans, and Puerto Ricans, Showing How Far They Are Behind Whites

Minority groups	Grade levels behind white students of nonmetropolitan areas		
	Verbal ability	Reading achievement	Math achievement
Grade 6			
Indian	1.3	1.8	1.8
Mexican-American	1.6	2.2	1.7
Negro	1.5	1.8	1.9
Puerto Rican	2.3	2.8	2.3
Grade 9			
Indian	1.4	1.9	2.1
Mexican-American	1.6	2.2	2.3
Negro	1.9	2.6	2.5
Puerto Rican	2.2	2.9	3.1
Grade 12			
Indian	2.5	2.6	3.0
Mexican-American	2.5	2.7	3.2
Negro	2.8	2.8	4.3
Puerto Rican	2.6	3.1	3.9

SOURCE: Adapted from Estelle Fuchs and Robert J. Havighurst 1973. *To live on this earth: American Indian education.* Garden City, N.Y.: Doubleday. Table 7, p. 125.

sociates from 1951 to 1954. The results were similar to those found in the Coleman study. In reading and math, Indian children were below national norms at the start, and they fell further and further behind in subsequent grades (Coombs *et al.*, 1958). Parmee found a similar gap between Anglo-Americans and the San Carolos Apaches: the Apache students were substantially lower in grade point average than Anglos of similar backgrounds in the same public schools (Parmee 1973:61; see also Berry 1971; Brophy and Aberle 1966:139–141; National Advisory Council on Indian Education 1974:59–63, 100).

Mexican-Americans. In addition to the Coleman study, other studies showing that Mexican-Americans lag behind Anglo-Americans in academic achievement are those of Carter (1970) and the U.S. Commission on Civil Rights (1974b). Carter found that Mexican-Americans attending the same school districts as Anglo-Americans have lower grade point averages and that the gap between the two groups increases substantially during the intermediate grades. He describes the situation as follows:

> Mexican American children start out in school fairly close to Anglos in measured achievement of all kinds. Although they fall slightly more behind the Anglos with each grade, the two groups remain in about the same relative position through the third or fourth grades. After beginning the intermediates, the Anglos continue their upward climb, approximating national norms. Sometime in the intermediate grades the Mexican American group begins to fall progressively and drastically further below the Anglo achievement. According to all reports gathered in the field, "mental withdrawal," manifest in boredom, failure to work, inattentiveness, and discipline problems, begins sometime from the third to the sixth grade [pp. 17, 20].

Puerto Ricans. "Mental withdrawal" is also characteristic of Indian and Puerto Rican children, resulting in the low academic achievement of these groups. For Puerto Rican children, Sexton (1972) reports that their reading scores in East Harlem decline with age. In one district, Puerto Rican students in grade 3 scored 2.8 on a reading test, compared with a citywide average of 3.5; and by grade 8 the Puerto Ricans were two full years below grade level. Sexton further reports that "in the junior high schools, 12% of the [Puerto Rican] students were reading above grade level, 8% at grade level, 10% one year below grade level, and 70% more than one year below grade level [p. 391]." In 1972, according to a recent study, 79% of the 8617 Puerto Rican children in grade 8 in New York City were reading below grade level (New York State, Department of Education 1972; cited in Fitzpatrick 1974). Because of their low academic achievement, most Puerto Ricans end up in vocational high school programs rather than academic. Thus Cordasco (1972:342) reports that in 1963 only 331 or 1.6% of the 21,000 high school graduates receiving academic diplomas were Puerto Ricans; and their share of vocational high school diplomas was 7.4%. During the same period, Puerto Ricans constituted 20% of the elementary school population and 18% of the junior high school enrollment. By 1968, the situation had improved slightly: The study by the New York State Department of Education (cited in Fitzpatrick 1974) shows that of the 10,142 Puerto Rican students in grade 10 in 1966, 43% or 4393 were enrolled in grade 12 in 1968. Of these, 19% reached grade 12 but either did not graduate or received general diplomas; 8% received commercial diplomas, and 16% or 1628, received academic diplomas which met college entrance requirements. Puerto Ricans in other cities such as Boston and Chicago are also considerably behind Anglo-Americans in academic achievement. (For the situation in Chicago in the 1970–1971 school year, see the report by the Illinois Advisory Committee on Civil Rights, 1974:43.)

Dropouts and Low Educational
Attainment Levels

In addition to their lower performance in formal tests, or perhaps partly because of it, disproportionate numbers of American Indians, Mexican-Americans, and Puerto Ricans terminate their schooling earlier than Anglo-Americans (see Carter 1970; Coombs 1970; Fitzpatrick 1974:2; Fuchs and Havighurst 1973:39–40, 116–117; Grebler *et al.* 1970; Szasz 1974; Washington State Advisory Committee on Civil Rights 1974; Wax 1967). Fewer of them attend or graduate from college. As a result, their general level of education is much lower than that of Anglo-Americans.

Comparison with Blacks. Group differences in the IQ and scholastic achievement test scores obtained in the Coleman study have often been used to compare the relative performance of American Indians, Mexican-Americans, and Puerto Ricans and show that some of them surpass blacks at the higher grades. Of the four minority groups, Indians scored highest and closest to the Anglos in the Coleman study; they were followed by Mexican-Americans, blacks, and Puerto Ricans in that order. But this comparison is deceptive and not very reassuring to those who use it to show that the Indian, the Mexican-American, or the Puerto Rican is "not low man on the totem pole" of academic achievement (see Coombs 1970:6). The reason is that the higher school dropout rates both before and after grade 9 (and in the case of Indians even before grade 6) make a meaningful comparison of the performance of these groups on tests given at grades 9 and 12 difficult. Many Indian, Mexican-American, and Puerto Rican students, whose very low scores would considerably lower the median scores of their groups, have already left before the tests are given, leaving behind members of their groups who are more like Anglo-Americans in performance (Carter 1970:18).

The high dropout rate of Puerto Rican students has already been cited. For Mexican-American students, the United States Commission on Civil Rights (1971b:11) reports that the estimated dropout rate for the five southwestern states is about 8.9% by grade eight and 39.7% by grade 12; for blacks in the same region it is 1.4% and 33.2%, respectively. The school dropout rate among Indians is even higher. Some school officials told the Washington State Advisory Committee on Civil Rights that the Indian dropout rate in the northwestern states is between 38% and 60%. Specific reports indicate considerably higher rates. For example, the superintendent of the Seattle public schools told the advisory committee that in the 1972–1973 school year there were 889 Indians enrolled in his district, of whom *only 29* were in grade 12; in the preceding year, there were only 13 Indians in grade 12, and 22 the year before that. (Washington State Advisory Committee on Civil Rights 1974:21–25.) According to the National Advisory Council on Indian Education (1974:29–30), the Indian dropout rate by grade 6 was 87% at an all-Indian public elementary school near Ponca City, Oklahoma. The overall Indian dropout rate is 90% in the Nome, Alaska, public schools; 62% in Minneapolis and between 45% and 75% throughout Minnesota; 70% in parts of California; and 90% in Klamath, Oregon. Although the situation varies according to regions, blacks are on the whole closer to Anglos in rate of school dropout than the other groups. For example, the Census Bureau report on national school enrollment in October 1973, shows that among 16- to 17-year-olds, 87.7% of blacks were still in precollege schools and another 3.4% were in college. Among Anglo-Americans, the figures were 88.3% and 3.5% respectively (cited in Levitan *et al.* 1975:83).

Current popular explanations of the lower performance of American Indians, Mexican-Americans, and Puerto Ricans emphasize that they are non-English-speaking minorities and that their cultures differ from that of the dominant Anglo caste. Other factors said to contribute to lower performance are lack of family and community support for education; the "culture of poverty" and "cultural deprivation"; and the educational policies and practices of the schools attended by these minorities (see Carter 1970; Illinois Advisory Committee on Civil Rights 1974; National Council on Indian Education 1974; Nava 1970; U.S. Commission on Civil Rights 1972a,b; U.S. Senate Select Committee 1970a,b). In the 1960s, the culture of poverty and cultural deprivation explanations were dominant, and their assumptions influenced many compensatory education programs for these minorities. These programs did not achieve any more success than they did in improving the performance of blacks. The explanation currently receiving the greatest official and unofficial attention is that these minorities fail to do well in school because they are non-English speaking and their cultures differ from Anglo-American culture. The linguistic and cultural explanations underlie efforts to develop and implement bilingual and bicultural education for these minorities, but the ability of such programs to improve academic achievement has not been demonstrated even in communities like Stockton, California, where they have been in operation for several years.

I do not, of course, mean to imply that language, culture, poverty, and the other variables listed above may not influence school performance. But it does not appear that cultural and language differences by themselves necessarily lead to generations of lower school performance. Therefore, when and where they are associated with persistent lower school performance, it is important to probe into the reasons. Consider, for example, the differences between the attitudes and school performance of native Mexican children and those of Mexican-American children born in the United States. My observations in Stockton lead me to conclude that the children from Mexico tend to have better attitudes toward school and probably do better in school than locally born Mexican-American children. Carter's (1970) observation for the southwestern states agrees with mine. He writes:

> As a general rule, children entering Southwestern schools directly from Mexico are reported to achieve better than the average local Mexican Americans. School personnel often are particularly proud of the performance of such children, who seem to learn English rapidly and well. The older the immigrant is, the better he appears to do in school [pp. 20–21].

Carter also notes that many explanations of the relatively better performance of children from Mexico appear to "violate the [generally assumed] relationship between acculturation and achievement [p. 21]." The children from Mexico are not necessarily from middle-class or upwardly mobile families; in Stockton at least, they are from farm-labor and lower-class families. But they resemble other immigrant minorities, like the Chinese, Japanese, and Philippinos in Stockton, more than they resemble local Mexican-Americans in attitudes and behavior in school.

Discussion with some members of the Puerto Rican community in Chicago in 1974 indicated a similar difference in attitudes and behavior between Puerto Ricans entering American schools directly from Puerto Rico and Puerto Rican students born and raised in the United States. This is not to say that "foreign" students from Mexico and Puerto Rico do not have problems adjusting to American schools. But their problems may be different in some important respects from those of American-born Mexican-Americans and Puerto Ricans.[2] The educational problems of the latter groups are closer to those of blacks than those of immigrant Mexicans and Puerto Ricans.

[2]A study of Puerto Ricans in New York City between 1953 and 1957 appears to contradict these impressionistic statements about the superiority of the students coming from Puerto Rico to those born in the United States. The study shows that in every measure (IQ test scores, achievment test scores in subject areas, and fluency in language) the American born, second generation Puerto Ricans appeared to be better students than those born in Puerto Rico and partially schooled there or receiving most of their schooling in the United States (New York City, Board of Education, 1972:178–181).

Indians, Mexican-Americans, and Puerto Ricans as Castelike Minorities

The significance of language and cultural differences is not to be underestimated, but I suggest that the lower school performance of American Indians, Mexican-Americans, and Puerto Ricans appears to be an adaptation to their castelike status and that it is within the framework of this adaptation that the language and cultural problems become pervasive and persistent. These minority groups share with blacks the experience of having been brought into United States society against their will and then relegated to subordinate status.

American Indians. The Indians lived in North America for centuries before the Anglos arrived and conquered them. After their subjugation, they became wards of the federal government. The wardship has at times been reorganized; some efforts have also been made to abolish it; and since the 1960s, Indians have increasingly asserted their desire for self-determination, but they have not completely emerged from wardship (see Brophy and Aberle 1966; Deloria 1974; Forbes 1964; National Advisory Council on Education 1974; Spicer 1962; Wax and Buchanan 1975).

Mexican-Americans. Mexican-Americans were also conquered and removed from power in the southwestern states. The conquering Anglos found a highly stratified society there in which the relationship between the upper-class Spanish and Mexican settlers on the one hand and the masses of the Mexican and Indian peoples on the other was decidedly castelike. The Anglos adopted and further stiffened the attitudes and discriminations of the local upper class toward the common people. Later immigrants from Mexico moved into the social and technoeconomic climate established between local Mexican-Americans and Anglos at the time of the conquest. World War II brought some changes in the castelike relationship. More Mexican-Americans moved into cities to escape from the rigid rural pattern of the caste system. Moreover, the need to maintain good relations with Mexico so as to continue recruiting Mexican farm laborers during the war years led the Anglos to introduce programs intended to foster better relationships with Mexicans and Mexican-Americans; it also led to the redefinition of the latter groups as *whites* or *Caucasians* by race. Other changes began in the 1960s after Mexican-Americans were "discovered" as a sizable minority group during the presidential campaign of 1960. Various federal and state programs for "disadvantaged" groups have also increased their visibility as a significant minority group. These events have in turn helped Mexican-Americans to discover themselves as an ethnic group, and with their new identity they have, like Indians, begun to demand further changes in their relationship with the dominant Anglos (see Acuna 1972; Forbes 1970; Knowlton 1975; Schmidt 1970; Studdard 1973).

Puerto Ricans. Puerto Rico became a colonial subject in 1898, when the United States took it from Spain, which had ruled the territory for nearly 400 years. The colony was first administered by the American military, then by civilian governors appointed by the president, and since 1948 by elected governors. In 1917, Puerto Ricans were granted United States citizenship; in 1948 they voted to remain under the United States as a commonwealth rather than become either one of the states or an independent nation.[3] Like Mexican-Americans, Puerto Ricans are officially classified as *whites* or *caucasians*. These changes did not, however, come as a benevolence bestowed on the Puerto Ricans by the United States; they were responses to the demands of politically conscious Puerto Ricans and probably represent the changes most acceptable to the United States rather than the aspirations of the political leaders demanding changes in their colonial status. For example, there was a small but vocal opposition to the abolition of Puerto Rican citizenship and its replacement with United States citizenship in 1917. Also, over one-third of the Puerto Rican voters in 1948 rejected commonwealth status (see McWilliams 1964; Meyerson 1972; Oliveras 1972; Senior 1972).

Most writers on Puerto Rican educational problems in the continental United States choose to emphasize that Puerto Ricans are recent immigrants to the mainland who frequently move back and forth between the mainland and Puerto Rico. The reason for the migration, the pattern of migration, and the problems of adjustment it involves need to be taken into account in studying why Puerto Ricans on the mainland do poorly in school. But Puerto Ricans are not immigrant minorities, as defined in this book, simply because, like those who truly are immigrant minorities, they migrated from somewhere else and differ from Anglo-Americans in language and culture. I suggest that their subordinate relationship to Anglo-Americans, both before and after they arrive on the mainland, contributes most significantly to their pattern of adjustment in American schools. The Puerto Rican migration

[3]Oliveras (1972) describes the commonwealth status of Puerto Rico: "Under its Commonwealth Status, Puerto Rico is a self-governing country in voluntary and close association with the United States of America based on common citizenship, common defense and free trade." He adds that "In a historic resolution adopted by the General Assembly of the United Nations on November 3, 1953, this Commonwealth was solemnly recognized as a self-governing political body [p. 247]."

to the mainland is like the migration of West Indians to Britain rather than the migration, for example, of Japanese to the United States (see Chapter 8). As citizens of the United States, Puerto Ricans expect an open reception and equal opportunities when the arrive on the mainland; and they become disappointed and disillusioned when their experiences turn out to be otherwise. This is particularly true of second-generation Puerto Ricans on the mainland, who have, like Indians and Mexican-Americans, increasingly demanded changes in their relationship with Anglo-Americans since the 1960s. They have also joined with some Puerto Ricans on the island to demand further changes in the political status of Puerto Rico.

Official Classification of whites versus Anglo-American Discriminatory Practices. Even though Mexican-Americans and Puerto Ricans are officially classified as *whites* or *caucasians*, Anglo-Americans do not usually treat them as such. Physical variations among Mexican-Americans, Puerto Ricans, and Indians, rather than the official classification, determine the attitudes and behavior shown toward them. Among Mexican-Americans, the majority are said to be *mestizos* or descendants of Indian and white (Spanish) mating; many are *mulattos*, the offspring of black and white parentage; some are *zambos*, or children of Indian and black mating; and some are more or less "full-blooded" whites (Spanish), Indians, or blacks. Thus their physical appearance varies from pure black to pure white (Nava 1970). The situation among Puerto Ricans is somewhat similar. One study of 1000 heads of households in Puerto Rico classified 608 as white, 307 as mulatto, and 80 as black, although this did not necessarily coincide with the way the Puerto Ricans classified themselves (Senior 1972:270). Indians are not officially classified as whites, but their population is just as racially mixed. For example, the Department of the Interior's tabulation of 52,908 Indian children enrolled in Bureau of Indian Affairs (BIA) schools in 1974 shows the degree of Indian blood as follows: full blood—76.9%; three-quarter blood—7.4%; one-half blood—9.9%; one-quarter blood—4.6%; and less than one-quarter blood—1.2% (U.S. Department of the Interior 1974).

Official and unofficial Anglo attitudes toward Indians, Mexican-Americans, and Puerto Ricans are heavily influenced by the folk ideologies or stereotypes supporting their historically subordinate status and by differences in the physical appearance of individual members of these groups. In the past, for instance, Indians were regarded as "simple-minded children," an uncivilized people obstructing progress and the westward move of civilization (Schmidt 1970:70). All three groups have traditionally been regarded as socially and mentally inferior. From the third decade of this century, Anglo psychologists began to "confirm" their mental inferiority "scientifically" by showing that Indians, Mexican-Americans, and Puerto Ricans did not score as high as Anglos on IQ tests. Moreover, these groups have traditionally been regarded as less then capable of managing their own affairs, much less the affairs of the wider society. Thus, until recently, Indians held few, if any, responsible positions in the Bureau of Indian Affairs; Mexican-Americans did not represent their communities in political bodies where decisions affecting them were made; and Puerto Ricans experienced a similar exclusion. In general, Anglo-American discrimination against Indians, Mexican-Americans, and Puerto Ricans, based on folk stereotypes and differences in physical appearance, manifests itself in matters of sex relationships, marriage, jobs, education, and the like. These are the same matters in which blacks experience restrictions, although to a greater degree. It is true, of course, that the wide variations in the physical appearance of Indians, Mexican-Americans, and Puerto Ricans permit a greater proportion who want to do so to pass as Anglos (e.g., by adopting Anglo names and moving to distant communities where their identities are not known) in order to overcome the social and economic barriers imposed on them by the caste system (see Nava 1970:131ff).

The Educational Implications
of Castelike Status

The lower caste status of Indians, Mexican-Americans, and Puerto Ricans affects their education in several ways. First, each group has traditionally received inferior education to prepare its members for their inferior social and technoeconomic positions in adult life. Second, they have, like blacks, faced the problem of the job ceiling; and this in turn has reinforced their inferior education and lower school performance. Like blacks, their perception of schooling is also affected by their perception of the job ceiling.

Access to Inferior Education. The experience of the Indians will illustrate the point that the castelike status of these minority groups determines the kind of education offered them at different periods.

Indian participation in formal education in the American West predates their status as a castelike minority group in the United States. They attended mission schools during their earlier contacts with Spanish settlers. The original British colonies did little to encourage formal education among the Indians; but when these colonies achieved independence, the new United States government became involved in Indian education because of its special relations with various Indian nations. Since that time, the kind of education provided for Indians has varied according to the conception of the status of Indians in American society at different times. The relationship between Indian status and the education of Indians can be seen by examining what happened in Indian education in various periods of Anglo-Indian relations.

During the Treaty Period (1788–1871), Indian tribes were treated as independent nations, and various treaties they signed with the United States contained provisions for the federal government to provide them with Western education. These provisions were usually carried out by Christian missionaries who were interested in converting and civilizing the Indians. The government supported the missionaries' efforts to use education to civilize the Indians and appropriated about $15,000 annually between 1819 and 1873 for that purpose.

The Allotment Period (1889–1924) began when most Indian tribes had been subjugated. The government's motive during this period apparently was to destroy Indian tribes as viable societies and integrate the Indians *as individuals* into the wider society. The federal government assumed that this was the best way to provide Indians with more opportunity to acquire Western civilization. One method it used to accomplish this was breaking up Indian communal lands and alloting them to individuals. Another was forcing Indian children to give up their language and way of life and learn the white middle-class language and way of life at school. Federal boarding schools were built to educate Indian children far away from their families and tribal communities. In these schools, there was an emphasis on vocational education, since it was assumed that Indians did not understand the value of work from the Anglo point of view the way Anglos did. But this strategy did not work: Indian children did not give up their tribal ways of life; and many dropped out of school after only a few years. The allotment policy also failed.

The failure of the allotment policy ushered in an era of criticism, research, and reappraisal of Indian administration policies. An overall study of the position of the Indian in American society was published in the *Meriam Report* (1928), which recommended that the land allotment policy be abandoned and that Indian tribal societies be strengthened rather than destroyed. The latter recommendation led to the establishment of Indian tribal goverments; the new conception that Indians would remain as Indians in American society led to the adoption of bilingual education, training of Indian teachers, development of in-service programs to help non-Indian teachers understand Indian cultures; some of the boarding schools were closed and many day schools were opened on the reservations.

A new policy toward Indians, the Termination Policy (1944–1960), began during World War II. It was like the policy of the allotment period in that the federal government wanted to end its special relationship with the Indians by relocating them in cities. The goal of Indian education at this time appeared to be that of making Indians better Americans rather than training them to be better Indians (National Advisory Council on Indian Education 1974). The strategies used in the allotment period were therefore reinstated, and many Indian children were transferred to distant boarding schools where they were taught to give up their Indian language and culture and learn English.

The current period of self-determination and development (1960 to the present) began in the early 1960s and has become part of the general social identity movement among America's minorities. In this period, the Indians are asserting their right to participate more fully and take the initiative in determining and implementing policies that affect their lives. The specific factors generating the movement toward self-determination are a series of studies and reports on the Indian situation published in the 1960s which criticized the termination policy of the 1940s and 1950s. These reports provided the initial basis of Indians' demands for more direct and active participation in running their own affairs. Later, various social programs of the Great Society era, such as programs under the Economic Opportunity Act (1964) and the Elementary and Secondary Education Act (1965), made it possible for Indians to show both their determination and ability to run their own affairs. The trend toward self-determination and development has influenced Indian education because many of the Great Society programs had to do with education. Indians are now playing a greater role in managing their own education; the curriculum of Indian education is also being redesigned to include aspects of Indian culture and to help Indian children achieve a more positive sense of being Indian.

The Job Ceiling and Education. Like blacks, Indians, Mexican-Americans, and Puerto Ricans in the United States have traditionally faced the job ceiling in adult life. Unfortunately, good accounts of the employment histories and experiences of these groups are rare. There are frequent references to their low occupational status with equally frequent assumptions that it is attributable to their low educational attainment. Less attention has been given to the barriers that exclude them from equal chances for employment, when compared with Anglos, and still less to the way they perceive the job ceiling. Of the three groups, information on these matters is most available for

Mexican-Americans. I therefore use this group to illustrate the nature of the job ceiling that affects all three minorities.

In a landmark study of Mexican-Americans in the Southwest, Grebler *et al.* (1970:209) found that Mexican-Americans tend to hold inferior jobs within nearly every major occupational group and that the earnings of Mexican-Americans in the same occupations are usually smaller than those of Anglo-American workers. The study also found that differences in occupational status between Mexican-Americans and Anglo-Americans are not caused merely by differences in educational attainment:

> It suffices to say here that, in general, schooling explains only part of the inferior occupational position of Mexican-Americans, though a larger part than in the case of non-whites. The unfavorable occupational patterns of [Mexican-Americans and nonwhites] result in considerable measure from factors not associated with education [p. 214].

These authors go on to say that the disproportionate representation of Mexican-Americans in menial and low-level jobs is attributable to "employee selection process," an aspect of the job ceiling. In the absence of adequate data, Grebler *et al.* were unable to provide a detailed history of the job ceiling against Mexican-Americans in the Southwest, but they suggest that historically there were similarities between the experiences of Mexican-Americans and those of blacks: Mexican-Americans, like blacks, made little occupational progress before World War II, when labor shortages forced Anglo-Americans to hire them for jobs from which they had previously been excluded. After the war, their advancement slowed down considerably until the social and economic reforms of the 1960s.

Schmidt's study (1970) of Mexican-American employment in the Southwest corroborates the findings of Grebler and his associates. Schmidt observes that Mexican-Americans were traditionally regarded as casual workers; and in the 1930s, when new industries such as petroleum, metal fabricating, and transportation began, they made only insignificant occupational gains. Their limited participation in the new industries was not attributable to lack of training, since Anglo-American Texas "farm boys," who also had no prior training, gained entry into the new jobs and received their training on the job. Mexican-Americans and other minorities were confined to "laborer jobs in mining, smelting, and low-paid operative jobs in the garment trades, textiles, and similar industries [p. 9]."

The focus of Schmidt's study was, however, the analysis of occupational data collected in 20 counties by the Bureau of the Census in mid-March 1966 and the first employment reports submitted to the

Equal Employment Opportunities Commission by companies in those 20 counties. The analysis of the companies' reports revealed an interesting pattern: Mexican-Americans and other minorities achieved "a considerably higher representation in skilled blue-collar craftsmen jobs than . . . in the least skilled white-collar jobs of clerical, office, and sales workers, which make up about one-half of all white-collar jobs [1970:13]." Their underrepresentation in the white-collar jobs was attributable not to lack of training but to the job ceiling. Schmidt's analysis of the Census Bureau data revealed the same kind of underrepresentation in white-collar jobs, especially for Mexican-American males. Furthermore, like Grebler and his associates, Schmidt found that even in the low occupational category of operatives, where Mexican-Americans were overrepresented, they mainly held the less desirable jobs (p. 19).

I argued previously that the job ceiling against blacks contributes to their lower school performance in many ways and thus helps to prepare them educationally for primarily low-status and menial jobs. The same argument can be made in regard to Indians, Mexican-Americans, and Puerto Ricans. American society and its school systems maintain, as they do in the case of blacks, that these groups need good educations to obtain the better jobs and social position enjoyed by Anglos. But neither society nor the schools provide them with the real opportunity to do so. The schools provide them with inferior education, and society uses the job ceiling to prevent them from benefiting more fully from their education (Education: Carter 1970; National Advisory Council on Indian Education 1974. Employment opportunities: Schmidt 1970). The policies and practices within schools prepare most of them primarily for low-status social and occupational positions in life. The devices by which the schools accomplish this are the same mechanisms, both gross and subtle, that schools with a majority of black students use in preparing blacks for inferior roles. A number of studies have documented these mechanisms in predominantly Indian schools (National Council on Indian Education 1974); in predominantly Mexican-American schools (Carter 1970; Grebler et al. 1970; Parsons 1965; Sanchez 1965; USCCR 1971a, 1972a, 1973a, 1974b; U.S. Senate, Select Committee 1970a); and in schools in which Puerto Ricans are in the majority (Moore 1964; U.S. Senate, Select Committee 1970b).

The Job Ceiling and Perception of Schooling. Besides its influence on the educational policies and practices of Indian, Mexican-American, and Puerto Rican schools, the job ceiling also affects the way these minorities perceive their schooling and their efforts in school. Although this problem has not been systematically studied, we can safely assume that these groups know and believe that they do not have chances for employment, advancement on the job, good wages, and other benefits of education equal to those of Anglos. They also know and believe that the primary reason for this lack of equal opportunity is discrimination against them. The fact that we do not have ethnographic or other documentation of how they perceive their schooling in relation to the job ceiling does not mean that the two are unrelated. In any case, one recent study suggests a possible unconscious link between them.

The study in question is that of Blair (1971, 1972), who investigated the employment and schooling experiences of Mexican-Americans in Santa Clara County, California. He compared the benefits, measured by wages, received by Anglo-Americans and Mexican-Americans of the same levels of education. He compared two paired groups of Mexican-Americans and Anglo-Americans based on areas of residence. One pair lived in predominantly Mexican-American barrios, and the other pair lived outside the barrios. In each case, Blair found that the Mexican-American group earned lower wages than the Anglo-American group, when the two groups had the same level of education. Among those living in the barrios, the Anglo-Americans earned $880 more per year than Mexican-Americans with the same level of education; among those living outside the barrios, the Anglo-Americans earned $1713 more. Blair calls the wage differential a "schooling penalty" against the Mexican-Americans. He points out that the average difference in the wages, the *schooling penalty*, is equivalent to what an average person in the county would expect to earn by acquiring an additional 2½ years of schooling. The study also shows that this schooling penalty is greater for younger Mexican-Americans than for older members of the group (Blair 1971:82–85).

What is an even more significant aspect of Blair's findings is that the schooling penalty is greater for Mexican-Americans who graduate from high school or college than for those who drop out short of graduation. That is, Mexican-Americans who stay long enough or persevere hard enough to graduate from high school or college experience a greater earning gap between them and their Anglo peers, whereas Mexican-Americans who drop out of high school or college experience less of a gap. Blair notes that in this way the caste system is transmitting different messages to Anglo and Mexican-American students. To the Anglo student the message is consistent with the American ideology that more education and hard work in school lead to greater self-improvement: It tells the Anglo student that he can expect increasing rewards from society if he stays long enough and works hard enough in school to obtain a high school diploma or a college degree. The Mexican-American student as well as castelike minority students in general receive the contrary message that they can expect to earn wages a little closer to what their Anglo peers earn if they drop out of school rather than stay long enough and work hard enough to obtain a high school diploma or college degree. Blair suggests that Mexican-American and other castelike minority people probably realize, albeit unconsciously, that additional schooling or graduation from high school or college brings less returns, when compared with the resources and effort they have to invest in the schooling. Perhaps because of these contradictory messages, castelike minority students adjust differently to schooling than do the Anglo students. Without implying that minority students should drop out of school, Blair says:

> This explanation of the dropout phenomenon would put less emphasis on socio-cultural determinants of school-taking behavior, such as childhood conditioning of parents' SES [socio-economic status], students' motivations and aspirations, educational quality, and academic ability (at the same time recognizing their partial role). It would, instead, place greater stress on the observed fact of real ethnic money-wage [and job] discrimination in the employment market for equal age and school-attainment qualifications.
>
> Apparently, only efforts to ensure that employers and unions pay employed Mexican-Americans of given school attainment and age the same money as their Euro-American counterparts and provide equal access to the same kind of work will close the ethnic income gap and equalize return investment in schooling [1972:98–99].

In other words, because the job ceiling (with its attendant income ceiling) stultifies the schooling efforts of minority people, the remedy lies in eliminating the job and income ceiling, not in changing the minority people.

That Indians, Mexican-Americans and Puerto Ricans, like blacks, perceive and react to the barriers against them in future employment and social positions probably accounts for the commonly observed phenomenon which Carter calls "mental withdrawal" (1970). Caste-minority children may or may not lag behind their Anglo peers in academic achievement in the first two or three grades, but during the intermediate grades, their performance begins to drop sharply, while that of Anglo children increases (see Carter 1970:178; Fuchs and Havighurst 1973:126; Sexton 1972). Bryde (cited in Fuchs and Havighurst 1973) reports that among Indians a sharp drop in achievement begins to occur at about grade 6 or grade 7, at the age of puberty, when the children become more aware of the "Indianness" and begin to feel more alienated, with the result that they lose self-confidence. They subsequently stop trying to do well in school, and thus their achievement drops. Fuchs and Havighurst argue (1973:128ff) that the drop in the Indian children's school achievement occurs well before the age of puberty, and they go on to explain this in terms of environmental factors, such as family background and culture conflict.

Carter (1970: 136–137) has reviewed various explanations of the phenomenon of declining achievement among Mexican-Americans, which he says is associated with "mental withdrawal." His preferred explanation links it to the nature of the education system or school itself. He seems to imply that the children do relatively well in the early grades because at that stage school curriculum and authority structure are flexible enough to make them enjoy school. From the intermediate grades, however, the curriculum becomes progressively more rigidly defined and controlled, and school becomes less relevant to children. At this point, their background becomes the crucial factor as to whether their academic achievement will drop or go up. He explains the ability of middle-class children to maintain or increase their achievement by saying that a middle-class background provides them the kind of support, reinforcement, and reward that generates increased academic achievement; the lower-class and minority children's background, on the other hand, fails to provide such stimuli, resulting in a drop in the academic achievement of lower-class children. Anglo middle-class children apparently persevere in school and do well, even though schooling per se is essentially uninteresting and unrewarding, according to this explanation, because their parents teach them to expect their reward in "future social success." In contrast, "poor parents may not support the idea that school is a series of steps that must be climbed regardless of the boredom or unpleasantness involved, nor are they able to guarantee their children significant future social rewards for perseverance in and graduation from school [Carter 1970:137]."

Although Carter's explanation has some merit, it fails to explain why non-middle-class, immigrant peasant minorities, including those from Mexico, do well in school and do not exhibit "mental withdrawal." Any explanation of the success of such immigrant children and the failure of Indian, Mexican-American, and Puerto Rican children, must account for the fundamental difference between the latter groups and the Anglo-American middle class in terms of experience with regard to jobs and social position under the caste system. If Anglo-American middle-class parents teach their children that they should persevere in school regardless of the boredom and unpleasantness involved *because they will be rewarded in the future with desirable social positions and jobs,* the behavior [teaching] of these parents is motivated by a belief system derived from the actual experience of white middle-class people which they "naturally" transmit to their children. If the Anglo-American middle-class children accept their parents' advice or teaching and behave accordingly, it is also because they know from the experiences of their parents and other adults in their communities that their success in school will surely bring social and occupational rewards. Now the experiences of Indian, Mexican-American, and Puerto Rican parents are different: Education has not usually brought the same desirable social and occupational rewards; and there is no reason to expect that the different experiences of the minority-group parents *will generate the attitudes, beliefs, and teaching about schooling* characteristic of Anglo-American middle-class parents. Nor does one have to be a member of the Anglo-American middle-class to share its attitudes, beliefs, and behavior. Immigrant parents, whether or not they are of middle-class background, tend to have similar instrumental attitudes, partly because they want their children to be educated in order to get better jobs than their parents and partly because they have not become disillusioned by repeated failure to achieve self-improvement through education because of caste barriers.

It should be added that children do not always persevere in school simply because their parents teach them to do so; nor do children always give in to peer-group pressures because their parents fail to teach them about future rewards through perseverance in school. Immigrant parents whose children achieve school success may have no good understanding of how American schools operate and may lack the knowledge of Anglo-American middle-class parents to teach their children what is required to succeed in American schools. Immigrant parents are not relevant models of school success or failure for their children. What is significant is not what these parents (or any other parents) can teach their children but what both parents and children believe or expect they can gain from their educational efforts. Castelike minority children, on the other hand, learn from the experiences of their parents and other adult members of their communities that education does not always lead to good social and occupational positions in adult life and that the reason for this is that they are members of caste minorities, that they are Indians, Mexican-Americans, Puerto Ricans, or blacks. As they get older, they are likely to compare their future chances with those of their Anglo-American peers, and they are likely to ask why they should work as hard now in school for smaller future rewards. Under these conditions they are more susceptible to peer-group influences than Anglo-American middle-class children. In other words, peer influence or pressure becomes an important link to school failure only when mental withdrawal from schoolwork has already taken place because of perceived limited future chances for employment opportunities and other benefits supposedly based on school success or education.

Summary and Conclusions

Like blacks, Indians, Mexican-Americans, and Puerto Ricans do less well in school than Anglo-Americans. Some people use the data from the Coleman study to show that Indians and Mexican-Americans are not the lowest achievers. Such comparisons have little meaning in view of the high dropout rates among these groups. Nor is maintaining that Indians, Mexican-Americans, and Puerto Ricans do less well than Anglo-Americans because of cultural and language differences an adequate explanation, since it appears that native Mexicans and Puerto Ricans, who differ even more from Anglo-Americans in terms of culture and language, tend to have more nearly white middle-class types of instrumental attitudes toward schooling and probably do better in school than second generation Mexican-Americans and American-born Puerto Ricans. I have suggested in this chapter that Indians, Mexican-Americans, and Puerto Ricans are, like blacks, castelike minorities and that their lower school performance is an adaptation to the requirements of their social and occupational positions in society. This does not mean that cultural and language differences are not relevant; what it does mean is that their castelike status makes it more difficult for them to overcome any problems created by cultural and language differences than it is for immigrant minorities. As castelike minorities, they have had access mainly to inferior education; they have experienced the job ceiling and other caste barriers that prevent them from maximizing their efforts in school in terms of future social and economic rewards; they have, generally speaking, responded to these barriers with "mental withdrawal," failing to persevere in their schoolwork. Although I have not explored such matters in this chapter, it is possible that the job ceiling and other caste barriers affect the institutions (e.g., family and status mobility systems) and personal attributes or skills (e.g., linguistic, cognitive, and motivational) of Indians, Mexican-Americans, and Puerto Ricans in a way that further contributes to their lower school performance.

The educational problems described thus far in this book are not unique to blacks, Indians, Mexican-Americans, and Puerto Ricans living in the United States. The same problems exist among castelike minorities wherever they are found in other societies. To substantiate this proposition in a rather limited way, we examine the educational experiences of castelike minorities in Great Britain, New Zealand, India, Japan, and Israel in Part II.

II

CROSS-CULTURAL STUDIES

Some issues in minority education in the United States will not be easily resolved so long as those debating them are unwilling to test their hypotheses against similar situations in other cultures. This is particularly true of the debate between those who believe that black–white differences in IQ test scores are caused by genetic differences and those who believe they are caused by differences in environmental influence. In spite of the significance the two groups attach to the issue and to their positions, and in spite of their claims to sophistication in research techniques, American educational psychologists on either side of the debate have not had the courage to test their hypotheses in diverse cultures with castelike minorities. Where studies bearing on the matter have been carried out, they have generally shown that the minority groups do not perform as well as the dominant groups both on the so-called intelligence tests and on scholastic achievement tests. This is true regardless of the racial affiliations of the minority and dominant groups involved.

Chapters 8, 9, 10, 11, and 12 examine various problems associated with minority school performance in other societies, namely, India, Israel, and Japan (where the minority and majority groups belong to the same races) and the United Kingdom and New Zealand (where the minority and majority groups belong to different races). The materials presented in these chapters generally confirm the findings on black education in the United States, that the school performance of caste-like minorities is much influenced by the castelike stratification system. In each of the five cases, we first show that the relationship between the dominant group and the minority is formed by a castelike principle that is not taken into account by a pervasive ideology of equality of opportunity through education which is based primarily on the experiences of the dominant group. Second, we describe the contrasting experiences of the castelike minority group. Chapter 13, which concludes Part II, compares the findings on the education of the caste-like minorities in the six societies studies, including the United States.

8

West Indians in Britain

Minority groups in Great Britain can be divided into several broad categories. First, there are the indigenous minorities such as the Scots, the Welsh, and the Northern Irish Roman Catholics. Except for the last, these are autonomous minorities. Second are the "white immigrants." The earliest of these groups are the Southern Irish, most of whom are Roman Catholics, and the Jews. The more recent white immigrants have arrived only since World War II from various Eastern, Western, and Southern European countries.

These latter immigrants fall into two groups: (a) political exiles and refugees such as the Poles, Ukranians, Balts, Czechs, Rumanians, Yugoslavs, and Hungarians; and (b) economically motivated labor migrants such as the Germans, Austrians, Italians, Spaniards and Greeks (Krausz 1971:99–100; Patterson 1968:20–24; 1969:2–5; Rose 1969:97).

The third category of minority groups in Britain are the "colored immigrants," made up of three principal groups: West Indians, East Indians, and Pakistanis (now including those from Bangladesh). Other colored immigrants come from Africa, the Middle East, and Southeast Asia. The three major colored communities in Britain differ from one another just as much as they differ from the dominant group. All the colored minorities are, however, accorded lower caste status, although the West Indians are most like black Americans in this respect and in their response to their situation. Unlike the other colored groups, West Indians came to Britain originally expecting to settle permanently, and the West Indian community in Britain has always included a sizable number of school age children. For these reasons, the following analysis focuses on West Indians rather than on the colored groups in general.

West Indians in British Society

Prior to World War II only a small number of West Indians from the British colonial possessions had settled in Britain. Their numbers increased rapidly after the war, beginning with many of the 700 soldiers who had served in the Royal Air Force in Britain and many of the 345 skilled craftsmen recruited from the West Indies to work in war-related industries. The labor shortages in Britain after the war further contributed to the immigration of West Indians, as British industries were forced to recruit thousands of workers from the islands. In fact, up to 1962, when Britain attempted to control foreign immigration, West Indian immigration was generally in direct response to the demands of the British labor market (see Davidson 1966: 104–120; Glass 1961:31; Krausz 1971:110; Patterson 1969:6; Rose 1969:419–433).

West Indians constitute the largest group of colored immigrants in Britain; and over 60% of them come from Jamaica. As in the case of the Indians and Pakistanis, the main reasons for their emigration are population pressures and the desire to improve their economic status. West Indians who immigrate, usually have higher educational and vocational skills than the general population of their home countries. The Parlimentary Select Committee (1973:59) reported an estimated illiteracy rate in Jamaica of about 25% in 1973; but Glass (1961:31–32) reported that illiteracy among some 16,089 immigrants in 1954 and 1955 was less than 2%—the test of illiteracy used being the ability of the immigrant to sign his name. A slightly higher rate of illiteracy is reported by Patterson (1969:145) who interviewed men who were collecting their passports in Kingston, Jamaica over a period of seven weeks in 1961; she found that 4% had no education at all.

Unlike immigrants from India and Pakistan, those from the Caribbean have always been individualistic rather than organized. No sponsors are required, either in Britain or in the Caribbean.[1] Generally, individuals finance their own passage, although they may receive some help from their families. From the beginning, West Indian immigration has included a high proportion of females and a significant number of children. Some of the households in Britain are headed by women, but the nuclear family consisting of father, mother, and children appears to be the norm. In contrast to Indians and Pakistanis, most West Indian women work, whether they are married or not and whether they have children or not.

West Indians are linguistically and culturally closer to the British than are the other two colored immigrant groups; they speak English as their first language, practice Christianity, and share other aspects of British culture. They also identify strongly with Britain, which they regard as their mother country. They regard themselves as British subjects, and not as foreigners; to them, a move to Britain is a kind of internal migration, just like a move from one part of the United Kingdom to another. They have come to Britain to stay and usually they have high expectations for full and immediate acceptance by the British.

Their communities in Britain are neither cohesive nor exclusive like those of the Indians and the Pakistanis. But these factors have not made them more acceptable than the other colored minorities to the dominant group (see Braithwaite 1968; Davidson 1966:104–120; Glass 1961:31; Krausz 1971:110; Patterson 1969:6; Rose 1969:419–433). In fact, the social and occupational barriers against West Indians are considerably more rigid.

To understand why the West Indians are kept in such a low position, it is essential to look at the role of color in British social values, a problem which has just begun to be acknowledged by British social scientists. Previously the latter regarded the problems of West Indian adjustment in Britain as of the same order as those of white immigrants. They stacked these problems within the framework of the "immigrant–host relation cycle" theory, which states basically that prejudice and discrimination against West Indians are part of the

---

[1]The immigration from some countries, like Pakistan, was highly organized and depended on a system of sponsorship and patronage. The sponsor was usually someone already in Britain who headed an all-male household or dormitory house. The sponsorship consists of sending money to pay the cost of bringing a male relative to Britain to work. The new immigrant is required to join the dormitory house, work to pay his debt to the sponsor, and send money back to Pakistan to support his family. He is also encouraged to save enough money to bring another male relative to Britain. Members of a dormitory house often form a work gang.

British cultural norm of discriminating against lower class people, strangers, and foreigners. According to the theory, as West Indians improved their economic status and learned appropriate British attitudes and behavior the prejudice and discrimination against them would disappear (Patterson 1968:2–4). But some social scientists recognized that the barriers against West Indians in terms of social participation, housing, jobs, and the like were caused by color.

The importance of color is more clearly recognized in every empirical study or speculative analysis of the position of West Indians (and other colored immigrants) in Britain (see Banton 1958; Braithwaite 1968; Davidson 1966; Goldman and Taylor 1966; Krausz 1971; Little 1968; Patterson 1968, 1969; Rose 1969). Various surveys, including Gallup polls, show varying degrees of prejudice against the colored immigrants (Goldman and Taylor 1966). A 1969 survey of race relations in Britain, commissioned by the Institute of Race Relations, began with a careful appraisal of the experiences of immigrants and blacks in the United States. This analysis led the project to reject the immigrant–host relationship framework which had dominated most of the previous studies of race relations in Britain. Rose (1969) states: "We felt that we must consider the possibility that color generates a response which cannot be satisfactorily explained in terms of class or the fact of strangeness [p. 6]." The primacy of color in determining the response of the British to the West Indian minorities is fully illustrated in a study of a colored settlement in Cardiff which was established immediately after World War I. The study, cited by Rose (1969:487 ff.), showed that few of the colored people—whatever their generation—had been able to leave their ghetto community or make significant advances in education and jobs. In contrast, European immigrants who arrived after World War II, although they experienced initial hardships, have achieved significant social and economic mobility and become fully integrated with the native white population.

Krausz (1971:118–122) also compares the experiences of white and colored immigrants and concludes that although both groups experienced social and economic barriers when they first arrived, the white immigrants have made greater social and economic progress. He attributes this difference partly to the fact that the colored immigrants are "newcomers," partly to the fact that the newcomers came with less resourcefulness and training, but mainly to the fact that they are discriminated against because of their color. Referring to the experience of the American blacks, Krausz (1971) notes that in Britain color plays a major role in retarding the progress of the colored immigrants. But he also thinks that Britain is not yet stratified by color, and that a "caste line" does not yet exist because "some colored people are in the top reaches of its (British) social scale; but (Britain) does have a 'color line' which prevents a quick adjustment to a 'normal' social class distribution among the new immigrants [pp. 120–121]." Krausz presents no evidence to show that some colored people are in the top reaches of the British social scale. Moreover, the data from the older settlements of minority immigrants certainly show that the colored minorities were disproportionately represented in the lower reaches of the British social scale but not because they had only recently arrived.

This prejudice and discrimination against the colored immigrants and the consequent hostilities between the white and the colored communities have resulted in two types of legislative actions: those intended to curtail the growth of colored populations and those intended to end the exclusion of the colored people from certain public facilities, such as hotels and boarding houses, and from housing and jobs and the like (Hill 1970; Rose 1969).

In conclusion, the available evidence strongly suggests that there is a color–caste stratification in Britain. Although the inferior position of the colored minorities is not maintained by a formal law, the stratification system contains many features associated with the color–caste system found in America and in South Africa (which goes a step further, to legalize discrimination). Whites of all social classes in Britain generally regard themselves as superior to the colored minorities, whatever the educational and occupational status of the latter. Intermarriage between whites and colored sometimes takes place, but the offspring of such marriages cannot affiliate with the dominant white group. Associated with the system of color–caste stratification are all kinds of stereotypes used to justify the advantages of the superior white caste and the disadvantages of the inferior colored caste. How this color–caste stratification influences West Indian education in Britain is discussed later. As a background to that discussion, let us look at the role of education in the British system of social mobility.

Education and Opportunity in Britain

It is widely believed in Britain that one's education determines one's position in adult society, particularly one's position in the occupational hierarchy. The people at the top of the hierarchy, like those at the bottom, are believed to have earned their respective places through education (Banks 1968:41). Among those without university education, the ability to achieve significant social mobility also depends on the *type* of secondary school attended. To obtain a university degree or complete other forms of higher education further enhances one's chances of getting a more desirable social and occupational position.

Because education is believed to have such an enormous influence on the status mobility system in Britain, several efforts have been made throughout the twentieth century to reform the British education system so that various forms of education and schools would be available to all groups, including West Indians.

Up to the early part of the twentieth century, there were two distinct systems of education in England, one for the working or lower class and the other for the middle and upper classes. The two systems were called elementary education and secondary education, respectively. Transfer from the elementary system to the secondary was possible for only a few working-class children who were considered to have exceptional ability and who "showed promise of successful assimilation to the middle classes (Banks 1968:46)." There were, however, a number of postelementary schools to which working class pupils could go by passing examinations administered at the age of twelve. Some working-class pupils selected for such schools received scholarships (Lacey 1970:5). But these postelementary schools were not as prestigious as the secondary grammar schools, nor did they prepare working-class students for higher education or university training, as did the latter. Attending the secondary grammar schools thus had distinct advantages: Graduates had more prestige; they had better opportunities for employment and promotion to high-status occupations; and they also qualified for university education.

A number of changes introduced both before and after World War I now make it possible for more working-class students to attend the grammar and other types of secondary schools on the basis of age, ability, and aptitude.

Today formal schooling in England is divided into three main stages: primary, secondary, and higher education. Preschool education is neither universal nor free nor compulsory. Beyond this, schooling is compulsory between the ages of five and fifteen. Primary school education is relatively uniform, although within a given educational district schools vary in quality and tend to be ranked. The proportion of the students in a given school passing the 11-plus examination largely determines the standing of the school in a district's public image (Lacey 1970:34). Middle-class parents often try to register their children in schools where more pupils are successful in the 11-plus examinations.

At the secondary school level, the education system is entirely selective. The selection into grammar, technical, comprehensive, and modern secondary schools is based on an examination taken at the age of eleven, consisting of tests of intelligence and achievement in English and arithmetic (Floud and Halsey 1961:86). The "superior" pupils go to the grammar and technical schools; others go to secondary modern and comprehensive schools. According to Floud and Halsey (1961), each of the four types of secondary schools "has more or less specialized relations with institutions of further education and [with] the occupational structure [p. 84]." Most students attending secondary modern and comprehensive schools and, to some extent, technical secondary schools tend to leave school after reaching the mandatory age of 15. Most of them go into unskilled and semiskilled jobs; some obtain apprenticeships leading to skilled crafts, and a few obtain minor clerical positions. Many technical and some grammar school pupils leave at the age of 16 to enter apprenticeship programs leading to skilled crafts; some start training for professional qualification in law, accountancy, surveying, and the like; and a few begin full-time employment. The superiority of grammar school education is shown by the fact that more grammar school students remain in school longer (to the age of 18) and that they have better opportunities to attend a university, where they train for administrative and professional jobs. Other grammar school graduates go into higher white-collar occupations in banks, insurance offices, civil service, and the like. Even those who attended but did not complete grammar school are able to obtain white-collar jobs (Floud and Halsey 1961:87).

The reforms described above have made the British education system more open than it was in 1900, so that more people are able to use formal education to achieve social and occupational mobility. Members of the working class, however, are still not able to do so to the same degree as those of the middle and upper classes; the former are still underrepresented among those selected for the grammar schools and other superior training institutions. Among the colored immigrants, particularly the West Indians, the situation is even worse.

The Education of West Indians in Britain

West Indians form the largest single colored minority in British schools. The government reported that in January 1972 there were about 280,000 children of immigrant communities in British schools. Of these, 40% were West Indians; Indians constituted 20%, Pakistanis 10%, Africans 10%, and other 20%.

West Indian students in Britain may be divided into those born in the West Indies and those born in Britain. Sometimes the latter are sent to the West Indies to be looked after by relatives and then brought back to Britain when they are about 10 years old or more. These are often referred to as "remittance children" who, like the immigrant children born in the West Indies, usually receive some of their early education in the Caribbean before entering school in Britain (Parliamentary Select Committee 1973:47).

A number of studies (Parliamentary Select Committee 1973:58–65; Rose 1969:45–46) indicate that there are both similarities and differences between education in the West Indies and education in Britain, the former being derived to some extent from the latter. Some of these similarities and differences serve as a background to the problems West Indians encounter when they go to school in Britain. Schools in the West Indies, like those in Britain, use English as the medium of instruction; but the English of the West Indian schools is different from the English spoken by West Indians at home. Schools in both Britain and the West Indies tend to use the same textbooks, and the teachers in the West Indies are said to have values typical of the British middle class. On the other hand, these teachers are not so well prepared for their profession as teachers in Britain, and at the primary school level, their classes are usually too large to permit effective teaching. The classroom participation of their pupils is also more limited than that of pupils in British schools.

In the West Indies, many children either do not complete primary school or do so much later than is the case in Britain. As in Britain, secondary school education is very selective: There are only a few places available, so that many who desire secondary education cannot find places to attend; furthermore, it is too expensive for most families. In recent years, some West Indian governments have made concerted efforts to increase opportunities for secondary education for their people. Thus West Indian parents who immigrate to Britain are familiar with some aspects of British education, as are West Indian children who already have had some schooling at home.

West Indian children born in Britain and those brought there at an early age usually enter and proceed through the British education system in the same way as native white children. That is, they begin school at the age of five and, on the basis of their performance in the 11-plus examination, proceed to the various types of secondary schools. Until recently, those who arrived from the West Indies with some education were assumed to be English speaking and placed in various classes on the basis of the results of standardized tests.

Up to 1965, neither segregation nor integration of colored and white children was a major issue of public debate. In fact, there was generally no attempt to document or debate, either publicly or in scholarly works, any deliberate policies to provide West Indians and other colored immigrants with inferior educations. This does not mean that colored immigrants received equal educations. Caste barriers, for instance, restricted West Indians to slum and ghetto residence, where the schools are typically substandard. Within these schools, many subtle devices, such as low teacher expectations and attitudes, the use of unsuitable standardized tests for assessing children's mental abilities, misclassification, and labeling, were utilized to reinforce the inferior education of West Indians.

The Education Gap. A topic of much discussion in Britain today is the fact that colored pupils, especially West Indians, are not doing as well in school as the native white pupils. Many writers talk about the problem of the colored pupils but present almost no statistical evidence to show the extent to which the problem exists, i.e., the extent of the difference in school performance between colored and native white pupils. The Department of Education and Science does not include information on school performance by ethnic origin in its annual census, and information on the actual school performance of West Indian pupils in Britain is therefore both sparse and unsystematized.

Such information as has been pieced together on the subject is predictable: Immigrant pupils, particularly West Indian pupils, are substantially underrepresented in the selective schools, especially in the grammar schools; on most standardized achievement and IQ tests, they score lower than English children. Their lower scores on such tests are usually explained by the test administrators as a result of their lack of competence in English (Goldman and Taylor 1966:168–174; see also Bowker 1968:64–67; Burgin and Edson 1967:65–76; Haynes 1971:14–15, 25–28, 72–78; Houghton 1966:147–156; Rose 1969:479–481, 698, 708; Parliamentary Select Committee 1973:13, 35–40).

The most detailed information on the school performance of West Indian children concerns their disproportionate representation in the schools and classes for the educationally subnormal (ESN) at both the primary and secondary levels. According to the report of the Parliamentary Select Committee (1973:38), some 5500 immigrant pupils were enrolled in special schools, mostly schools for the retarded, in England and Wales in 1971. Of these children, 70% were of West Indian origin. The figures varied according to regions. In greater London, for example, 25% of all West Indian children were in the schools and classes for the retarded, although nationally only 7% of West Indian children were in such classes and schools. In one London borough, Brent, West Indian children represented about 60% of the children in a primary school for the educationally subnormal, and over 70% of the children in a secondary school for such children. In another London borough, Haringey, West Indian children accounted for 25% of the retarded children, although they made up less than 10% of the school population. A similar high representation of West Indian children among the educationally subnormal is reported for Sheffield, but the figures for other cities are much lower. Even those West Indian pupils who are not in special schools and classes tend to be concentrated at the bottom streams of the regular classes in a given grade.

Not only do West Indian children perform less well than English children, they also perform less well than other immigrant children. Rose (1969:480) reports, for example, that a study by the Inner London Education Authority in 1966 found that among the 10-year-olds, 85% of the West Indian children were rated below the median in mathematics, compared to 68% of the Indian and Pakistani children. The Parliamentary Select Committee (1973) made a similar observation regarding the representation of West Indian and other immigrant children in the schools and classes for the educationally subnormal:

> While all these statistics should . . . be treated with some reserve, they reveal that in some parts of Greater London, and in Greater London alone, the number of West Indian children in ESN schools is wholly disproportionate both to the number of other immigrant children in ENS schools and to the West Indian population [p. 38].

West Indian children perform less well than English children, at both the primary and secondary school levels. They have comparatively little chance of attending the more selective secondary grammar schools. This reduces their chances of obtaining higher education and training for the more desirable occupations in the nonmanual labor sector.

Explaining the Gap. A significant number of West Indian children have been attending British schools since the middle of the 1950s. The scholastic gap between them and English children was not recognized as a problem until the influx of non-English-speaking pupils from India, Pakistan, and Southern Europe (e.g., Greek and Turkish Cypriots) after measures were introduced in 1962 to control immigration from the Commonwealth countries. Even since then, most of the efforts to understand the problems of the colored pupils have been focused on non-English-speaking pupils, so that there are hardly any systematic studies of the causes of lower school performance among West Indian children (see Glass 1961:64; Burgin and Edson 1967:88; Rose 1969:281–285). The following explanations have therefore been pieced together from the reports of social scientists and others working with

the schools to develop programs for immigrant pupils, from commen-
taries by social scientists and others on the responses of government
and local education authorities to the influx of colored immigrant
pupils in the 1960s, and from the education report of the Parliamentary
Select Committee on Race Relations and Immigration (1973). The explanations fall into five broad categories: language, culture, race relations, ability (i.e., IQ), and job ceiling.

Writing in 1961 (p. 64), Glass noted that the most important factor
in teaching West Indian pupils in British schools was the absence of a
language barrier. The consensus now, however, is that West Indian
children in British schools do have a language barrier which is probably more serious than that of the non-English-speaking Indian and
Pakistani pupils because it is hidden: The ostensibly English-speaking
West Indian pupils speak an English dialect, different from the language of the British schools (see Parliamentary Select Committee
1973:12; Bowker 1968:173–174; Hill 1970:77; Houghton 1966:152–153;
Patterson 1969:268 n. 1, 270 n. 2; Rose 1969:280–285). Two types of
language problems—dialect language and inadequate language
development—have now been identified.

The language barrier associated with dialect differences is characteristic of native West Indian pupils. These children speak a patois, a
Creole dialect that differs from the standard English of the British
schools in vocabulary, grammatical structure, and intonation (Burgin
and Edson 1967:89; Parliamentary Select Committee 1973:12). On the
other hand, inadequate language development is said to be characteristic of second- and third-generation West Indian pupils (Parliamentary
Select Committee 1973:9). It is said that these children do not fully
develop their language skills because they do not have sufficient contact with adults who could stimulate their language development,
since most of their mothers work. According to the committee report, a
West Indian lecturer in education "estimated that some 95% of West
Indian children born in this country needed special language treatment
[p. 9]." If such a situation exists, it necessarily creates learning problems for West Indians born in Britain. There are, however, no studies to
confirm the existence of this type of language problem or the nature of
its influence on school achievement.

Cultural disadvantage ranks next to the language barrier among the
explanations given for the lower performance of West Indian children.
The list of the cultural disadvantages varies according to different
writers, but the following are often included: West Indians have different attitudes toward school, teachers, and learning; West Indian parents do not give their children adequate preschool training; the expec-

tations of West Indian families in Britain in matters of discipline are in conflict with those of British schools; West Indian parents are not involved in their children's education; West Indian pupils have high expectations which are not matched with efforts; the children suffer from "multiple deprivations," including poverty, inadequate housing, and the like (see Parliamentary Select Committee 1973:15–17; Bowker 1968:19–20; Burgin and Edson 1967:20, 90–92; Goldman and Taylor 1966:170–171; Hill 1970:77–78; Rose 1969:284). There are, however, very few empirical studies to confirm the existence of these putative cultural disadvantages or the way in which they influence the school performance of West Indian children.

Discrimination and prejudice are also said to affect the school performance of West Indian children. Rose (1969) points out that these factors can affect the education of West Indian children even when they do not originate directly with their teachers or the school system but in the wider society. "The problems of discrimination and expressions of racial prejudice in the wider society must inevitably affect the relationship which can be formed in the classroom, between pupils of different racial origin, and between teacher and pupil [pp. 284–285]." Racial problems in the schools are further complicated by what many educators see as unreasonable demands on the schools from society with regard to race issues. As racial tensions have increased in the wider society since the 1960s, there has been a tendency to look upon the schools as the place to solve these problems by teaching children proper attitudes which would promote the "integration" or "assimilation" of the immigrants and the growth of a "multi-racial society [Parliamentary Select Committee 1973:20–25]."

The placement of a disproportionate number of West Indian children either in schools and classes for the retarded or at the bottom streams of the regular classes is usually based on their performance on standardized tests designed for English children. Given the emphasis on grading and selection in the British education system and given the prevailing stereotype about the intellectual superiority of the white race, the lower scores of West Indian pupils were not regarded as a problem until recently. As Bowker (1968) notes, it was sometimes argued that colored people were less intelligent than white people. "Put in terms of racial stereotypes, the argument [held] that Caucasians [were] more intelligent than either Negroids or Mongoloids [pp. 64–66]."

But the influx of non-English-speaking immigrant pupils forced some reevaluation of the test scores of different groups. It was soon realized that for children who did not speak English and came from radically different cultural backgrounds, the standardized tests for English children had little validity (Burgin and Edison 1967:65–68). With increasing recognition in recent years that West Indian pupils do have language problems, there has been a growing skepticism about the validity of their scores on the standardized tests (see Goldman and Taylor 1966; Houghton 1965; Vernon 1965a; Parliamentary Select Committee 1973). The present trend is to interpret their low performance on the standardized tests as a result of "hidden language" problems, as well as "cultural handicaps [Parliamentary Select Committee 1973:13, 38]."

Closing the Gap. Just as the recent discovery of West Indian school problems came as a result of efforts to deal with the problems of the more recent non-English-speaking immigrant pupils, so also the policies and efforts to improve the school performance of West Indian pupils are both recent and inseparable from those directed toward improving the school performance of these other colored pupils.

Since the early 1960s, a number of national and local bodies have been involved in dealing with immigrant pupils in British schools. Among these are the Department of Education and Science, teacher training colleges and institutes, local education authorities and their directors and inspectorates, and the personnel of particular schools. The efforts of these bodies were initially directed at the problems created by the presence of immigrant pupils for normal school routines; it was only later that the focus shifted to the educational problems of the immigrant pupils themselves, especially those of the non-English-speaking pupils from Asia and Southern Europe (Bowker 1968:58–79; Burgin and Edson 1967; Glass 1961:63; Goldman and Taylor 1966:167–174; Gummer and Gummer 1966:78–87; Haynes 1971:12–15; Hill 1970:80–81; Hooper 1965:99–101; Patterson 1969:253–285; Rose 1969:264–293; Parliamentary Select Committee 1973).

The British response to immigrant education, particularly of the West Indians, can be divided roughly into three periods. The first period, which lasted from the 1950s to 1962, when controls on immigration were introduced, may be called a period of indifference during which West Indians were the only significant colored minority group in British schools. As indicated earlier, their generally lower academic achievement was not perceived as a problem. There were therefore no formal attempts to bridge the scholastic gap between West Indian and English children.

The years between 1962 and 1965 may be called a normalizing period. The influx of immigrant pupils, especially non-English-speaking Asians and Southern Europeans, was seen by the education establishment and the public alike to disrupt the normal routine of the schools or of particular classes receiving such pupils. During this period, the schools were expected to perform the important social role of helping the immigrants become "integrated" or "assimilated" into British society by teaching them the English language and British values and social conventions. Thus emphasis was placed on developing better social or race relations rather than on improving the academic achievement of the immigrants. Local white parents often protested that teachers devoted too much time to immigrant pupils at the expense of their own children's education.

Such protests led the Department of Education and Science to formulate the policy of "dispersal." By this was meant that local education authorities were not to permit immigrant pupils to constitute more than one-third of the pupils in a particular class or school. Any immigrant children in excess of the 33% quota should be "dispersed," that is, transported to other schools. The government justified the dispersal policy on the grounds that the presence of more than 33% immigrant children in a class or school created a "strain" on the system and made their integration difficult. The dispersal policy was controversial because only immigrant pupils were dispersed or transported. Some local education authorities ignored it and adopted one of two alternatives. The first was "laissez-faire," which its advocates considered a more radical alternative to "forced integration" (i.e., dispersal). The laissez-faire policy was described as a "policy of segregation" or "educational apartheid" by its opponents because some schools were allowed to become predominantly or totally "immigrant schools." The second alternative was "streaming"; that is, immigrant children were separated into special classes within a school according to their educational needs (such as additional language courses) during certain hours of the normal school day. At other times, they were allowed to mix with white pupils. Although they adopted different approaches toward the influx of immigrant pupils—quota system by dispersal, laissez-faire, and streaming—until 1965 the schools emphasized socializing immigrant pupils into middle-class, aspiring Britons and attempted to avoid becoming immigrant schools and to preserve their normal functions (Bowker 1968:58–64; Hill 1970:80–82; Patterson 1969:255–268; Rose 1969:265–278).

The third phase, which began in 1965, may be called the remedial education period. During this period, attention has shifted to the treatment of the specific educational needs of immigrant children, particularly their language difficulties. This period began with the establishment of the Schools Council, which immediately (1965) funded a

3-year project at Leeds University (the Leeds Project) to study the needs of Asian and Southern European (non-English-speaking) pupils and to provide materials, books, and in-service training for teachers of children with inadequate backgrounds in English. Two years later, in 1967, the Schools Council funded a similar project at the University of Birmingham to study the problems of West Indian pupils and devise appropriate remedial programs. Until 1967, no specific attention had been directed toward West Indian education problems, even though, as Rose (1969) points out,

> Children of West Indian parents, the largest group of all the immigrant groups, have been a source of bafflement, embarrassment, and despair in the educational system. They have complicated the attempt to define the term "immigrant pupil" and to assess the linguistic needs of immigrant pupils; in class, they have often presented problems which the average teacher is not equipped to understand, let alone overcome [p. 281].

The literature on immigrant pupils in Britain suggests that since 1965 remedial programs have been developed to deal with their problems as they are perceived by the educational establishment. These programs have emphasized the linguistic and cultural handicaps of immigrant pupils, and they have been directed primarily toward non-English-speaking children from Asia and Southern Europe. There is no doubt that West Indian pupils have benefited, if indirectly, from the growing national awareness that immigrant pupils have special educational needs and are not merely disrupting the normal routine of the schools. Some schools, like Spring Grove in Huddersfield, provide English tutoring for West Indian pupils "when staff conditions permit [Burgin and Edson 1967:89]." Huddersfield provides two special teachers of English for them (Patterson 1969:270); and classes in teaching English as a second language are offered at Birmingham (Rose 1969:277–278). The general effort to deal with the educational problems of West Indian pupils, however, lags considerably behind those marshaled to deal with the problems of Asian and Southern European pupils, although the school performance of West Indian pupils falls considerably behind that of the latter groups.

There are no studies showing the extent to which the various programs have succeeded in improving the school performance of West Indian pupils. Commenting on the prospect of closing the gap between immigrant pupils in general and the native whites, Rose suggests that the end is not near and that there may be some dangers ahead. He points out that because immigrants generally live in ghettolike communities there is a danger that their problems will be misinterpreted

and that immigrant schools will be equated with inferior schools. Thus
he writes (1969):

> So long as present housing policies are continued some neighborhoods will
> increasingly become colored quarters and there will be a growing number of pre-
> dominantly immigrant schools. *In fact, if we look ahead, the danger which may
> face the predominantly immigrant schools is not that they will be different but that
> the differences will be misinterpreted. It is that those in authority—local adminis-
> trators, head teachers—will perceive an identity between colour and inferiority,
> and as a result the schools and the children in them will receive inferior treat-
> ment.* . . . If the multi-racial schools are as good as any others and, equally impor-
> tant, are perceived to be so, then the self-fulfilling prophecy linking colour and
> inferiority will be invalidated [pp. 292–293; emphasis added].

At the moment, it cannot be categorically stated that the gap is closing
or that it is likely to close in the near future.

Education and the Future

According to Bowker (1968) the level of skills and knowledge demanded by modern industrial and technological societies dictates that
talents should be selected and trained "wherever they may lie in the
social order [pp. 73–77]." The task of selecting and training has therefore been transferred from the family to schools, colleges, and universities. To qualify for various occupations in Britain, a person must now
pass written examinations to obtain certificates which become the
visible symbols of proficiency. These certificates not only provide
members of society with access to particular occupations but also act as
a means of social advancement.

Bowker further states that it is for these reasons that so much prestige is attached to grammar-school education: Grammar school has traditionally provided the major access to white-collar jobs and professions. He then goes on to say that political and legislative actions have
added to the pressures on the educational system from the economic
and industrial sector to detect and develop talents from all sections of
society. He implies that the same pressures—political and economic—
can force the schools to facilitate the absorption of West Indians and
other immigrants into contemporary Britain. In this respect, he sees the
task of the schools as twofold: to detect and train talent among the
immigrants as they do among the native whites and to teach these
immigrants the values, norms, and social conventions of their new
society.

Bowker, like most members of the dominant caste who write about
the educational problems of the minority caste, may overemphasize

the importance of *selecting and training talents* from the minority group. He recognizes that West Indian talents already selected and trained are not fairly and adequately used by the larger society. For example, grammar-school certificates do not guarantee West Indians access to the kinds of white-collar jobs and professions open to whites.

A number of field studies, as well as data from secondary sources, show that West Indian immigrants to Britain are confronted with a *job ceiling* which results both in occupational downgrading and in actual exclusion from the more desirable occupations (see Glass 1961; Krausz 1971; McPherson and Gaitskell 1969; Patterson 1963, 1965, 1968, 1969; Rose 1969; Parliamentary Select Committee Report 1973). In her study of the employment experiences of West Indians in the London area, Glass (1961:30, 72) found that in most cases the jobs held by the immigrants were generally inferior to those they held prior to their immigration. She also found that occupational downgrading was most prevalent among those who held white-collar jobs in the West Indies, 86% were employed in London as manual workers, and over half as unskilled laborers. Among those who did skilled work in the West Indies, 40% were holding unskilled jobs in London, and 7% were in semiskilled jobs. The proportion of West Indian immigrants able to obtain professional and skilled jobs was considerably smaller than would be expected in view of their occupational backgrounds. Other studies during the same period and much later confirm these findings. Patterson (1965:77–81) reports that before 1964, when government employment agencies were ordered to restrict their service to employers discriminating against colored immigrants, the latter were prevented from holding white-collar jobs by the color bar and considerably smaller quotas in many firms. She also reports that in the white-collar jobs there was definitely "a total bar." A survey of 12 private employment agencies in Croydon (Gaitskell 1966) showed that few firms outside London were prepared to hire colored immigrants for white-collar jobs and that those who did had small quotas for them. The employment agencies estimated that the proportion of firms they served that would consider hiring *qualified colored applicants* ranged from 2% to 15% (cited in Patterson 1969:185).

Even in London, where West Indians supposedly have always had better opportunities, Rose (1969) reports that their occupational status changed little between 1961 and 1966:

> Finally, and most crucially, an examination of the data for London in 1961 and 1965 showed no sign of occupational structure of immigrants coming in any way closer to the occupational structure of the total population. What changes there were, as far as West Indian men were concerned, showed very slight moves toward greater concentration in certain occupations; there was no evidence that between

1961 and 1966 they were moving into those occupations in which they were markedly under-represented [p. 166].

Nor are West Indians promoted on the same basis as their white co-
workers. Employers contend that white workers do not like to work
under West Indians. Thus West Indians not only face barriers in finding
suitable jobs or jobs commensurate with their training and skills, but
they cannot be given the promotions they deserve if such promotions
involve the direct supervision of white workers (Patterson 1969:170;
see also Glass 1961:75; Patterson 1965:83).

Some of the reasons often given for the disproportionate representation of West Indians in unskilled jobs include lack of skills or
qualifications, lack of industrial background, low adaptability or poor
attitudes toward work, and the color bar or prejudice. Systematic inves-
tigations tend, however, to cast doubt on the validity of some of these
(see Glass 1961:31–32; Krausz 1971:110–111; Patterson 1963:389;
1965:80–82; 1969:145–147, 186–195; Rose 1969:166). While there are
some differences between the skills of West Indian immigrants and
those of British workers (Glass 1961:73; Patterson 1965:80, 1969:145–
147), both Glass and Krausz have shown that the lower occupational
status of West Indian immigrants cannot be explained primarily in
terms of their lower level of skills. Glass (1961) argues that West Indian
immigrants are generally better educated than the general population
of the Caribbean and that they tend to have fewer illiterates among
them "in comparison to the illiteracy ratios in the adult population of
advanced Western countries [pp. 31–32]." She also suggests that the
immigrants' claim that they are skilled or white-collar workers is supported "by the only detailed study of the performance of a group of
West Indian workers over a period of several years [pp. 31–32]." This
was a study by the British Ministry of Labor of the job performance of
309 West Indian workers over approximately four years. The evaluation
took into account such factors as the men's general work ability,
knowledge of their particular trades, and their workmanship. The findings were then compared with the occupational status the men had
claimed for themselves. According to Glass (1961):

> Although a perfect correlation between the two classifications could not be ex-
> pected since the Ministry's assessment also took innate ability into account, a sig-
> nificant correlation was, in fact found. Thus 77.5 percent of the skilled workers (in
> terms of occupational status) were graded by the Ministry as being "very skilled" in
> their actual performance [p. 73].

Refuting the same "low skills hypothesis," Krausz (1971:110–111)
compared the occupational status of West Indian immigrants and other

groups with the levels of skill attributed to them by the managers of British firms. According to the census data of 1966, West Indians had the lowest proportions of employees as managers, professionals, and other nonmanual workers of any immigrant group in Britain. Table 8.1, however, shows that the West Indians were assessed to have higher levels of skill than the other immigrant groups. Thus the low occupational status of West Indians is not consistent with their levels of skill. Rose (1969) also makes a similar point when he examines the overrepresentation of West Indian women in all categories of the nursing profession and their underrepresentation among the "white-blouse" workers of the West Midlands. He notes that the representation of West Indian women in these two jobs is at a ratio of 4:1. In the general population, this representation is reversed, with a ratio of 1:16. Rose concludes that the underrepresentation of West Indian women in "white-blouse" jobs cannot be explained in terms of lack of education or skills:

> The reasons for these immense differences are complex, but it seems fair to suppose that the reasons why West Indian women are markedly under-represented in white-blouse-occupations, cannot be solely their lack of suitable qualifications, but must also include in some measure the disinclination of the general population to see them in these occupations. It is also unlikely that the skill levels of West Indian men and women are so disparate that the under-representation of West Indian men in "white-collar" jobs is not also due in part to the same reason [p. 166].

Many analysts stress the fact that West Indians are *new immigrants* and that this may account for their inability to get good jobs like other British residents. But studies of older settlements of colored immi-

Table 8.1
A Comparison of the Occupational Skills of Minorities, Assessments of Managers of British Firms

	Percentage of British managers offering assessment			
Immigrant group	More skilled than British workers	About the same as British workers	Less skilled than British workers	Number of firms responding
West Indians	0	44	56	39
Pakistanis	0	21	79	19
Indians	0	37	63	33
Arabs	0	23	77	13
Africans	0	27	73	11

SOURCE: Ernest Krausz, 1971. *Ethnic minorities in Britain.* London:MacGibbon and Kee. P. 111.

grants, some dating from the end of World War I, show that the color bar and the job ceiling restrict the opportunities of the second- and third-generation colored residents from competing for desirable jobs on the basis of their training and ability (Rose 1969:487–490).

Furthermore, although few systematic studies exist, there are strong indications that the children of the postwar West Indian immigrants who were born in Britain and have received most of their education in British schools are treated just like their parents in matters of jobs, housing, and the like (Krausz 1971:105, 110–118; Patterson 1966:83–84; 1969:151–158; Rose 1969:481–484). With the second generation of West Indian secondary school graduates language is not nearly so much of a handicap as it is among Indians or Pakistanis, so that the exclusion of these West Indians from desirable employment is largely attributable to discrimination or the color bar. According to Rose (1969), "Sometimes whole sectors which supply typical school-leaving employment, such as the retail trade, discriminate against coloured workers [p. 482]." West Indian secondary school graduates are not readily employed in hairdressing, catering, or office work. Their chances of being employed in banks, insurance companies, or other high-status white-collar and professional jobs are even slimmer. Patterson (1969) reports a study of employment agencies in 1966 in which it was found that 52 firms out of 147 served by the agencies listed "N.C." (No Colored) on their cards and 22 others were unlikely to accept colored secondary school graduates. The study also found that

> Most vacancies for trainee draftsmen were N.C., as were fourteen out of twenty-seven clerical jobs. Some youth employment offices were said to put green stars (cut in half for Cypriots and Pakistanis in one area) to indicate that an applicant was coloured. Other qualifying marks in use were: black star for Borstal, red star for educationally sub-normal, red disc for physically handicapped, yellow disc for deaf and blind. Firms that would employ coloured labour were said to be labeled as such, and there was a tendency to send too many coloured applicants in proportion to white, until they either put on quotas or became "black firms" [p. 153].

In another study, also reported by Patterson (1969) white and colored grammar school leavers were matched "for jobs advertised in banks, insurance companies, and similar establishments [p. 157]." The study showed "marked differences" in the way the same firms treated the white and colored grammar school leavers.

The employment barriers against the colored school leavers are not merely attributable to lack of qualification. In fact, Rose (1969) points out that barriers are usually more rigid against those with higher qualifications:

> The higher qualifications of the second generation will not necessarily lessen discrimination. The findings for the P.E.P. [Political and Economic Planning] Report were not reassuring. *Although employers felt that the better educated immigrant would find employment more easily than the illiterate, P.E.P. found that the more qualified the immigrant, the more likely he was to experience discrimination.* There is already a feeling that the dice is loaded. In the words of a West Indian youth leader in Britain, "There is a lot of fear and a lot of frustration among our young people" [p. 484; emphasis added].

Krausz (1971) confirms that the job ceiling against the more qualified colored minorities is causing much concern: "What many regard as disturbing, however, is the fact that the second generation of coloured minorities, the young people who were born in this country, who had their schooling here and have become anglicized, are still discriminated against particularly insofar as white-collar employment is concerned [p. 105]." The situation led the Community Relations Commission to set up the Advisory Committee on Employment in 1969 specifically "to encourage equality of opportunity in all aspects of employment."

Available evidence thus strongly suggests that the color bar or caste barriers directly and indirectly restrict the opportunities open to West Indians to obtain jobs commensurate with their education and abilities. The color bar also retards their chances for promotion on the job. Even the research of Patterson, who appears to be a strong advocate of the differential-skills hypothesis, is full of references to the restrictive influences of the color bar (Patterson 1963:389; 1965:77–78; 1968:xviii, 203; 1969:170, 185–186; see also Braithwaite 1968; Glass 1961:74; Krausz 1971:111, 115–119; McPherson and Gaitskell 1969:55f).

It is not only in the field of employment and promotion that British society fails to reward West Indians equitably for their education and abilities. A probe into the areas of income, housing, and social positions in general also shows the same pattern of discrepancy between what education does for the dominant white group and what it does for West Indians. Education simply does not function as a bridge to the same adult status for the two groups.

The response of West Indians to the job ceiling and other barriers that prevent them from achieving social and technoeconomic status commensurate with their education and abilities is not unlike that of black Americans to their similar situation. We have seen that West Indians, unlike Indians and Pakistanis, have always been eager to be integrated and assimilated into the British society and that they had high expectations that they would be fully received by the British. The realities of the color bar, the job ceiling, and their experiences in Britain proved therefore to be very disappointing. Partly because of this, and partly because discrimination is severest against the West Indians, Rose (1969) reports that disillusionment and disenchantment are more prevalent in this group than among Indians and Pakistanis. He goes on to describe a survey by the P.E.P. which found that

> over half of the West Indians had found life in Britain worse than they had expected, while only 12 percent said that it was better. Their greater sources of disappointment was the racial and colour prejudice they had experienced, and unfriendliness to foreigners. Others mentioned difficulties in getting housing and jobs—difficulties sometimes caused by prejudice. The consensus of West Indian opinion revealed by the P.E.P. Report reflected two aspects of life in Britain for the black man or woman: the problem of survival and the problem of respect [pp. 434–435].

Rose suggests (1969:439) that this subjective evaluation of their position in Britain may cause West Indians to withdraw into a sort of defensive avoidance, perhaps within the enclave of the Pentecostal Church movement, which he reported to be growing among them. Others may take refuge in cultural nationalism in the context of negritude or the black power movement.

There is as yet no systematic study of the extent to which the response of West Indians to the color bar affects the school performance of their children. But the possibility that the situation *does depress their school performance* is suggested by a number of observers (Braithwaite 1968:231; Bowker 1968:68, 70–71; Rose 1969:481; Parliamentary Select Committee 1973). Bowker suggests that the lack of equal employment opportunities may cause colored pupils to withdraw from actively seeking to maximize their school performance, because "the child who sees his elder brothers and sisters failing to get jobs in competition with equally qualified English children will hardly be inspired by this to take his education seriously. He is much more likely to lower his sights toward the kind of jobs more readily available to him [p. 68]." He adds that this withdrawal is particularly likely to happen when the more academically successful colored minorities fail to get the jobs "available to 'white' youngsters of similar educational level [p. 71]." This demoralization is already occurring, as is indicated by the following statement by a youth employment officer: "No matter how we try to advise and help them they are aware of a colour problem once they have to go out into the world to earn a living [Rose 1969:481]."

Thus while there are no good studies on the subject, there are some

indications that the color bar and the job ceiling have a definite influence on the school performance of West Indian children in Britain. This
is particularly true of the older children whose perception of the color
bar and job ceiling and their own approaching entrapment are likely to
raise the level of disillusionment and disenchantment.

9

Maoris in New Zealand

The main groups in New Zealand are the Pakeha (Europeans) and the Maoris (the natives). There is a third group, a small but increasing number of "islanders." These are other Polynesians such as students and migrant laborers, who have recently come to New Zealand for temporary or permanent residence. Each of the three groups can be further divided into subethnic groups, but that is not relevant to the present study. Although the islanders certainly constitute a minority group, it is generally the Maoris that New Zealanders refer to when they talk about "minority-group problems." The present study is therefore concerned with the Maoris as a distinct minority group, rather than with the islanders.

Maoris in New Zealand Society

The earliest Maori contact with Europeans was with Tasman, the Dutch explorer (1642), and Captain Cook (1796), both of whom landed in New Zealand by accident and mistook the Maoris for East Indians (Hawthorn 1944:7). The contact between the Maoris and Europeans

increased with the arrival of European missionaries and settlers after
1800. The initial Maori–European relationship was friendly, but it later
proved destructive to Maori society and culture. The Maoris acquired
muskets from the Europeans to replace fists and clubs as their weapons
of war; and with the new weapons they soon began to depopulate their
country through intensified intertribal warfare. In order to obtain muskets and other European goods, the Maoris had to sell their lands to the
Europeans, whose conception of land ownership was markedly different from theirs. To prevent further acquisition of their lands by
European settlers, the Maoris, on the advice of some missionaries,
ceded their country to Queen Victoria in 1840 in return for her promise
fully to protect them and their rights as "English subjects." The Maoris
probably did not understand the full implications of this treaty. According to Sutherland (1947), "The nearest the Maoris came to com-
prehending the treaty was expressed in the saying of one of their
number: 'The substance of the land remains with us. Its shadow goes to
the Queen' [p. 57; see also Buck 1950; Hawthorn 1944]."

Following the treaty, more Europeans began to arrive, so that by
1856 there were about 45,000 settlers in the country. In violation of the
treaty of 1840, the Europeans continued to buy Maori lands until "the
Maoris saw both the substance and the shadow of their land passing
from them [Sutherland 1947:58]." The Europeans interpreted a new
constitution granted to them by Parliament in such a way that the
Maoris had the right neither to vote nor to be represented in the colony's legislative assembly, although they were heavily taxed. The only
government department that was really interested in the Maoris was
the Land Purchase Department of the New Zealand colonial government. As a result of these developments, the Maoris lost most of their
lands.

Experiencing at this point what Barber (1941:664) has called
"harsh times," the Maoris reacted in two ways: First, they developed a
"revitalization movement," the *Hauhau*, the goal of which was to drive
the Europeans from their country (Ritchie 1963:22; Sutherland
1947:60); second, finding that the *Hauhau* was not particularly effective, some of the tribes united to form one Maori "kingdom" ruled by
an elected Maori king. The new king provided leadership against the
settlers, but in 1872 the Maoris were defeated by a combined army of
European settlers and British troops, and more of their lands were
appropriated as punishment (Metge 1964:12; Ritchie 1963:24; Sutherland 1947:60). The Maoris then withdrew into the hinterlands both
physically and psychologically. They gave up their recently acquired

Christian religion in preference for nativistic cults with a strong anti-European bent. For a while, the Maoris appeared to be a dying people, with a rapidly declining population, partly from the war and partly from European diseases they had contracted for which they had no cure. According to Sutherland (1947):

> The Maori now saw the white man growing in power in the land while they felt themselves to be passing away. A mood of profound depression resulted. Lack of interest in life led to a disregard for the future. Through subtle interrelations of mind and body in a people more than usually imaginative and suggestible, it led to physical deterioration and affected birthrate and numbers.

Maori withdrawal from participation in New Zealand society was partially ended at the close of the nineteenth century, when a group of young, educated Maoris initiated a movement for new Maori identity. The Young Maori party, under the leadership of such men as Sir Peter Buck and Sir Apirana Ngata, emphasizing the virtues of *Maoritanga* (Maorihood), revived Maori interest in New Zealand society. Side by side with renewed vitality and hope came an increase in the Maori population (Metge 1964:12; Ritchie 1963:24; Sutherland 1947:62–69). Metge (1967) reports that the Maoris were granted the franchise in 1893 and the secret ballot in 1936. They were also given four reserved seats in the New Zealand Parliament, to be filled by members elected from a separate Maori electoral roll. Socially, the official policy of the New Zealand government, until quite recently, was one of "assimilation." Since 1960, this has changed to a policy of "integration"; but today the Maori minority remains neither assimilated nor integrated into New Zealand society.

Maori identity is legally defined, although this definition is not consistent. For example, for electoral purposes anyone who is more than 50% Maori by ancestry must register on the Maori roll to vote. "Half-castes," that is, people with less than 50% Maori ancestry, may register on either the Pakeha or the Maori roll.[1] The Census Bureau, on the other hand, defines the Maoris differently.

The New Zealand constitution and its laws now recognize the Pakeha and the Maoris as equal citizens with the same basic rights. But this has not always been the case. Until recently, there were laws which

[1]In 1960 the four Maori electoral districts had an average of 12,000 electors compared with 16,500 for the non-Maori districts. However, the Maori districts covered larger territories inhabited by many different tribal groups. Furthermore, the above figure did not accurately reflect the proportion of Maori electors because increasing number of Maoris were registering on the non-Maori roll, perhaps because it was easier or because local members of Parliament were more accessible (Metge 1967).

discriminated against the Maoris in such matters as the registration of births, marriages, and deaths; jury service; and liquor sales. Such laws thus confirmed the inferior status of the Maoris vis-a-vis the Pakeha.

Pakeha attitudes and behaviors toward the Maoris are determined by a social rather than a legal definition of the latter. The Pakeha define a Maori as anyone who "looks Maori," whatever the degree of his Maori ancestry and regardless of his cultural or social background. Furthermore, although intermarriage is not uncommon, persons of known mixed ancestry are invariably classified as Maori. This definition is based on skin color. The Pakeha not only accord lower value to the darker color of the Maoris but regard it as a sign of biological and mental inferiority. On the basis of skin color, the Pakeha rank the Maoris as "far more intelligent than the American [black], but not as intelligent as the Europeans" [Ausubel 1960:166]. The Pakeha and the Maoris are therefore stratified into superior and inferior castes on the basis of color. The color line is the primary factor that differentiates the two groups in terms of marriage, education, jobs, housing, social interaction, and the like. According to Ausubel, there is discrimination against Maoris in housing, hotel accommodations, employment, credit, and ordinary social interaction. Open discrimination is rare; most of it is subtle, covert, and extralegal (Ausubel 1960). Metge states that although most Pakeha deny believing in an innate superiority of whiteness, their ordinary conversations and behavior quickly show assumptions of racial superiority. Such assumptions are enshrined in stereotypic descriptions of the Maoris as dirty, happy-go-lucky, lazy, improvident, and the like—stereotypes used to rationalize discriminatory practices against them, which in turn influence their behavior.

It is not only the dominant Pakeha public that denies the existence of racial stratification but also government officials and the intellectual elites. Only since the mid 1960s have the latter begun to acknowledge that their society is stratified by color castes. Previously, they even overlooked the discriminatory laws against the Maoris, pointing instead to more favorable laws, such as those concerning reserved seats in Parliament, which the Pakeha interpreted as "privileges." On the whole, there was a general assumption that the Pakeha and the Maoris had the same legal and constitutional rights. Because of this belief, as well as the long-standing government policy of assimilation, there developed what Ausubel (1960:156) calls a kind of "national self-delusion," which denied the existence of racial stratification and racial problems. In recent years, particularly since the publication of the *Hunn Report* in 1961, some Pakeha have begun to reassess more critically the nature of their society. They are beginning to acknowledge that although the two races now have equal legal and constitutional rights, the Maoris clearly have occupied an inferior social position largely because of their color (see Ausubel 1960:159; 1961; see also Forster 1968; Metge 1967).

Education and Opportunity in New Zealand

The present educational system in New Zealand has evolved from the British system established in colonial days and in response to both the manpower needs of the society and the requirements of the status mobility system of the dominant white caste. Early in the colonial days, few people required more than primary school educations to make their livings or hold various positions in society. The primary school in those days consisted of a two-year infant period, followed by a six-year elementary school period. As the colony developed and began to require more educated workers, the Education Act of 1877 established a national system of free education up to the age of 15, with compulsory attendance to the age of 13. The period of compulsory schooling was later extended to age 15.

The secondary schools of the colonial period also initially followed the British pattern. Some were public and others private, principally mission schools. Some developed as selective academic secondary schools, while others emphasized technical training. The division was never quite rigid, however, because some schools, especially the district (county) high schools, were so located that they were forced to serve as both academic and technical high schools. Since 1945, the two types of schools have come to resemble one another in many respects. Before World War II, admission to the secondary schools was by entrance examination. In the 1920s, another development saw the introduction of intermediate schools, which were similar to junior high schools. For higher education, New Zealanders usually sent their children to England, until universities and other institutions of higher education were established locally.

The present system reflects the social, economic, and technological realities of contemporary New Zealand. Various positions in society require not only longer periods of education but also higher and more specialized training. Below the university level, the system is organized into the kindergarten, primary, intermediate, and secondary schools. Schooling begins at the age of five with a two-year infant school, which is not compulsory. The government provides most of the funds for this program, but the services are sponsored by two private organizations—the Kindergarten Association and the Nursery Play Centre's Association. The infant schools are subject to inspection by the New Zealand Department of Education. The programs serve only a small proportion of the children of this age, including some Maori children.

Regular primary school begins in the first grade at the age of 7, but some children are admitted at five or six. After four years, the children proceed to the fifth and sixth grades (forms I and II), which are held in separate schools or in schools attached to the secondary schools. Upon completion of the intermediate grades, the children proceed to the secondary schools for grades seven, eight, and nine (forms III, IV, and V).

Some students leave school when they reach 15 (during or at the end of form III, as tuition is charged after form III). Others remain to take the Secondary School Certificate Examination at the end of form V. Among those who pass this examination, some spend their secondary school training for two more years in forms VIA and VIB to prepare for university education or to obtain certificates that qualify them for some professional career. Until recently, the number of students continuing into the sixth form was relatively small. Only 30% of the students who entered secondary school (form III) in the 1957–1958 school year continued into the sixth form in 1960–1961. This represented an increase of 5% over the previous two years. After completing the sixth form, students usually need three years to complete the degree course at university. Those who gain admission to university by passing the entrance examination rather than attending the sixth form take about four years to complete their degrees (New Zealand Government 1962:198–222), thus in effect shortening their schooling by a year.

New Zealand considers itself an egalitarian and democratic society in which an individual achieves his or her social and occupational position in life on the basis of training and ability rather than on the basis of birth or membership in a particular racial group. It is assumed that more education will lead to better chances for obtaining jobs associated with higher wages and higher social prestige. It is further assumed that the children of poor families, new immigrants, and minority groups will be able to achieve more desirable jobs, higher wages, and higher standards of living in adult life than their parents. The importance of education in providing New Zealanders with the skills to adapt to their changing economic and technological society, and especially in helping disadvantaged groups to achieve better positions in life, is stressed in the following statement from the Education Commission (New Zealand Government 1962):

It can, however, be assumed with some confidence that as mechanization of primary and secondary industry increases, the demand for unskilled labour is likely to decrease steadily and a higher premium for both Maori and non-Maori will be placed on the skills and knowledge of the technician and the professional worker. From one point of view, therefore, there is an urgent need to advance Maori education sufficiently to prevent the development of an unemployable proletariat; from another it is urgent that we develop the almost untapped professional talent of the Maori people for the benefit of all. Elsewhere, the Commission has emphasized that the nation cannot afford to waste any of the ability of the country's children: in the Maori pupil lies the greatest reservoir of unused talent in the population.

Educational credentials are, therefore, important in New Zealand both in terms of the needs of society and in terms of the needs of the individual citizen. Education is almost a prerequisite for self-improvement.

The Education of the Maoris

Schools were first established for Maoris by the Church Missionary Society in 1816. When these schools began to receive government subsidies in about 1857, the colonial government required them to follow its policy of assimilation, that is, of making Europeans out of the Maoris. The education ordinance of 1847, for instance, required schools receiving government aid to teach Maori children both in English and in the Maori language. Previously, the mission schools had conducted instruction only in Maori because these schools were intended to train Maori children to live and work among their own people according to the Maori way of life rather than to Europeanize them. Beginning in 1867, the government began to set up its own "native schools," where it put its policy of assimilation more fully into practice.

These new government schools located mainly in rural areas, were intended to Europeanize the Maoris and were therefore required to teach them only in English. The Native Schools Amendment Act of 1871 specifically permitted English as the only language of instruction in the government village schools (see Biggs 1968:74; Metge 1967; Powell 1955). A more elaborate policy of assimilation for these schools, drawn up in 1881, remained in force until 1930. Under this policy, Maori schools and European schools (public schools) were to use the same syllabus or curriculum, and English was to be the language of instruction. Maori children were required to clean their school buildings and grounds as a part of their training in the Pakeha or European way of life. Where possible, Maori and Pakeha children attended the same schools, either public or Maori.

The policy of assimilation in education was modified in 1930 with the introduction of selected aspects of Maori culture into the Maori curriculum. These included Maori history, rhythms, and crafts. There was also a shift in Maori schools from purely academic to more "practical" education (Metge 1967; Parsonage 1956). The teaching of the Maori language *as a language* (but not as a means of instruction) was made compulsory at the postprimary level in 1935. Since 1956, more fundamental changes have taken place, including the current emphasis on integration rather than assimilation in education. In 1956, a committee on Maori education recommended the following changes: (a) that Maori and public schools be gradually integrated, with the consent of the Maori people (Maori schools have traditionally been small rural schools, and since 1930 the number of Maori children attending public rather than Maori schools has been increasing—see Table 9.1); (b) that Maori history, legend, songs, arts, and crafts be taught *in all schools;* and (c) that Maori school boards be given the same powers as the public school boards. All three recommendations were implemented to some degree. Also as a result of the committee's report, a senior education officer for Maori education was appointed by the Department of Educa-

Table 9.1

Decreasing Proportion of Maori Children Attending Maori Schools, 1930 to 1958 (selected years)

	1930	1940	1950	1958
Primary				
Maori village schools	6,220	9,471	10,841	11,051
Private schools (Maori)	520	659	826	840
Maoris attending public schools	8,172	12,477	18,699	26,404
Total	14,912	22,607	30,366	38,295
Postprimary				
Maori district high schools			261	725
Private schools (Maori)	512	405	817	755
Maoris attending public schools	—	—	2,711	5,597
Total	—	—	3,789	7,077
TOTAL (all schools)	—	—	34,155	45,372

SOURCE: J.K. Hunn 1961. *Report on Department of Maori Affairs.* Wellington: Government Printer. P. 157.

tion in 1956, and in 1963 a Maori was appointed as assistant education officer to supervise Maori education in all schools.

Maori education is no longer regarded as an instrument with which to transform the Maori into a Pakeha. Today the idea is that the Maori can be educated "to take his place on terms of equality [with the Pakeha] as a New Zealand citizen" while retaining his racial and cultural dignity and pride (New Zealand Government 1962:415). The schools are therefore attempting to provide the Maoris with a *bicultural education*.[2] But its implementation is made difficult by the elimination of Maori schools and the increasing participation of Maoris in the public schools. According to the commission, in 1960 only 28.4% of Maori children attending state-supported primary schools were in Maori schools and only 8.5% of Maori high school students were attending Maori district high schools. The Education Commission also reports that these Maori schools embodied a sizable number of non-Maori students, a total of 1089 Pakeha in Maori primary schools and 33 in Maori high schools. The commission further adds that "there is a Maori school where the majority of the pupils is European and there are likewise a number of board [public] schools that are almost completely Maori in racial composition [p. 419]." About 40% of the teachers in Maori schools are Maoris; there is no information regarding Maori public school teachers. One effect of the gradual desegregation of both Maori schools and the public school system is the decrease in Maori participation in the administrative control of the schools.

The changes in Maori education are the results of the failure of government educational policies, especially the policy of using education to make Maoris into Europeans. The failure of these policies is symbolized in the wide educational gap between the Maoris and the Pakeha, a problem to which I turn next.

The Education Gap. There are probably no differences between the Maoris and the Pakeha in literacy rates;[3] but other data show that the

---

[2]Teaching the Maori language to Maori children is also a part of this bicultural education. The purpose of the language teaching is to help the Maori maintain his "cultural identity and the security that such feelings of identity confer" [New Zealand Government 1962:427]. I have no information about the extent to which the Maori language is still the first language of most Maoris, but it appears to be more widely used than is suggested by the Education Commission, which reports that in some parts of the country it is used only for ceremonial purposes. Thus Parsonage (1956:10) reports that Maori school children often use their native language in the playground, to produce plays, hold simple debates, and deliver "historical lecturettes." In the nursery schools, children sing with zest and carry out other verbal activities in their native language. Both he and the education commission, however, point out that contemporary Maori has been modified with features borrowed from English.

[3]Schooling has been compulsory for the Maoris as for the Pakeha since the late nineteenth century, and this accounts for the similarity in literacy rates between the two groups.

Maoris are behind the Pakeha in the number of students continuing their education beyond the compulsory school age (7–15), and in their performance on standardized tests.

Proportionately fewer Maori students proceed beyond the primary schools, i.e., beyond the fourth grade. For example, in 1956 about 85% of Maoris and 95% of Pakeha went on to the postprimary schools. Among Maori postprimary students, 35% did not continue beyond form III (i.e., seventh grade); but among the Pakeha, only 13% did not continue (Ausubel 1961:79). According to the Hunn Report (New Zealand Government 1960:24) only 18% of Maori students continued their high school education beyond the optional school-leaving age of 15 in 1956, and this figured dropped to 17.3% in 1958.

During the same period, the proportion of non-Maori students in the same age range continuing their education increased from 18% to 21%. Differences in attrition rates between the Maoris and the Pakeha become even more marked with each additional year of high school beyond the optional school-leaving age (see Table 9.2).

Table 9.2

Number of Maori and Non-Maori Students in Various Grades of Secondary School, Showing High Attrition Rates Among Maori Students, 1955–1958

	1955	1956	1957	1958
Form III				
Maori	2,145	2,179	2,579	2,601
Non-Maori	26,623	26,056	27,071	28,936
Form IV				
Maori	1,429	1,504	1,569	1,856
Non-Maori	22,118	23,103	22,399	23,847
Form V				
Maori	870	1,003	1,089	1,061
Non-Maori	14,074	16,127	17,674	17,143
Form VI				
Maori	66	74	81	76
Non-Maori	4,584	5,177	6,300	7,147
Total				
Maori	4,510	4,760	5,318	5,597
Non-Maori	67,399	70,463	73,390	77,073

SOURCE: J.K. Hunn 1961. *Report on Department of Maori Affairs.* Wellington: Government Printer. P. 157.

In 1958, there were only 76 Maori students in form IV, .5% of the Maori population between the ages of 12 and 18; but among the Pakeha, there were 7147 students, 3.78% of the Pakeha population of that age range. Had the Maori children continued their schooling in the same proportion as the Pakeha, according to the Hunn Report (New Zealand Government 1960:24), their number in form VI in 1958 would have been 890. At the university level, the Maori are also grossly underrepresented. Ausubel (1961) reports that "whereas 3.5 percent of the original group of Pakeha Third-Formers go on to the university, only 0.2 percent of the corresponding group of Maori Third-Formers do likewise [p. 79]." The figures given in the Hunn Report (1960:24) show that in 1956 there were only 89 Maori undergraduates at the university; their proportional representation would have been 741.

During the compulsory school period of ages 7 to 15, there are no marked differences between Maori and Pakeha school enrollment. Beyond this period of compulsory schooling, however, the attrition rate is much greater for the Maoris than for the Pakeha.

Systematic studies that compare actual classroom performance of Maori and Pakeha children are rare. But there are some indirect clues that the performance of Maori children is markedly lower than that of the Pakeha in basic school subjects at the primary and postprimary levels (Ausubel 1961; Schwimmer 1968). Commenting on the inferior quality of the academic skills acquired by Maori children in the classroom, the Hunn Report (New Zealand Government 1960) states:

> A serious flaw in Maori education is the lack of tuition in mathematics. It is very evident, for example, among the 30 trainees at the Panmure Carpentry School, where an hour a day has to be given up to repairing this deficiency. Their school record cards show that the boys did little, if any, mathematics previously. Yet an understanding of mathematics is basic to most apprenticeships, as it is to the professions of engineering, architecture, surveying, and science. Apparently the children are too often allowed to take "soft" options at school, without regard to their vocational future—which, in the case of Maoris, is likely to lie more and more in skilled trades [p. 26].

Stronger evidence of the performance gap is contained in Ausubel's study (1961). In a rural high school, he found that Maori third-formers had scored lower than the Pakeha on both English and arithmetic entrance tests. In 1958, the Maori students in the same school averaged 31 points on English in the Secondary School Certificate Examination, while the average score of Pakeha students was 47 points. Over a four-year period, only 17% of the Maori candidates were successful in the School Certificate Examination, as compared to 56% of the Pakeha candidates (1961:91). Ausubel (1961:79, 91) further reports that a similar pattern of Maori–Pakeha performance existed in Hawkes Bay High School, where the Maoris made up 50% of the student population: the Maoris consistently gained less than 10% of the places in the top third–form class; but they constituted more than 90% of the places in the lowest of the six third-form classes.

The two races also differ in their performance on standardized intelligence tests (Ausubel 1961; Lovegrove 1964; James Ritchie 1957). In the rural high school studied by Ausubel, the mean Otis IQ for all entering third-form Maori students was 83; for the Pakeha it was 96. In Ausubel's matched sample in the same school, the figures were 84.9 for the Maoris and 92.8 for the Pakeha. The Maori–Pakeha difference in mean Otis IQ was much smaller in a matched urban sample where it was 90.3 for the Maori and 94.3 for the Pakeha (Ausubel 1961:90). Lovegrove (1964:71) found "significant differences between [the two] races" when he administered a battery of the New Zealand Standardized Otis Intermediate Form B and other tests to a matched sample. Table 9.3 gives the average scores of Maori and Pakeha pupils in IQ points on the Wechsler-Bellevue Test (Children's Scale) administered by Ritchie to Maori and Pakeha children in Rakau.[4] Maori children scored lower than the Pakeha on both the verbal and performance tests.

However, there are two reported studies in which this pattern of racial differences in standardized tests does not hold. Lovegrove (1964:71), who also gave a battery of scholastic achievement tests to his sample, reports that there was no significant difference in performance between the two races. Both Ausubel (1961:90) and Lovegrove (1964:70) report a study by Leone Smith in which she found no differences in IQ between Maori and Pakeha children of 11–13 years to whom she gave the General Ability Test of the Australian Council for Educational Research. There were no reports of other studies using the tests administered by Smith. Apart from these two instances, all other studies report significant differences between the Maoris and the Pakeha in tests of intelligence or scholastic achievement.

Explaining the Gap. Popular explanations among the Pakeha of the lower Maori school accomplishments and their lower educational attainment are in line with their explanation of the generally lower status of Maoris in health, occupation, income, housing, and the like. The Pakeha *blame* the Maoris and their "nature" for their situation in these matters. The study by Archer and Archer (1970:201–218) shows that in

---

[4]Rakau is a pseudonym for a semirural Maori community in which New Zealand and some American social scientists—primarily psychologists—studied various aspects of Maori life, such as childrearing practices, "basic personalities," and so on.

Table 9.3

A Comparison of Maori and Pakeha Pupils in Rakau on the Wechsler-Bellevue Test (Children's Scale)

	Averages scores in IQ points		
	Verbal scale	Performance scale	Full scale
Pakeha females	95.7	98.2	96.7
Pakeha males	99.8	94.7	97.1
Pakeha combined (N = 22)	97.5	96.6	96.8[a] (SD)
Maori females	82.5	89.9	86.8
Maori males	87.5	91.25	88.25
Maori combined (N = 18)	84.7	90.5	87.2[a] (SD)

SOURCE: James E. Ritchie 1957. Some observations on Maori and Pakeha intelligence test performance. *Journal of the Polynesian Society* **66**:352.

[a] Significant at the .05 level (t = 3.55).

New Zealand the Pakeha use racial stereotypes associated with material success and upward mobility, such as instrumental attitudes toward time, work, money, property, and education to describe themselves but use stereotypes that deemphasize such instrumental attitudes to describe the Maoris. They say that Maoris lack those qualities which promote *individual success*, including success in formal education (see also Ausubel 1960, 1961; Archer and Archer 1970; Ritchie 1968).

Some school officials not only share these general beliefs or stereotypes but also hold more specific stereotypes about Maori educability. They believe, for instance, that the Maoris perform more poorly than the Pakeha in their schoolwork because they are *inherently inferior*. The same reason—the inherent inferiority of the Maori—is sometimes given to explain why Maori students do less well than other non-European students or why they do better in "practical work" than in academic subjects like mathematics (Ausubel 1961:43, 45, 49, 89, 92).

Social science theorizing about lower Maori school performance began to appear in the 1950s. It generally followed explanations similar to those American social scientists offered for minority school performance in the United States. New Zealand social scientists first explained Maori school performance as a consequence of faulty socialization which resulted in an inadequate development of both "intellectual functioning" and achievement motivation. This position was most clearly formulated in the Rakau studies, a project designed originally to study the "basic personality" of the Maoris (Beaglehole and Ritchie 1961; James Ritchie 1956a). The project was greatly influenced by the "culture-and-personality" school of American anthropology and psychoanalysis. The Rakau project included ethnographic studies of the Maori community; study of the socialization of Maori children of different age groups (Jane Ritchie 1957; Earle 1958); the administration of the Rorschach projective instrument (Beaglehole and Ritchie 1961; Ritchie 1956a), and study of Maori achievement motivation (Ausubel 1961; Williams 1960).

According to these scholars, Maori children find their parents quite indulgent and permissive during the first two years of life. After that, however, the children are rejected and forced to rely on peer groups for their gratification. Yet the peer group provides them with no opportunities to develop trust or commitment to long-range goals. Such a situation forces Maori children to develop some defenses,

> chief amongst which is non-achievement, in Maori social situation; recourse to practical rather than abstract tasks; a belief in the ultimate validity of self-evaluations, and counter-rejection which expresses itself chiefly through attacking achievers by gossip or by interpreting their actions as egocentric rather than altruistic [Beaglehole and Ritchie 1961:507].

From their observations, Beaglehole and Ritchie conclude that there are basically three reasons why Maori children do less well in school than the Pakeha: First, they have lower intellectual functioning; second, their achievement motivation is lower; and third, group support is lacking. As for Maori intelligence, these authors argue that the Maoris have an " 'imagination deficiency' which may have as many repercussions for the Maori success in secondary and advanced education as would vitamin deficiency for the proper care and health metabolism functioning of the body" [Adcock *et al.* 1954 quoted in Beaglehole and Ritchie 1961:498]. Turning to the lack of achievement motivation, these scholars point out that it is attributable to the fact that the Maori personality is characterized by a weak ego, so that Maoris cannot defer immediate impulse gratification in order to achieve long-range goals. Finally, Beaglehole and Ritchie (1961) argue that Maori students, especially those in higher education, fail because they lack strong group support which would make them persevere in their studies year after year.

The above formulation did not go uncriticized. Some critics point out that it is an error to try to use Rorschach responses as a measure of the level of Maori intellectual functioning. Others, Metge and Campbell (1958:352–386), state that the authors of the Rakau studies have generalized too much from findings concerning the childrearing practices of an unrepresentative sample of Maori families. They also point out that these authors define achievement too narrowly, primarily in terms of economic status, while neglecting many areas of Maori life in which achievement is traditionally sanctioned.

David P. Ausubel, an American ethnopsychologist (1961), provided another elaborate explanation of the scholastic gap between Maoris and the Pakeha. Although his study deals with Maori high school adolescent boys, some of his findings are applicable to other Maori pupils. Ausubel's study, conducted in 1957–1958 as a part of the Rakau studies, focused on the educational and vocational goals of Maori and Pakeha adolescent boys and on the extent to which these goals were achievable (1961:14). He found that Maori and Pakeha adolescent boys had similar educational and occupational goals; but after analyzing the influence of various forces in Maori life, he concludes that it is more difficult for Maori boys to achieve their educational goals than it is for Pakeha boys. He notes from past records that Maori boys did considerably worse than Pakeha in various tests of scholastic ability.

More important, however, Ausubel says that Maori boys were more disadvantaged because they received little encouragement from their families to do well in school; their peer groups placed little emphasis on academic success for assigning status to individual members, in contrast to the Pakeha peer groups. Maori culture had in fact lost its traditional value of formal learning and actually encouraged disillusionment with and withdrawal from Pakeha education. Maori culture also emphasized derived [inherited] status rather than achieved and did not particularly encourage long-range academic goals.

The study also suggests that Maori students had more difficulties in adapting to the secondary school environment, which in many cases was radically different from the primary school environment from which they had come. Other reasons for the lower academic performance of Maori children included racial prejudice on the part of Pakeha teachers and the Pakeha community, "retarded" verbal intelligence, bilinguilism, and excessive absenteeism on the part of Maori boys. Thus while Maori adolescents have the same educational goals as the Pakeha, Ausubel concludes that they have not learned the attitudes and work habits that would make them equally successful in school (Ausubel 1961:78–95). Ausubel further states that fewer Maoris continue their education beyond the school-leaving age of 15, especially through the university, because of economic hardships. Education beyond Form III is a commodity that the individual must purchase at his or her own expense, so that Maori families, who are generally poorer than Pakeha families, either cannot afford to purchase higher education for their children or need their children to work in order to contribute to the support of the family (Ausubel 1961; Hunn Report 1960:25; Schwimmer 1968:344).

Closing the Gap. Some of the historical changes in Maori education previously described were not based on either the popular or the social science conception of Maori educational problems. Also, prior to the 1960s, most of the changes in educational policy were intended not so much to close the educational gap between Maoris and the Pakeha as to promote better relations between the two racial groups through assimilation or integration. For example, the first radical change in Maori education, introduced in 1931, came in direct response to the Maori "racial rejuvenation," a clear recognition that "the policy of assimilation had failed to produce the desired results [Parsonage 1956:6]. The Maoris had not only reemerged from their physical, social, and psychological withdrawal (1872–1927) but were also beginning to show increasing and renewed interest in their cultural, artistic, and ceremonial ways of life. Under these circumstances, the Maori schools were used as an instrument to promote the new Maori identity and pride in past Maori achievement (Ausubel 1961:104–105; Metge 1967:48–50; Parsonage 1956:6–7). The campaign to eradicate the Maori language was also softened and Maori language study was made compulsory in Maori secondary schools and teacher training colleges and taught in some Maori primary schools. In 1945, Maori became one of the subjects in the High School Certificate Examinations. That these changes were not intended to improve the academic performance of Maori children can be seen from the fact that teachers already teaching in the schools were not given any special training in Maori language or culture, although they were encouraged to utilize such community resources as Maori volunteers fully (Biggs 1968:73–77).

In the 1950s, some measures were taken toward integrating the Maori schools with the public school system, primarily because the dual school system was considered potentially harmful to race relations (Parsonage 1956:8). The Hunn report (1960) makes the same point in recommending the abolition of the Maori schools in the 1960s. It states, "School is the nursery of integration. Children mix naturally where their less adaptable elders stand apart. The cause of race relations would, therefore, be best served by absorbing as many Maori children as possible into the board [public] schools [p. 25]."

Since Maori schools are considered equal to the public schools in terms of syllabus, their abolition has not been discussed in terms of improving the school performance of Maori children. In fact, it has even been suggested that their special emphasis on Maori culture should be transferred to the public schools to serve all Maori children.

The concern about the scholastic gap between the Maori and the Pakeha became a major theme only in the 1960s, especially with the publication of the Hunn Report (1960) and the subsequent report by the Education Commission (New Zealand Government 1962). These reports stressed the need to improve the quality of academic skills acquired by Maori children and to increase the proportion of Maoris receiving secondary and university education.

Prevailing remedial educational programs for the Maori are now mostly administered through the Maori Education Foundation. The foundation was established in 1961 on the recommendation of the Hunn report, with funds raised from the public (both Maori and Pakeha) and an equal subsidy from the government. Its programs cover three broad areas of Maori education. The first of these is the preschool: The foundation has established Maori play centers, staffed with trained Maori supervisors and Maori mothers as aides, to offer preschool programs. The purpose of the programs is to minimize Maori "educational handicaps at the pre-school stage." In these centers, Maori mothers are taught how to raise their children as the Pakeha do, so that their children will succeed in Pakeha schools and society. The preschool program is probably not adequately coordinated, for Ritchie and Ritchie (1968) state that

> Many voices now direct the Maori mother where she should now go, how she should now act: the district nurse, the local doctor, the Play Centre, not to mention radio talks, other mass media and, we understand, the Maori Education Foundation. We have confidence in the intention of parents and their ability to formulate and follow a policy in these matters, in the influence and thoughtful reflection on how one was reared and the shaping of a new pattern out of the old pattern, rather than some revolutionary adoption of a new pattern that may not fit the personality of the mother [p. 327].

The Maori play center movement is growing; Metge (1967:109) reports that in 1967 there were 83 centers catering to about 1650 Maori children. But there are as yet no evaluations of the effectiveness of the program (see also Schwimmer 1968:343).

The second program might be termed *special facilities*, intended to "help remove the cultural handicaps under which the Maori child suffers when he tries to compete in the general New Zealand school system [Schwimmer 1968:343]." According to Schwimmer the special facilities were recommended by the Education Commission report of

1962 and consisted of "additional reading advisers, additional staff for remedial work at Forms I and II, special guidance counsellors (6), more visiting teachers, extra allowances for reading materials, etc." [p. 343].

Although these programs have not yet been adopted as the official policy of the Department of Education, Schwimmer reports that many of them are being provided. In addition, a new method of teaching English based on structural linguistics has been introduced into some Maori schools. Again, there are no data indicating the extent to which these programs are effective in closing the scholastic gap between the Maori and the Pakeha. But Schwimmer reports that they have generated much public interest and support for Maori education (1968:343).

Another approach is an attempt to increase the number of Maoris receiving secondary and university education. This program consists essentially of financing a full postprimary and university education for some Maori students through a system of competitive scholarships. The program is run by the Maori Education Foundation which, according to Metge (1967:109), by the end of 1964 had awarded such scholarships to 886 secondary and 100 university students and to 25 apprentices (see also Schwimmer 1968:343). The Hunn report estimated that through such a scholarship program it would be possible in 10 years to bring Maori students to the university in the same proportion as Europeans (New Zealand government 1961:25). Although the scholarship program is easy to evaluate in terms of the number of awards, there are no data on the number of students who dropped out of the program. The underlying assumption of the remedial programs seems to be that the problem lies in the cultural, social, economic, and psychological background of the Maoris. The programs intended to close the academic gap are therefore directed at these background factors among Maori children and young people.

Education and the Future

As in other societies, the educational problems of the Maori are discussed and treated almost without reference to the actual opportunities in adult life for educated members of the group. The popular and social science theorizing about the causes of lower Maori school performance and the policy discussions about possible changes in Maori education all begin with the assumption that Maoris do not have good jobs, earn high wages, or live in good houses like the Pakeha because they have less education. Why the Maoris are not as educated as the Pakeha is attributed to their way of raising their children, their lack of desire to succeed in school, their lower IQs, their language, and their relative lack of money. The presumed greater opportunities available to those with more education becomes the justification for recent efforts to improve Maori education, as the following statement in the Hunn (1961) report indicates:

> The practical measures that induce closer integration move around a circle in a chain of reaction. Better education promotes better housing, which promotes better health and social standing, which promotes better education and thus closes the circle [p. 28].

It is probably true that better educated Maoris have better jobs, better health, better housing, and the like than the less educated, but achieving the same level of education as the Pakeha does not give the Maoris and the Pakeha equal access to good jobs, good housing, and other benefits.

There is little specific information on the employment of Maori and Pakeha people with similar educations. However, what information exists suggests that the more highly educated Maoris are employable primarily in the civil service, especially in positions which have to do with direct services to the Maori community (Ritchie 1968:293). They are largely excluded from the more desirable jobs in the wider society *because they are Maoris* regardless of their educational achievement. This exclusion is aptly described by Ausubel (1961):

> Among the Pakeha population at large, prejudice in employing Maoris stems from strong colour bias, from popular stereotype of the Maoris as lazy, happy-go-lucky, undependable, and capable of only rough manual labour, and from unfavourable experience with one or more individuals that is uncritically generalized to the entire race.
>
> Thus, apart from unskilled labour and Public Service jobs, Maoris encounter considerable prejudice in most fields of employment, particularly in banks, shops, and offices. Hostile reactions from other employees may also tend to bar them from managerial and supervisory positions. *Generally speaking, with the exceptions noted above, Pakeha employers consider a Maori job applicant if no European is available.* It is true, of course, that since World War II, the job market has been generally favourable for Maoris as a result of underemployment situation. Nevertheless it is perfectly clear that in many instances they were hired with great reluctance—simply because employers had no other choice—and that they will be the first employees to be laid off in the event of an economic recession [pp. 75–76; emphasis added].

Thus the phenomenon of *job ceiling* prevents formal education in New Zealand from serving the same function for the Maoris as for the Pakeha.

Differences in employment opportunities represent only one area of inequality in adult life which Maori educational accomplishments do not overcome; there are also inequalities in housing, social prestige, and so on. Yet the influence of racial stratification, particularly the influence of the job ceiling, on Maori education began to be openly discussed only after Ausubel wrote about the castelike status of the Maoris in modern New Zealand society in the 1960s.

Maori reaction to these inequities has not been systematically studied, either. However, it is reasonable, even in the absence of such studies, to suggest that this situation is one of the major causes of lower Maori school performance, the high Maori dropout rate at the post-primary level, and other school problems. The Maoris' disillusionment with and withdrawal from Pakeha education because of the way they are treated in society goes back to their defeat in the Maori–Pakeha wars. The government policy of using education to transform the Maoris into Europeans taught the Maoris to replace their own way of life with that of the Europeans; but that policy did not include providing the Maoris with the social and occupational opportunities which would have enabled them to live as the Europeans did. Thus the Maoris were offered, as it were, the shadow but not the substance of assimilation education: They were not provided with any material incentives to overcome their disillusionment or to work as hard as the Pakeha in school.

The Maoritanga movement of the early part of the twentieth century was led by some educated Maoris from tribes that had not taken part in the Maori–Pakeha war. But neither the Maoritanga movement nor the gradual shift from assimilation education to integration education altered the basic problem: New Zealand society was still attempting to offer the Maoris equal access to formal education with the Pakeha but not equal opportunity in terms of employment and other social and economic benefits in adult life which depend on educational accomplishments. The consequences of a continuing job ceiling and other inequities are not merely that the Maoris are "under-represented in professional, clerical, and commercial occupations, in farm ownership, skilled trades, and are over-represented in agricultural and unskilled labor"; and that "the mean annual income of the Maoris is only three-quarters that of the Pakeha, and relatively fewer Maoris than Pakeha are in the moderate and upper income brackets [Ausubel 1961:72]." Another consequence is that Maori students, especially as they get older, are not motivated to work as hard in school or to stay longer in school, especially during periods of increasing difficulties with school studies. Although there has been no consistent, formal policy fostering education different from or inferior to that offered to the Pakeha, low teacher expectations and biased textbooks and curriculums are among the subtle devices which have contributed to lower Maori school performance.

10

Scheduled Castes in India

Many groups in India, using such criteria as rates of literacy or relative economic status, consider themselves as minority groups. But the following are the ones more generally accorded minority status: scheduled castes, scheduled tribes, other backward classes, lower castes (i.e., castes that are "clean" but low in the pollution hierarchy), women, and in some places, Muslims. The scheduled tribes, scheduled castes, and other backward classes receive most attention in government policies toward minority groups.

Only the education of the scheduled castes will be dealt with in this chapter, partly because there is more information about their education than there is for any other minority group in India, but, more important because the position of the scheduled castes in Indian society most closely approximates that of black Americans.

Scheduled Castes in Indian Society

The term *scheduled castes* was first used in 1935 by the British colonial government when it prepared a list of low-ranking Hindu castes for purposes of statutory safeguards and other benefits. After independence, the Indian government modified the caste list. The criteria for selecting the castes included in the lists are specified in the Indian constitution. They were drawn up by the central government and can be revised—with some groups added or dropped—only by presidential authorization. There is also a permanent office of the Commission of the Scheduled Castes to look after their affairs. The term *scheduled castes* is meaningful, however, only in the context of legal provisions and government policies and actions. The diverse groups included on the list prefer to identify themselves by their traditional caste names.

Unlike the scheduled tribes, the scheduled castes live not in isolated communities but in multicaste villages where they are residentially segregated. They are found in every state and district, and in 1971 they numbered over 80 million or about 15.54% of the total population (Dushkin 1972:166). Scheduled castes include diverse groups, and there is no uniform criterion for identifying them except that they are generally groups which suffer from both ritual and secular stigma. In the past they were prevented from full participation in many collective village activities, and today they are still restricted to some extent.

Social stratification in traditional Indian society was based on a fivefold division of society, under which four of the groups fell within the Hindu religion, according to a Rig-Vedic hymn of the first millennium B.C. These social strata consisted of the Brahmin, the Kshatriya, the Vaisya, the lower but nonpolluting castes, and the still lower, ritually polluting castes—the untouchables (the scheduled castes). The first three groups received the highest social prestige, the greatest secular power, and the greatest material wealth in that order. The lower nonpolluting castes performed various services for the three upper castes, especially in the field of agriculture. The untouchables, regarded as ritually polluting, were confined to the least desirable occupations from both social and economic standpoints: scavengers, sweepers, washermen, and laborers. Their occupational status resulted in extreme poverty, in addition to the social stigma attached to such occupations. Because they were regarded as polluting, the untouchables were prevented from intermarrying with other groups or eating with them, and they were residentially segregated.

This traditional system of caste stratification was rationalized by the Hindu religion. For each individual, as well as for the group to which he belonged, the present life was seen as a continuation of his previous life before birth, and his present status was seen as a result of the way he had performed his duties in his previous life. Duties assigned to a person born into a particular caste were considered his rightful activities, and the way he performed them was believed to determine his position in the next life. In theory, no individual could achieve upward social mobility within a single lifetime. Since this closed system of stratification received religious sanction, social inequality was accepted as a value of society (Chauhan 1967; Srinivas 1962).

Some modifications began to occur during British colonial rule. In 1935, the British government passed the British Indian Act, which led to the compilation of a list of groups with untouchable status. Subsequently, these groups were designated as the scheduled castes. The act also provided some statutory safeguards and other benefits for the untouchables, especially in the areas of civil rights, education, and employment. When India became independent in 1947, the national government expanded these safeguards and took further steps to improve the conditions of the untouchables. More important, the Indian constitution abolished untouchability, and in 1955 a new law, the Untouchability Offences Act, granted former untouchables the right to enter any Hindu or religious structure, draw water from any tap, tank, stream, or well, and use any public restaurant, hotel, place of entertainment, or other facility. In addition to the national legislation, individual states have also passed legislation aimed at broadening the civil rights of the scheduled castes.

Since independence, three methods have been used, especially by the central government, to improve the status of the scheduled castes. The first is a series of legal provisions, the most important of which were the abolition of untouchability by the Indian constitution, i.e., emancipation, and the Untouchability Offences Act of 1955 (Mahar 1972a).[1] The second method embodies the programs of community development and welfare. Some of these programs are aimed at aiding landless agricultural laborers, urban slum dwellers, and other low-income groups, regardless of caste origin; but since the scheduled castes are disproportionately represented among such groups, they benefit greatly from the programs. The third method is what many Indian and foreign writers call "protective discrimination." These pro-

---

[1]The emancipation of their scheduled castes was in the constitutional provisions eliminating their ritual and legal disabilities imposed by traditional Hindu Society. The constitution declared that scheduled castes were not ritually polluting and granted them the same rights as other citizens, such as the franchise; it provided them seats in the national and state legislatures in proportion to their population; and it provided them with quotas in the civil service of the national, state and local governments. The civil rights act of 1955 (The Untouchability Offences Act) not only removed the remaining ritual barriers, but also made ritual discrimination against the scheduled castes punishable by law (see Beteille 1969:94–97; Chandrasekhar 1972; Dushkin 1972).

grams embody *preferential treatment* for the scheduled castes. Theoretically, this preferential treatment, the quota system, is supposed to continue until the scheduled castes have achieved their proportionate share of the political, social, and economic opportunities in modern India (Beteille 1967; Chandrasekhar 1972; Dushkin 1972).

Although the legislative and administrative measures noted above have resulted in some political and economic changes in the status of the scheduled castes in the past few decades, they have not resulted in the abolition of the caste system or the transformation of the scheduled castes into ordinary Indian citizens who can strive for and achieve self-improvement on the basis of individual training and ability. Nor have the legal safeguards protecting the scheduled castes made the dominant castes more willing to accept them as equals.

Education and Opportunity in India

Formal education in traditional India was essentially directed toward perpetuation of the system of closed caste stratification. The children of each of the three upper castes were trained to take their places in the adult world according to the existing values: Brahmin children learned to read the sacred texts and interpret them to the masses; Kshatriya children studied war, statecraft, and government organization as future secular rulers of the community; and Vaisya children learned arithmetic, the writing of business transactions, and how to keep records and maintain accounts, skills needed in managing their wealth and business. The lower castes, both clean and untouchables, were excluded from formal education (Chauhan 1967:230).

Under British colonial rule, the three upper castes monopolized the newly introduced Western education up to the first decade of this century. Thus modern education tended to strengthen the position of the traditionally privileged groups in emergent Indian society. The British first introduced Western education into the traditional Arabic and Sanskrit colleges which catered exclusively to the upper castes. The latter soon saw the relevance of Western education to their traditional roles as religious specialists, administrators, and businessmen as well as the new opportunities it offered them in the colonial administration. Not only did they dominate the educational institutions which came to be provided by the British missionaries, private organizations, and individuals with government grants, but by the end of the nineteenth century they also began to build schools themselves to enable their children to achieve a good education. They clearly perceived

Western education as a means to acquire the skills, valued and highly rewarded by the colonial government in the civil service, the teaching profession, and mercantile fields. The standards of efficiency and life-style of colonial administrators became objects of emulation for the upper castes (Chauhan 1967:232). Before the end of colonial rule, for-mal education at the elementary level was extended to most groups in India, although it was not free.

Indian people today desire formal education as in the old days because it enhances their chances of achieving social and occupational positions that are associated with material rewards and social prestige. Various positions in the civil service, business, and industry, for in-stance, require different amounts and kinds of education. From the point of view of the individual, formal education is now viewed throughout India as the *major means* of achieving significant social and occupational positions in adult life. The lower castes regard educa-tion as a means of escaping from their traditionally ascribed menial occupations; but all segments of society place a very high value on white-collar occupations, which are regarded as passports to respecta-bility (Beteille 1967:107). Education is positively associated with white-collar and professional occupations and negatively associated with manual occupations. The state of Madras has even gone so far as to pass a law that no one with a secondary school diploma should be employed to do manual labor (Mencher 1972). It is generally believed that the more education one has, the better are one's chances of obtain-ing a better job, higher wages, promotions, and social respectability. It is also believed that competition for these benefits of education should be free and based on individual training and ability, not on caste origin. But as will be seen later, in the case of the scheduled castes, the role of formal education in social mobility is still greatly influenced by caste membership.

Since India became independent, it has made some serious efforts both to provide free universal elementary school education and to ex-pand the opportunities for secondary school and higher education for those groups largely excluded from the colonial education system. The present system of education varies somewhat from state to state, but a more uniform national system begun in 1975 consists of five years of primary education and five of secondary, followed by two years of preuniversity training and a three-year university degree course. Most secondary schools are presently state schools, but the best are privately managed. Fees charged by the latter are usually so high that only well-to-do families can afford to send their children to them. These private secondary schools are chiefly preparatory schools for higher education, and they use English rather than one of Indian languages as the medium of instruction. In state primary and secondary schools, the dominant local language (e.g., Gujarati, Hindi, Urdu) is the medium of instruction. However, both state and private secondary schools follow the state syllabus and are subject to state inspection (see Parliamentary Select Committee 1973:71; Shukla 1974:237).

In most parts of India, schooling is free and universal for the first five years (Parliamentary Select Committee 1973:70; Postelthwaite 1974:160). Only a small proportion of children proceed to the secondary schools and not many of these graduate. The Parliamentary Select Committee on Race Relation study (1973:71) in the state of Gujarati in 1969 illustrates the high rate of attrition associated with the Indian system of education. In 1969, there were 4 million primary and secondary school students in the state. Of these, 1.4 million were in the first grade; the first and second grades accounted for about 50% of the total student population; and the ninth grade population was less than 10% of the first grade population. The proportion of those reaching the university was even smaller, partly because of the inability of many students to meet the entrance requirements (such as passing the Secondary School Certificate Examination), and partly because of their inability to meet the financial expense of attending either the state university or a private university.

Education of the Scheduled Castes

The exclusion of the scheduled castes from the Western education of the colonial period until the first decade of this century (Beteille 1967) resulted from the fact that they were confined to menial occupations for which formal education had little relevance and that they lived mainly in rural villages where schools were introduced very late.

Chauhan (1967:237–238) reports a number of important historical developments in the education of the scheduled castes. The first was the effort by some voluntary agencies (Christian missions, private societies, and individuals) to establish separate schools for them toward the end of the nineteenth century. These schools received some grants-in-aid from the colonial government, which also assumed some supervision over them. The Education Commission of 1881–1882 recommended that the special schools for the scheduled castes be abolished and that the untouchables be admitted to the standard public schools. However, the separate schools continued to exist well into the twentieth century.

The second development was an attempt to desegregate the multiple separate schools at the beginning of this century. At first, the scheduled caste children were assigned to sit in the back rows of designated classrooms, especially in the village schools. Although desegregation occurred as a result of government policy, integration was not fully achieved because of persistent prejudice and discrimination against scheduled-caste children in their new school environment.[2] Many teachers of upper-caste origin were openly prejudiced against children of scheduled-caste origin, nor have those children even now been fully accepted by upper-caste pupils and parents.

One other development was the launching of several government programs during the second decade of this century, whose purpose was to expand and strengthen the education of the scheduled castes. These programs came as a response to the increasing demands by Gandhi and the leaders of the scheduled castes themselves that they should be provided with more opportunities for formal education. The programs have been greatly expanded since India achieved independence, and the extension of basic education to the scheduled castes has been partially met by making primary education universal and free, although not compulsory. Government scholarship programs and other measures (e.g., special hostel facilities, lower eligibility requirements for scholarships, college admission, and so on) have been instituted since 1944 to encourage the education of the scheduled castes beyond high school (Chauhan 1967; Dushkin 1972:178).

The primary and secondary schools and colleges administered by the municipal, district, or state agencies are open to all children regardless of caste origin. In some places, the public primary school attendance of the scheduled castes equals that of the upper castes. But beyond this level, there is a great difference in the school attendance of the two groups (Mencher 1972:33). The scheduled castes attend public schools almost exclusively, while there is a tendency for the upper castes to send their children to private schools, some of which were founded by members of a particular caste to serve their own needs. The abandonment of the public schools by the well-to-do upper-caste members and the proliferation of private schools are due to the widespread belief among them that educational standards in the public schools have fallen considerably. This belief arises, in part, because of the government policy of reserving a certain proportion of the teaching and other positions in the public schools for members of the scheduled castes (Rao 1967).

[2]See p. 101 for the distinction between desegregation and integration. See also Pettigrew 1969a,b.

In theory then, the scheduled castes have had equal access to the public schools in their local communities since the abolition of the separate schools in 1948. In practice, however, they attend schools that are regarded as inferior, while many upper-caste parents pay to send their children to the superior private schools in India or to colleges in foreign countries. This is one of the reasons why the scheduled castes continue to lag behind the upper castes in education (see Chauhan 1967:239; Dushkin 1972:178–179; Mahar 1972c:33; Mencher 1972).

The Education Gap. The following description of the lag in the education and school performance of the scheduled castes is based on the sketchy and sometimes indirect evidence available. Scheduled castes have lower school enrollment and attendance at the primary, secondary, and college levels than do the upper castes. Although primary school education is free, many scheduled-caste families are too poor to provide their children with the books and other supplies they need to go to school. More important, families of these castes often need the labor of their school-age children in order to subsist. For example, in his study of a northern Indian village, Lewis (1958:179) found that the only scheduled-caste groups with high primary school attendance were the Nais and the Khatis, whose occupations (as barbers and carpenters) did not require the labor of children under 14 years of age. The attrition rate after primary school is considerably higher among the scheduled castes than among the upper castes. Enrollment of scheduled-caste children at the secondary school level has only recently increased because of government scholarship programs and special pre-secondary school training programs. This is also true at the college level, where the central government scholarship program plays a major role. However, the proportion of scheduled caste college students is still small (see p. 101; see also Chauhan 1967:240; Dushkin 1972:187).

Indirect evidence that the standard of classroom performance is much lower among scheduled castes than among upper castes comes from the fact that scheduled-caste candidates are permitted lower requirements for admission to colleges and universities and for qualifying for government scholarships; that leaders of their communities are insisting that the government strengthen the education of their children because they themselves received inferior educations and found it difficult to compete with the upper castes; that there is a drive to recruit teachers of scheduled-caste background. This campaign is based partly on the belief that the presence of such teachers in the classrooms would encourage scheduled-caste students to improve their school performance (Chauhan 1967:238).

The only comparative study of the performance on IQ tests of scheduled caste members with those of the upper castes is that of Bhatia (1955). He compared the performance of rural and urban, literate and nonliterate, and high-caste and low-caste children with scheduled-caste children. His study showed no significant differences between the high and low castes, perhaps because the items on the IQ tests were foreign to both groups. But there were significant differences among the various occupational groups, as well as between the rural and urban groups. However, the occupational and the rural–urban groups were not broken down by caste, so that it is not possible to compare the schedule castes with the upper castes on the basis of occupational status or place of residence.

In terms of literacy and educational attainment, the scheduled castes, as would be expected, rank lower than the general population and much below the upper castes. The Indian census for 1961 showed that although the national rate of literacy was 24%, it was 10.3% for the scheduled castes. It was highest in the states with the smallest concentrations of scheduled castes, such as Kerala, Assam, and Gujarat. Those living in urban areas were also more literate than those in the villages (Dushkin 1972:179–182).

Because of the high attrition rate among the scheduled castes in elementary school, many do not reach the secondary school level, and of those who do, very few graduate. I do not have the total school enrollment of the scheduled castes, but the proportion of those classified in the census as literate or said to have completed various levels of schooling gives a relatively good indication of their lag in education. Thus in 1961, out of a total scheduled-caste population of 64,417,366 the literate or educated proportion was 10.27% (6,616,203); 2.52% (1,622,816) had completed primary education, .27% (176,493) were high school graduates, and .01% (6,307) were college graduates. About 40% of the scheduled-caste college graduates came from two states, Uttar Pradesh and Delhi (Dushkin 1972:181).

Explaining the Gap. There is as yet no great body of literature examining critically the causes of the differences in education between the scheduled and upper castes. This may be attributed to (a) the relatively undeveloped state of the social sciences in India; (b) the preoccupation of Indian social scientists with other problems; (c) the recognition of the general problem of illiteracy among all groups in a country where nearly 76% of the people were reported to be illiterate in 1961; or (d) the refusal of Indian social scientists to acknowledge that the problem of untouchability still exists because it was formally abolished by the Untouchability Offences Act of 1955. Nevertheless, there are explanations for the lower educational accomplishments of the scheduled castes, which break down roughly into traditional and modern views.

The traditional view holds that inequalities exist in educational accomplishments and other areas of life because the scheduled castes are living out their Karma, i.e., their destined inferior status. At one time it was even believed that the scheduled castes belonged to a different race, although that view is not supported by anthropometric studies. Scheduled castes do not represent a homogeneous physical type, but the stereotype persists that they differ from the upper castes in skin color and facial type. Hence their lower educational accomplishments and their lower social, economic, and political status are interpreted by the traditionalists as the result of racial inferiority.

The modern view of the scheduled castes' problems in education is that they are associated with their *lower class status*, not caste status. There is a tendency to deny that untouchability still exists because the scheduled castes were emancipated by the constitution, and the Untouchability Offences Act of 1955 was intended to remove the last vestiges of the problem. The modernists point to the preferential treatment given to the scheduled castes in scholarships, college admission, and government jobs as evidence that the problem of untouchability is no longer a factor; but beneath these denials lies the powerful assumption that the scheduled castes are inferior to the upper caste, that every member of a scheduled caste holding a scholarship or a good job got it because of government preferential treatment and not because of his own ability. It is generally believed that members of the scheduled castes are incompetent, so that those who hold scholarships or good jobs are expected to prove themselves; and whenever a case of incompetence or failure occurs among them, it is taken as a general attribute of the scheduled castes.

Some Indian social scientists point out a number of ways in which the caste system adversely influences the education of the scheduled castes. During the colonial period, they were excluded from equal participation in the education system; education was not made available to the older generation of the scheduled castes in the same measure as it was to the older generation of the upper castes. And even after the schools were desegregated, the scheduled castes were still made to receive inferior education or forced to drop out of school because of the ritual prejudice of upper-caste pupils, parents, and teachers. Ritual prejudice persists in the schools today, even at the college level (Mahar 1972a).

The way in which the government scholarship program is administered discourages some scheduled-caste members from applying.

Among those who manage to go beyond the primary grades, there is always the question of employment, an issue I take up in a later section. Let us now look at what is being done to improve the educational accomplishments of the scheduled castes.

Closing the Gap. One of the earliest measures to improve the education of the scheduled castes was the abolition of their separate schools in 1948, which enabled them to attend the same schools as the general population in their local communities. The introduction of free universal primary education further ensured that this level of education was available to the members of all castes, irrespective of economic status. Here again there are some problems. Although primary school education is free, many scheduled-caste parents cannot afford the few materials their children need in school. To remedy this situation, state governments now provide scheduled-caste pupils with slates, books, school lunches, and other necessities. These children also attend secondary schools at the expense of the state, i.e., they pay no tuition fees, and they usually receive grants for books and other expenses, although these grants are often inadequate. The central government is responsible for all postsecondary school education of the scheduled castes. The government's scholarship program for higher education was initiated in 1944.

Scholarship programs, admission quotas, lower admission requirements, and reserved places in residence halls at the institutions of higher education, as well as other aids at the preuniversity levels, constitute a part of the "protective discrimination" programs. To be eligible for these programs, the applicant must present proof of his scheduled-caste membership. As mentioned previously, these programs are theoretically supposed to continue until the members of the scheduled castes have reached their proportionate share of various levels of educational achievement (see Chauhan 1967; Dushkin 1972; Mahar 1972b,c,d).

There is no general assessment of the sources of these programs, but available data indicate many positive results. First, the rate of illiteracy among the scheduled castes seems to have decreased appreciably, especially in those states where they constitute only a small proportion of the total population. Second, the number of members of the scheduled castes attending high schools and universities is increasing significantly. For example, in the 1950–1951 school year, the scheduled castes constituted only .32% of the total university population. By the 1960–1961 school year, their proportion had risen to 5.3%. The number receiving government scholarships increased from 75,000 in 1964–1965 to 103,000 in 1967–1968. Chauhan (1967) estimated that by the middle of the 1970s the scheduled castes' "share in the college population [would reach] half of their proportionate population in India [p. 240]." There are no adequate data to support this optimistic view.

On the whole, these advances have reduced the differences in educational attainment between the scheduled castes and the upper castes only slightly. But simultaneously the gap in quality of the education between the two groups may have widened: As mentioned earlier, the increasing participation of the scheduled castes in public school education has tended to be associated with deterioration in the quality of these schools and the withdrawal of the upper castes into private schools. Even those upper-caste children who remain in the public schools often have private tutors to supplement their education and thus better prepare them for higher education. That a gap exists in the quality of school performance between the scheduled castes and the upper castes is further supported by the continued use of lower qualification requirements for government scholarships and for secondary and college admissions for the scheduled castes.

Education and the Future

The scheduled castes initially attempted to use education to improve their position as castes, not as individuals, within the traditional hierarchy. Their new literacy skills enabled them to learn directly from the Sanskrit classics about the ritual life of the upper castes, and the relative improvement in their material resources enabled them to afford the symbols associated with upper-caste lifestyles. But even with their modern education, the scheduled castes were unable to achieve upward mobility in the traditional caste system.

The reason for this failure, according to Srinivas (1962), is that "however thoroughgoing the Sanskritization of an Untouchable group may be, it is unable to cross the ritual barriers of untouchability." Srinivas goes on to say, "It is indeed an anachronism that while groups which were originally outside Hinduism such as tribal groups, or alien ethnic groups have succeeded in entering the Hindu fold, and occasionally at a higher level, an Untouchable Caste is always forced to remain untouchable [p. 59]." Beteille (1967) suggests that the scheduled castes fail to achieve upward group mobility through Sanskritization, partly because of the great *structural distance* between them and the upper castes, which continues to be maintained through

the rules of endogamy, and partly because of the barriers of untouchability, which often remain even after intermarriage takes place.[3]

Because the scheduled castes have not succeeded in improving
their positions as groups in the traditional caste hierarchy through
formal education and Sanskritization, the younger generations of these
castes are increasingly rejecting the traditional upper castes as models
for emulation. They are also rejecting Sanskritization and the Hindu
model of social mobility and converting to Buddhism, Islam, Sikhism,
and Christianity. Older members of the scheduled castes still hold to
the traditional model of social mobility, but any member of the younger
generation who aspires to political leadership usually finds it advan-
tageous to repudiate Sanskritization and the Hindu social structure.

The scheduled castes now desire education primarily because it
enables them *as individuals* to achieve self-improvement in the
technoeconomic system of modern India. In particular, they regard
education as a route by which the individual can escape from the traditionally ascribed menial occupations. Not only the scheduled castes,
but all Indian groups, attach a very high value to nonmanual work,
viewing a white-collar job as a passport to respectability and education
as a passport to a white-collar job. The scheduled castes, however,
desire white-collar jobs more strongly than other Indians, probably
because they were excluded from such occupations in the past. Beteille
(1967:107) thinks that the value the scheduled castes attach to white-
collar jobs is so strong that they refuse to enter government-sponsored
crafts-training schools.

Competition for white-collar and other highly rewarding jobs, such
as jobs in government, in the modern sector of Indian society is theoret-

---

[3]In the traditional hierarchical organization of Indian caste system, the structural distance between any two castes was the number of segments by which the castes were separated from each other.
The greatest structural distance existed between the scheduled castes, who were at the bottom of this
hierarchical organization, and the upper castes, who were at the opposite end. This structural distance
was maintained partly by rules prohibiting intercaste marriage, partly by rules proscribing intercaste
commensality (eating together) and other forms of social interaction, and partly by distinctive lifestyles developed by each caste and sanctioned by the system. Sankritization offered one legitimate
means by which the structural distance between castes could be reduced. Essentially, Sankritization
involved the adoption of the lifestyles of a caste higher in the social hierarchy by a lower caste. Castes
on the middle and lower-middle rungs of the hierarchy successfully used Sankritization to achieve
social mobility within the hierarchical organization (i.e., reduce the structural distance between them
and the higher castes), but Sankritization did not fulfill this function for the scheduled castes. This
was partly because the scheduled castes usually did not have the economic and political power by
which they could validate their claims of changed lifestyles, partly because they possessed a far too
inferior ritual status, and partly because the upper castes opposed their social mobility, which they
interpreted as a threat not only to their own social status but also to their economic and political
power (Beteille 1967:94–103).

ically based on individual ability and education, not on caste origin. That is, members of the upper castes and members of the scheduled castes compete for these positions on the basis of training and ability. But in this competition the scheduled castes fare rather badly. First, the upper castes have had a head start in education and are therefore more likely to possess higher qualifications for the same positions. Second, and perhaps more important, traditional caste barriers intrude into the modern Indian economic system to prevent members of scheduled castes from getting jobs for which they are qualified if these are outside their traditionally ascribed occupations.

Thus a job ceiling exists in modern India to deny members of the scheduled castes equal opportunities to benefit from education as the upper castes do. In both rural villages and urban centers, Indian society places a lower value on the academic credentials of scheduled castes and denies them employment in jobs commensurate with their education.

In the rural villages where more than 80% of the scheduled castes still live, social and economic conditions make no provision to accommodate educated members of these castes, except for a few teachers. In these rural communities, the upper castes manipulate government-sponsored rural development programs to ensure their continued political and economic domination of the scheduled castes. Srinivas (1962) points out that

> While the leaders of the dominant castes are sensitive to economic and political opportunities, they are socially conservative. They do not, for instance, like the conditions of the Harijans to improve.[4] They have a vested interest in keeping Harijans poor and ignorant. At the present time Harijans are their most important sources of agricultural labor, and if they become educated and conscious of their rights they will be a threat to the position of the dominant castes. Anti-Harijan sentiments are freely expressed in the rural areas. Attempts by Harijans to exercise the rights given to them by the Constitution have led to violent attacks on them by the dominant castes. They have been beaten up and their huts burned down, and in addition, they have been subjected to economic boycott. Harijans are among the poorest sections of our agricultural population and many of them are agricultural servants of the land-owing castes.

Because of such conditions in the rural villages, educated scheduled-caste members have no alternative other than to migrate to

---

[4]The term *Harijan*, originally coined by Gandhi, means *Children of God*. It is a term the educated elites of the dominant castes prefer to use for the scheduled castes because they consider the term *untouchables* to be derogatory and because untouchability was officially abolished by the constitution. Educated members of the scheduled castes, on the other hand, rarely refer to themselves as *Harijans*; instead, they freely use the term *Untouchables*.

the cities. But in the cities they also face many social and occupational barriers, and most of them work only as scavengers, sweepers, truck and bus drivers, or railroaders. They are rarely hired for jobs above these categories except for those positions traditionally held by members of their group. They are excluded from better jobs in private industry, partly because employees in such industries are hired through regional caste and family connections. But the scheduled castes are excluded mainly because of their ritual status: few high-caste Hindus would knowingly hire a member of the scheduled castes for more than a menial job (Isaacs 1972:372).

Isaacs (1972:377) notes also that until recently neither the academic institutions nor the professions in India offered educated scheduled-castes members any appreciable opportunities. He estimates that in 1953 there were probably no scheduled-caste members with Ph.D. degrees but that in 1963 there were about 100 such people, some of whom now hold junior positions in academic institutions. In teaching, it is only at the primary and secondary levels that the number of the scheduled castes has grown rapidly in recent years.

The civil service has, however, provided the educated scheduled-caste members the best opportunity for employment through the system of "protective discrimination" described previously (see Beteille 1967; Chandresekhar 1972; Dushkin 1972; Isaacs 1964, 1972). Usually a certain percentage of various jobs at each level of the civil service is reserved for qualified members of those castes. This reserved quota system was begun toward the end of the colonial period and has continued in an expanded form in independent India because the constitution mandates the government to transform Indian society into a nation based on "justice, equality, and fraternity" (Chauhan 1967). The current quota for direct recruitment of the scheduled castes to central government jobs is 16.6%, although for positions where the candidates are selected through competitive examinations the quota is 12.5% (Dushkin 1972:185).

The actual representation of the scheduled castes in government jobs falls far short of what might be expected from the quota system: First, jobs above the clerical level are filled by promotions, where quotas do not usually apply; second, bureaucratic manipulation intervenes. Thus Dushkin (1972:183) says that the figures from the employment exchanges in 1966 showed that only 3.84% (6621 out of 172,227 positions) of all vacancies reported to the exchanges were reserved for scheduled-caste members, although the statutory reservations ranged from 12.5% to 16.6%. The third reason for the discrepancy is that reservation orders do not apply to all jobs, especially to menial jobs. Because of this, those who seek employment through the exchanges are often channeled into the unreserved vacancies in both government and private industries, and these are usually menial jobs.

Channeling scheduled-caste members into menial jobs by the employment exchanges means that they are overrepresented in the least desirable occupations and underrepresented in the most desirable. For example, almost all the sweepers—the lowest category of government employees—came from the scheduled castes in 1966; in the same year, they constituted only 1.77% of the senior administrative civil servants (Dushkin 1972:183).

Protective discrimination seems to work best at the lower echelons of the white-collar jobs. Because many scheduled caste members are able to meet the educational requirements for these jobs, most of them perceive their best chances of being employed at all occurring at this level and therefore tend to seek employment there. At this level, they are permitted even more than their proportionate representation, perhaps to compensate for their exclusion from higher job categories through the job ceiling.

In addition to their exclusion from higher categories of government jobs, it appears that scheduled-caste candidates are expected to demonstrate more than educational qualifications for the jobs they want. Many government jobs reserved for the scheduled castes are left unfilled, while many scheduled-cast members with the requisite educational qualifications remain unemployed. For example, it was reported that in 1966 only half of the 9605 government jobs reserved for scheduled caste members were filled because of a lack of qualified candidates, although, as Dushkin (1972) points out, there were also nearly 64,000 high school and college graduates still looking for work:

> "[This] does not mean "a dearth of candidates" with the minimum qualifications [exam marks] stipulated for the job.... It apparently means that they have not demonstrated additional qualifications deemed desirable for the maintenance of efficient operations. It is difficult to regard 60,260 high school and 3,480 college graduates still seeking jobs in 1966 as a "dearth" of any other sort. The fact that Scheduled Caste candidates sometimes passed written qualifying exams and then failed the oral personality tests suggests that they were still suffering from the very class differentials which reservations are intended to overcome [p. 185]."

In the private sector, the job ceiling is extremely low, so that the chances of scheduled-caste members being employed in white-collar jobs are very slim. Here they face both stiff competition and resistance from members of the dominant castes. The low job ceiling in the private sector is shown in Table 10.1 which compares the employment of scheduled-caste members as clerks and other officials in government (where reservation applies) and in the private sector (where reservation does not apply).

The fact that Indian society does not offer the scheduled castes social and occupational rewards commensurate with their education and abilities contributes to their lag in school performance. Being restricted to menial occupations, they are unable to achieve incomes high enough to purchase better education for their children in the private schools or through tutoring services.

However, the lack of equitable rewards for their education has not led the scheduled castes to develop serious fatalistic attitudes toward education. One reason for this is that formal education is a relatively recent phenomenon among many of the castes. Another reason is that while the educated scheduled-caste members do not have the same opportunities for good jobs and incomes as do educated members of the upper castes, they are still able to get better jobs with higher wages than is possible for the uneducated members of their own castes. So they continue to desire education and work hard in school to escape from their traditionally ascribed menial positions as landless agricultural laborers or menial urban workers. It will be recalled that in the state of Madras, the law forbids the employment of anyone with a high school

Table 10.1

Employment of Scheduled Castes in Class I–III Jobs in the Private Sector and in the Central Government Civil Service of India, January 1966

	Private sector		Central government	
Class of post	Total employed	Scheduled castes as percentage of total	Total employed	Scheduled castes as percentage of total
Class 1: Senior administrators	35,512	0.20	20,379	1.77
Class II: Other administrators	15,820	1.07	30,379	3.25
Class III: Clerical workers and stenographers	126,166	0.92	1,117,754	8.86

SOURCE: Adapted from Dushkin, 1972. Scheduled caste politics. *The untouchables in contemporary India,* edited by J. H. Mahar. Tucson: Univ. of Arizona Press. P. **183**.

diploma as a manual laborer. The alternative to manual labor is a white-collar job, and a white-collar job of any kind is enough incentive for schooling.[5]

The third, and perhaps the most important reason why scheduled-caste members have not developed a collective fatalism toward education is the system of protective discrimination. Because certain government legal, social, and economic programs are designed to favor them as a matter of constitutional responsibility, they tend to perceive the government as supportive of their cause. Even though the quota system in scholarships, school admissions, and jobs has many imperfections in its actual operation, the system works adequately enough to sustain their expectations of the government. There is no indication in the literature that scheduled-caste members or those sympathetic to their cause have tried to pressure private employers to hire more educated members of their groups or to hire them in higher job categories. Nor is the reason for this lack of pressure on private employers evident in the literature.

Finally, scheduled-caste members do not seem to have developed a serious fatalistic attitude toward education because they appear to have found several alternative uses for education. At first, they tried to use it to improve their relative position as a group, rather than as individuals, within the traditional caste hierarchy. When this approach failed, they began to use education to achieve individual self-improvement in the modern sector of Indian society. They have not found this path easy. As Table 10.1 shows, they are discriminated against when they compete with the upper castes for the same jobs and other positions for which their education qualifies them. Some try to overcome this difficulty by "passing" as members of the higher castes. In order to do this, they usually move to other parts of India, where they can conceal their caste origins. But passing has its own problems, and therefore it is not an ideal solution (Isaacs 1972). The political arena is also opening up other opportunities for them to experience benefits from education. As the scheduled-castes, often in coalition with other castes, gain political strength in local councils, state legislatures, and the national parliament, they are able to bring about new laws which create better opportunities for the educated members of their groups (Beteille 1967; Dushkin:1972; Isaacs 1972). It thus appears that they have not yet exhausted the number of ways in which they can use education profitably.

---

[5]The threat of growing unemployment may also act as an incentive for the scheduled castes to strive for education.

In conclusion, there is a gap in school performance between the scheduled castes and the upper castes. The gap is attributable to the fact that formal education was introduced late to the scheduled castes; that the education offered to them is generally inferior to that offered to the upper castes; and that a job ceiling prevents them from utilizing their academic skills to the same degree and deriving the same material and psychic rewards from their training as do the members of the upper castes. But unlike similar minorities in other societies, the scheduled castes in India have not yet developed a serious fatalistic attitude toward education because they have not exhausted alternative uses of education.

11

The Buraku Outcastes of Japan

As in India, there were castes in premodern Japanese society, of which the Burakumin constituted the lowest caste of outcastes. This outcaste minority group was previously called *Eta*, meaning literally "full of filth." Today the term *Eta* has the same pejorative connotation as the term *nigger* in the United States (Donoghue 1967). The accepted term for the group in contemporary Japan is *Burakumin*, which means "people of special or unliberated communities."

The Burakumin differ from both the Korean and the Ainu minorities. Unlike the Koreans, they are not immigrant minorities. Furthermore, although in contemporary Japan Koreans are ranked lower than the dominant group in the social hierarchy (Mitchell 1967), they rank higher than the Burakumin. Mitchell points out that Japanese–Korean intermarriage goes further back, to premodern times. At that time, "More than a third of the families of the Japanese nobility were descendants of Korean and Chinese immigrants [p. 3]." Today Japanese–Korean intermarriage is on the increase. In contrast, there is little intermarriage between the Burakumin and the dominant Ippan group, and in the past intermarriage was legally forbidden.

The Buraku outcastes differ from the Ainu, who also rank above them. Cornell reports (1964) that the Ainu have always been respected as human beings, although their culture was deprecated. Thus while the Ainu culture has been regarded as expendable, steps have been taken to assimilate the Ainu population. In contrast, the Burakumin were historically ranked as subhuman (De Vos 1973:310).

Further historical background will help to clarify the present position of the Buraku outcastes. In the past, Japanese society was divided into four "human" classes, consisting of the samurai (i.e., the ruling warrior elite), the peasant masses (farmers), the artisans, and the merchants. Below these were two "subhuman groups, the *Hinin* ("Non-people," consisting of itinerant entertainers, prostitutes, and quasi-religious itinerants), and the Eta, an artisan group who also handled the dead (De Vos 1973; Price 1967; Wagatsuma 1967a). The Eta were considered lower than the Hinin because their occupation was "polluting." Some of them were leatherworkers and engaged in slaughtering and skinning animals, tanning leather, and making leather goods. Because Shinto tradition regarded the handling of carcasses as polluting and because Buddhism forbade the killing of animals, the Eta leatherworkers were avoided by other members of Japanese society. They had to live in separate communities, "away from the communities of decent common people" [Wagatsuma 1967b:119].

In the early part of the seventeenth century, during the Tokugawa era, the status of the Eta as an untouchable group was firmly established through an official classification: they were declared untouchable and became a hereditary caste. By government edict, they were forced to wear special costumes and reside in special communities away from others; they were also forbidden to intermarry with other Japanese (De Vos 1973:311; Price 1967; Wagatsuma 1967a:120).

The Eta were formally emancipated in 1871 by another government edict, which abolished their pariah caste status and proclaimed them as "new commoners" (De Vos 1973:312; Price 1967; Wagatsuma 1967a). This edict did not produce any radical changes in their social and economic conditions, nor did it change the attitudes of the dominant Japanese groups toward them. The "emancipated" Eta remained in their segregated communities not only because of social and economic ties but also because they were prevented from entering the dominant society through informal sanctions against integrated residence and intermarriage. In rural areas, they survived either as owners of inferior farmland or as tenant farmers. Those who lived in or near the cities either continued to follow their traditional occupations as butchers and tanners or took up other menial jobs. Their emancipation adversely affected their economic status in two ways: They lost their legal monopoly on some of their more lucrative traditional occuaptions, and they began, for the first time, to pay taxes like other Japanese.

The Burakumin population is now estimated to number between 1.5 and 3 million. They still live in about 6000 segregated communities, located in both rural and urban areas (De Vos 1973; Wagatsuma 1967a). The dominant groups still regard them as physically different and racially inferior, even though they are not racially different, and their identity can be firmly established only through place of birth. Wagatsuma (1967a:118–119) summarizes the beliefs and attitudes of the dominant society toward the Burakumin as follows:

> The Burakumin are considered mentally inferior, incapable of high moral behavior, aggressive, impulsive, and lacking in any notion of sanitation or manners. Very often they are "the last hired and the first fired." Marriage between a Buraku individual and a member of the majority society, if not impossible, is frequently the cause of tragedy and ostracism.

Since the beginning of the twentieth century, the Burakumin, with the help of sympathetic elites of the dominant Ippan caste, have formed a number of civil rights organizations to counter the prejudice and discrimination of the dominant society. Although the Japanese government subsidizes the activities of some of these organizations, there has been no national legislation to deal with the prejudice and social and economic barriers against the Burakumin (see Totten and Wagatsuma 1967:38–63; Wagatsuma 1967a:122; 1967b:68–87).

Education and Opportunity in Japan

Traditional Japanese culture strongly encouraged achievement through individual ability. Nakane (1970:111) reports that the Japanese much admired a man born into poverty who achieved great social and economic success through hard work. Dore (1967) describes the evolution of the belief, dating from the Tokugawa period, that one can achieve social and economic success through personal courage, energy, and ability. He also shows how formal education developed as the principal mechanism of social mobility. He suggests that the widespread ambition "to get ahead" can be seen in the post-World War II intensification of the competition for educational credentials (1967:138–139). Whether in competition for academic success or in other kinds of competition, the Japanese do not believe that success is determined chiefly by innate ability. Instead, they believe that anyone who works hard enough can succeed in spite of any "natural deficiencies" he may have (1967:140).

Contemporary Japanese society strongly encourages educational achievement as a prerequisite for attaining desirable social and occupational positions in adult life. It regards educational credentials as the true evidence of a person's ability, to be rewarded by jobs and social position. Nakane (1970:111–112) notes that the belief that a person should be fully rewarded for his or her educational accomplishments is particularly strong in the area of employment, although it is also pertinent to other areas of adult life. He states that the length and quality of a person's education are important criteria in judging ability.

> By such standards, a man with only qualifications up to high school level, whatever his ability and experience, cannot compete with a university graduate in obtaining employment or in climbing the promotion ladder. Three or four years in earlier life make a significant difference in Japan. *Indeed, society in general regards educational background as one of the most important yardsticks of ability and social significance and there is little regard for what a man has done outside school education.* Educational qualifications are obvious and perceivable, and can be used as a clear measurement and open indication, while it is difficult for everyone to judge individual achievements outside school by generally accepted and acknowledged standards [pp. 111–112; emphasis added].

This ideology that education is the best evidence of a person's ability and that it acts as the best bridge to desirable social and occupational roles in adult life is reflected both in the development of the modern Japanese education system and in the Japanese quest for education. Before the Meiji Restoration in 1868, most children did not attend school. For instance, only 28.13% of the children of elementary school age were enrolled in school in 1872 (Kaigo 1965:65). Before 1868, the few schools and colleges supported by the government were intended mainly to train members of the samurai ruling class. Some commoners obtained educations in private schools housed in temples or private homes (Hall 1965).

Following the Meiji Restoration, a universal system of elementary education based on the French model was introduced. The schools were administered by prefectural and local officials but received subsidies from the national government. By 1890, the national school system had become firmly established; at the same time, it was reorganized into a four-year ordinary elementary school followed by a two-year upper elementary school. Later it was further reorganized into a six-year ordinary elementary school followed by a two-year upper elementary school. Then compulsory education was extended from four to six years, that is, through the six-year ordinary elementary school (Dore 1967:131–132; Kaigo 1965). Although these schools were tax supported, they were not free. The elementary schools continued to charge tuition fees until 1898, when the fees were abolished (Dore 1967:131). By 1907 enrollment had reached 97.38% of the population of elementary school age.

Postelementary education was organized into various types of high schools, including academic high schools (i.e., middle schools for boys), girls' high schools, and vocational schools. Superimposed on this was a system of higher education consisting of government-sponsored and private colleges and universities. The number of these colleges and universities, as well as their student enrollment, expanded very rapidly between 1935 and 1945. Neither the secondary schools nor the institutions of higher education were free or compulsory (Kaigo 1965:64–65, 92, 106).

In 1947, the entire system from the elementary schools to the universities was reorganized on the American model of 6–3–3–4, that is, it contained six years elementary school followed by three years of lower secondary school, three years of senior secondary school, and four years of university. The first nine years of public school, elementary through the lower secondary level, are now free and compulsory. Although upper secondary school is neither free nor compulsory, about 50% of the lower secondary school graduates are reported to be proceeding to various types of upper secondary schools. Some go to special five-year technical schools which combine high school and junior college courses geared for technical training. Some continue their education by correspondence courses or part-time studies. Recent reforms of secondary education have attempted to provide a more uniform system of secondary education and thus abolish "privileged connections" as criteria for admission to higher educational institutions (Kaigo 1965:92). Postsecondary educational institutions themselves are now organized into four basic types: five-year higher technical colleges, two-year junior colleges, four-year universities for the baccalaureate degree, and universities with graduate training.

These reforms, together with postwar economic prosperity, have resulted in a national increase in the level of education. By 1960, the percentage of children attending elementary school had reached 99.82%. Most proceed to the free and compulsory three-year junior secondary schools. In 1960, about 6 million children were in such schools. The percentage of graduates of the lower secondary schools going on to the upper secondary schools rose from 45% in 1950 to 60.2% in 1960 and 70.6% in 1964; and the number of students receiving higher education has increased by more than 50% since the reforms of 1947 (Hall 1965; Kaigo 1965). These developments, however, do not necessarily reflect the experience of the Buraku outcastes.

Education of the Buraku Outcastes

It is not certain that the Burakumin participated in any formal education before they were emancipated in 1871. After emancipation they were included in the new comprehensive system of universal education established in 1873. Because the official policy was nondiscriminatory, no separate schools were built for the Burakumin; but in practice there was strong discrimination against them. Wagatsuma (1967b) reports that "there were numerous instances of de facto exclusion of outcaste children from participation in school programs [p. 100]." Some Buraku communities established their own private schools, but they had difficulty staffing them. Most teachers were members of the samurai and landowning classes and were prejudiced against the Burakumin and unwilling to teach in Buraku communities. Until the Buraku schools were incorporated into the national public school system, they were staffed mainly by young volunteers motivated in part by the idea of educating indigenous Buraku leaders. These educators also hoped to teach the Burakumin "the right attitudes and behavior" that would make them more acceptable to the dominant Ippan group. It was thought that the achievement of such educational goals "would naturally lead to a removal of discriminatory attitudes and practices" held by the dominant group [Wagatsuma 1967b:100].

The outcastes had considerable interest in education, but formal education spread more slowly among them than among the dominant group, partly because outcaste families were generally more impoverished and could not afford to send their children to school. Their participation began to increase when fees were abolished for the compulsory education period. The extension of the period of free compulsory education and other developments in Japanese education since the end of World War II have also increased Buraku participation.

· Today the children of the Buraku outcastes and the children of the Ippan attend the same schools. Exceptions can probably be found where the Buraku outcastes live in segregated communities large or remote enough to have their own schools. Specific information on the education of Buraku outcastes is difficult to find because of the official and conventional Japanese attitude of denying that they can still be classed as outcastes. But enough information is available from various sources to indicate the degree of their school performance.

The Education Gap. A few studies show that there are significant differences between the Buraku outcastes and the Ippan in literacy rates, truancy rates, school dropout rates, and performance on standardized tests of scholastic achievement and IQ. De Vos and Wagatsuma (1967c:263–264) cite a number of studies which show that long-term absenteeism, truancy, and school dropout are more prevalent among Buraku students. For example, in Nara prefecture between 1950 and 1953, about 30% (162 out of 503) of the Buraku students failed to complete junior high school, compared to only 3% (8 out of 237) of the other students. Brameld's study (1968:101) in another prefecture showed that in one community, although the Buraku represented 35% of the primary school enrollment (105 out of 300), their proportion dwindled to a mere 5% at the junior high school. At the senior high school, there were only six Buraku students, and at the college level only two. Most Buraku children drop out of school soon after reaching the legal school-leaving age of 15. Brameld (1968:101) found that in general only 10% of the Buraku students completing junior high school proceeded to senior high, whereas among the Ippan students approximately 85% did so. Furthermore, he found that the Buraku students were overrepresented in junior high prevocational rather than academic courses. He also reports that in two of the schools he studied the Buraku students were disproportionately represented in special education classes for slow learners (1968:101). De Vos and Wagatsuma (1967c:260–263) cite some studies in which Buraku students scored lower than other students on both scholastic achievement tests devised by the Ministry of Education and standardized intelligence tests (IQ tests). At the elementary school level, the grade-point average of Buraku students ranged from 2.29 for boys to 2.51 for girls; for other students it was 3.29 and 3.16, respectively. At the junior high school level, it was 2.2 for Buraku students and 3.3 for others. On standardized achievement tests, Buraku students at the junior high level scored 46.5 in Japanese, 46.6 in humanities, 36.4 in mathematics and 41.0 in science. For other students, the scores were 55.5, 61.8, 49.9, and 51.1, respectively.

Intelligence tests are not popular in Japan, but reports of a few cases where such tests have been given to both Buraku and non-Buraku students indicate that the former consistently score below members of the dominant group. Tables 11.1 and 11.2 indicate this pattern: Table 11.1 shows the results of a Tanaka-Binet group of IQ tests administered in Takatsuki City; Table 11.2 shows the results of the same tests given to smaller groups of children in Fukuchiyama City (De Vos and Wagatsuma 1967c:260–162; De Vos 1973:314–315).

Thus the minority outcastes in Japan, as in the other societies examined here, consistently perform lower than the dominant group on tests of both intelligence and scholastic achievement. They also generally have lower educational attainments than the dominant group.

Explaining the Gap. How the Japanese explain the lower educational standards of the Burakumin is even more difficult to describe. The published literature in English contains very little information about it. Indirect evidence suggests that there are popular stereotypes: The outcastes are lazy, lacking in persistent efforts, unreliable, and dependent. These and other stereotypes tend to imply that the outcastes differ from other Japanese and that they are inferior (Brameld 1968; Cornell 1967b:348; Donoghue 1967; Price 1967; Wagatsuma 1967a). One school superintendent added to the stereotypes by saying that the outcastes in his schools are overrepresented in special classes for slow learners because they have a high rate of endogamy (Brameld 1968).

As for Japanese social scientists, it can generally be said that they do not explain the lower Buraku educational standards in terms of lower IQ. On the whole, the Japanese believe that hard work and persistent efforts can compensate for such innate deficiencies (see Dore 1967:140).

Another kind of explanation is provided by De Vos and Wagat-

Table 11.1

*A Comparison of the Scores of Buraku and
Non-Buraku Students on the Tanaka-Binet
Intelligence Test, Takatsuki City
(percentage groupings)*

IQ	Buraku children (N = 77)	Non-Buraku children (N = 274)
125 or higher	2.6	23.3
109–124	19.5	31.8
93–108	22.1	23.3
77–92	18.2	11.7
76 or lower	37.6	9.9

SOURCE: George A. De Vos and Hiroshi Wagatsuma, eds. 1967 *Japan's invisible race*. Berkeley: Univ. of California Press. P. 261.

Table 11.2
A Comparison of the Scores of Buraku and
Non-Buraku Primary School Pupils on the
Tanaka-Binet Intelligence Test, Fukuchiyama
City

	N	Average IQ
Buraku boys	10	89
Buraku girls	9	87
Non-Buraku boys	10	105
Non-Buraku girls	12	103

SOURCE: George A. De Vos and Hiroshi
Wagatsuma, eds. 1967. Japan's invisible race.
Berkeley: Univ. of California Press. P. 261.

suma (1967c:263). In their discussion of the problems of absenteeism
and school dropout, they point out that the general poverty of the
outcaste families probably accounts for these phenomena among them.
Not only is it difficult for the outcaste families to support their children
in school beyond the compulsory years, but these families often need
the extra money the children earn in order to help support the family.

   Closing the Gap. There are no special programs to ensure educational equality between the Burakumin and the larger society, either by
increasing their proportional representation at various levels or by improving their classroom performance. Those aspects of national educational policy that seem to favor the Burakumin are that Buraku and
non-Buraku children appear to have the same curriculum and
textbooks and, where possible, attend the same schools; that segregation is unconstitutional; that special classes are provided for slow learners which ideally could benefit Buraku students who are disproportionately represented in such classes; and that a large number of
Burakumin receive financial aid from government welfare programs for
poor children in the junior high schools (see Brameld 1968; Wagatsuma
1967a).

   Since 1926, the Japanese government has attempted to use educational institutions as instruments of integrating and assimilating
Buraku outcastes into the dominant society. Between 1926 and 1938,
the government instituted special "integration" programs, including
the teaching of values and attitudes intended to eliminate the prejudice
and discriminatory treatment of the majority toward the Burakumin.
These programs were instituted in response to the criticisms of the
Levellers' Association, a Buraku civil rights organization, against

the educational system, which emphasized the military aspects of Japanese culture (Wagatsuma 1967c:102).[1]

In 1938, the government introduced what it called "assimilation education" for the purpose of eliminating discrimination against the Burakumin. But the real purpose of assimilation education, according to a government pamphlet published in 1941, was to promote the solidarity and unity of the Japanese nation for the purpose of winning the war. It was thought that assimilation would be achieved under this program both by teaching the majority group to give up their prejudice and discrimination against the Burakumin and by teaching the Burakumin to give up those features of their lives which caused discrimination, such as "untidy manners, bad speech, and lack of moral attitudes" (Wagatsuma 1967b:103). Assimilation education continued after the war, and since 1959 it has received increased financial support from the national government. Current emphasis in assimilation education includes not only courses of study in the schools to teach children the causes of discrimination and the nature of Buraku problems but also programs geared to change teachers' attitudes toward the problems. Recent studies cited by Wagatsuma (1967b:106–197) indicate that teachers are becoming more aware of these problems and are developing more positive attitudes to help solve them.

How effective assimilation education and other programs are in improving the school performance of the Buraku outcastes is unknown. Indeed, because of the reluctance of both the government and Japanese social scientists to admit the existence of a Buraku problem, the situation has never been seriously studied in a way that would provide an objective basis for evaluating the effects of various programs of Buraku education. The data I presented above in discussing the school performance gap suggest, however, that the programs have been relatively ineffective in closing the education gap between Buraku outcastes and the Ippan majority.

Education and the Future

Although kinship and personal connections are still important for getting a good job in modern Japan, a good educational background is a

---

[1]The Levellers' Association (Zenkoku Suiheisha) was the first civil rights organization formed by the Burakumin themselves with the objective of achieving equality with the dominant Ippan group through political action. It was first organized in 1922 as a "leveling" movement (suihei undo) because its purpose was to remove "all social and political distinctions and inequalities" between the Burakumin and the rest of society (Totten and Wagatsuma 1967:43–44).

prerequisite for many important occupational positions. But the situation is not the same for the Buraku outcastes as for members of the dominant group. In the first place, because the outcastes are extraneous to the kinship systems and personal connections of the dominant society, they are excluded from positions where such ties are necessary or important. In the second place, the outcastes are subject to prejudice in hiring practices. Because discrimination is unconstitutional, no employer will publicly reject a Buraku applicant simply because of an outcaste background; but several studies show that employers are most reluctant to hire Burakumin except for the positions of menial labor traditionally associated with their outcaste status (see Brameld 1968; Cornell 1967; De Vos 1973; De Vos and Wagatsuma 1967c; Donoghue 1967; Wagatsuma 1967a).

An example of the unequal opportunity in obtaining jobs for educated Burakumin is described by De Vos. He cites a study by Mahara (1959) of junior high school graduates in Kyoto. Among the Buraku graduates, about 29.8% obtained jobs with small-scale industries; only 1.5% obtained jobs with large-scale industries where the working conditions are much better. For the other graduates, the figures were 13.1% and 15.1% respectively. The average starting salary for the two groups was different: 4808 yen for Burakumin and 5196 yen for others. Employers often rationalize this discriminatory treatment by saying that Buraku applicants are "not as qualified" as non-Buraku applicants for the same jobs. However, De Vos (1973) notes that "many employers are unwilling to hire Buraku applicants even when they are well qualified. Several of the largest companies in the Osaka region are said to exclude all Burakumin as a matter of policy [pp. 313–315]."

Japanese society also offers the more highly educated Burakumin few rewards for their educational efforts. They have only two options: They can pass into the dominant society in order to benefit more fully from their education or they can, perhaps reluctantly, direct their energies into the Buraku ghetto to fight against the discrimination and injustice done to Burakumin as a group. Passing is not an easy solution to the problem; It involves social and psychological costs that many are unwilling to pay. To pass successfully requires moving to a distant part of the country and cutting oneself off from kinship and personal ties. One must manipulate the bureaucracy, for example, by moving at least four times to escape identification with residence in an outcaste area because one is required to carry an identification card that lists three previous places of residence.

A more difficult problem to overcome is the practice of investigating a person's background prior to employment or marriage. The *koseki* (family record) of any individual can be obtained from city hall files by anyone, either a company or an individual, by simply paying a fee of 14 cents. Theoretically, an investigation is not to be made without the authorization of the person being investigated; however, the practice appears to be prevalent throughout the country. Although the *koseki* does not specifically identify anyone as a Burakumin, it does give his family connections and place of birth, which suggest whether his identity is that of a Buraku (Wagatsuma 1967a,b:142).

Those who elect to remain within the Buraku community become leaders of their people and attempt to persuade the less educated to change their way of life so that their position in society will improve. The fate of the educated individuals is thus tied to the fate of the group as a whole (Donoghue 1967). Within the Buraku community there are few rewards such as desirable occupations for the highly educated.

On the whole, because of the job ceiling against them, Burakumin are excluded from many desirable occupations and social positions held by other Japanese citizens by virtue of education. The educated Burakumin are forced to occupy many low technoeconomic positions in both the private and public sectors of the Japanese economy; and many are forced to continue the traditional Buraku occupations. In rural areas, they become subsistence farmers, fishermen, and unskilled laborers. In the cities, their marginal economic position makes them heavily dependent, as unskilled laborers, on government-sponsored public works projects or government welfare payments (Wagatsuma and De Vos 1967:122).

The facts that Japanese ideology proclaims education as the route to self-improvement and that society supposedly offers education to the Burakumin education but at the same time denies them the social and economic rewards and symbols of self-improvement commensurate with their education and abilities pose a problem for the Burakumin unknown to other Japanese, even the lower-class members of the dominant Ippan caste. Although this unique situation has forced some Burakumin to divert their energies and other resources from the pursuit of educational achievement into fighting discrimination on behalf of themselves and their group as a whole (Cornell 1967b:352), the response of many Burakumin has been a kind of collective fatalism toward education. They tend to withdraw from actively seeking to maximize their educational accomplishments, a response that no doubt contributes to the generally lower school performance of the Burakumin and thus reinforces the influence of inferior education and inadequate social and occupational rewards for their educational accomplishments. Their lower school performance is functionally adaptive to their menial jobs and low social and occupational positions in adult life.

The fact that some Buraku outcastes have migrated from Japan (where they are excluded from full participation in adult life because of their lower-caste status) to the United States (where the Buraku and Ippan immigrants are treated more or less alike by the dominant white group) provides an opportunity to study the effects of caste barriers on Buraku education in Japan. The lower school performance of the Buraku outcastes, which continues to exist in Japan, is not found among those who have migrated to the United States or among their descendants. In a study conducted in the early 1950s, Ito (1967) found that outcaste and nonoutcaste immigrants had come from similar backgrounds with respect to education, age, economic status, and the like. Both groups were from rural Japan and from families of generally low economic status. The outcaste groups tended to be a little younger; they also had "a bit more education partly because they came later, after the extension of the length of compulsory education in Japan [pp. 205–206]."

In the United States, the rejection of the outcastes by the dominant Ippan group continued. For example, intimate personal friendships and intermarriage were rare between members of the two groups. The outcastes tended to avoid taking up occupations traditionally associated with their outcaste status in Japan; they also avoided occupations that would increase their overt rejection by other Japanese in the United States. On the whole, the study revealed that compared to the other Japanese immigrants, the Burakumin achieved superior economic status in the United States.

In the area of formal education, the study found no differences in achievement between outcaste and nonoutcaste Japanese children in American schools (Ito 1967:208). In the Japanese language schools, the outcaste children were rated superior to the children of the nonoutcaste immigrants (1967:210).[2] Ito goes on to say that

[2]The language schools (usually called "Japanese Schools" as opposed to the public or "American Schools") were privately organized by the Japanese communities. Children are sent to these schools after regular school hours or during the weekends to learn the language and culture of Japan. Apart from formal lessons in these subjects, films about Japan may be shown and Japanese nationals are invited to speak on some aspects of Japanese culture or on topics of current interest. One expressed purpose of the langauge school is to help the children develop their cultural (i.e., Japanese) identity. As an Issei (first generation) parent told one student, "School [i.e. American public school] is good and necessary to get ahead, but you also need Japanese school to remember who you are" (Kobori 1972:12). Language schools (though they may be called by various terms) are also found among such other U.S. groups as the Chinese and Jews. And during my field work in Stockton, California (1968–70), I encountered one Mexican parent who regularly sent his son to the local Chinese language school because he believed it would help him develop self-discipline and good study habits.

"according to teachers of Nisei [second generation] and Sansei [third generation] at Japanese language schools in the ethnic communities, it seems that outcaste children were slightly more conscientious than non-outcastes in their language studies, and were somewhat less reluctant to participate in student programs, oratorical contests, and the like in which demonstrated ability and achievement were the criteria of success [p. 210]."

The situation in Japan thus seems somewhat reversed in the United States. In the United States, the outcastes appear to have increased their efforts in both scholastic and economic pursuits. The reason for this is that the outcaste immigrants and their children are no longer overwhelmed by the traditional prejudice and discrimination *associated with caste status per se.* In their new environment, they have as much opportunity as the other Japanese immigrants to improve their social and occupational status through individual efforts, whether through formal education or other means.

12

Oriental Jews in Israel

One of the major social problems in Israel is the position of its minority groups. This "minority problem" among Jewish immigrants has developed recently and rapidly, and it constitutes a crisis in the ideological foundations of the state of Israel to which the government has responded by instituting a number of measures to eliminate the problem. At first these measures were intended to westernize the minorities, and now they are intended to prevent the development of a castelike society.

The state of Israel is made up of a number of groups with distinct ways of life. Among these are the Moslem and Christian Arabs, the Veterans, the Ashkenazim, and the Oriental Jews.[1] The Arabs include

[1]The term *Oriental Jews*, according to Eisenstadt (1954:90–91), is applied to diverse ethnic groups who migrated from the former Ottoman Empire, including the Sephardim, Persians, Kurds, Babylonians, Yemenites, Moghrebites (from Morocco), Jews from Bukhara, Haleb, Urfa, Georgia, Afghanistan, and so on. The Sephardim (a term originally applied to Jews who originated in Spain) form somewhat a distinct group within the Oriental Jewish population and came mainly from North Africa, Turkey, Greece, Egypt, and elsewhere. All these groups are called Oriental Jews not only because they came from the same general geographical area, but also because they share certain common cultural features which set them apart from other Jews in Israel. Among their unique cultural features, according to Eisenstadt (1954:91) are their tendency to cluster in special residential quarters or slums, their relative poverty, and a high degree of endogamy.

Palestinians indigenous to the area before the state of Israel came into being in 1948, as well as the residents of various territories which the Israelis have seized since then. The veterans were Jewish residents of the area in the prestate period. The Ashkenazim are Jewish immigrants from Europe, the Americas, Oceania, China, and Japan since statehood, and the Oriental Jews are those who have migrated from other parts of Asia and from Africa. One other group, which constitutes 6–7% of the population, are the Sabras, the Israel-born children of immigrants. For the purpose of this study, they are classified as either Ashkenazim or Orientals according to the geographical origins of their forebears.

Any of these groups may rightly claim the status of a minority group by employing one of several criteria such as their percentage of the total population or their share of power, prestige, or wealth; but in Israel the two groups generally accorded the status of minorities are the Arabs and the Oriental Jews. The present study is concerned with the Oriental Jews because the general emphasis in the literature surveyed here is that this group has threatened to transform Israel from a homogeneous, predominantly Western society to a heterogenous society plagued by increasing social tension. Second, the available literature on educational problems deals primarily with differences in cognitive skills and school performance between the European Jews and the Oriental Jews. Finally, one of the main objectives of the present research is to discover the extent to which minority and majority groups in one country, who do not regard themselves as belonging to different racial groups, differ in IQ and scholastic achievement as well as to discover the reasons for the existence of their differences.[2] The Oriental Jews in Israel satisfy this requirement better than the Arab minorities.[3]

Oriental Jews in Israeli Society

In order to understand the present position of Oriental Jews in Israel's social stratification system it is necessary to look at the ideological basis of the state of Israel and the changes which have occurred in ideology and social structure since the state was founded. This comparison is important because many Israelis continue to think of their soci-

[2]Here as elsewhere in this book, *race* is defined from the point of view of the groups involved. Thus the Oriental Jews are not classified as a separate race because the Israelis believe that all Jews belong to the same race.

[3]Perhaps one reason why the Oriental Jews are not more castelike is the presence of the Arab minorities who are yet below them. Furthermore, Arab–Israeli relations in the Middle East in general probably militate against rigid stratification of the Jewish groups on the basis of country of origin, ethnicity, or physical appearance (i.e., color).

ety in terms of the ideology and social structure of the prestate period, even though the present social and economic realities are radically different.

The prestate society, the *Yishuv* (Jewish community), was a strongly egalitarian and open society, partly because of the homogeneity of its population, partly because of the low level of economic development, and partly because of the strong socialist orientation of the pioneers.

The Eastern European immigrants of the prestate period were mainly unmarried young men who had been students, artisans, teachers, writers, or professionals in Europe. They were motivated by the idea of Zionism, the primary goal of which was to establish a Jewish state in Palestine. Two features of the immigrants' ideology shaped the social structure of the prestate period. One was the disapproval of association and stratification based on differences in religious observances, traditions, country of origin, and so on, on the ground that such distinctions would prevent the immigrants from becoming integrated into one nation; the other was the insistence of the immigrants on making the new society egalitarian and open, that is, a society in which individuals would have the opportunity for professional, intellectual, and civil achievements irrespective of their economic and social backgrounds (Lissak 1970:143). Early attempts to translate the ideology into practice included the establishment of agricultural communities such as the *Kibbutzim* (collective farms) and the *Moshavim* (private farmholds) where classlessness was a primary value (Weingrod 1966:16). These agricultural communities also fulfilled an important vision of the pioneers, which was to become farmers, to "take up the plow and sickle."

The socialist conception of the sociopolitical organization of the Jewish community began to be challenged in the 1930s with increasing economic development. Growing differences in wealth eventually led to incipient social stratification, which the pioneer immigrants had sought to avoid. Since Israel achieved statehood in 1948, the gap between rich and poor has been increasing, thus strengthening the system of stratification based on wealth. For example, although the population experienced a general rise in standard of living between 1950 and 1956, the family income of the top 10% of the population rose by 2.7% during that period while that of the bottom 10% declined by 2.3%. There was also an increase in occupational differentiation resulting from the opening up of new and expanded occupations in the civil service, the military, and the new industries.

Oriental Jews who immigrated to Palestine in the prestate period differed from the immigrants from Europe in their motives as well as in the position they occupied in the Yishuv. According to Eisenstadt (1954:92–93), the Oriental Jews immigrated for two reasons: the desire to escape from economic and political persecution recurrent in the various countries of the Ottoman Empire,[4] and "vague messianic aspirations," which were especially revived by the rumors of the Balfour Declaration, the establishment of the National Home, and so on. Katz and Zloczower (1970:339) add, however, that as far back as 1909 Oriental Jews (e.g., those from Yemen) were being encouraged to immigrate to Palestine by the European immigrants (Ashkenazim), who wanted to use them as cheap farm labor.

Unlike the Jews who came from Europe and America, very few of the Oriental Jews who immigrated in the prestate period were inspired by the secular Zionist ideals of founding a socialist state. Moreover, once they arrived in Palestine they were not fully integrated into the Yishuv. They often lived in city slums, performed menial tasks in the city, or worked as farm laborers in the farm settlements and private farmholds. Thus while the Zionist ideology of the prestate period proclaimed a classless society and the equality of the "one people of Israel," there existed a system of social stratification in which the Oriental Jews occupied the lower stratum.

Oriental Jewish immigration greatly increased after Israel became a state in 1948. This was a response to the formalization of the immigration principle, especially the Law of Return (1950) which proclaimed the right of all Jews to immigrate to Israel (Matras 1970b:312). The motives for immigration among the Oriental Jews since 1948 are probably no different from those of other immigrants. For some it is a sort of prophetic fulfillment; and for many it is an escape from economic and political persecution, as well as the opportunity for economic advancement. Contemporary immigrants, whether Oriental Jews or the Ashkenazim, are no longer primarily motivated by the desire to establish or live in a classless society. Official ideology aside, Israel is a Western, capitalist, industrial nation (Bar Yosef 1970; Lissak 1970; Weingrod 1966).

In social stratification that has emerged in Israel since statehood, there is a tendency for economic and occupational classes to coincide

---

[4]Eisenstadt (1954) cites no empirical evidence to support his assertion that the Oriental Jews suffered political and economic persecution in the Ottoman Empire. He simply states that one of the two main reasons for their migration was "economic and political persecution, of the recurrent type traditional in the various countries of the Ottoman Empire." And he later states that "although suffering from temporary persecution and economic vicissitudes, the Oriental Jews were still able to follow their traditional occupations—minor handicrafts, peddling, small-scale trade, sometimes unskilled labors, and, at the other end of the scale, banking and large-scale commerce [p. 93]."

with ethnic divisions, so that the Veterans occupy the top positions, the Ashkenazim the next position, and the Oriental Jews and Arabs the bottom (Lissak 1970:152–153).[5] Insofar as Oriental Jews, like the Ashkenazim, regard Israel as their only homeland, this pattern of stratification is significant to the understanding of their educational problems. For Oriental Jews, though they have immigrated to Israel from some Asian and African countries, are not—strictly speaking— immigrants. Like the Ashkenazim, they have no other homeland to which to return and they therefore constitute an indigenous, subordinate minority group.

The rapid increase in the number of Oriental immigrants, as well as their higher birthrate, has thus changed the ethnic composition of Israel. In 1948, Oriental Jewish immigrants constituted only 10% of the Jewish population, the Ashkenazim about 55%, and the Sabra about 35%. By 1960, the Orientals had increased to 28% of the total population, the Ashkenazim had decreased to 35%, and the Sabra had slightly increased to 37%. A combination of Israeli-born Orientals, Oriental immigrants, and their children now constitute more than 50% of the total Jewish population.[6] Furthermore, the children of the Oriental group now make up about 65% of the school-age population, a significant factor with respect to educational problems as the Israelis see them.

Education and Opportunity in Israel

Early in the prestate period, the dominant ideology in Israel undervalued individual social position based on ability and training, including formal education. The dominant Zionist ideology of the period extolled "collective enterprise," so that the position of an individual in society was judged in terms of his ideological commitment and membership of a collective group, not in terms of his educational qualifica-

[5]Another important factor contributing to the emerging pattern of ethnic composition in Israel is outmigration from Israel. This is easier for the Ashkenazim and more common among them than it is for the Orientals. The San Francisco *Examiner-Chronicle* (March 21, 1976) reported that from 1971 to 1976 about 20% of all new immigrants remigrated from Israel, but among the Ashkenazim the outmigration was twice as high.

[6]These figures refer only to the Jewish population of Israel. It should be noted, however, that in 1948 when Israel became a state there were 700,000 Arabs within her borders. This number soon declined to 156,000 because of the migration of about 550,000 Arabs to the West Bank and Gaza regions during the Jewish–Arab conflict of 1948–1949. By 1969, the Arab population in Israel had increased to 414,000 or 14.3% of the total population of the state (Gottheil 1973:237, see also Bastuni 1973).

tions and occupational status (Lissak 1970:143). This ideology changed, however, with the economic and technological development of Israel and with its concomitant occupational differentiation. In Israel today, social and occupational positions are based on individual achievement, especially in formal education. Most significant social and occupational positions in society require specified amounts and types of formal education on the part of their incumbents. According to Lissak (1970:153), the social and occupational roles highly valued by Israelis are those which provide the individual with access to high income and a high standard of living, social prestige, power, or various combinations of these. The least valued occupations are associated with manual labor, especially occupations that do not require extensive formal training. Although agricultural labor was among the most highly valued occupations during the prestate period, it is now one of the least acceptable to the children of the immigrants.

These changes in Israeli ideology regarding the relationship between education and social status reflect the realities of the social and economic development of Israeli society; and they are in turn reflected in the development of the education system. In the prestate period, schools were maintained in the Jewish community by various agencies of the Zionist movement. During the period of the British Mandate (1919–1948) the schools, which were private, tended to reflect the views of the three divergent political blocs which sponsored them. However, in spite of the ideological differences reflected in the curriculums of these schools, they adequately served the needs of the *Yishuv*. Education was valued highly within the community, and a high standard was stressed. Apparently most children, especially those of European immigrants, went as far as the system permitted (Ackerman 1973:397; Adler 1970:287–288; Bentwich 1965; Eisenstadt 1954).

The establishment of the state of Israel brought several changes in the education system. The number of pupils rapidly increased because of the influx of immigrants. Likewise the diversity of the children's ethnic and cultural backgrounds increased, adding to the strain on the schools to help some groups of children adapt successfully. In order to use the schools to integrate the diverse immigrant populations, the state legislature passed the Compulsory Education Law in 1949, which provided for free compulsory schooling from the ages of 5 to 13.[7] These

---

[7]The free compulsory schooling law of 1949 was for both Jews and Arabs, although the two groups were allowed to attend different schools which emphasized their respective cultures. Bastuni, one of 200 Arabs out of a total Arab population of 100,000 who remained in Haiffa after the state of Israel was established, describes the schooling situation as follows:

9 years included kindergarten and an eight-year elementary school. Adolescents who could not complete the nine years of compulsory schooling in the regular elementary schools were to attend special classes in the late afternoons and evenings. Secondary school education covered four years (ages of 14 through 17). It is still neither free nor compulsory, but primary school graduates are encouraged to attend by tuition grants and other incentives. There are also evening classes for those who cannot attend during the day. A reform in 1968 introduced the middle school concept, so that the precollege education now includes one year of kindergarten, six years of elementary school, three years of middle school or junior high, and three years of secondary or senior high school. In addition, free and compulsory education has been extended through the middle school, i.e., through the ninth grade. At the age of 18, all Israelis must enter compulsory national service lasting three years.[8] Higher education for Israelis also begins when they are 18 (Ackerman 1973; Adler 1970; Bentwich 1965).

School attendance during the compulsory school years (ages 5–14) is nearly 100% until the last one or two years, when there is a noticeable decline. In 1962, more than 80% of the primary school graduates were reportedly proceeding to one of several types of secondary schools (Bentwich 1965). Not only the amount but also the kind of education a person receives influences his or her social and technoeconomic opportunities in adult life. This differentiation in the kinds of education begins at the secondary school level.

The secondary schools are stratified into two basic types: academic or preuniversity (admitting about 50% of the primary school graduates) and vocational and agricultural (admitting about 35%). To gain admission to the academic secondary schools, candidates must pass the survey examination administered to nearly all eighth-grade pupils and must maintain good records in their classwork. The admission requirements for the two-or three-year vocational schools are not as high.

The Arabs have made great progress in education since the establishment of the state because the compulsory education applies to everybody in Israel, regardless of nationality or race. Every child must go to school or his parents face penalties, even imprisonment. This creates problems among the Arabs because Arab girls' fathers don't like them to go on to higher grades. But the girls must go to school, and thus the educational level of all Israeli Arabs rises [1973:412–413].

In 1948–1949, there were 140,817 students enrolled at all levels of education in Israel, of whom 11,129 or 7.9% were Arabs. In 1970 there were 825,786 at all levels of education, of whom 110,537 or 13.39% were Arabs (Ackerman 1973:399).

[8]For Israelis, compulsory national military service and higher education both begin at the age of 18. Some 18-year-olds are granted academic deferments and have to fulfill their national service after their university education. The majority, however, go into the national service at the age of 18, after which some proceed to the university or other institutions of higher education (Schild 1973:419–420).

Many children who go to the agricultural schools are actually sent there by the Welfare Office and the Youth *Aliyah*.[9] Thus the agricultural schools rank low in the secondary school system (see Adler 1970; Bentwich 1965).

The Education of Oriental Jews

In the prestate period, when different ideological groups maintained schools to serve their needs, Oriental Jews also had their own schools, established as a part of their orthodox religious organizations rather than to serve as the basis for teaching socialist ideals. Some Oriental Jewish children also attended other kinds of schools, but they were apparently not very successful there (Eisenstadt 1954:99–100).

The education of the Oriental Jews changed considerably after 1948, when a large wave of immigrants began to arrive in Israel. The new state, which was dominated by Jews of European origin, regarded the schools as an important agency in the absorption of immigrants. They were to teach the Oriental Jewish immigrants and immigrants from other parts of the world the Western values and skills desired by the new state. It was feared that because so many Oriental Jews were coming to Israel, the nation might one day become dominated by their values and culture. To prevent this, (i.e., to prevent Israel from becoming "Levantized"), the schools were expected to help transform Oriental Jewish immigrants into Western Jews as rapidly as possible. This emphasis on the "westernization" of Oriental Jews did not particularly help the latter to succeed in school. It ultimately resulted in increasing the academic gap between them and the general population. As this gap became more and more obvious, some changes were introduced to help the Oriental students. Nevertheless, the emphasis in the education of Oriental Jews has now shifted from education for assimilation to education for cultural pluralism. Instead of trying to change the Oriental child to fit the existing education system, some attempts are being made to adapt the system to the needs of the Oriental Jewish child.

These changes are discussed more fully in connection with efforts to improve the school performance of Oriental Jews and increase their representation at various levels of the education system. It can generally be observed that the kind of education provided to Oriental Jews

[9]Youth *Aliyah* is an agency which supervises the absorption of children and youth among the immigrants. The organization was founded in 1934 to cater to children of immigrants from Germany and Central Europe who were not accompanied by their parents or could not be sponsored by their parents (Eisenstadt 1954:72–73; Gittelman 1973:87).

has varied according to what the dominant group perceived to be their educational needs at different periods.

The Education Gap. The differences in scholastic achievement among the various ethnic groups in Israel, but particularly between the Oriental Jews and the Ashkenazim, have been a dominant concern of educators, social scientists, and the government since statehood (see Ackerman 1973; Adler 1970; Avineri 1973; Bentwich 1965; Eisenstadt 1954; Guttman 1963; Lissak 1970; 1973; Ortar 1967; Patai 1958; Rosenfeld 1973; Similansky and Similansky 1967; Weingrod 1966). Educational differences between the Ashkenazim and the Orientals show up whether achievement is measured by IQ tests, scholastic achievement tests, school attrition rates, or admission to prestigious secondary schools and universities. In all these measures, the Orientals rank lower than the Ashkenazim.

Some of these differences probably existed even in the prestate period. Although there is no statistical record for this period, Eisenstadt (1954:99) describes the Oriental Jews of the prestate period as showing a low percentage of school attendance, a high percentage of school absenteeism and backward pupils, and a high percentage of early school leavers. Similansky and Similansky (1967:410–411) also refer to the difficulties of the Orientals in adjusting to the schools in the *Yishuv*. They point out that "a vicious cycle" was begun with the first-generation Oriental immigrants, whose low education and vocational skills confined them to low paying jobs, slum dwelling, and poverty. They further point out that the descendants of these immigrants rejected their parents' values but lacked the cultural, educational, and emotional resources to succeed in school and thus achieved to higher status. Between 25% and 30% of the Oriental children were said to repeat first grade, and their academic retardation increased year after year. This contributed to their high and early school dropout rate. Another indication of the school problems of the Oriental pupils in the prestate period was the disproportionate number of Orientals among juvenile delinquents. Orientals constituted 25% of the youth group, but 80% of the delinquent groups (Similansky and Similansky 1967:411).

With the achievement of statehood and the influx of Oriental immigrants, the problem of Oriental school failure not only increased in magnitude but also began to attract more public and official attention. There are few good statistical records describing the magnitude of their difficulties in school, even though everyone writes about "the problem." The following are therefore intended to give only an indication of the nature of the current educational problems of Oriental Jews in Israel.

With regard to IQ differences between the Ashkenazim and the Orientals, there is little specific information. Patai (1958:31) quotes a 1953 study by Ortar in which the Wechsler Intelligence Scale was administered to three different groups of children: Ashkenazim, Israelized Orientals, and new Oriental immigrants. The Ashkenazim were superior in language skills, while the Israelized Orientals were superior in "their mastery of numbers." There were no ethnic differences in their powers of "abstraction." But in an analysis of the results of annual eighth-grade examinations, Guttman (1963) presents a graph which shows Oriental students scoring lower than Ashkenazim in most subjects. Ortar (1967) has also analyzed the results of the same eighth-grade examinations given over a period of 12 years. She concludes that Orientals perform more poorly than Ashkenazim, whether or not the Oriental students have received all their schooling in Israel (see Table 12.1). She further concludes that, subject to certain qualifications, "it appears that no discernible trend can be found in the fluctuation of the consecutive differences between the two main cultural groups. The difference amounts, on the average, to one standard deviation [p. 37]."

It should be pointed out, however, that these examinations given to the eighth grade every year are not, strictly speaking, the standard IQ tests but a combination of IQ test items and achievement tests (Bible study, history, and geography). The two tests were initially administered separately, but in subsequent analysis "the intercorrelation showed insufficient basis for a differentiation of achievement tests from the tests of intelligence [Ortar 1967:25]." Ortar further adds (p. 32) that although the scores resemble deviation in IQ, they are not referred to as such because of age differences within the groups and because of the noninclusion of many pupils reluctant to participate in the test. Although they present no tables showing differences in IQ between the Ashkenazim and the Orientals, Similansky and Similansky (1967), Rosenfeld (1973), Bentwich (1965), and Pelled (1973) discuss various compensatory education programs which have been instituted in order to raise the IQs of Oriental children, especially at the preschool level.

There are indications that in actual classroom work, Oriental Jewish students do less well than the Ashkenazim. Many more Oriental pupils repeat grades, drop out of the regular elementary schools in the last two years, and are enrolled in special classes for out-of-school youths who have not completed their elementary educations. Among those reaching the eighth grade, fewer Orientals pass the matriculation examination. For example, Ackerman (1973:400) reports that in 1966 only 33.3% of the Oriental candidates passed the matriculation examination compared to 75% of the Ashkenazim.

Table 12.1
Mean Scores on the Eighth Grade Survey Test, by Country of Origin and By Father's Level of Education, Israel

Father's level of education	All pupils	Father's birthplace (pupils born in Israel)			Fathers birthplace (pupils born outside Israel)	
		Israel	Europe or America	Oriental country	Europe or America	Oriental country
All levels	100	100	107	92	102	92
No schooling	89	88	92	89	94	89
Primary school[a]	97	96	104	93	100	92
Secondary school[a]	105	106	107	102	103	96
Higher education[a]	109	110	111	107	107	100
Number of pupils	20,168	1,465	8,768	1,702	2,906	5,327
Correlation with level of education tetrachoric r	.33	.41	.16	.19	.22	.21

SOURCE: Gima R. Ortar 1967. Educational achievement of primary school graduates in Israel as related to their socio-cultural background. *Comparative Education*, **4**, 31.

[a] Any level within this range.

Statistics for secondary school attendance also show that the Orientals lag behind the Ashkenazim. Adler (1970:296) reports that in 1963–1964, 1964–1965, and 1965–1966, Orientals constituted between 50% and 55% of the 14–17-year-olds (i.e., the secondary school age group). In the same years, they made up 25.9%, 28.5%, and 32.0%, respectively, of the secondary school population. He further suggests that in the 1965–1966 school year, Orientals probably made up only 16% to 18% of the twelfth grade (i.e., the graduating class) because many of them dropped out before the twelfth grade. The differences between the Ashkenazim and the Orientals at the secondary school level are also evident in the type of schools they attend. According to Adler (1970:296), in the 1963–1964, 1964–1965, and 1965–1966 school years, Orientals made up about 17.8%, 20.0%, and 23.4%, respectively, of the student population in the academic secondary schools. Again, he suggests that because of the high dropout rate among the Orientals they would constitute in 1965–1966 only about 12% or 13% of the twelfth grade population. Available data do not indicate what proportion of Oriental students who reach grade 12 actually pass the matriculation examination from the academic secondary schools. Bentwich (1965) reports that in the general population only about 15% of the

18-year-olds who enter these schools successfully graduate. The figure for the Orientals is certainly considerably lower, since they represent only about 12% of the student body in the 12th grade in such schools.

The matriculation certificate from the academic secondary schools is a prerequisite not only for many desirable positions in the wider society, but also for admission to the universities and other institutions of higher learning. It follows that because fewer Orientals achieve this matriculation certificate they are subsequently underrepresented among university students. Data on the proportion of the 20- to 29-year-olds attending the university and on the ethnic composition of the university student population appear to confirm this. Thus Avineri (1973:298) reports that among the general population the proportion of 20- to 29-year-olds attending the university was 4.1% in 1964 and 6.4% in 1970. Among the Orientals of the same age group, university attendance was .8% in 1964 and 1.6% in 1969. Orientals constituted 5% of the total university student population in 1964 and 14% in 1969. This increase in the number of Orientals attending the university began in the late 1960s as a result of special programs for the Orientals in the secondary schools, at the Hebrew University, and in the army.

In a recent report on remedial education programs for Oriental children, Rosenfeld (1973) summarizes the differences between the Ashkenazim and the Orientals in educational achievement as follows:

> According to the most recent figures, 61 percent of children entering primary schools have fathers born in Afro-Asian countries [i.e., are Orientals], 25 percent have fathers born in Western countries [i.e., are Ashkenazim] and the remaining children (14 percent) have native-born fathers. The 61 percent share of Afro-Asian children in the total population of first graders dwindles to 43 percent of high school pupils and 31 percent of high school graduates. Only 6 percent of Afro-Asian children pass their matriculation examination compared to 35 percent of the Western population. Only 1.4 percent of the Afro-Asian population completed university studies compared with 8.2 percent of the Western population. These figures are obviously a source of very serious concern [p. 1].

The extent of this concern can be seen in recent efforts to close the school performance gap.

Explaining the Gap. There are both popular and social scientific explanations for the position of Oriental Jews in Israel and their lower school performance. The popular explanation preceded any scientific study, and it probably influenced early attempts to improve it. The folk explanation asserts, for instance, that Oriental Jews are socially and culturally backward and that they are too religious in comparison with the modern "Western" Israelis. Oriental Jews are considered "primitive" (Weingrod 1966:133–134). They are also considered "inferior" to

the Ashkenazim, and these labels often result in a kind of racial prejudice toward them. In his study of a *kibbutz*, Spiro (1958:319–320),
found the negative label, *shchorim* ("black ones") often used to describe the Orientals. Such labels become the basis for explaining differences between the behavior of Orientals and that of Ashkenazim
both in and out of school.

The perception of Oriental Jews as primitive people underlies the
popular explanation of their lower school performance. The schools
and other institutions (e.g., the army) are given the responsibility of
transforming the Orientals into more "advanced" Western Israelis, but
Orientals are not able to learn the "higher cultures" and skills taught by
the schools because their cultural backwardness and the "negative"
influences of their families and neighborhoods all combine to produce
inferior mental capacity. Rosenfeld (1973) mentions a report about the
stereotypes held by middle-class women volunteers in a kindergarten
project in Tel Aviv. These women believed that the Oriental children in
the slums were mentally retarded; but they changed their views after
they "worked with individual Afro-Asian children [p. 96; see also
Spiro 1958; Weingrod 1966]."

Some social scientific explanations of the lower performance of
Oriental Jews are similar to the popular explanations, although they are
more sophisticated. Most writers usually begin by observing that
Oriental immigrants are, on the average, less educated than European
immigrants. From this they conclude that Oriental Jews either did not
value education in their countries of origin or do not value education in
Israel, at least not as much as the Ashkenazim do. Bentwich suggests
(1965:48–49) that the negative attitudes of the parents made it necessary for Israel to have compulsory elementary education; otherwise
poorer and backward parents would have tended to keep their children
at home or send them out to earn money. This suggestion is not supported by ethnographic studies of Oriental communities. Bar Yosef
(1970) reports, for instance, that before the Moroccan Jews immigrated
to Israel, education was one of their principal means of social mobility.
Katz and Zloczower (1970) also report that their Yemenite informants
were very much concerned about the quality of their children's education.

It is also said that some of the children do not receive adequate
help in their schoolwork from their parents because the latter do not
have enough education themselves to be able to help their children, or
because they do not understand the Israeli education system, especially
if they themselves have language problems. Lack of parent education is
invoked by those who attribute the lower school performance of Oriental Jews to cultural deprivation.

Others explain their lower school performance in terms of deficiencies in IQ or cognitive skills (Ackermann 1973; Pelled 1973; Rosenfeld 1973; Similansky and Similansky 1967). Some of these authors say that Oriental children do not develop adequate cognitive skills because they are culturally deprived. Some suggest that lower IQs among the Oriental Jews are caused by the cultural backwardness of the countries from which they immigrated to Israel. Still others assert that Oriental Jews have lower IQs because of the way Israeli society treats their parents (see Rosenfeld 1973).

Israeli social scientists do not usually explain differences between the Ashkenazim and the Oriental Jews in cognitive skills in terms of biological differences; specifically, Similansky and Similansky (1967:415) reject the notion of biologically limited ability as the reason for the lower peformance of Oriental students. They also point out that differences between Oriental Jews and Ashkenazim are not biological or genetic but cultural (1967:242).

The literature further suggests that Oriental pupils tend to leave school earlier than Ashkenazim for a number of reasons: They have difficulties in school; there is a real need for them to earn money to help out their families; and their families cannot support them financially after they have completed the years of compulsory free primary schooling.

A number of authors (Ackerman 1973; Adler 1970; Lissak 1970; Ortar 1967; Similansky and Similansky 1967) blame the lower performance and other educational problems of the Oriental Jews partly on the school system which, they assert, until very recently had not made sufficient allowance for the students with Oriental cultural backgrounds. They point out that the schools should have adapted their organizational structure and their curriculum to meet the special needs of Orientals. Instead, the schools expected the Oriental pupils to change. The posture of the schools and their selective nature have been influenced by the official egalitarian ideology about Israeli society which, as Adler (1970) and Lissak (1970) point out, until very recently failed to recognize that present Israeli society is both heterogeneous and stratified. Adler (1970:296) specifically argues that fewer Orientals go beyond the nine years of free and compulsory education because the uniformity of the school system and the process of selection for post-primary, and later postsecondary, education work against them. He goes on to say that this state of affairs nullified the concept of equality of educational opportunity embodied in the establishment of the education system (1970:297). In her analysis of the test scores of Ashkenazim and Oriental pupils in the eighth grade annual survey examination over a 12-year period, Ortar (1967) also points out that the gap between Ashkenazim and Orientals is partly caused by the fact that "an egalitarian school system and curriculum" are superimposed on a heterogeneous school population.

These writers may differ about the specific handicaps of Oriental pupils: It may be cultural deprivation or cultural differences and their attendant cognitive consequences; or it may be parents' indifference or their inability to help their children with schoolwork; or it may be poverty or other problems of identity. Whatever the specific handicaps, these authors blame the schools for not adjusting to the needs of the Oriental children.

On the basis of her own field study and her review of published literature on disadvantaged Oriental children in Israel, Rosenfeld (1973) implies that certain aspects of the cognitive inadequacies of the Oriental children, such as lack of abstract exploration of 'how and why,' formal reasoning and problem solving, may be related to the treatment of Oriental immigrants in Israel [p. 95]. She notes, for example, that during the early days of mass immigration, "absorption" programs tended to deprive Oriental Jews of their sense of autonomy and initiative. The resulting sense of frustration and powerlessness continues to be reinforced today by their contact with welfare offices, housing agencies, and other public institutions. Many Oriental parents have thus not achieved a sense of mastery over their own fate, and they do not fully understand how the system works, nor have they succeeded in making decent livings. They are unable to see the world as improvable and themselves as actors within such a world. All these experiences influence the cognitive skills parents transmit to their children.

Closing the Gap. These explanations have had varying degrees of influence on the programs instituted to improve the school performance of Oriental Jews. The earlier programs were, however, influenced more by the popular explanations than by the findings of modern social science. Authors differ in their accounts of the measures taken to close the gap and the extent to which they have been successful; they agree, however, that the elimination of the gap has been of great concern to the Israeli government and that these measures have passed through three phases.

The first phase, from 1953 to 1957, may be called a period of administrative manipulation and student adaptation. Measures focused on getting more Oriental students into the secondary schools, especially the academic secondary schools. Entrance to these schools was based on the results of the eighth-grade matriculation examination; tuition fees were graded so that parents in the lower income groups paid little or no fees for their children. However, few Oriental students obtained marks high enough to qualify them for these schools or for the graded tuition fees. To increase the number of Oriental students admitted into the academic secondary schools and the number receiving the graded tuition fees, a lower passing mark (Norm B) was introduced for the Oriental community. This approach succeeded in increasing the number of Oriental students enrolling in the academic secondary schools without eliminating the *cause* of the scholastic gap between Ashkenazim and Orientals (Adler 1970:297–298; see also Bentwich 1965:48–49; Pelled 1973:391; Similansky and Similansky 1967:413).

Furthermore, it did nothing to ensure that the students admitted to the academic high school would successfully complete their studies, as they were not really qualified to study there. There was, therefore, a high rate of dropout among Oriental Jewish students in the academic secondary schools, a problem partially remedied later by instituting tutoring programs for these students.

The continued existence of the scholastic gap led to new measures in 1958, under the slogan of "national protectionism," which meant that solving the problems of Oriental Jewish adjustment in Israel, especially closing the educational gap, was crucial for achieving the ideals upon which the state of Israel had been founded. The advancement of the Oriental Jewish population was given top government priority.

During this second period, 1958–1968, the lower performance of Oriental pupils was seen as primarily due to "cognitive deprivations" in their early childhood training (Ackerman 1973:399). Consequently, compensatory programs were introduced to prevent such cognitive deprivation or to compensate for the deprivation which had already occurred. These programs included: (a) preschool/nursery programs for the 3- and 4-year-olds which were intended to prepare them for the regular kindergarten; such programs were heavily subsidized so that they were practically free for the low-income Oriental families, and (b) primary school programs which involved extended school days in the regular schools; tutoring in homework; enrichment programs; remedial instruction techniques for grades two through five; special instructional materials; new methods of language teaching; school-wide homogeneous groupings for instruction in the Hebrew language, English, and mathematics in the seventh and eighth grades; and preacademic secondary boarding schools for "the most talented and promising students" in the seventh and eighth grades. In these boarding schools, the students were given special attention and groomed not only for successful attendance at the academic secondary schools but also for subsequent admission to the universities.

The state protection programs were only partially successful. Adler (1970) notes that in terms of scholastic achievement the preacademic secondary boarding schools were very successful: the students participating in these schools did not fail their eighth-grade matriculation examinations. But he adds that *their success was limited because only a few students were involved:* "Since only a small proportion of the students from these groups can be classified at the end of elementary school as highly talented and thus qualified for such projects, it hardly seems possible that this method could produce change [p. 298]."

Although the state protection measures increased the number of Oriental students attending academic secondary schools and universities, they did not significantly improve the performance of Oriental students at the primary school level. Ackerman (1973) states that toward the end of the period, a disturbingly large number of Oriental students "remained incapable of mastering the skills and techniques required for postelementary education and economic self-sufficiency in a technological society [p. 400]." He reports, for instance, that in 1966 about 66.6% of the Oriental students failed to pass their eighth-grade matriculation examinations, in contrast to only 25% of the Ashkenazim.

Critics of the state protection programs point out that although the educational system was more willing than in the past to utilize different education programs in order to close the scholastic gap between Orientals and Ashkenazim, the goal of these programs was still to change or adapt Oriental students to the established educational structure. The critics point out that the existing structure of the educational system was quite elitist and was largely responsible for the failure of many Oriental students (Adler 1970:298; see also Bentwich 1965; Pelled 1973; Similansky and Similansky 1967).

The current phase in the efforts to close the scholastic gap between Orientals and Ashkenazim began in 1968 and consists of two parts: One part involves reforming or restructuring the educational system itself; the other involves intensified rehabilitative compensatory programs at various levels.

By 1965 it had become apparent that the scholastic gap was not closing fast enough. This led to the appointment of a commission (the Praver Committee) to study the possibility of extending compulsory free schooling to the ninth grade. The committee decided that merely requiring free education up to grade nine would not solve the problem of Oriental school failure. Instead, it recommended a restructuring of the educational system below the university level. Specifically, it recommended that the schools be reorganized into 6–3–3 systems, i.e., six years of primary school, followed by three years of middle school and three years of secondary school. It also recommended the development of new curriculums for the middle school and the development of new programs for training teachers that would meet the needs of the middle school pupils. Debate over the committee's recommendation led to the appointment of a parliamentary committee to study the same problem. The latter made recommendations similar to those of the Praver Committee. The reports of the two committees thus form the basis of the current efforts to close the scholastic gap between Orientals and Ashkenazim.

The school reform aspects of the present phase include the following features. The first is the establishment of regional comprehensive middle schools and upper schools (i.e., secondary schools). The middle schools are being organized in such a way as to integrate students from different economic, ethnic, and social backgrounds. Heterogeneous grouping is encouraged in various grades. All students study the same subjects until the ninth grade, when tracking begins and the "common subject" of study represents only 25% of the school curriculum. Students in grade 9 are tracked into three broad groups: those going to academic secondary schools or to four-year agricultural or vocational secondary schools and eventually to the university; those going to academic secondary schools to obtain a diploma but not necessarily proceeding to the university; and those going to the three-year agricultural and vocational secondary schools. Another group consists of those who will receive a terminal diploma at the end of the ninth grade; they represent the least academically able students. The second aspect of the new school reform involves a reorganization and improvement of the curriculum. The new curriculum is to emphasize "cognitive development and learning by inquiry and discovery" methods. Ackerman (1973:401) reports that the new curriculum is heavily influenced by recent American ideas and practices in curriculum development. A third aspect deals with teacher training: The training of teachers for the new middle schools is to emphasize academic skills (Ackerman 1973).

Compensatory education programs include both preschool programs and remedial programs for elementary and secondary school pupils, or what some writers call "second chance programs." The preschool program is based partly on the report of a special task force appointed to find ways to strengthen early childhood education. These programs include teaching parents how to teach their children. In the remedial programs, especially for adolescents, parents are also encouraged to learn how the programs work. There are also some programs for gifted children (Similansky and Similansky 1967). The overall emphasis in the compensatory education programs at the preschool level is to prevent "developmental retardation," and at the higher age levels to "raise" the IQs of the students (Rosenfeld 1973; Similansky and Similansky 1967).

Because the programs in this phase are relatively new, there are as yet no evaluation studies of their effectiveness. Ackerman (1973) notes, however, that judging from the American experience with compensatory education it may not necessarily be wise to place so much emphasis on building academic skills as the new programs in Israel are attempting to do.

Education and the Future

There are hardly any direct and systematic studies of the way in which education affects the opportunities for Oriental Jews in adult life. However, there are comparisons of the educational attainment and occupational status of Oriental and Ashkenazic immigrants as well as studies of intergenerational mobility in Israel. These studies show that it is easier for immigrants from Europe and America and people born in Israel to obtain high-status jobs than it is for Oriental immigrants. Furthermore, although in general few Israeli sons follow their fathers' occupations, a higher proportion of the sons of Oriental Jews do so than is the case among the Ashkenazim (Matras 1970a).

The lower occupational status of the Oriental immigrants is usually attributed to their lower rate of literacy and their lack of technological sophistication. Sometimes it is even said that they have low-status jobs because they come from nonindustrialized societies and have difficulty doing the kind of work available in a "Western" democratic society. But Katz and Zloczower (1970:400) observe that these rationalizations do not explain why certain Oriental Jews (e.g., the Yemenites) with the same level of education have a considerably lower occupational status than the Ashkenazim.

One recent study (Ben-Porath 1973) has compared the educational attainments of Oriental Jews and Ashkenazim, as well as their occupational status both in their countries of origin and in Israel. The study shows that Oriental Jews are generally less educated than Ashkenazim. For example, more than 25% of the Oriental Jewish immigrants had no schooling, and only 25% had more than nine years of schooling. Among the Ashkenazim, the figures were about 0% and 50%, respectively (Ben-Porath 1973:223). A comparison of the occupational status of the two groups in their countries of origin (i.e., before they moved to Israel) shows that their occupational distribution was more nearly similar than the differences in their educational attainment suggest. Ben-Porath explains the similarity by saying that it "probably reflects the much lower educational requirements of white-collar occupations [p. 225]" in the countries of origin of the Oriental Jews. In Israel, both groups suffered declines in their occupational status, so that fewer than 25% of the Oriental Jews with white-collar backgrounds were holding white-collar jobs in Israel. Among the Ashkenazim, the decline was about 50%.

However, the most relevant finding in Ben-Porath's study for my purpose is that for a given number of years of schooling completed by both Oriental Jews and Ashkenazim, the occupational distribution of the Ashkenazim went "higher" than that of the Oriental Jews. Within each of the two groups, of course, "people with higher education acquired abroad have 'higher' occupational distribution also in Israel [1970:228]." But in general, Oriental Jewish immigrants with educational backgrounds similar to those of Ashkenazim tend to have lower occupational status.

The studies by Ben-Porath (1973) and Matras (1970b) show that all groups of immigrants are heavily represented in agriculture, service, and unskilled occupations. Matras (1970b:223) found that among the Oriental Jews, about 50.6% of the new immigrants were employed in agriculture and unskilled occupations, compared to 36.2% of the new Ashkenazic immigrants and 17.4% of the Veterans. In contrast to their heavy representation in agricultural work, according to Ben-Porath's (1973:224) findings, in their countries of origin only 1.9% of the Oriental Jews and 2.6% of the Ashkenazim had been farmers. Thus the immigrants were channeled into occupations other than those for which they had been trained in their countries of origin.

With increasing numbers of years of residence in Israel, the occupational status of immigrants tends to improve, so that they move into jobs with higher wages and more social prestige.[10] For example, in a study cited previously, Ben-Porath (1973:233) found that Oriental Jewish immigrants gradually move out of agricultural labor and into higher

---

[10]A comparison with the Arab population is difficult. It seems, however, that about half the Arab population was initially engaged in agriculture as peasant farmers rather than as farm laborers. Oriental Jewish immigrants participate in agriculture primarily as farm laborers. The percentage of Arab population engaged in agriculture has been decreasing since 1950 for several reasons, including the Land Acquisition Act of 1953 and the settlement of semirural Jewish communities adjacent to Arab communities. These two factors have resulted in the loss of Arab agricultural lands. The inability of traditional Arab peasants to compete with the mechanized and irrigated farms of the Kibbutz and the Moshav also contribute to the decrease in the proportion of Arabs engaged in farming. One effect of this shift away from farming activities is that the distribution of the Arab labor force in Israel is gradually converging with that of the Jewish labor force. This trend is shown in Table 12.2 (see Gottheil 1973:241–242).

Table 12.2

Percentage Distribution of Employed Arabs in Israel According to
Category of Employment, 1931–1969, Selected Years

	Arabs			Jews
	1931	1950	1969	1963
Agriculture	57.0	50.0	31.5	12.1
Industry and				
handicrafts	10.0	10.0	18.8	25.5
Construction	3.0	6.0	21.3	9.1
Electricity				
and water	—	—	0.6	1.8
Transport	6.0	6.0	6.6	7.2
Commerce and				
banking	8.0	—	8.1	13.3
Public services	7.0	28.0	—	—
Personal				
services	9.0	—	13.1	31.0
Total	100.0	100.0	100.0	100.0

SOURCE: Fred M. Gottheil: "On The Economic Development Of The Arab
Region In Israel." in Michael Curtis and Mordecai Chertoff, eds.: *Israel:
Social Structure and Change.* New Brunswick, N.J.: Transaction Book. P. 242.

jobs. But Lissak (1970) suggests that this does not necessarily narrow the
occupational gap between Oriental Jews and Ashkenazim, since the
latter also improve their own occupational status.

A study by Matras (1970b) shows that the occupational advantages
and disadvantages experienced by immigrant parents are to a large
extent passed on to their children: Children of immigrants who obtained high-status jobs in Israel (e.g., professional and technical positions) are more likely to achieve high-status occupations themselves
than are children whose immigrant parents ended up as manual workers. Matras points out that the major factors which determine whether
the children of immigrants will be employed in better jobs than those
held by their parents are ethnic origin (e.g., Oriental Jews versus
Ashkenazim) and the duration of their residence in Israel (e.g., new
immigrants versus Veterans). The ethnic factor works against the
Oriental Jews. Oriental immigrants are less likely to be employed in the
occupations in which they were engaged before they immigrated than
Ashkenazim; and within each occupation in Israel, Oriental immigrants obtain the least desirable jobs. These disadvantages subsequently make it difficult for Oriental children to obtain better jobs

than their parents (1970b:246–247). Lissak (1970: 152–153) makes a similar observation.

It appears, then, that among new immigrants, Oriental Jews do not have equal opportunities to compete with Ashkenazim of similar educational background for similar jobs, wages, and other benefits of formal schooling. This discrimination is not necessarily eliminated by duration of their stay in Israel; and their children tend to inherit many of the same social and occupational disadvantages.

How Oriental Jews respond to their social and occupational disadvantages is shown in some ethnographic studies of their communities. For example, Bar Yosef (1970:426–427) found that the Moroccan Jewish immigrants were frustrated because of the way they were treated both in the wider society and in the education system. Like the Ashkenazim, they had come to Israel with high hopes for economic and sociopolitical betterment and with the expectation that they would be accepted as full citizens of the state of Israel by the rest of the society; but their actual experiences have been quite different, resulting in a deep sense of disappointment and frustration which in the educational context has resulted in their children's withdrawal from active academic competition and in the social context has sometimes resulted in violent protests and riots. The emergence of the Black Panthers movement among Oriental Jewish youth in 1970 has further brought into the open the magnitude of the problem of the Oriental Jews.

Occupational and social barriers against Oriental Jews have existed since the prestate days and undoubtedly both indirectly and directly influenced their education. How hard they work in school and how far they strive in their education are affected by the way they perceive their chances in adult life. Moreover, the skills Oriental parents transmit to their children depend partly on those they themselves have been permitted to develop in Israel.

As Rosenfeld (1973) aptly points out, the limited opportunity for Orientals to hold decent jobs and make decent livings, as well as their disfavored relationships with employers and public agencies, are often associated with a deep sense of frustration and powerlessness. These feelings affect the kinds of perceptual, cognitive, and motivational skills they are able to transmit to their children. They also affect the extent to which the children, particularly as they grow older, see formal education as the ideal route to self-improvement and the extent to which they are willing to invest their efforts in acquiring education. The response of the Oriental Jews to their situation in Israel reinforces the effects of the barriers in school and society in lowering their school performance.

13

The Education of Castelike Minorities in Six Societies: A Comparison

A Synoptic Comparison

The minority groups studied in this book are in varying degrees to be found in castelike relationships with the dominant groups of their societies. Three distinctive features of this type of minority group are that membership is permanently determined by birth; that social and occupational roles of its members are determined by caste, not by education and ability; and that the group occupies a permanent place in society from which its members can escape only through "passing" or emigration—if these routes are open to them. These criteria describe the situation of blacks in the United States. The scheduled castes in both traditional and modern India are a pariah minority par excellence, and the same is true of the Buraku outcastes in Japan. While all the colored groups in Britain occupy inferior positions in the British system of color castes, the position of the West Indians is the most extreme, both objectively and subjectively. In New Zealand, there is also a color-caste stratification, in which the Maoris occupy an inferior, pariah position. Of all the minority groups examined in this study, the Oriental Jews in Israel are the least castelike.

Obviously the minorities chosen for this study are not the only minority groups in their respective societies. I selected for comparison the most castelike for which there is also adequate documentation of their educational problems. In addition, the minority groups in India, Israel, and Japan are regarded in these countries as members of the same racial groups as the dominant groups; whereas those in Britain, New Zealand, and the United States are regarded as members of separate racial groups.[1]

Social Mobility Ideology and Education. The dominant members of the societies studied here share the following beliefs: First, they strongly believe that various positions (occupational roles) in a modern technological society require different skills and knowledge that can be acquired primarily through formal education and that educational credentials demonstrate the possession of such skills, knowledge, and ability. Second, they believe that educational attainment—as evidenced by one's credentials—determines one's position in adult life, especially in the technoeconomic structure, so that those with more education are found at or near the top while those with less education are found at or near the bottom. This relative position is also associated with other benefits of education, such as the ability to earn high wages, own a good house in an attractive area, and achieve social prestige. The ability to improve one's social and economic status, i.e., to achieve social mobility, thus depends on the amount and type of one's education. Third, the dominant group's belief that education determines a person's position in adult life is generalized to include members of the minority groups, whose experiences may be quite different from those of the dominant group. Hence, in these societies the economic inequality between the minority and the dominant groups is usually attributed by members of the dominant groups to differences in education.

Access to Education. Historically, there were marked differences in the education of the minorities and of the dominant groups in each of the six societies studied. In the past, the minority groups were either first denied formal education and later given inferior education or given inferior education from the beginning. Only since the 1950s have these societies begun to emphasize the need to provide equal access to high quality education for both minority and majority groups. In most cases, however, this is far from being an accomplished fact, so that the minority groups still do not have equal access to quality education.

---

[1]Rhodesia, Rwanda, and South Africa, among others, are probably more castelike than the United States or Israel. I have not included them in this study partly because there is no adequate information on the education of their minorities.

Education Gap. There is a wide gap in educational achievement between the minority group and the dominant group in each of the six societies. This is true whether the gap is measured in terms of classroom performance, performance on standardized tests of cognitive skills and scholastic achievement, or levels of educational attainment. The education gap between blacks and whites in the United States is the most fully documented of the six cases. The gap in performance on tests of cognitive skills and scholastic achievement exists alike when both groups belong to the same race and when they belong to different races. Unfortunately, data on the performance of various groups on IQ tests are too meager and uneven to allow for more rigorous comparison.

Explaining the Gap. Within each of the societies examined, four typical explanations of the lower school performance of minority groups can be identified: folk and scientific theories offered by members of the dominant group and folk and scientific theories offered by members of the minority group. For each group, the folk explanations probably appeared first and often determined the course of the "scientific theories." There is a feedback relationship between the two, so that in the course of time the folk theory becomes modified to look more "scientific," especially as "scientific findings" are mass produced and mass consumed. Available literature is usually heavily biased in favor of the dominant-group theories. Where minority-group members develop both popular and scientific theories of minority school performance, as in the United States, they tend to differ significantly from those offered by the dominant group. In particular, both the folk and scientific explanations emanating from the minority group tend to locate the source of their educational problems in the inequities of the prevailing caste or castelike stratification system and in the legal or extralegal discriminatory policies and practices of the dominant group. In contrast, dominant-group explanations by and large locate the source of these educational problems in the personal, familial, cultural, or biological inadequacies of the minority group. The cases surveyed in this study also suggest that in contrast to the dominant group, minority-group members almost never explain their school performance difficulties and differences in terms of genetic differences. The dominant group almost always does *when there is a belief (real or not) that the minority and the majority groups actually belong to different races,* as in Britain, New Zealand, and the United States.

Closing the Education Gap. The societies studied here differ in the degree to which they have attempted to deal with the school performance deficiencies of the minority group. Reasons for this variability include the recency of the "discovery" of the problem (or the admission that it is a problem) and the degree of social science theorizing about the problem. In all cases, attempts to deal with the problems of minority school performance deficiencies preceded any systematic social scientific efforts to theorize about their causes and solution. But once social science theorizing begins, it tends to become allied with political considerations as the guiding principle.

In most of these six societies, major efforts to improve minority-group school performance revolve around changing or rehabilitating their members, i.e., making up for certain "deficits" minority-group children are supposed to take with them to school as a result of their unique biological makeup, their family upbringing, or their cultural background. Even where reform efforts include changes in the education system itself, they are based on the assumption that minority-group children are not as capable of learning effectively under the existing system as dominant-group children are. Efforts to improve minority-group school performance are only indirectly linked to other efforts made in recent years to break down the social and technoeconomic barriers minority groups face. The reason is that neither social scientists nor policymakers see these barriers as a major determinant of minority-group school performance.

Postschool Rewards and Recent Reform. None of the societies studied has a history of rewarding minority-group members equally for equivalent training and ability. In almost every case, the minorities have become disillusioned with the prevailing belief that the way to get ahead is through hard work and success in school. This disillusionment contributes significantly to their academic retardation and lower educational attainment.

In the past few decades, some of the six societies have introduced specific measures to eliminate the job ceiling and other barriers against minorities. These measures seem to fit into Burkey's typology of four general types of public policies "designed to reduce and eliminate racial (minority) discrimination and social inequality [Burkey 1971:98, also pp. 38–39, 98–99]." The first type is *civil rights policy,* which is concerned with guaranteeing equal rights for all citizens. Burkey (1971:99) notes that the public policy of the United States since World War II has primarily been of the civil rights type. In the past few years, Britain has also begun to enact civil rights legislation intended to eliminate discriminatory barriers in housing, jobs, public accommodation, and the like (Hill 1970). India's Untouchability Offences Act of 1955 was basically a civil rights law. Civil rights policy, in general, assumes that such a strategy will eventually reduce or eliminate inequality in jobs, income, housing, education, and the like. However, the civil rights strategy may simply freeze the gap at its present level and prevent it from widening. It does not necessarily encourage the gap to close because it does not take into account the effects of past discrimination. Furthermore, civil rights legislation and related programs are rarely enforced effectively by the dominant group.

The second type is *affirmative action*, which goes one step beyond the guarantee of equal rights. Affirmative action policy encourages those who control the coveted social and technoeconomic positions of society to take positive steps to make such positions available to minorities by giving preference to qualified individual members of minority groups and by seeking out such individuals. Affirmative action may or may not involve quotas. The United States has adopted this strategy to some degree in the area of employment since the passage of Title VII of the Civil Rights Act of 1964, particularly as amended in 1972. Some aspect of the secondary and higher education programs for Oriental Jews in Israel and the higher education programs for Maoris under the Maori Education Foundation in New Zealand exemplify the affirmative action approach. As with the civil rights strategy, the effectiveness of the affirmative action approach depends upon the degree of its enforcement. It may be weakened by the opposition of dominant-group members. In the United States, this opposition is expressed vigorously in arguments against quotas and allegations of lack of qualifications among minority-group members.

The third type of policy, *discrimination in reverse*, exists only in India, where it is called *protective discrimination*. This policy may include quotas, as in India. It gives preferential treatment to identifiable members of caste minorities in matters of employment, housing, scholarships, and the like. In India, discrimination in reverse is limited to institutions and programs directly under government control: civil service jobs, government scholarships, admission to government colleges and universities, and seats in the state and central legislatures. But except for the reserved seats in the legislatures, discrimination in reverse is not effectively enforced in these public institutions and programs.

The fourth type of policy encourages *reduction of social class inequality* in general. It is not directed specifically at helping minority group members, but since the latter are usually overrepresented in the lower classes, it will reduce the minority–majority inequality, provided that it is accompanied by adequately enforced civil rights programs. In the United States, the New Deal of the 1930s and the recent War on Poverty (MDTA, WIN, etc.) and Model Cities programs are examples of this type of policy. This fourth type of policy also exists in varying degrees in Britain, Israel, and Japan, usually in the form of welfare and various social programs to assist the poor in general.

All four types of public policies do have some positive effects on minority education. For example, they tend to prevent the social and technoeconomic gap from widening, and thus they indirectly provide some material resources to enable minority-group children to continue their education (e.g., financial aid to families). Civil rights and affirmative action policies, when adequately designed and enforced, tend to reduce the disillusionment of minority-group youths and increase their educational and occupational aspirations. Eventually they may influence the youths to work harder in school. But the degree to which these policies encourage improvements in school performance is limited by the fact that they are often inadequately designed and are not often vigorously and consistently enforced.

All four types of policies are limited in their capacity to improve minority school children's performance because they are not really designed with that goal in mind. Policymakers concerned with reducing acknowledged discrimination in jobs, income, housing, and the like tend to see the lower school performance of the minorities as a drawback in their own reform efforts. In fact, they generally come to see the minority-group "lack of educational qualification" or other skills as the major barrier preventing the minorities from taking advantage of newly opened social and technoeconomic opportunities.

The task of explaining why minorities are not educationally qualified for these opportunities and deciding what can be done to provide them with such qualifications is usually left to another group of policymakers—those concerned with education. This group is aware of the barriers against the caste minorities, but seems to proceed on the assumption that the minorities could do better in school in spite of these barriers, were it not for certain presumed handicaps or deficits in their learning skills. The educational policymakers further assume that the deficits in learning skills are attributable to the biological, familial, or cultural backgrounds of the caste minority children. Since the crucial policy issue for this group is what to do about the deficits in learning skills, and since the source of the deficits is located in the background of the caste minority group children, education policymakers direct most of their efforts toward the rehabilitation of these children.

Policymakers concerned with the elimination of social and technoeconomic barriers need to go beyond their observation that minority groups lag behind in education. They need to see the educational problem as a consequence of the barriers they are trying to eliminate. The elimination of such barriers should therefore be seen both as a means of giving educationally qualified minorities new opportunities and as a strategy for improving minority efforts in school and thereby of increasing the number qualified. Likewise, policymakers concerned with educational reforms must come to realize the futility of expecting lower-caste school performance to rise to the level of that of the dominant group through programs designed to change or rehabilitate individual minority-group children. Overall improvement in the school performance of the minorities is not likely to occur so long as the social and technoeconomic barriers to equality in later life remain.

Some Generalizations

In this section I enumerate some general features of caste and castelike minorities and their education. These generalizations are presented as hypotheses that can be tested either by further studies of the cases described in this book or by studying the education of caste minorities in similar societies. The further testing of these hypotheses is necessary because of the uneven data on the societies reviewed in the present study.

Differential Status Mobility Systems. In general, a society characterized by caste or castelike stratification is also characterized by two different systems of social mobility, one for the dominant group, usually based on education, ability, initiative, and competitive skills; the other for the caste minority, based on patronage and sycophancy. This encourages the development in caste minorities of such personal qualities as dependency, compliance, and manipulation rather than independence, industriousness, initiative, foresight, and individualistic competitiveness for achievements in the wider society—all of which to some degree or other characterize members of the dominant group. This does not mean that caste minorities lack competitive skills or are not competitive. They are very competitive and industrious *outside* the channel of social and economic competition.

Noneducational Determinants of Occupational Status. The status of the caste minority is defined as inherently inferior by the dominant group. The latter generally develops an ideology that rationalizes its political, social, and economic domination over the caste minority. The inferior status assigned to the latter then determines the social and occupational roles open to them. Through a job ceiling, the members of a caste minority are restricted to the least desirable occupational roles and are prohibited from competing freely for the more desirable positions above the job ceiling on the basis of individual training and ability. Thus, the inferior social, political, and economic positions occupied by members of the caste minority are not attributable to the fact that they have less education than members of the dominant caste, contrary to Jensen's contention (1969:76–79).

Ascribed Status and Access to Inferior Education. The kind of education provided to caste minorities in general is determined by the prevailing or anticipated definition of their social and occupational status. When caste minorities are defined as inferior to the dominant group and restricted to menial social and occupational roles (as most of them are), they are provided with education considerably inferior to that of the dominant group. When their status changes, when for a variety of reasons efforts are made to raise their social, economic, and political status, there are usually simultaneous or (in most cases) subsequent efforts to improve their education.

Adaptive Function of Castelike Minority Education. The purpose of caste minority education is twofold: One is to prepare members of the group for their ascribed social, occupational, and political roles; the other is to equip them with appropriate attitudes and motivation for the kind of social mobility characteristic of their group. The two objectives are, of course, interrelated. Whether caste minorities and the dominant groups receive their education in the same or separate facilities, the schools usually succeed in teaching the minority children the personal qualities and attitudes, values, knowledge, and skills generally regarded as appropriate for performing their inferior roles in adult life. This learning may be accomplished by various means: biased textbooks and learning materials, watered down curriculum, tracking into low ability groups, different standards of academic performance, and different systems of rewards in the classroom and in the wider society, as well as attitudes and behavior in day-to-day interactions and expectations that effectively communicate to caste-minority children their proper place in adult life. There has been little systematic study in this area, even in the United States, because it is believed that the function of the schools is to equip blacks with the skills, values, and motivations characteristic of the white middle class.

Ascribed Status and Adaptive Socialization. Like school training, the home training of minority children reflects values and practices determined by the inferior social and occupational roles adult members of the group play in the wider society.

The experiences of caste minority adults in their places of work and in their communities influence their child training values and skills. At work, their menial and low-level positions require them to obey others and conform to external authorities. They have few opportunities to make decisions or take the kind of initiative required by the higher-level jobs of middle-class workers from the dominant group. Specifically, the positions occupied by members of caste minorities in the community and in the technoeconomic organizations of their society do not require from them the kind of self-direction, ability to make decisions, initiative, competitiveness, and problem-solving skills or the high degree of self-confidence in controlling their environment that are associated with the positions held by members of the dominant group, positions which also include better opportunities of advancing to higher positions in life. Restricted to menial and low-level social and technoeconomic roles for generations, and generally unable to improve their positions in life through their own abilities, training, and initiative, members of caste minorities develop values, attitudes, and skills (including cognitive and problem-solving skills) compatible with the demands of their position in society.

But the problem is not merely that what the children of caste minorities learn in their homes and communities is *different* from what the children of the dominant group learn in their homes and communities. What immigrant minority children learn may be just as different, and yet they tend to do better in school than children of caste minorities. *The major difference (and the source of the problem) is that objectively and subjectively caste minorities perceive the barriers against their full participation in society as either not changing at all or changing only at a discouragingly slow pace.* This is why the child training of caste minorities is adaptive to their inferior social and occupational positions while the child training of immigrant minorities is not. Immigrant minorities have certain crucial characteristics which shield them from such an adaptation: They lack internalization of conventional stereotypes in the stratification system; they have instrumental attitudes and beliefs that formal education leads to self-improvement and group advancement; and they have the symbolic option of using their education to improve their position in life elsewhere.

Self-Fulfilling Prophecy in Ascribed Status. Caste minorities gradually come to be defined by the dominant group as "naturally suited" for only the inferior social and economic roles to which they are restricted through legal or extralegal devices. They also come to be regarded as incapable of performing other roles associated with higher status. In the course of time, caste minorities become adapted to such roles, a development which often lends credibility to "scientific evidence" later marshaled by members of the dominant group to prove that the caste-minority group and the dominant group are different.

The situation is further reinforced by a companion belief that because caste minorities are different from the dominant group they are not capable of benefiting from the same kind of education.

Limited Opportunity and the Development of Human Potential. There is no proof that differences in genetic potential between the minority and the dominant groups account for the academic gap between the two. The genetic potential of any group cannot be fully assessed until that group has been given the maximum opportunity to develop such potential. In none of the six cases studied in this book has such an opportunity been given to the minority group. That school performance may be directly related to the kinds of opportunities available to caste minorities for developing their potential is suggested by the fact that such minorities tend to improve their school performance when they move to situations or settings where opportunities are greater.

The cross-cultural data we have examined suggest that deficiencies in school performance among caste minorities and the academic gap between them and the dominant groups arise from four related sources: late inclusion in formal education, inferior education, limited access to the rewards of formal education in adult life, and the child-training values and practices of caste minorities, all of which result from the inferior status assigned to caste minorities by dominant groups.

Reforms and Rehabilitation: Inadequate Strategies for Change. Because caste and castelike societies recruit members of the dominant group to adult status on the basis of individual ability and training but recruit members of the castelike minorities to adult status on the basis of caste origin, school reforms and efforts to change the way minority parents raise their children prove relatively ineffective as ways of improving minority school performance. The school is an agent of society, and it is doubtful that it can altogether abandon its exclusionary policies and practices unless changes in the larger society force it to do so. In other words, it is not certain that schools can be effectively reformed without simultaneously or even previously breaking down social and economic caste barriers in adult life and providing the same modes of recruitment to adult roles for caste minorities as for dominant groups. School reform is an important part of any strategy to bring about an overall and lasting improvement in the school performance of caste minorities, but it represents only part of the solution to the problem.

As for the rehabilitation approach, it is essentially a conservative strategy, whether it takes the form of resocializing individual children or changing the way their parents train them. The approach places the responsibility for change on individuals who have no mastery over the forces that created and maintain their situation. For this reason, the strategy almost ensures that very little improvement will actually take place in the schoolwork of minority children or that the pace of change will be so slow as to be discouraging in spite of the inordinate number of programs. Such lack of improvement in turn tends to exonerate the schools and society at large and blame caste minorities for their continued academic retardation. It is significant, however, that there is no empirical evidence that changes in the way parents train their children among any group have led to a major change in the school performance of that group. Indeed, it seems that the weight of evidence supports the proposition that changes in child-training patterns generally follow changes in adult roles and the system of recruiting incumbents to such roles, all of which contribute to improvement in the school performance of the group (see Aberle 1968:316).

Breaking the Caste Barriers: New Forces of Change. Modern caste societies do not adhere rigidly to the principle of caste membership in role recruitment for three reasons. The first is economic: An expanding economy, industrialization, and occasional wartime manpower needs often lead to labor shortages that necessitate a limited opening of opportunities in those adult roles traditionally closed to lower-caste members. The second reason is political: The existence of an official ideology about the equality of all citizens is directly related to the political history of many such societies. Some of them, such as India and the United States, having fought for and won their independence from foreign domination have promised equality to all citizens in the new society; when this promise was written into the constitution, it assumed the status of an official doctrine. Although such doctrines have never displaced the folk ideology of the higher castes which asserts that there is an inherent inequality among members of the various castes, today's international political realities are forcing castelike societies to introduce reforms that reduce social and technoeconomic barriers against the minority castes. Except for the Republic of South Africa, which legalizes discrimination, few societies maintain officially that there is a "natural" inequality among their component castes.

Finally, members of the lower castes have begun to engage in protests and civil rights activities. Often with the help of sympathetic members of the dominant castes, lower castes have organized to protest against discriminatory barriers and to fight for their constitutionally guaranteed rights. They demand that society live up to its official ideology.

From time to time, such protests are successful in opening up positions traditionally closed to caste minorities. Increasingly the lower-caste members are being permitted to occupy adult positions in the wider society that were not previously open to them; and increasingly they are being inducted into various roles on the basis of individual training and abilities. But these changes have neither gone far enough nor lasted long enough in the United States and elsewhere to alter the basic situation I describe in this study. There has not been a total shift to the principle of role recruitment on the basis of individual training and ability among all castes. What seems to be evolving is a combination of role recruitment based on caste membership and recruitment based on individual training and ability. Thus in the United States, members of minority groups are increasingly being inducted into various roles on the basis of ability and training as a result of legislative and other pressures. In some situations, the criteria of training and ability are becoming accepted as the norm rather than as a matter of conformity to outside pressures. In some situations, however, caste considerations remain paramount and will require further legal and other pressures to change. These two bases of role recruitment will therefore coexist until such time as caste considerations are rejected as a valid basis of role recruitment in any given situation. We next consider the latter in more detail in the context of social policy.

III

POLICY IMPLICATIONS

The final chapter, which forms Part III of this book, examines the policy implications of the analyses presented in the foregoing chapters. It deals with the extent to which the caste system can be dismantled and how this may be achieved in order to improve the school performance of castelike minorities. It also makes some specific suggestions about the elimination of caste barriers in jobs, schools, and elsewhere and how to minimize the lag among castelike minorities in responding to the breakdown of caste barriers. The chapter ends with some personal remarks about specific policy issues that were discussed at meetings of the Carnegie Council on Children. These include preferential treatment for castelike minorities, cultural homogeneity versus cultural pluralism, and equality versus diversity. Because my analyses and conclusions are likely to generate these same issues in the minds of some readers, I think it is appropriate to make my own views very explicit.

14

Elimination of Caste Barriers: How to Close the Gap in School Performance

The principal causes of black academic retardation, as I argued in the preceding chapters, are that the schools translate the inferior social and technoeconomic status of blacks into inferior education; that caste barriers do not permit blacks to translate their academic skills into good jobs, income, and other benefits; and that both conditions result in blacks developing attitudes and skills less favorable to white middle-class type of school success.[1] Therefore the lower school performance of blacks is not itself the central problem but an expression of a more fundamental one, namely caste barriers and the ideologies that support them. *The elimination of caste barriers is the only lasting solution to the problem of academic retardation.* Programs that seek to change school policies and practices and to help blacks develop new attitudes and skills are necessary but auxiliary components of this strategy and cannot by themselves prove effective in solving the problem of school failure among castelike minorities in the United States and elsewhere.

[1]Although I refer only to blacks in this chapter, it should be understood that the policy issues discussed are applicable to all the castelike minorities, including American Indians, Mexican-Americans, mainland Puerto Ricans, and native Hawaiians.

Education and Social Change

Before going on to discuss what to do about caste barriers, I will briefly review the relationships among education, social structure, and social change in order to emphasize the structural basis of the problem. Schools everywhere, in caste and noncaste societies, reflect the basic organization of society. The dominant group in each society organizes and controls the schools; it also determines what they teach and how they teach it. Under these circumstances, schools are not usually set up to offer an education designed to change the basic organization of society, official ideologies to the contrary. In a castelike society like the United States, the success of the schools lies in their ability to equip members of different groups with the knowledge and skills appropriate for the social and technoeconomic positions occupied by their members. Schools are therefore not agents of the equalization of caste status.[2]

So long as caste remains the principle of social organization, no efforts to use the schools to equalize the social and occupational status of different minority and majority castes can succeed because the social system demands that both desirable and undesirable social and occupational positions be filled on an ascriptive basis. The schools therefore

[2]This statement requires some qualifications implicit in the analysis in some of the preceding chapters. Schools in castelike societies do contribute to equalization of caste status indirectly in the following ways:

1. In societies like the United States where schools *teach the same social ideals* to the minority and majority castes they help to undermine the acceptance of the principles of the system and encourage minority demands for change. For example, when American schools teach blacks and whites that social rewards should be distributed on the basis of individual ability and training, regardless of caste, blacks become much more aware of the unfairness of the job ceiling and other caste barriers and demand that the barriers be eliminated.

2. Although castelike minorities may have only marginal, if any, participation in the desirable social and technoeconomic roles of the wider society, some nevertheless perform similar roles within their own groups which are forced to develop parallel institutions like schools, churches, hospitals, insurance companies, news media, and the like, duplicating some of the roles from which their members are excluded in the wider society. The education of castelike minorities provides for those who will occupy these positions, who therefore receive more than average education for their groups. These relatively well educated minority elites not only provide services and leadership for their groups but also become important agents of social change, a function that arises from the fact that their education enables them to perceive the inequities of the caste system much more sharply, to experience it much more painfully, to articulate the problem much more clearly, and to organize much more effectively for a change through political and other channels.

[3] I previously referred to the conscious efforts now being made by castelike societies like India and the United States to improve the status of their castelike minorities through education. India is doing this because of the constitutional mandate to build a casteless society; in the 1960s, the United States made a deliberate choice to eliminate poverty through education. The success of these two approaches to the education of castelike minorities depends, of course, on the extent to which the job ceiling and other caste barriers are removed to enable the minorities to experience the social and technoeconomic rewards of education to the same degree as the dominant caste and to develop a new belief system about schooling and future chances in life.

continue to prepare a disproportionate number of lower-caste groups for their traditional menial positions, although they may not do this consciously. Likewise, without a fundamental change in the caste system, efforts to rehabilitate castelike minority members by teaching them to develop the attitudes and skills of the white middle class prove relatively unsuccessful—for two reasons: First, blacks still perceive and respond to their schooling, both consciously and unconsciously, in terms of how they see their chances in the future to use and benefit from education like their white peers; second, the cognitive and other school- and job-related attributes blacks develop continue to be those adaptive to their social and occupational roles rather than those demanded by the positions occupied by the dominant whites and stressed by their education.

To change this situation—to eliminate black academic retardation—requires, first a total destruction of the caste system—that is, the creation of a new social order in which blacks do not occupy a subordinate position vis-a-vis whites. If we destroy the caste system, both schools and blacks will begin to manifest changes compatible with the new social order, and academic retardation will disappear. Under the new social order, schools have no choice but to change their policies and practices and train blacks as effectively as they train whites because the new society will demand the same degree of competence from both. Destroying the caste system will have important consequences for blacks' response to schooling. Basically, it will increase (a) black *experience* with equal chances for employment, promotion, wages, good housing, and the like; (b) their *perception* of equal chances to benefit from education; (c) their *belief* that more education and better education leads to better jobs, advancement, wages, housing, and general self-improvement; (d) their *belief* that they are judged for social and occupational positions as individuals on the basis of training and ability; (e) their *belief* that their chances in life depend to the same extent as the chances of whites on their individual competitive ability in school and society. The new social order will not only drastically alter the way blacks perceive their schooling and increase their striving to succeed, it will also result in their development of new skills necessary both for white middle-class type success in school and for performing competently their newly acquired social and occupational roles. Many of the cognitive, linguistic, and motivational skills which American society has tried unsuccessfully to teach black children over the past decade are actually acquired *on the job*, that is in performing the highly desirable social and occupational roles from which most blacks have long been excluded. When these are as open to blacks as they are to whites, the former will be able to transmit their newly acquired skills or attributes to their children in the course of their child training. The problem of fade-out will not arise because these skills will be functional or adaptive. They will have a survival value for blacks.

To summarize, the first step toward raising black school performance is to eliminate all caste barriers so that American society can offer blacks the same desirable social and occupational positions it offers to whites for their training and ability. Schools will respond to this change by altering their policies and practices in order to train blacks as effectively as they train whites. For their part, blacks will respond to their new opportunities by persevering in their schoolwork and by developing behavior patterns compatible with high academic achievement. As blacks find their efforts in school better rewarded by society, as they find their behavior rewarded more and more within the schools in terms of better grades and school completion, they will find schooling itself more rewarding. And if under this situation they do not find schooling intrinsically rewarding (as some white middle-class children apparently do not), they will, like middle-class whites, develop more tolerant attitudes toward academic aspects of schooling because of the social and occupational rewards they can expect from it in the future.

Can the Caste System Be Dismantled?

Whether a modern society like the United States can undo its caste system is, of course, another matter. I know of only one instance—and it was a small and localized one—in which an ongoing community changed from a caste system to a class system. This is the case of the Peruvian sierra town of Muquiyauyo, reported by Adams (1953). The town's caste system was based on a Mestizo–Indian distinction and lasted until about the end of the nineteenth century. The two factors responsible for its destruction were first, that the members of both castes wanted to destroy the system and made serious efforts to do so, and second, that outside forces such as higher education and industrial development produced new status ranks in the town which were incompatible with the caste system. Although no modern castelike society has succeeded in abolishing its caste structure, I have indicated in Chapter 13 three principal forces currently working to alter the structure of these societies. These are the manpower requirements of expanding economies; the inclusive political ideologies of formerly colonial societies like the United States and India; and the increasing demands for changes by the lower castes themselves. Burkey (1971:34–37) lists the following factors as responsible for changes in the United States caste system since World War II: employment opportunities created by the war; changes in the American economy; increased urbanization of blacks; the decline in the political power of the Democratic party in the South; the emergence of the United States as a world power since World War II; nationalism in Africa and Asia; developments in social sciences which have undermined the doctrine of biological racism; the increased development of black competitive ability and black power; and public policies to combat racial discrimination. The last item—the public policies—Burkey notes, are generally *reactions* to the other forces of change. The difficulty of eliminating the job ceiling and other caste barriers in castelike societies is that the people who have the power to do so are the very people who benefit disproportionately from these barriers and who therefore stand to lose most when the caste system is dismantled.[3]

All caste systems in the modern world contain the seeds of their own destruction because the subordinate castes not only reject (as they always have) the rationalization of the system but also increasingly persist, ever more vehemently, in their demands to change the system. In this inevitable change, the difference between one castelike society and another lies in whether the change will be constructive or destructive; and here each society has a choice. In some cases, the choice has already been made. For example, the legitimacy that the South African constitution and government policy bestow on the caste structure of that society leaves little room for constructive change. In contrast, India and the United States have written into their constitutions the principle of equality among all citizens, regardless of caste membership. And the governments of these countries have the obligation to carry out policies

[3]White individuals and white businesses profit from discrimination because *discrimination against* blacks often turns out to be *discrimination in favor* of whites. For example, as I showed in an earlier chapter, separate and unequal schools of the past usually involved channeling money and other facilities from black schools to white schools, thereby maintaining a high standard of education for whites which would have been impossible under a more equitable distribution of the school funds. In the area of jobs and wages, the job ceiling against blacks gives even less qualified white workers access to better jobs, better wages, and promotions which they might otherwise not have achieved if blacks were permitted to compete for these things on the basis of training and ability. White real estate agents derive inordinate profits from housing segregation. And white business corporations derive substantial financial profits from their discriminatory employment practices against blacks. For example, the Equal Employment Opportunities Commission (EEOC) studied the employment practices of the Bell Telephone Company in 30 metropolitan areas and found that black employees of the company lost $225,000,000 a year and employees with Spanish surnames lost $137,000,000 a year because of the company's discriminatory practices. In other words, the Bell Telephone Company gained $362,000,000 a year from its discrimination against the two castelike minority groups (EEOC 1972, cited in Perlo 1975:145).

that enable their citizens to realize their constitutionally guaranteed rights. As already noted, however, because those who have the power to formulate and enforce such public policies in both societies are also those who benefit from the barriers, the policies are often formulated in reaction to forces of change and half-heartedly enforced.

Americans, however, have a unique opportunity to create a society free of caste barriers, a society in which blacks and whites have equal chances to develop their potentials for the benefit of all. There are three reasons for this optimistic view: there is a constitutional basis for dismantling the caste system; some significant changes have occurred in that direction in the past few decades; and a growing proportion of the dominant white caste is increasingly becoming ideologically committed to such changes, if not in practice.

How the Caste System Can Be Dismantled

Becuase there are no precedents of modern societies that have successfully dismantled their caste systems, one cannot state the best way to do it. However, numerous studies of the problems of caste and race relations, special commissions on the same problems, the kinds of changes demanded by lower-caste members and their sympathizers, as well as some public policies on these issues, all provide ample suggestions for constructive ways to dismantle the system (see Burkey 1971; Levine 1972; Parsons and Clark 1966; U.S. Commission on Civil Rights 1967; U.S. National Advisory Commission on Civil Disorders 1968; Wallace 1973). What seems to be lacking are both the political commitment and the will to do it on the part of the powers that be. Yet a national commitment to eliminate caste barriers is necessary in order to formulate and effectively implement the relevant policies. By national commitment I mean that the federal, state, and local governments, the business community, and the general public as well as the black community must commit themselves to such a goal. The analysis presented in earlier chapters shows that such a commitment has never been made. Past improvements in black occupational status, housing, education, and the like have occurred primarily as a result of the uncoordinated efforts of individuals and organizations, of court orders in civil suits against discrimination, and of federal, state, and local legislation, which is often reluctantly passed and most reluctantly enforced.

The haphazard approach to the problem of caste barriers is well illustrated by efforts to eliminate the job ceiling against blacks. The

importance in American society of a job that brings good material rewards and social prestige and the opportunity to develop one's cognitive and other potentials cannot be overemphasized. Miller (1971:195)
notes correctly that "it is the job that counts" in American society. Yet
it is precisely here that the caste barriers against blacks have been most
pervasive and persistent. Black occupational advances in the past were
not associated with the normal development which has characterized
jobs for the white population. (By normal development is meant that
advances in occupational status are a function of concomitant advances
in formal education and increases in the number and types of available
jobs.) As noted earlier, blacks advanced occupationally only in times of
national crises and labor shortages and because of external pressures.
Neither the statutes governing the federal Fair Employment Practices
Commission nor those of some states and local governments nor Title
VII of the Civil Rights Act of 1964 (amended in 1972) is a part of any
carefully planned national policy to eliminate the job ceiling, nor are
they vigorously enforced. If this haphazard approach continues, blacks
will never achieve equal occupational opportunity with whites, although they will continue to make some advances here and there.

The federal government will have to play the dominant role in the
commitment to the policy of eliminating the caste barriers. Many communities and states do not have the financial and other resources to
plan and implement the kind of comprehensive programs envisioned
here. Moreover, there are communities and states, as well as business
establishments, that are not yet willing to commit themselves to equal
opportunities for blacks and whites but will probably do so if there is
federal power behind such a policy. Finally, a strong and committed
leadership at the national level is necessary to generate and sustain the
kind of attitudes and responses within the black community that help
to break down caste barriers once and for all.

Eliminating Caste Barriers

Programs to eliminate the caste barriers will have to focus on
eliminating the job ceiling against blacks, improving their economic
opportunities in general, eliminating housing discrimination and promoting interracial communities and housing, increasing black access
to higher education and professional training, and increasing their
political participation not only as voters but also as decision makers.
Changes of these kinds will result in the general improvement of black

communities and families because they will reduce black unemployment and underemployment, their disproportionate representation among the poor, and their dependence on welfare; they will also reduce the various forms of social pathology that now prevail in black communities. These changes are bound to have other ripple effects: They will influence parents to train their children so as to be more likely to succeed in school; black attitudes toward American society and the schools, their self-conceptions, and their motivation and learning habits are also likely to be influenced. In short, the breakdown of caste barriers will change the skills and motivations blacks take with them to school learning and thus will increase their academic achievement. The breakdown of caste barriers will also change the way the schools perceive and train blacks: There will be a drastic reduction in their discriminatory policies and practices against blacks.

The effects on black school performance of removing caste barriers can be illustrated with what could happen if job ceilings were eliminated. All through this book I argue that the development of human potential depends on the opportunity to utilize the derivative skills. For members of a particular group in a modern industrial and technological society like the United States, the development of cognitive and academic skills is no different. Specifically, the ability of a group of people to maximize their cognitive and academic skills depends on the opportunity they have to use these skills in the world of work. In a technological and money-oriented society like the United States, a lack of opportunity to perform highly skilled jobs stunts the development of such skills. Furthermore, the absence of such an opportunity for any group deprives its members of their sense of self-worth, frustrates their efforts to improve themselves, and ruins their ability to maintain normal family life and raise their children adequately. Eliminating the job ceiling will improve the economic status of black families, reduce the blight and social pathologies of their communities, improve their general health and nutritional level, increase their belief that they can succeed in American society by individual initiative and hard work, enable them to raise their children to be more successful in school, and enable black children to develop more fully those skills needed for school learning. It should be added that the breakdown of caste barriers would also mean the end of the selective unemployment of black teenagers which, in turn, would result in a reduction in petty thievery and drug addiction. The effectiveness of the prevailing policy of hiring more policemen to curb these problems is questionable and does nothing to solve the larger underlying problems of a society aligned between the haves and the have nots.

Eliminating Caste Barriers in Schools

Caste barriers permeate American educational institutions, and therefore school reforms should be a part of the overall effort to dismantle the caste system. The goal of school reform should be to eliminate both the obvious and the subtle ways by which the schools prevent blacks from receiving the kind of education that would enable them to play "a constructive, competitive and contributory adult role in the economy and society as a whole [Clark 1972:21]." Some of the exclusionary policies and practices are described in Chapter 4, and the methods of achieving this goal have been suggested in a number of previous studies (Clark 1972; U.S. Senate Select Committee 1972; Brazziel 1974; Marburger 1970; Webster 1974). For example, there is a need to strengthen the curriculum so that children will be taught early the necessary skills they need to function adequately in adult life. Programs could be developed to enable school personnel, especially teachers and counselors, to understand the needs of black children and to improve their attitudes and behavior toward these children. Equally important are programs to increase the participation of students and their parents in the educational process itself. Other programs will be aimed at equalizing the resources of urban and suburban schools and of black and white schools. Internship programs should be used to increase the number of black school personnel at all levels of the education system.

Apart from these broad areas, there is a need to study and eliminate the many subtle ways in which schools exclude blacks from effective education. Among these are the ways that testing, classification, tracking, and disciplinary techniques effectively operate against blacks. Finally, the reforms of the schools should include a careful study and revision of the contents of textbooks and curriculums to remove biases which overtly and covertly reinforce the lower-caste status of blacks by what they teach black and other children.

Facilitating Positive Black Response to Change

As long as caste barriers remain a major feature of American social structure, the adaptive qualities blacks develop cannot be termed "deficient," even though they are different from those of middle-class whites and even though they constitute one more factor contributing to black academic retardation. They are normal in the sense that they are

functionally adaptive to the caste barriers. As caste barriers are eliminated and the schools change to reflect changes in the caste system, the
adaptations cease to be useful and become a source of learning problems. While I believe that school reforms and the elimination of caste
barriers will eventually influence blacks to develop new sets of attitudes, self-conceptions, learning habits, and other skills that promote
success in school, I also believe that it is necessary to develop programs
that will speed up the process. Unless this is done, there is likely to be a
considerable time lag between the elimination of caste barriers and the
school reforms on the one hand, and changes in the influences of the
home and community on black educational efforts on the other.

Some cultural factors associated with difficulties in school learning among black children which originally arose in response to caste
barriers will eventually disappear when the caste barriers are eliminated, but among the areas where remedial programs would help to
speed up the desired change are attitudes toward schooling, learning
habits, and self-image in relation to learning. Other matters that require
remedial action arise from the fact that many ghetto parents come from
rural backgrounds and themselves attended schools quite different
from the urban schools their children attend. These parents have a
tendency to see the functions of urban schools and the nature of learning in ways considerably different from the ways these schools operate,
which often makes it difficult for them to help their children successfully adjust. Caste barriers further complicate the situation by barring
these parents from opportunities and incentives to acquire better
knowledge of the urban school system.

Changes in socialization patterns and linguistic, cognitive, and
motivational skills will probably take a longer time to occur and will be
more dependent on black participation in higher social and occupational roles than on remedial efforts. It should also be pointed out that
the attitudes, skills, and behavior patterns which the remedial programs I am recommending are intended to change have developed over
many generations, if not centuries. Some of them are not likely to
change because of short-term treatment during one summer or even one
full year. The effectiveness of such innovative programs cannot, therefore, be fully judged by the usual method of evaluation, i.e., by ad-
ministering psychometric and other tests at the end of a few weeks, a
few months, or even a full year.

New programs will be designed, although some of the programs
under existing compensatory education can be used, perhaps in modified form, to accomplish the same purpose. Many current programs

may be unsuitable, however, because of their assumptions and techniques. From the programs developed since the mid 1960s it should be possible to select those which have proved effective in dealing with problems of academic retardation arising from home and community environments and utilize them on a nationwide scale with modifications wherever necessary to meet local conditions. The programs so selected should be regarded as transitional, as intended to help blacks make the transition from attitudes, skills, and behavior patterns appropriately acquired and adaptive for education under the influence of caste barriers to another set of attitudes, skills, and behavior patterns for education in an American society free of such caste barriers.

More Than Equal Treatment Is Required

Some members of the dominant white caste (and some minority castes, too) will object to the idea of setting up a special public policy to eliminate the caste barriers against blacks and other castelike minorities; they will object on moral grounds because the policy involves "preferential treatment." (It should be pointed out, however, that the discriminatory practices of the past and present generations constitute preferential treatment for the dominant group.) Opponents of this kind of policy will also regard it as politically unsound because the dominant white power structure will not accept it.

It will also be suggested by opponents that programs developed specially for particular groups like the poor and minorities are often ineffective because these programs are stigmatized by the middle class. People who raise these objections suggest an alternative policy designed to improve the education of all groups and all children in American society. They argue that if we can show that the education system is failing white middle-class children and white children generally, and not just black and other minority-group children, then we can find the political and moral leverage to get Congress and other centers of power to initiate reforms that will in the end benefit blacks and everybody else and at the same time avoid the odious issue of preferential treatment. From this point of view, the key to eliminating caste barriers and, eventually, academic retardation among black children is the policy of universal and equitable treatment in employment, housing, education, and the like. This argument combines the first and fourth types of public policy discussed in Chapter 13, *civil rights* policy and the policy of *a general reduction of class inequality*. But civil rights strategy, even if firmly implemented (which it rarely is) merely freezes the existing gap and does not close it. Blacks might benefit somewhat disproportionately from a well-implemented policy of general reduction of class inequality because they are overrepresented in the lower class. However, such a disproportionate gain is doubtful because the problems of unequal opportunity created by caste barriers are not of the same order as those created by class barriers and are not necessarily subject to the same solutions. This unrealistic approach fails to take into account the fact that although past universal programs (e.g., the New Deal, the War on Poverty, Model Cities, compensatory education) helped both blacks and whites, they were ineffective tools for closing the social, economic, and educational gaps between the two races.

It is true that on moral and political grounds there is no easy choice between universal treatment and special treatment. But on the basis of the analysis of the causes of black academic retardation presented in this book, I think that it is necessary to make a clear distinction between a strategy that can effectively eliminate black academic retardation and a strategy that will be politically and morally acceptable to the dominant white group. I am convinced that the first strategy calls for the kind of comprehensive policy recommended in the present study.

Members of the dominant white caste who have the power to initiate and implement the strategy also have the power to define what is morally and politically acceptable. Since they have benefited disproportionately from past and present discriminatory social, economic, and educational policies and practices, they can be expected to oppose any public policies that will radically alter the existing social structures on such grounds as preferential treatment, quota systems, or other "reprehensible" concepts (see note 3). The evidence reviewed earlier in the present study shows that major improvements which have occurred in the social, economic, political, and educational status of blacks, especially since World War II, have taken place only in times of national crises or in direct response to civil rights initiatives of black people and their white supporters. It seems likely that these initiatives, as well as pressures for priorities and preferential treatment as a compensation for generations of discriminatory exclusion, will have to increase before the white power structure will design and implement a comprehensive policy for total elimination of the caste barriers and their supporting ideologies and thereby eliminate black academic retardation.

Conclusions

This book began with an examination of the various explanations offered for the academic retardation of black children and of the gap between blacks and whites in school performance. Current theories tend to stress the personal and social inadequacies of blacks and the inadequacies of the schools they attend, or both, as the causes of their academic retardation. They ignore the system of racial castes under which blacks must live and study—the source of their personal, social, and institutional adaptation. There has never been a serious effort to examine systematically how the American system of racial stratification contributes to black academic retardation. Instead, most research and programs focus on the *symptoms* of black subordination and exclusion under the caste system, such as poverty; childrearing practices; and differences in culture, language, cognition, and motivation, which distinguish them from the white middle class. Predictably, the remedial programs generated by these theories do not focus on eliminating black subordination and exclusion as a way of eliminating their academic retardation. Instead they focus on rehabilitating individual blacks from the supposed bad influences of their families and communities on their development of school-related skills. This is essentially a conservative approach. Other, more recent proposals emphasize the need to reform the schools in the belief that better schools can be created where, in spite of the caste barriers and other forces outside the schools, black children will not experience academic retardation.

I have suggested an alternative explanation of black academic retardation, taking into account both historical and structural influences which shape the lives of black Americans. In this formulation, I have tried to balance the overemphasis of prevailing theories on personal, social, and institutional inadequacies by tracing the origins of these inadequacies to the American system of racial stratification with its concomitant subordination and exclusion of blacks from full participation in society. The caste system which relegates blacks to the pariah status and excludes them from full social and technoeconomic participation in adult life determines black economic status: child-training practices; and linguistic, cognitive, and motivational skills. The latter, in turn, influence black school performance more directly. The problem of black academic retardation is not merely one of poverty. There is abundant evidence that within the caste system blacks with requisite education have not traditionally had access to the more desirable social and occupational roles in society nor have they been permitted to advance to higher positions in life on the basis of their education and abilities. A study of the education of similar caste minorities in five other societies shows that the same kind of academic retardation occurs among these groups. The study also strongly suggests that the academic retardation of these minority groups is caused by historical and structural conditions similar to those in the United States which affect black education. The latter suggestion is strengthened by the further finding that when these same minorities escape from the historical and structural barriers through emigration to other societies they no longer experience academic retardation.

I have stressed in this chapter the need to develop a comprehensive national policy aimed at eliminating caste barriers. Within this planned policy, there should be programs dealing simultaneously and in a coordinated way with the three sources of the retardation: caste barriers, school discriminatory policies and practices, and the "dysfunctional" influences of the home and community environment on black school children. Neither programs aimed at changing or rehabilitating the individual nor those aimed at reforming the schools can by themselves, or even combined, significantly and permanently eliminate black academic retardation. What is required to achieve this is a comprehensive policy with the clearly defined goal of incorporating blacks into the mainstream of American society, and this amounts to nothing less than a total elimination of caste barriers.

Bibliography

Aberle, David F. 1961. Culture and socialization. In *Psychological Anthropology*, edited by F. L. K. Hsu. Evanston, Ill.: Dorsey Press. Pp. 381–399.

———. 1968. The influence of linguistics on early culture and personality theory. In *Theory in anthropology*, edited by Robert A. Manners and David Kaplan. Chicago: Aldine. Pp. 303–317.

Aberle, David F., and K. D. Naegele. 1952. Middle-class fathers' occupational role and attitudes toward children. *American Journal of Orthopsychiatry* **22**:366–378.

Ackerman, Walter. 1973. Reforming Israeli education. In *Israel: Social structure and change*, edited by Michael Curtis and Mordecai Chertoff. New Brunswick, N.J.: Dutton. Pp. 397–408.

Acuna, Rodolfo. 1972. *Occupied America: The Chicanos's struggle toward liberation*. San Francisco: Canfield Press.

Adams, Arvil V. 1972. *Toward fair employment and the EEOC: A study of compliance procedures under Title VII of the Civil Rights Act of 1964: Final Report*. Washington, D.C.: U.S. Government Printing Office.

Adams, R. N. 1953. A change from caste to class in a Peruvian town. *Social Forces* **31**:238–244.

Adcock, C. J., J. R. McCreary, J. E. Ritchie, and H. C. A. Somerset. 1954. An analysis of Maori scores on the Wechsler Bellevue. *Australian Journal of Psychology* **6**:16–29.

Adcock, Cyril, and James Ritchie. 1958. Intercultural use of Rorschach. *American Anthropological* **60**:881–892.

Adler, Chaim. 1970. The Israeli school as a selective institution. In *Integration and development in Israel*, edited by S. N. Eisenstadt, Rivkah Bar Yosef and Chaim Adler. New York: Praeger. Pp. 287–301.

Alland, Alexander, Jr. 1973. *Human diversity*. Garden City, N.Y.: Anchor Press/ Doubleday.

Anastasi, Anne, and Fernando A. Cordova. 1972. Some effects of bilingualism upon the intelligence test performance of Puerto Rican children in New York City. In *The Puerto Rican community and its children on the mainland: A source book for teachers, social workers, and other professionals*, edited by Francesco Cordasco and Eugene Bucchiono. Metuchen, N.J.: Scarecrow Press. Pp. 318–332.

Andreas, Burton G. 1968. *Psychological science and the educational enterprise*. New York: Wiley.

Archer, Dane, and Mary Archer. 1970. Race, identity, and the Maori people. *Journal of the Polynesian Society* **79**,2:201–218.

Armstrong, G. P., E. M. Achilles, and M. J. Sacks. 1935. Reactions of Puerto Rican children in New York City to Psychological test. In New York State Chamber of Commerce, *Report of Special Commission on Immigrants and Naturalization*.

Ashmore, Harry S. 1954. *The Negro and the schools*. Chapel Hill: Univ. of North Carolina Press.

Austin, Ernest. 1965a. Cultural deprivation—a few questions. *Phi Delta Kappan* **46**:67–70.

——. 1965b. A parting shot from a still skeptical skeptic. *Phi Delta Kappan* **46**:75–76.

Ausubel, David P. 1960. *The fern and the Tiki: An American view of New Zealand national character, social attitudes and race relations*. New York: Holt.

——. 1961. *Maori Youth: A psychoethnological study of cultural deprivation*, New York: Holt.

——. 1964. How reversible are cognitive and motivational effects of cultural deprivation? Implications for teaching the culturally deprived. *Urban Education* **1**:16–39.

Avineri, Shlomo. 1973. Israel: Two nations? In *Israel: Social structure and change*, edited by Michael Curtis and Mordecai Chertoff. New Brunswick, N.J.: Dutton. Pp. 281–306.

Bailey, F. G. 1957. *Caste and the economic frontier*. Manchester: Manchester Univ. Press.

Bakan, D. 1967. *On method: Toward a reconstruction of psychological investigation*. San Francisco: Jossey-Bass.

Banks, O. 1968. *The sociology of education*. London: Batsford.

Banton, M. 1958. *White and coloured*. London: Jonathan Cape.

Bar Yosef, Rivkah. 1970. The Moroccans: Background to the problem. In *Integration and development in Israel*, edited by S. N. Eisenstadt, Rivkah Bar Yosef, and Chaim Adler. New York: Praeger. Pp. 419–428.

Baratz, Joan C. 1970. Teaching reading in the urban Negro school system. *Language and poverty: Perspectives on a theme*, edited by Frederick Williams. Chicago: Markham. Pp. 11–24.

Baratz, Stephen S., and Joan C. Baratz. 1970. Early childhood intervention: The social-science base of institutional racism. *Harvard Educational Review* **40**:29–50.

Barber, B. 1941. Acculturation and Messianic movement. *American Sociological Review* **6**:662–668.

Bastuni, Rustum. 1973. The Arab Israelis. In *Israel: Social structure and chance*, edited by Michael Curtis and Mordecai Chertoff. New Brunswick, N.J.: Transaction Book. Pp. 409–418.

Baughman, E. Earl. 1971. *Black Americans.* New York: Academic Press.

Beaglehole, Ernest, and James Ritchie. 1961. Basic personality in a New Zealand Maori community. In *Studying personality cross-culturally,* edited by Bert Kaplan. Evanston, Ill. Row, Peterson. Pp. 493–517.

Beardsley, Richard K., John W. Hall, and Robert E. Ward. eds. 1959. *Village Japan.* Chicago: Univ. of Chicago Press.

Becker, Garry. 1957. *The economics of discrimination.* Chicago: Univ. of Chicago Press.

Ben David, Joseph. 1970. Ethnic differences or social change? In *Integration and development in Israel,* edited by S. N. Eisenstadt, Rivkah Bar Yosef, and Chaim Adler. New York: Praeger. Pp. 368–387.

Ben-Porath, Yoram. 1973. On East-West differences in occupational structure in Israel. In *Israel: Social structure and change,* edited by Michael Curtis and Mordecai Chertoff. New Brunswick, N.J.: Dutton and Co. Pp. 215–236.

Bentwich, Joseph Solomon. 1965. *Education in Israel.* London: Routledge and Kegan Paul.

Bereiter, C. 1965. Academic instruction and preschool children. In *Language programs for the disadvantaged,* edited by R. Cobin and M. Crosby. Champaign, Ill.: National Council of Teachers of English.

Bereiter, Carl, and Siegfried Engelman. 1966. *Teaching disadvantaged children in the preschool.* Englewood Cliffs, N.J.: Prentice-Hall.

Bereiter, C., Jean Osborne, S. Engelmann, and P. A. Reidford. 1965. An academically-oriented preschool for culturally deprived children. In *Preschool education today,* edited by Fred M. Hechinger. New York: Doubleday.

Berg, Ivar. 1969. *Education and jobs: The great training robbery.* New York: Praeger.

Berger, Monroe. 1967. *Equality by statute: The revolution in civil rights.* New York: Doubleday.

Bernstein, Basil. 1961. Social class and linguistic development: A theory of social learning. In *Education, economy, and society,* edited by A. H. Halsey, J. Floud, and A. Anderson. New York: Free Press.

———. 1970. A sociolinguistic approach to socialization, with some reference to educability. In *Language and poverty: Perspectives on a theme,* edited by Frederick Williams. Chicago: Markham.

———. 1971. Education cannot compensate for society. In *School and society: A sociological reader,* edited by Cosin, Dale, et al. Cambridge, Mass.: M.I.T. Press. Pp. 61–67.

Berreman, Gerald D. 1960. Caste in India and the United States. *American Journal of Sociology* LXVI:120–127.

———. 1967a. Structure and function of caste system. In *Japan's Invisible Race,* edited by George DeVos and Hiroshi Wagatsuma. Berkeley: Univ. of California Press. Pp. 277–307.

———. 1967b. Concomitants of caste organization. In *Japan's Invisible Race,* edited by George DeVos and Hiroshi Wagatsuma. Berkeley: Univ. of California Press. Pp. 308–324.

———. 1972. Race, caste, and other invidious distinctions in social stratification. *Race* **23,** No. 4.

Berry, B. 1969. *The education of the American Indian—final report.* Project No. 7-0813-U.S. Dept. of Health, Education and Welfare, Office of Education, Washington, D.C.

Berry, J. W. 1966. Temne and Eskimo perceptional skill. *International Journal of Psychology* **1**:207–229.

———. 1971. Ecological and cultural factors in spatial perceptual development. *Canadian Journal of Behavioral Science* **3**:324–336.

Beteille, Andre. 1967. The future of the backward classes: The competing demands of status and power. In *India and Ceylon: Unity and diversity,* edited by Philip Mason. New York: Oxford Univ. Press. Pp. 83–120.

———. 1969. *Castes: Old and new.* New York: Asian Publishing House.

———. 1972. Pollution and poverty. In *The untouchables in contemporary India,* edited by J. M. Mahar. Tucson: Univ. of Arizona Press. Pp. 411–420.

Beteille, Andre, and M. N. Srinivas. 1969. The Harijans of India. In *Castes: Old and new,* edited by Andre Beteille. New York: Asian Publishing House. Pp. 87–102.

Bhatia, C. M. 1955. *Performance tests of intelligence under Indian conditions.* London: Oxford Univ. Press.

Biggs, Bruce. 1961. Maori affairs and the Hunn Report. *Journal of the Polynesian Society* **70**:361–364.

———. 1968. The Maori language past and present. In *The Maori people in the nineteen-sixties,* edited by Erik Schwimmer. New York: Humanities Press. Pp. 65–84.

Blackman, Robert. 1939. *The language handicap of Spanish-American children.* Unpublished master's thesis, Univ. of Arizona, Tuscon.

Blair, Philip M. 1971. *Job discrimination and education: An investment analysis.* New York: Praeger.

———. 1972. Job discrimination and education. In *Schooling in a corporate society: The political economy of education in America,* edited by M. Carnoy. New York: David McKay. Pp. 80–99.

Blauner, Robert. 1972. *Racial oppression in America.* New York: Harper.

Bloom, B. S. 1964. *Stability and change in human characteristics.* New York: Wiley.

Bloom, Benjamin S., Allison Davis, and Robert Hess. 1965. *Compensatory education for cultural deprivation.* New York: Holt.

Bohannon, Paul. 1963. *Social anthropology.* New York: Holt.

Bond, Horace Mann. 1966. *The education of the Negro in the American social order.* New York: Octagon.

———. 1969. *Negro education in Alabama: A study in cotton and steel.* New York: Atheneum.

Bowker, Gordon. 1968. *The education of coloured immigrants.* New York: Humanities Press.

Bowles, Samuel, and Henry M. Levin. 1968. The determinants of scholastic achievement—an appraisal of some recent evidence. *Journal of Human Resources* **3**:393–400.

Braithwaite, E. R. 1968. The "colored immigrant" in Britain. In *Color and race,* edited by John Hope Franklin. Boston: Houghton-Mifflin. Pp. 218–233.

Brameld, Theodore. 1968. *Japan: Culture, education, and change in two communities.* New York: Holt.

Brazziel, William F. 1974. *Quality education for all Americans: An assessment of gains of black Americans with proposals for program development in American schools and colleges for the next quarter-century.* Washington, D.C.: Howard Univ. Press.

Brazziel, W. F., and Mary Terrel. 1962. An experiment in the development of readiness in a culturally disadvantaged group of first grade children. *Journal of Negro Education* **31**:4–7.

Brigham, Carl C. 1923. *A study of American intelligence.* Princeton, N.J.: Princeton Univ. Press.

Brimmer, Andrew F. 1974. Economic development in the black community. In *The great society: Lessons for the future,* edited by Eli Ginzberg and Robert M. Solow. New York: Basic Books. Pp. 146–163.

Brookover, Wilbur B., and Edsel L. Erickson. 1965. *Society, schools, and learning.* Boston: Allyn and Bacon.

Broom, Leonard, and Glenn Norval. 1967. *Transformation of the Negro American.* New York: Harper.

Brophy, William A. and Sophie D. Aberle. 1966. *The Indian: America's unfinished business.* Norman, Okla.: Univ. of Oklahoma Press.

Bryde, John S. 1970. *The Sioux Indian student: A study of scholastic failure and personality conflict.* Vermillion, S. Dak. Dakota Press.

Buck, Peter H. 1950. *The coming of the Maori.* Wellington: Maori Purposes Fund Board.

Buck, Solon J., and Elizabeth Buck. 1939. *The planting of civilization in Western Pennsylvania.* Pittsburgh: Univ. of Pittsburgh Press.

Bullock, Henry Allen. 1970. *A history of Negro education in the South: From 1619 to the present.* New York: Praeger.

Burgin, Trevor, and Patricia Edson. 1967. *Spring Grove: The education of immigrant children.* London: Oxford Univ. Press for the Institute of Race Relations.

Burkey, Richard M. 1971. *Racial discrimination and public policy in the United States.* Lexington, Mass.: D.C. Heath.

Burma, John H., ed. 1970a. *Mexican-Americans in the United States: A reader.* New York: Schenkman.

———. 1970b. Mexican American, prejudice and discrimination. In *Mexican-Americans in the United States: A reader,* edited by John H. Burma. New York: Schenkman. Pp. 57–62.

Burt, Sir Cyril. 1963. Is intelligence distributed normally? *British Journal of Statistical Psychology* **16**:175–190.

———. 1969. Intelligence and heredity. *New Scientist* **1**:226–228.

California, State of. 1972. City of Stockton: Affirmative action survey. Sacramento: California Fair Employment Practice Commission. Unpublished Manuscript.

Caliver, Ambrose. 1935. Some problems in the education and placement of Negro teachers. *Journal of Negro Eduation* **4**:99–112.

Callis, H. A. 1935. The training of Negro physicians. *Journal of Negro Education* **4**:32–41.

Campbell, Ronald F., Luvern L. Cunningham, and Roderick F. McPhee. 1965. *The organization and control of American schools.* Columbus, Ohio: Merril.

Carnegie Quarterly. 1974. Racism and sexism in children's books. *Carnegie Quarterly* **22**,4:1–4.

Carter, Thomas P. 1970. *Mexican Americans in school: A history of educational neglect.* New York: College Entrance Examination Board.

Castle, E. B. 1964. *Ancient education and today.* Baltimore, Md.: Penguin.

Chandrasekhar, S. 1972. Foreward-personal perspectives on untouchability. In *The Untouchables in contemporary India,* edited by J. M. Mahar. Tucson: Univ. of Arizona Press. Pp. xi–xxviii.

Chauhan, Brij Raj 1967. Special problems of the education of the scheduled castes. In *Papers in the sociology of education in India,* edited by S. M. Gore and I. P. Desai. New Delhi: National Council of Educational Research and Training. Pp. 228–249.

Children's Defense Fund. 1974. *Children out of school in America.* Washington, D.C.: Washington Research Project.

Clark, Kenneth B. 1965. *Dark ghettos: Dilemmas of social power.* New York: Harper.

———. 1967. Sex, status, and underemployment of the Negro male. In *Employment, race, and poverty: A critical study of the disadvantaged status of Negro workers from 1865 to 1965,* edited by Arthur M. Ross and Herbert Hill. New York: Harcourt. Pp. 138–148.

———. 1971. Education in the ghetto: A human concern. In *Urban education in the 1970's,* edited by A. Harry Passow. New York: Teachers College Press.

———. 1972. *A possible reality: A design for the attainment of high academic achievement for inner-city students.* New York: Marc Corporation.

Clark, Kenneth B., and Talcott Parsons, eds. 1965. *The Negro American.* Boston: Beacon Press.

Clausen, John A. 1968. Perspectives on childhood socialization. In *Socialization and society,* edited by John A. Clausen. Boston: Little, Brown.

Clement, Dorothy C., and Patricia A. Johnson. 1973. The "cultural deprivation" perspective. In *Beyond 'compensatory education': A new approach to educating children,* edited by Glen P. Nimnicht and James A. Johnson, Jr. San Francisco: Far West Laboratory for Educational Research and Development. Pp. 1–26.

Cloward, Richard, A., and J. A. Jones. 1963. Social class: Educational attitudes and participation. In *Education in depressed areas,* edited by A. H. Passow. New York: Teachers Press.

Coers, W. C. 1935. Comparative achievement of White and Mexican junior high school pupils. *Peabody Journal of Education* 12:157–262.

Cohen, David K., Thomas F. Pettigrew, and Robert T. Riley. 1972. Race and the outcome of schooling. In *On equality of educational opportunity,* edited by Frederick Mosteller and Daniel P. Moynihan. New York: Random House.

Cohen, Rosalie A. 1969. Conceptual styles, culture conflict, and nonverbal test of intelligence. *American Anthropologist* 71:828–856.

Cohen, Yehudi A. 1971. The shaping of men's minds: Adaptation to the imperatives of culture. In *Anthropological perspectives on education,* edited by Murray L. Wax, Stanley Diamond, and Fred Gearing. New York: Basic Books.

Cohn, Bernard S. 1955. The changing status of a depressed caste. In *Village India: Studies in the little community,* edited by Marriott McKim. Chicago: Univ. of Chicago Press. Pp. 53–77.

Cole, Michael, John Gay, Joseph A. Glick, and Donald W. Sharp. 1971. *The cultural content of learning and thinking: An exploration experimental anthropology.* New York: Basic Books.

Cole, Michael, and Sylvia Scribner. 1973. Cognitive consequences of formal and informal education. *Science* 182:553–559.

———. 1974. *Culture and thought: A psychological introduction.* New York: Wiley.

Coleman, James S. 1969. The concept of equality of educational opportunity. In *Equality of educational opportunity,* edited by Harvard Educational Review. Cambridge, Mass.: Harvard Univ. Press. Pp. 9–24.

Coleman, James S., Ernest R. Campbell, Carol J. Hobson, James McPartland, Alexander M. Mood, Frederic D. Wernfield, and Robert L. York. 1966. *Equality of educational opportunity.* Washington, D.C.: U.S. Government Printing Office.

Conant, James Bryant. 1961. *Slums and suburbs.* New York: McGraw-Hill.

———. 1965. Social dynamite in our large cities: Unemployed, out of school youth. In *The schools and the urban crisis,* edited by August Kerber and Barbara Bommarito. New York: Holt. Pp. 170–185.

Conrad, Earl. 1966. *The invention of the Negro.* New York: Paul S. Erikson.

Cook, J. C. and G. Arthur. 1955. Intelligence ratings for 97 Mexican children in Saint Paul, Minnesota. *High School Journal* **38**:24–31.

Coombs, M. 1970. The Indian student is not low man on the totem pole. *Journal of American Indian Education* **9**:1–9.

Coombs, M., Ralph E. Kron, E. Gordon Collister, and Kenneth F. Anderson. 1958. *The Indian child goes to school.* Lawrence, Kansas: Bureau of Indian Affairs, Haskell Institute.

Cooper, Bruce. 1971. *Free and freedom schools: A national survey of alternative programs.* Washington, D.C.: U.S. Government Printing Office.

Cooper, R., and J. Zubek. 1958. Effects of enriched and restricted early environments on the learning ability of bright and dull rats. *Canadian Journal of Psychology* **12**:159–164.

Cordasco, Francesco. 1972. The Puerto Rican child in the American school. In *The Puerto Rican community and its children on the mainland: A source book for teachers, social workers, and other professionals.* Metuchen, N.J.: Scarecrow Press. Pp. 341–348.

Cornell, John B. 1964. Ainu assimilation and cultural extinction: Acculturation policy in Hokkaido. *Ethnology* **11**,3:287–304.

———. 1967a. Buraku relations and attitudes in a progressive farming community. In *Japan's invisible race,* edited by George DeVos and Hiroshi Wagatsuma. Berkeley: Univ. of California Press. Pp. 154–182.

———. 1967b. Individual mobility and group membership: The case of the Burakumin. In *Aspects of social change in modern Japan,* edited by R. P. Dore. Princeton, N.J.: Princeton Univ. Press. Pp. 337–372.

Cosin, B. R., I. R. Dale, G. M. Esland, and D. F. Swift. 1971. *School and society: A sociological reader.* Cambridge, Mass.: M.I.T. Press.

Costello, Joan, and Ellice Peyton. 1973. The socialization of young children's learning styles. New Haven: Yale University Child Study Center. Unpublished Manuscript.

Cox, Oliver. 1945. Race and caste: A distinction. *American Journal of Sociology* **50**:360–368.

Crossland, Fred E. 1971. *Minority access to college.* New York: Schocken Books.

Crow, James F. 1969. Genetic theories and influences: Comments on the value of diversity. *Harvard Educational Review, Reprint Series No. 2.* Pp. 153–161.

Curtis, Michael, and Mordecai Chertoff, eds. 1973. *Israel: Social structure and change.* New Brunswick, N.J.: Dutton.

Daniels, John. 1969. *In freedom's birthplace.* New York: Arno Press.

Dasen, P. R. 1973. The influence of ecology, culture and European contact on cognitive development in Australian Aborigines. In *Culture and cognition: Readings in cross-cultural psychology,* edited by J. W. Berry and P. R. Dasen. London: Methuen. Pp. 381–408.

Davidson, Robert Barry. 1966. *Black British: Immigrants to England.* London: Oxford Univ. Press for the Institute of Race Relations.

Davis, Allison, and John Dollard. 1964. *Children of bondage: The personality development of Negro youth in the urban South.* New York: Harper.

Davis, Allison, Burleigh B. Gardner, and Mary R. Gardner. 1965. *Deep South: A social anthropological study of caste and class.* Chicago: Univ. of Chicago Press.

Dawson, J. L. M. 1967. Cultural and physiological influences upon spatial perceptual processes in West Africa. *International Journal of Psychology* **2**:115–128.

De Avila, Edward A., and Barbara E. Havassy. 1975. Piagetian alternative to IQ: Mexican-American study. In *The future of children. Vol. 2: Issues in the classification of children*, edited by Nicholas Hobbs. San Francisco: Josey-Bass. Pp. 246–265.

Deloria, Jr., Vine. 1974. *Behind the trail of broken treaties: An Indian declaration of independence*. New York: Dell.

Dennenberg, Victor H. 1970. *Education of the infant and young child*. New York: Academic Press.

Dennis, Wayne. 1970. Goodenough scores, art experience, and modernization. *Cross-cultural studies of behavior*, edited by Ihsan Al-Issa and Wayne Dennis. New York: Holt. Pp. 134–152.

Dentler, Robert A., Bernard Mackler, and Mary Ellen Warshauer, eds. 1967. *The urban R's: Race relations as the problem in urban education*. New York: Praeger.

Desai, A. R. 1967. Social change and educational policy. In *Papers in the sociology of education in India*, edited by S. M. Gore and I. P. Desai. New Delhi: National Council of Educational Research and Training. Pp. 91–126.

Deutsch, Cynthia. 1964. Auditory discrimination and learning: Social factors. *Merril-Palmer Quarterly*. **10**:277–296.

Deutsch. M. 1963. The disadvantaged child and the learning process: Some social and developmental considerations. In *Education in depressed areas*, edited by A. H. Passow. New York: Teachers College Press. Pp. 163–179.

Deutsch, Martin, Irwin Katz, and Arthur R. Jensen, eds. 1968. *Social class, race and psychological development*. New York: Holt.

Deutsch, Martin, and associates. 1967. *The disadvantaged child: Selected papers of Martin Deutsch and associates*. New York: Basic Books.

De Vos, George A. 1973. Japan's outcastes: The problem of the Burakumin. In *The fourth world: Victims of group oppression*, edited by Ben Whitaker. (Eight Reports from the Field Work of the Minority Rights Group) New York: Schocken Books. Pp. 307–327.

De Vos, George A., and Arthur Hippler. 1969. Cultural psychology: Comparative studies of human behavior. In *Handbook of social psychology*, Vol. IV, edited by G. Lindzey and E. Aronson. Cambridge, Mass.: Addison-Wesley.

De Vos, George A., and Hiroshi Wagatsuma, eds. 1967a. *Japan's invisible race*. Berkeley: Univ. of California Press.

———. 1967b. Group solidarity and individual mobility. In *Japan's invisible race*. Berkeley: Univ. of California Press.

———. 1967c. Minority status and attitudes toward authority. In *Japan's invisible race*. Berkeley: Univ. of California Press.

Dillard, J. L. 1972. *Black English: Its history and usage in the United States*. New York: Random House.

Dollard, John. 1957. *Caste and class in a southern town*. (3rd ed.) Garden City, N.Y.: Doubleday.

Donoghue, John. 1967. The social persistence of an outcaste group. In *Japan's invisible race*, edited by George De Vos and Hiroshi Wagatsuma. Berkeley: Univ. of California Press.

Dore, R. P. 1958. Educational normative standards in Israel: A comparative analysis. *International Review of Education* **IV**:389–408.

———. 1967. Mobility, equality, and individuation in modern Japan. In *Aspects of social change in modern Japan*, edited by R. P. Dore. Princeton, N.J.: Princeton Univ. Press. Pp. 113–150.

Drake, St. Clair. 1968. The ghettoization of Negro life. In *Negroes and jobs*, edited by Louis A. Ferman, Joyce L. Kornbluh, and J. A. Miller. Ann Arbor: Univ. of Michigan Press. Pp. 112–128.

Drake, St. Clair, and Horace R. Cayton. 1970. *Black metropolis: A study of Negro life in a northern city.* Vols. 1 and 2. New York: Harcourt.

Dreger, Ralph Mason. 1973. Intellectual functioning. In *Comparative studies of blacks and whites in the United States,* edited by Kent S. Miller and Ralph Mason Dreger. New York: Seminar Press. Pp. 185–229.

Druding, Aleda. 1965. Stirring in the big cities: Philadelphia. In *The schools and the urban crisis,* edited by August Kerber and Barbara Bommarito. New York: Holt. Pp. 244–251.

Du Bois, W. E. B. 1900. *The college-bred Negro.* Atlanta, Ga.: Atlanta Univ. Press.

———. 1911. *The common school and the Negro.* Atlanta, Ga.: Atlanta Univ. Press.

———. 1967. *The Philadelphia Negro.* New York: Schocken Books, 1967 (originally published in 1899).

Dumont, L. 1961. Caste, racism and "stratification": Reflections of a social anthropologist. *Contributions to Indian Sociology no. 5.,* 20–43.

Dunca, Otis Dudley. 1975. Patterns of occupational mobility among Negro men. In *Racial discrimination in the United States,* edited by Thomas F. Pettigrew, New York: Harper. Pp. 167–187.

Dunklin, L. D. 1935. A study of the intelligence of some recent Puerto Rican immigrant children in a first grade in a New York City school. Unpublished M.A. dissertation, Teachers College, Columbia Univ.

Durham, Joseph T. 1972. Who needs it? Compensatory education. In *Urban education.* (rev. ed.), edited by Richard R. Heidenreich. Arlington,Va.: College Readings. Pp. 47–57.

Dushkin, Lelah. 1972. Scheduled caste politics. In *The untouchables in contemporary India,* edited by J. M. Mahar. Tucson: Univ. of Arizona Press. Pp. 165–226.

Earle, Margaret J. 1958. *Rakau children from six to thirteen years.* Wellington: Victoria Univ. Publicaton in Psychology, No. 11.

Eisenstadt, Samuel N. 1954. *The absorption of Immigrants: A comparative study based mainly on the Jewish Community in Palestine and the state of Israel.* London: Routledge and Kegan Paul.

———. 1970a. Israel: Traditional and modern social values and economic development. In *Integration and development in Israel,* edited by S. N. Eisenstadt, Rivkah Bar Yosef, and Chaim Adler. New York: Praeger. Pp. 107–122.

———. 1970b. The process of absorption of new immigrants in Israel. In *Integration and development in Israel,* edited by S. N. Eisenstadt, Rivkah Bar Yosef, and Chaim Adler. New York: Praeger. Pp. 341–367.

Eisenstadt, S. N., Rivkah Bar Yosef, and Chaim Adler, eds. 1970. *Integration and development in Israel.* New York: Praeger.

Fantini, Mario, Marilyn Gittell, and Richard Magat. 1970. *Community control and the urban school.* New York: Praeger.

Farber, Bernard, and Michael Lewis. 1972. Compensatory education and social justice. In *Urban education,* edited by Richard R. Heidenreich. Arlington, Va.: College Reading. Pp. 47–57.

Farley, Reynolds, and Karl E. Taeuber. 1968. Population trends and residential segregation since 1960. *Science.*

Farmer, James. 1968. Stereotypes of the Negro and their relationship to his self-image. In *Urban schooling,* edited by Herbert C. Rudman and Richard L. Featherstone. New York: Harcourt.

Fein, Leonard. 1970. The centers of power. In *Integration and development in Israel,* edited by S. N. Eisenstadt, Rivkah Bar Yosef, and Chaim Adler. New York: Praeger. Pp. 47–90.

Ferguson, C. O. 1917. The psychology of the Negro. *Archives of Psychology*, No. 36. New York: Columbia Univ. Press.

Ferguson, Harold A., and Richard L. Plaut. 1954. Talent: To develop or to lose. *Educational Record*.

Ferman, Louis, A., Joyce L. Kornbluh, and J. A. Miller., eds. 1968. *Negroes and jobs: A book of readings.* Ann Arbor: Univ. of Michigan Press.

Findley, Warren G. 1973. How ability grouping fails. *Inequality in Education* **14**:38–40.

Fitzpatrick, Joseph P. 1971. *Puerto Rican American: The meaning of migration to the mainland.* Englewood Cliffs, N.J.: Prentice-Hall.

———. 1974. Puerto Ricans in New York. El Verde de Rio Grande, seminar on migration. Unpublished manuscript.

Floud, Jean, and A. H. Halsey. 1961. English secondary schools and the supply of labor. In *Education, economy, and society: A reader,* edited by Jean Flood, A. H. Halsey, and C. Arnold Anderson. Glencoe, Ill.: Free Press. Pp. 80–92.

Forbes, Jack D., ed. 1964. *The Indian in America's past.* Englewood Cliffs, N.J.: Prentice-Hall.

———. 1970. Mexican-Americans. In *Mexican-Americans in the United States: A reader,* edited by John H. Burma. New York: Schenkman.

Forman, Robert E. 1971. *Black ghettos, White ghettos, and slums.* Englewood Cliffs, N.J.: Prentice Hall.

Forster, John. 1968. The social position of the Maori. In *The Maori people in the twentieth-century,* edited by Erik Schwimmer. New York: Humanities Press.

Frazier, E. Franklin. 1940. Negro youth at the crossways: Their personality development in the middle states. Washington, D.C.: American Council on Education.

———. 1957. *The Negro in the United States.* New York: Macmillan.

Fuchs, Estelle, and Robert J. Havighurst. 1973. *To live on this Earth: American Indian education.* Garden City, N.Y.: Doubleday.

Garrett, H. E. 1928. The relation of tests of memory and learning to each other and to general intelligence in a highly selected adult group. *Journal Educational Psychology* **19**:601–613.

———. 1971. *Heredity: The cause of racial differences in intelligence.* Kilmarnock, Va.: Patrick Henry Press.

Garth. T. R. 1931. *Race psychology: A study of racial mental differences.* New York: McGraw-Hill.

Garth, T. R., and H. D. Johnson. 1934. The intelligence and achievement of Mexican children in the U.S. *Journal of Abnormal and Social Psychology* **29**:222–239.

Gartner, Alan, and Frank Riessman. 1973. The lingering infatuation with I.Q.: A review of Arthur R. Jensen's *Educability and group differences.* Unpublished manuscript.

Gay, John, and Michael Cole. 1967. *The new mathematics and an old culture: A study of learning among the Kpelle of Liberia.* New York: Holt.

Gearing, Fred O. 1972. *Where we are: Where we might go: Steps toward a general theory of cultural transmission.* Unpublished manuscript.

Geber, M. 1958. The psycho-motor development of African children in the first year, and the influence of maternal behavior. *Journal of Social Psychology* **47**:185–195.

Geber, M., and R. F. A. Dean. 1957. The state of development of newborn African children. *Lancet* 1216–1219.

Ginzberg, Eli. 1956. *The Negro potential.* New York: Columbia Univ. Press.

———. 1964. *The Negro challenge to the business community.* New York: McGraw-Hill.

————. 1967. *The middle-class Negro in the white man's world.* New York: Columbia Univ. Press.

Gittelman, Zvi. 1973. Absorption of Soviet immigrants. In *Israel: Social structure and change,* edited by Michael Curtis and Mordecai Certoff. New Brunswick, N.J.: Transaction Book. Pp. 47–66.

Glass, Ruth. 1961. *London's newcomers: The West Indian migrants.* Cambridge, Mass.: Harvard Univ. Press.

Goldberg, Miriam L. 1971. Socio-psychological issues in the education of the disadvantaged. In *Urban education in the 1970's,* edited by A. Harry Passow. New York: Teachers College Press. Pp. 61–93.

Goldman, R. J., and Francine M. Taylor. 1966. Coloured immigrant children: A survey of research, studies and literature on their educational problems and potential in Britain. *Educational Research* **8,**3:163–183.

Goldschmidt, Elisabeth, ed. 1963. *The genetics of migrant and isolate populations.* Baltimore: Williams and Wilkins.

Goldschmidt, Walter. 1971. Introduction: The theory of cultural adaptation. In *The individual in cultural adaptation: A study of four East African peoples,* edited by Robert B. Edgerton. Los Angeles: Univ. of California Press. Pp. 1–22.

Goldwin, Robert A., ed. 1964. *100 years of emancipation.* Chicago: Rand McNally.

Gordon, Ira J. 1968. *Parent involvement in compensatory education.* Urbana: Univ. of Illinois Press.

Gore, M. S., and J. P. Desai, ed. 1967. The scope of sociology of education. In *Papers in the sociology of education in India,* edited by M. S. Gore and I. P. Desai. New Delhi: The National Council of Educational Research and Training. Pp. 1–32.

Gottfried, Nathan W. 1973. Effects of early intervention programs. In *Comparative studies of blacks and whites,* edited by Kent S. Miller and Ralph Mason Dreger. New York: Seminar Press. Pp. 273–293.

Gottheil, Fred M. 1973. On the economic development of the Arab region in Israel. In *Israel: Social structure and change,* edited by Michael Curtis and Mordecai Chertoff. New Brunswick, N.J.: Transaction Book. Pp. 237–248.

Grebler, L., J. W. Moore, and Ralph Guzman, eds. 1970. *The Mexican-American people, the nation's second largest minority.* New York: Free Press.

Gray, Susan W., and A. R. Klaus. 1963. *Interim report: Early training project.* George Peabody College and Murfreesboro, Tenn. City Schools. (Summary in *Compensatory education for cultural deprivation,* edited by Benjamin Bloom, Allison Davis, and Robert Hess. New York: Holt, 1965.)

Greene, Lorenzo, and Carter G. Woodson. 1930. *The Negro wage earner.* Washington, D.C.: The Association For The Study of Negro Life and History.

Greenfield, Patricia Marks. 1966. On culture and conservation. In *Studies in cognitive growth,* by Jerome S. Bruner, Rose R. Oliver, and Patricia M. Greenfield. New York: Wiley. Pp. 225–256.

Greer, Colin. 1971. *The great school legend: A revisionist interpretation of American public education.* New York: Basic Books.

Griffith, J. A. G., Judith Henderson, Margaret Usborne, and Donald Wood. 1960. *Coloured immigrants in Britain.* London: Oxford Univ. Press for the Institute of Race Relations.

Grindal, Bruce. 1972. *Growing up in two worlds: Education and transition among the Sisala of Northern Ghana.* New York: Holt.

Gummer, Canon S., and John S. Gummer. 1966. *When the Coloured People come.* London: Old Bourne.

Gurin, Patricia, Gerald Gurin, Rosina C. Lao, and Muriel Beattie. 1969. Internal-external control in the motivational dynamics of Negro youth. *Journal of Social Issues* **25**,3:29–53.

Guthrie, James W., George B. Kleindorfer, Henry M. Levin, and Robert T. Stout. 1971. *Schools and inequality.* Cambridge, Mass.: MIT Press.

Guttman, Ruth. 1963. A test for a biological basis for correlated abilities. In *The genetics of migrant and isolate populations.* edited by Elisabeth Goldschmidt. Baltimore, Md: Williams and Wilkins. Pp. 338–39.

Haddad, William F., and G. Douglas Puch, eds. 1969. *Black economic development.* The American assembly. Englewood Cliffs, N.J.: Prentice-Hall.

Hall, John Whitney. 1965. Education and modern national development. In *Twelve doors to Japan,* edited by John Whitney Hall and Richard K. Beardsley. New York: McGraw-Hill.

Haller, John S. Jr. 1971. *Outcasts from evolution: Scientific attitudes of racial inferiority, 1859–1900.* Urbana: Univ. of Illinois Press.

Harlan, Louis R. 1968. *Separate and unequal: Public school campaigns and racism in the Southern seaboard states, 1905–1915.* New York: Atheneum.

Harrington, Michael. 1967. The economics of protest. In *Employment, race, and poverty: A critical study of the disadvantaged status of Negro workers from 1865 to 1965,* edited by Arthur M. Ross and Herbert Hill. New York: Harcourt. Pp. 234–257.

Harrison, Bennett. 1972. *Education, training, and the urban ghetto.* Baltimore, Md.: Johns Hopkins Univ. Press.

Hawkridge, D. G., A. B. Chalupsky, and A. O. H. Roberts. 1968. *A study of selected exemplary programs for the education of disadvantaged children.* Washington, D.C.: U.S. Department of Health, Education and Welfare.

Hawthorn, H. B. 1944. *The Maori: A study in acculturation.* Menasha, Wis.: American Anthropological Association, Memoir, No. 64.

Haynes, Judith. 1971. *Educational assessment of immigrant pupils.* London: The National Foundation for Educational Research in Engla ᴵ and Wales.

Heber, Rick, and Richard B. Dever. 1969. Research on education and habilitation of the mentally retarded. In *Social-cultural aspects of mental retardation,* edited by H. C. Haywood. New York: Appleton.

Heller, Celia S. 1973. The emerging consciousness of the ethnic problem among the Jews of Israel. In *Israel: Social structure and change,* edited by Michael Curtis and Mordecai Chertoff. New Brunswick, N.J.: Dutton. Pp. 313–332.

Henderson, Vivian W. 1967. Regions, race, and jobs. In *Employment, race and poverty,* edited by Arthur M. Ross and Herbert Hill. New York: Harcourt. Pp. 76–102.

Herrnstein, Richard J. 1971. I.Q. *Atlantic Monthly* **228**:43–64.

———. 1973. *The I.Q. in the meritocracy.* Boston: Little, Brown.

Hess, Robert D., and Virginia C. Shipman. 1967. Early experience and the socialization of cognitive modes in children. In *Problems of children and youth in modern society,* edited by Gene R. Medinnus, Harold Keely, Karl Mueller, and Eldred Rutherford. New York: Selected Academic Readings.

Hicks, John D. 1937. *The federal union.* Boston: Houghton-Mifflin.

Hiernaux, J. 1968. *La diversité humaine en Afrique Subsaharienne.* Editions de l'Institut de Sociologie Université Libre de Bruxelles.

Hill, Clifford. 1970. *Immigration and integration: A study of the settlement of coloured minorities in Britain.* Oxford: Pergamon.

Hill, Herbert. 1968. Twenty years of state fair employment practices commissions: A critical analysis with recommendations. In *Negroes and jobs: A book of reading*, edited by Louis A. Ferman, Joyce L. Kornbluh, and J. A. Miller. Ann Arbor: Univ. of Michigan Press. Pp. 496–522.

Hill, H. S. 1936. Correlation between IQ's of bilinguals of different ages on different intelligence tests. *School and Society* **44:**89–90.

Hillson, Maurie, Francesco Cordasco, and Francis P. Purcell. 1969. *Education and the urban community.* New York: American Book.

Hippler, Arthur E. 1974. *Hunter's point: A black ghetto.* New York: Basic Books.

Hobbs, Nicholas. 1975. *The futures of children.* San Francisco: Jossey-Bass.

Hooper, Richard, ed. 1965. *Colour in Britain.* London: British Broadcasting Corporation.

Houghton, V. P. 1966. Intelligence testing of West Indian and English children. *Race* **8,**2:147–156.

Houston, Charles H. 1935. The need for Negro lawyers. *Journal of Negro Education* **IV:**49–52.

Huff, Sheila. 1974. Credentialling by tests or by degrees: Title VII of the Civil Rights Act and Griggs v. Duke Power Company. *Harvard Educational Review* **44:**246–269.

Hughes, John F., and Anne O. Hughes. 1972. *Equal education: A new national stragey.* Bloomington: Indiana Univ. Press.

Hull, C. L. 1943. *Principles of behavior.* New York: Appleton-Century-Crofts.

Hunn, J. K. 1961. *Report on Department of Maori Affairs.* Wellington: Government Printer.

Hunt, J. McVicker. 1961. *Intelligence and experience.* New York: Ronald Press.

———. 1964. The psychological basis for using preschool enrichment as an antidote for cultural deprivation. *The Merrill-Palmer Quarterly* **10:**209–248.

———. 1969a. Has compensatory education failed? Has it been tried? *Harvard Educational Review, Reprint Series,* No. 2. 130–152.

———. 1969b. *The challenge of incompetence and poverty: Papers on the role of early education.* Urbana: Univ. of Illinois Press.

Ingle, D. J. 1970. Possible genetic basis of social problem: A reply to Ashley Montagu. *Midway* **10:**105–121.

Inkeles, Alex. 1955. Social change and social character: The role of parental mediation. *Journal of School Issues* **11:**12–23.

———. 1968a. Social structure and the socialization of competence. *Harvard Educational Review, Reprint Series,* No. 1, 50–68.

———. 1968b. Society, social structure and child socialization. In *Socialization and society,* edited by John A. Clausen. Boston: Little, Brown. Pp. 73–129.

Inner London Education Authority. 1967. *The education of immigrant pupils in primary schools.* The ILEA Report. London.

Isaacs, Harold R. 1964. *India's Ex-Untouchables.* Cambridge, Mass.: MIT Press.

———. 1972. The Ex-Untouchables. In *The Untouchables in contemporary India,* edited by J. Michael Mahar. Tucson: Univ. of Arizona Press. Pp. 375–410.

Ito, Hiroshi. 1967. Japan's outcastes in the United States. In *Japan's invisible race: Caste in culture and personality,* edited by George De Vos and Hiroshi Wagatsuma. Berkeley: Univ. of California Press. Pp. 200–221.

Jackson, Jacquelyne Johnson. 1973. Black women in a racist society. In *Racism and mental health,* edited by Charles V. Willie, Bernard M. Kramer, and Bertram S. Brown. Pittsburgh: Univ. of Pittsburgh Press. Pp. 185–268.

Jackson, Reid E. 1947. The development and character of permissive and partly segregated schools. *Journal of Negro Education* **15**:301–310.

Janssen, Peter. 1972. OEO as innovation: No more rabbits out of hats. *Saturday Review* **55**:40–43.

Jencks, Christopher. 1969. Slums and schools—I & II. In *Education and the urban community: Schools and the crisis of the cities*, edited by Maurie Wilson, Francesco Cordasco, and Francis P. Purcell. New York: American Book. Pp. 26–40.

———. 1972. *Inequality: A reassessment of the effects of family schooling in America*. New York: Basic Books.

Jensen, Arthur R. 1961. Learning abilities in Mexican-American and Anglo-American children. *California Journal of Educational Research* **12**:147–159.

———. 1968. Social class and verbal learning. In *Social class, race and psychological development*, edited by Martin Deutsch, Irwin Katz, and Arthur R. Jensen. New York: Holt.

———. 1969. How much can we boost I.Q. and scholastic achievement? *Harvard Educational Review*, Reprint Series No. 2:1–123.

———. 1970a. Another look at culture fair testing. In *Disadvantaged child*. Vol. 3: *Compensatory education: A national debate*, edited by Jerome Hellmuth. New York: Brunner/Mazel. Pp. 53–101.

———. 1970b. Can we and should we study race differences? In *Disadvantaged child*. Vol. 3. *Compensatory education: A national debate*, edited by Jerome Hellmuth. New York: Brunner/Mazel. Pp. 124–157.

———. 1971. The race × sex × ability interaction. In *Intelligence: Genetic and environmental influences*, edited by Robert Canero. New York: Grune and Stratton. Pp. 107–161.

———. 1972a. Senate Select Committee on Education Statement of Dr. Arthur R. Jensen February 24, 1972. Unpublished manuscript.

———. 1972b. *Genetics and education*. New York: Harper.

———. 1973. *Educability and group differences*. New York: Harper.

Johnson, Charles S. 1930. *The Negro in American civilization: A study of Negro life and race relations in the light of social research*. New York: Holt.

———. 1935. The Negro college graduate: How and wher he is employed. *Journal of Negro Education* **4**:5–22.

———. 1938. *The Negro college graduate*. Chapel Hill: Univ. of North Carolina Press.

———. 1943. *Backgrounds to patterns of Negro segregation*. New York: Crowell-Collier.

———. 1966. *Shadow of the plantation*. Chicago: Univ. of Chicago Press.

Johnson, George M., and Jane Marshall Lucas. 1947. The present legal status of the Negro separate school. *Journal of Negro Education* **XVI**:280–289.

Jordan, Winthrop D. 1968. *White over black: American attitudes toward the Negro, 1550–1812*. Baltimore: Penguin Books.

Kagan, Jerome. 1973. What is intelligence? *Social Policy* July/August: 5:88–94.

Kahn, Tom. 1968. The economics of inequality. In *Negroes and jobs: A book of readings*, edited by Louis A. Ferman, Joyce L. Kornbluh, and J. A. Miller. Ann Arbor: Univ. of Michigan Press. Pp. 15–28.

Kaigo, Tokiomi. 1965. *Japanese education: Its past and present*. Tokyo: Kokusai Bunka Shinkokai (The Society for International Cultural Relations).

Kain, John F., ed. 1969. *Race and poverty: The economics of discrimination*. Englewood Cliffs, N.J.: Prentice-Hall.

Kane, Michael B. 1970. *Minorities in textbooks: A study of their treatment in social studies texts.* Chicago: Quadrangle Books.

Kaplan, David, and Robert A. Manners. 1970. *Culture Theory.* Englewood Cliffs, N.J.: Prentice-Hall.

Katz, Elihu, and Abraham Zloczower. 1970. Ethnic continuity in an Israeli town: Relations with parents. In *Integration and development in Israel,* edited by S. N. Eisenstadt, Rivkah Bar Yosef, and Chaim Adler. New York: Praeger.

Katz, Irwin. 1967. Socialization of academic achievement in minority group children. In *Nebraska symposium on motivation,* edited by D. Levine. Lincoln, Neb.: Univ. of Nebraska Press.

———. 1969. A critique of personality approaches to Negro performance, with research suggestions. *Journal of Social Issues* 25:13–27.

Katz, Irwin, and Patricia Gurin, eds. 1969. *Race and the social science: A survey from the perspectives of social psychology, education, political science, demography, economics and sociology.* New York: Basic Books.

Katz, Irwin, T. Henchy, and H. Allen. 1968. Effects of race of tester, approval-disapproval, and need on Negro children's learning. *Journal of Personality and Social Psychology* 8:38–42.

Katzman, David M. 1973. *Before the ghetto: Black Detroit in the nineteenth century.* Urbana: Univ. of Illinois Press.

Keesing's Research Report, #4. 1970. *Race relations in the USA.* New York: Scribner.

Kerber, August, and Barbara Bommarito, eds. 1965a. *The schools and the urban crisis.* New York: Holt.

———. 1965b. Preschool education for the developing cortex. In *The schools and the urban crisis,* edited by A. Kerber and B. Bommarito. New York: Holt. Pp. 345–349.

Killingsworth, Charles C. 1967. Negroes in a changing labor market. In *Employment, race, and poverty: A critical study of the disadvantaged status of Negro workers from 1865 to 1965,* edited by Arthur M. Ross and Herbert Hill. New York: Harcourt. Pp. 49–75.

———. 1969. Jobs and income for Negroes. In *Race and the social sciences: A survey from the perspectives of social psychology, education, political science, economics, and sociology,* edited by Irwin Katz and Patricia Gurin. New York: Basic Books.

Kirkpatrick, James J. 1973. Occupational aspirations, opportunities and barriers. In *Comparative studies of blacks and whites in the United States,* edited by Kent S. Miller and Ralph Mason Dreger. New York: Seminar Press. Pp. 355–373.

Kitano, Harry H. L. 1969. *Japanese Americans: The evolution of a subculture.* Englewood Cliffs, N.J.: Prentice-Hall.

Klineberg, O. 1935. *Negro Intelligence and Selective Migration.* New York: Columbia Univ. Press.

Kneller, George F. 1965. *Educational anthropology: An introduction.* New York: Wiley.

Knowles, Louis L., and Kenneth Prewitt, eds. 1969. *Institutional racism in America.* Englewood Cliffs, N.J.: Prentice-Hall.

Knowlton, Clark S. 1975. The neglected chapters in Mexican-American history. In *Mexican-Americans tomorrow: Educational and economic perspectives,* edited by Gus Tyler. Albuquerque: Univ. of New Mexico Press. Pp. 19–59.

Knox, Ellis O. 1947. The origin and development of the Negro separate school. *Journal of Negro Education* XVI:269–279.

Kobori, Larry S. 1972. What features of Japanese cultures and Japanese American history lend to their successful adaptation in American schools. Unpublished manuscript, Univ. of California, Berkeley.

Kohl, Herbert. 1969. *The open classroom*. New York: Random House.

Kohn, Melvin L. 1969. Social class and parent-child relationships: An interpretation. In *Life cycle and achievement in America*, edited by Rose Laub Coser. New York: Harper. Pp. 21–48.

Konvitz, Milton R. 1961. *A century of civil rights*. New York: Columbia Univ. Press.

Kozol, Jonathan. 1966. *Death at an early age*. Boston: Houghton-Mifflin.

———. 1972. *Free schools*. Boston: Houghton-Mifflin.

Kraus, Michael. 1966. *Immigration, the American mosaic*. Princeton, N.J.: Van Nostrand-Reinhold.

Krausz, Ernest. 1971. *Ethnic minorities in Britain*. London: MacGibson and Kee.

Krugman, Morris. 1965. Educating the disadvantaged child. In *The schools and the urban crisis*, edited by August Kerber and Barbara Bommarito. New York: Holt. Pp. 240–244.

L'Abate, Luciano, Yvonne Oslin, and Vernon W. Stone. 1973. Educational achievement. In *Comparative studies of blacks and whites in the United States*, edited by Kent S. Miller and Ralph Mason Dreger. New York: Seminar Press. Pp. 3235–354.

Lacey, C. 1970. *Hightown grammar: The school as a social system*. Manchester: Manchester Univ. Press.

Labov, William. 1972. *Language in the inner city: Studies in the black English vernacular*. Philadelphia: Univ. of Pennsylvania Press.

Ladenburg, Thomas J., and William S. McFeeley. 1969. *The black man in the land of equality*. New York: Hayden.

Leacock, Eleanor, B. 1969. *Teaching and learning in city schools: A comparative study*. New York: Basic Books.

Levine, Marvin J. 1972. *The untapped human resources: The urban Negro and unemployment*. Morristown, N.J.: General Learning Corporation.

Levine, Robert A. 1967. *Dreams and needs: Achievement motivation in Nigeria*. Chicago: Univ. of Chicago Press.

———. 1970. Cross-cultural study in child psychology. In *Carmichael's manual of child psychology*, (3rd ed.) Vol. 2, edited by P. Musson. New York: Wiley. Pp. 559–612.

Levine, Robert A., Nancy H. Klein, and Constance R. Owen. 1967. Father-child relationships and changing life-styles in Ibadan, Nigeria. In *The city in modern Africa*, edited by Horace Miner. New York: Praeger.

Levitan, Sar A. 1969. *The great society's poor law: A new approach to poverty*. Baltimore: Johns Hopkins Univ. Press.

Levitan, Sar A., William B. Johnson, and Robert Taggart. 1975. *Still a dream: The changing status of blacks since 1960*. Cambridge, Mass.: Harvard University Press.

Lewis, Oscar. 1958. *Village life in northern India: Studies in a Delhi village*. Urbana: Univ. of Illinois Press.

Lipset, Seymour Martin. 1973. The Israeli dilemma. In *Israel: Social structure and change*, edited by Michael Curtis and Mordecai Chertoff, New Brunswick, N.J.: Dutton. Pp. 349–362.

Lissak, Moshe. 1970. Patterns of change in ideology and class structure in Israel. In *Integration and development in Israel*, edited by S. N. Eisenstadt, Rivkah Bar Yosef, and Chaim Adler. New York: Praeger. Pp. 141–161.

———. 1973. Pluralism in Israeli society. In *Israel: Social structure and change*, edited by Michael Curtis and Mordecai Chertoff. New Brunswick, N.J.: Dutton. Pp. 363–378.

Little, Allan, and George Smith. 1971. *Strategies of compensation: A review of educational projects for the disadvantaged in the United States.* Paris: Organization for Economic Co-operation and Development.

Little, Kenneth. 1968. Some aspects of color, class, and culture in Britain. In *Color and race,* edited by John Hope Franklin. Boston: Houghton Mifflin. Pp. 234–248.

Loehlin, John C., Garner Lindzey, and J. N. Spuhler. 1975. *Race differences in intelligence.* San Francisco: W. H. Freeman.

Logan, Frank A. 1971. Incentive theory, reinforcement and education. In *The nature of reinforcement,* edited by Robert Glasser. New York: Academic Press.

Logan, Rayford W. 1933. Educational segregation in the North. *Journal of Negro Education.* **2.**

Long, Larry H. and Lynne R. Heltman. 1974. Income differences between blacks and whites, controlling for education and region of birth. A paper prepared for the 1974 Annual Meeting of the Population Association of America, April 18–20, New York City.

Lovegrove, M. 1964. Maori underachievement. *Journal of the Polynesian Society* **73:**70–72.

Luria, A. R. 1971. Towards the problem of the historical nature of psychological processes. *International Journal of Psychology* **6:**359–272.

Lyman, Stanford M. 1970. *The Asian in the West.* Las Vegas: Western Studies Center, Desert Research Institute, University of Nevada System; Social Science and Humanities Publications, No. 4.

————. 1973. *The black American in sociological thought: A failure of perspective.* New York: Capricorn Books.

Lynch, Owen. 1958. The politics of untouchability: A case from Agra, India. In *Structure and change in Indian society,* edited by Milton Singer and Bernard Cohn. Chicago: Aldine. Pp. 209–240.

Mabogunje, Akin L. 1972. *Regional mobility and resource development in West Africa.* Montreal: McGill-Queens Univ. Press.

Macarov, David. 1970. *Incentives to work.* San Francisco: Jossey-Bass.

Mack, R. 1968. Functions of institutionalized discrimination. In *Race, class, and power,* edited by R. Mack. New York: American Book. Pp. 341–344.

Mahar, J. Michael, ed. 1972. *The untouchables in contemporary India.* Tucson: Univ. of Arizona Press.

Manley, Douglas. 1960. The West Indian background. In *The West Indian comes to England,* edited by S. K. Ruck. London: Routledge and Kegan Paul. Pp. 3–50.

Maquet, Jacques. 1971. *Power and society in Africa.* New York: World University Library.

Marburger, Carl L. 1971. America's last frontier. In *Urban education in the 1970's,* edited by A. Harry Passow. New York: Teachers College Press. Pp. 141–153.

Marris, P., and M. Rein. 1967. *Dilemmas of social reform: Poverty and community action in the United States.* London: Routledge and Kegan Paul.

Marshall, Ray. 1967. *The Negro workers.* New York: Random House.

————. 1968. Industrialization and race relations in the southern United States. In *Negroes and jobs: A book of readings,* edited by Louis A. Ferman, Joyce L. Kornbluh, and J. A. Miller. Ann Arbor: Univ. of Michigan Press. Pp. 28–52.

Marshall, Ray, and Vernon M. Briggs, Jr. 1966. *The Negro and apprenticeship.* Baltimore: John Hopkins Univ. Press.

Mason, Philip, ed. 1967. *India and Ceylon: Unity and diversity: A symposium.* New York: Oxford Univ. Press, Institute of Race Relations.

Matras, Judah. 1970a. The Jewish population: Growth expansion of settlement and changing composition. In *Integration and development in Israel,* edited by S. N. Einstadt, Rivkah Bar Yosef, and Chaim Adler. New York: Praeger. Pp. 307–340.

——. 1970b. Some data on intergenerational occupational mobility in Israel. In *Integration and development in Israel,* edited by S. N. Eisenstadt, Rivkah Bar Yosef, and Chaim Adler. New York: Praeger. Pp. 223–248.

Mayo, M. J. 1913. The mental capacity of the American Negro. *Archives of Psychology* **5:**109–146.

McCreary, J. 1955. Maori age grouping and social statistics. *Journal of the Polynesian Society* **64,**1:16–21.

McEntire, Davis. 1960. *Residence and race.* Los Angeles: Univ. of California Press.

McPherson, Klim, and Julia Gaitskell. 1969. *Immigrants and employment: Two case studies in East London and in Croydon.* London: Institute of Race Relations.

McWilliams, Carey. 1964. *Brothers under the skin.* Boston: Little, Brown.

Means, John E. 1968. Fair employment practices legislation and enforcement in the United States. In *Negroes and jobs: A book of readings,* edited by Louis A. Ferman, Joyce L. Kornbluh, and J. A. Miller. Ann Arbor: Univ. of Michigan Press. Pp. 458–496.

Meer, Bernard, and Edward Freeman. 1966. The impact of Negro neighbors on white homeowners. *Social Forces* **45:**11–19.

Mencher, Joan P. 1972. Continuity and change in an ex-untouchable community of South India. In *The Untouchables in contemporary India,* edited by J. Michael Mahar. Tucson: Univ. of Arizona Press. Pp. 37–56.

Mercer, Jane R. 1973. *Labeling the mentally retarded: Clinical and social system perspectives on mental retardation.* Berkeley: Univ. of California Press.

Meriam, Lewis, ed. 1928. *The problem of Indian administration.* Baltimore: Johns Hopkins Univ. Press.

Metge, Joan. 1964. *A new Maori migration.* London: Athlone Press.

——. 1967. *The Maori of New Zealand.* New York: Humanities Press.

Metge, Joan, and Dugal Campbell. 1958. The Rakau Maori studies. *Journal of the Polynesian Society* **67:**352–86.

Meyerson, Michael. 1972. Puerto Rico: Our backyard colony. In *The Puerto Rican community and its children on the mainland: A source book for teachers, social workers, and other professionals,* edited by Francesco Cordasco and Eugene Bucchioni. Metuchen, N.J.: Scarecrow Press. Pp. 68–75.

Michelson, Stephan. 1972. Rational income decisions of blacks and everybody else. In *Schooling in a corporate society: The political economy of education in America,* edited by Martin Carney. New York: David McKay. Pp. 100–119.

Miller, D., and G. Swanson. 1958. *The changing American parent.* New York: Wiley.

Miller, Harry, L., ed. 1967. *Education for the disadvantaged.* New York: Free Press.

Miller, Herman P. 1971. *Rich Man, Poor Man.* New York: Thomas Y. Crowell.

Mingione, A. 1965. Need for achievement in Negro and white children. *Journal of Counseling Psychology* **29:**108–111.

Mitchell, Richard H. 1967. *The Korean minority in Japan.* Berkeley: Univ. of California Press.

Moore, Alexander. 1964. Realities of the urban classroom. Garden City, N.Y.: Doubleday.

Morris, Albert. 1955. Some aspects of delinquency and crime in New Zealand. *Journal of the Polynesian Society* **64,**1:5–15.

Mosteller, Frederick, and Daniel P. Moynihan, eds. 1972. *On equality of educational opportunity.* New York: Random House.

Myrdal, Gunnar. 1944. *An American dilemma: The Negro problem and modern democracy.* New York: Harper.

Nakane, Chie. 1970. *Japanese society.* London: Weidenfeld and Nicolson.

NAACP & Washington Research Project. 1969. *Title 1 of ESEA: Is it helping poor children?* (rev. ed.) New York: Washington Research Project and NAACP Legal Defense and Educational Fund.

National Advisory Council on Indian Education. 1974. *First annual report.* Washington, D.C.: U.S. Government Printing Office.

Nava, Julian. 1970. Cultural backgrounds and barriers that affect learning by Spanish-speaking children. In *Mexican-Americans in the United States: A reader,* edited by John H. Burma. New York: Schenkman. Pp. 125–134.

Newsom Report. 1963. *Half our future.* London: H.M.S.O.

New York City, Board of Education. 1972. *The Puerto Rican study, 1953–1957.* New York: Orioe Education.

New York State, Commission Against Discrimination. 1960. *Apprentices, skilled craftsmen and the Negro: An analysis,* New York City.

New York State, Department of Education. 1972. *Bilingual education.* Albany, N.Y.: Regents of the Univ. of the State of New York.

New York Times. 1974. *High court ruling blocks city-suburb school links.* July 26, p. 1.

New Zealand Government. 1961. *The Hunn Report: Report on Department of Maori Affairs.* Wellington: New Zealand Government Printer.

———. 1962. *Report of the Commission on Education in New Zealand.* Wellington: New Zealand Government Printer.

Norgren, Paul H., and Samuel E. Hill. 1964. *Toward fair employment.* New York: Columbia Univ. Press.

Northrup, Herbert R., and Richard L. Rowan, eds. 1965. *The Negro employment opportunity.* Ann Arbor: Bureau of Industrial Relations, Univ. of Michigan.

Ogbu, John U. 1973. *A new look at ghetto education: An alternative interpretation of black–white differences in academic achievement.* A paper delivered at the 73rd Annual Meeting of the American Anthropological Association, New Orleans.

———. 1974a. *The next generation: An ethnography of education in an urban neighborhood.* New York: Academic Press.

———. 1974b. Black school performance as an adaptation. Unpublished manuscript. Carnegie Council on Children, New Haven.

———. 1975. Castelike minorities. Unpublished manuscript, Carnegie Council on Children, New Haven.

———. 1976. *Socialization of competence in a doubletrack system.* Unpublished manuscript, Univ. of California, Berkeley.

Ohlin, Lloyd E., and Richard A. Cloward. 1960. *Delinquency and opportunity: A theory of delinquent gangs.* New York: Free Press.

Oliveras, Candido. 1972. What are the educational needs of Puerto Ricans who come to New York: In *The Puerto Rican community and its children on the mainland: A source book for teachers, social workers, and other professionals,* edited by Francesco Cordasco and Eugene Bucchioni. Metuchen, N.J.: Scarecrow Press. Pp. 246–251.

Orem, R. C., ed. 1967. *Montessori for the disadvantaged: An application of Montessori educational principles to the war on poverty.* New York: Capricorn Books.

Ortar, Gina R. 1967. Educational achievement of primary school graduates in Israel as related to their socio-cultural background. *Comparative Education* **4**:23–34.

Ovington, Mary White. 1911. *Half a man: The status of the Negro in New York.* New York: Schocken Books.

Padilla, Amedo M., and Rene A. Ruiz. 1973. *Latino mental health.* Rockville, Md.: National Institute of Mental Health.

Palmier, Leslie. 1967. Educational systems of southern Asia and social stratification. In *Papers in the sociology of education in India,* edited by S. M. Gore and I. P. Desai. New Delhi: National Council of Educational Research and Training. Pp. 147–172.

Parlimentary Select Committee on Immigration and Race Relations, Session 1972–3. 1973. *Education, Volume 1: Report.* London: H.M.S.O.

Parmee, E. A. 1973. *Formal education and culture change.* Tuscon, Arizona: Arizona Univ. Press.

Parsonage, William. 1956. The education of Maoris in New Zealand. *Journal of the Polynesian Society* **65**:5–11.

Parsons, Talcott. 1968. The school class as a social system: Some of its functions in American society. *Harvard Educational Review, Reprint Series,* No. **1**:69.-90.

Parsons, Theodore W., Jr. 1965. *Ethnic cleavage in a California school.* Unpublished Ph.D. thesis. Stanford Univ.

Passow, A. H., ed. 1963. *Education in depressed areas.* New York: Bureau of Publications, Teachers College, Columbia Univ.

———. 1971. *Urban education in the 1970's.* New York: Teachers College Press.

Patai, Raphael. 1958. *Cultures in conflict: Three lectures on the sociocultural problems of Israel and her neighbors.* New York: Herzl Institute Pamphlets 1.

———. 1973. Western and oriental culture in Israel. In *Israel: Social structure and change,* edited by Michael Curtis and Mordecai Chertoff. New Brunswick, N.J.: Dutton. Pp. 307–313.

Patterson, Sheila. 1963. *Dark strangers: A sociological study of the absorption of a recent West Indian migrant group in Brixton, South London.* Bloomington: Indiana Univ. Press.

———. 1965. Work. In *Colour in Britain,* edited by Richard Hooper. London: British Broadcasting Corporation. Pp. 75–89.

———. 1968. *Immigrants in industry.* London: Oxford Univ. Press, Institute of Race Relations.

———. 1969. *Immigration and race relations in Britain 1960–1967.* New York: Oxford Univ. Press, Institute of Race Relations.

Pechstein, L. A. 1929. The problem of Negro education in northern and border cities. *The Elementary Education Journal* **30**:192–199.

Pelled, Elad. 1973. Education: The social challenge. In *Israel: Social structure and change,* edited by Michael Curtis and Mordecai Chertoff. New Brunswick, N.J.: Dutton. Pp. 389–396.

Perrucci, Robert. 1967. Education, stratification, and social mobility. In *On education-sociological perspectives,* edited by Donald A. Hansen and Joel E. Gerstl. New York: Wiley. Pp. 105–155.

Pettigrew, Thomas F. 1964. *A profile of the Negro American.* Princeton: N.J.: Van Nostrand-Reinhold.

———. 1969a. The Negro and education: Problems and proposals. In *Race and the social sciences,* edited by Irwin Katz and Patricia Gurin. New York: Basic Books. Pp. 49–112.

———. 1969b. Race and equal educational opportunity. In *Equality of educational op-*

portunity, edited by Harvard Educational Review Editors. Cambridge, Mass.: Harvard Univ. Press. pp. 69–79.

Perlo, Victor. 1975. *Economics of racism, U.S.A.: Roots of black inequality.* New York: International Publishers.

Pierce, Truman M., James B. Kincheloe, R. Edgar Moore, Galen N. Drewry, and Bennie E. Carmichael. 1955. *White and Negro schools in the South: An analysis of biracial education.* Englewood Cliffs, N.J.: Prentice-Hall.

Ploski, Harry A., and Coscoe C. Brown, Jr. 1967. *The Negro almanac.* New York: Bellwether.

Plotnicov, L., and Arthur Tuden, eds. 1970. Introduction. In *Essays in comparative social stratification*, edited by L. Plotnicov and Arthur Tuden. Pittsburgh: Univ. of Pittsburgh Press, Pp. 3–25.

Pollitzer, William S. 1958. The Negroes of Charleston (S.C.): A study of hemoglobin types, serology, and morphology. *American Journal of Physical Anthropology* **16**:241–263.

Porteus, S. D. 1939. Racial group differences in mentality. *Tabulae Biologicae* **18**:66–72.

Postelethwaite, T. Neville. 1974. Introduction. *Comparative Education Review* **18**:157–163.

Pounds, Ralph L., and James R. Bryner. 1973. *The school in American Society.* (3rd ed.) New York: Macmillan.

Powdermaker, Hortense. 1968. *After freedom: A cultural study in the deep South.* New York: Atheneum.

Powell, Guy. 1955. The Maori school: A cultural dynamic? *Journal of the Polynesian Society* **64**:259–266.

Powledge, Fred. 1967. *To change a child: A report on the Institute for Developmental Studies.* Chicago: Quadrangle.

Price, John. 1967. A history of the outcaste: Untouchability in Japan. In *Japan's invisible race*, edited by George De Vos and Hiroshi Wagatsuma. Berkeley: Univ. of California Press.

Price-Williams, William Gordon Douglas, and Manuel Ramirez III. 1969. Skills and conservation: A study of pottery-making children. *Developmental Psychology* **1**:769.

Pyle, William Henry. 1915. The mentality of the Negro child compared with whites. *Psychological Bulletin* **12**:12,71.

Quarles Benjamin. 1964. *The Negro in the making of America.* New York: Macmillan.

Ramirez, Manuel, and Alfredo Castañeda. 1974. *Cultural democracy, bicognitive development and education.* New York: Academic Press.

Rao, M. S. 1967. Education, social stratification and mobility. In *Papers in the sociology of education in India*, edited by S. M. Gore and I. P. Desai. Delhi: National Council of Educational Research and Training. Pp. 127–146.

Reddick, L. D. 1947. The education of Negroes in states where separate schools are not legal. *Journal of Negro Education* **6**:290–300.

Rees, Helen E. 1968. *Deprivation and compensatory education: A consideration.* Boston: Houghton Mifflin.

Reich, Michael. 1972. Economic theories of racism. In *Schooling in a corporate society: The political economy of education in the United States*, edited by Martin Carnoy. New York: David McKay. Pp. 67–79.

Remba, Oded. 1973. Income inequality in Israel: Ethnic aspects. In *Israel: Social structure and change*, edited by Michael Curtis and Mordecai Chertoff. New Brunswick, N.J.: Dutton. Pp. 199–214.

Rex, John, and Robert Moore. 1967. *Race, community, and conflict: A study of Sparkbrook.* London: Oxford Univ. Press for the Institute of Race Relations.

Riessman, Frank. 1962. *The culturally deprived child.* New York: Harper.

Riles, Wilson, C. 1973. A master plan for urban education: The 1970 urban education task force. In *Black manifesto for education,* edited by Jim Haskins. New York: William Morrow. Pp. 41–56.

Rist, Ray C. 1972. *Restructuring American education. Innovations and alternatives.* New Brunswick, N.J.: Transaction Books.

Ritchie, James. 1956. Human problems and educational change in a Maori community; A case study in the dynamics of a social decision. *Journal of Polynesian Society* **65:** 13–34.

———. 1957. Some observations on Maori and Pakeha intelligence test performance. *Journal of the Polynesian Society* **66:**351–356.

———. 1963. *The making of a Maori.* Wellington: Victoria Univ. Publication in Psychology, No. 15.

———. 1968. Workers. In *The Maori people in the nineteen-sixties,* edited by Erik Schwimmer. New York: Humanities Press.

Ritchie, James, and Jane Ritchie. 1968. Children. In *The Maori people in the nineteen-sixties,* edited by Erik Schwimmer. New York: Humanities Press. Pp. 311–327.

Ritchie, Jane. 1957. *Childhood in Rakau: The first five years of life.* Wellington: Victoria Univ. Publication in Psychology, No. 10.

———. 1964. *Maori families.* Wellington: Victoria Univ. Publication in Psychology, No. 18.

Roberts, S. O., and Carrell P. Horton. 1973. Extent of and effects of desegregation. In *Comparative studies of blacks and whites in the United States,* edited by Kent S. Miller and Ralph Mason Dreger. New York: Seminar Press. Pp. 296–323.

Rose, E. J. B. 1969. *Colour and citizenship: A report on British race relations.* New York: Oxford Univ. Press for the Institute of Race Relations.

Rosen, B. 1959. Race, ethnicity, and the achievement syndrome. *American Sociological Review* **24:**417–460.

Rosenfeld, Eva. 1973. *A strategy for prevention of developmental retardation among disadvantaged Israeli preschoolers.* Jerusalem: The Henrietta Szold Institute. Research Report No. 175.

Rosenham, David L. 1967. Cultural deprivation and learning; an examination of method and theory. In *Education for the disadvantaged,* edited by Harry L. Miller. New York: Free Press. Pp. 38–45.

Rosenthal, Robert, and Lenore Jacobson. 1968. *Pygmalion in the classroom: Teacher expectation and pupils' intellectual development.* New York: Holt.

Ross, Arthur M. 1967. The Negro in the American economy. In *Employment, race and poverty,* edited by Arthur M. Ross and Herbert Hill. New York: Harcourt. Pp. 3–48.

Ross, Arthur M., and Herbert Hill. 1967. *Employment, race, and poverty: A critical study of the disadvantaged status of Negro workers from 1865 to 1965.* New York: Harcourt.

Ross, Arthur R. 1973. Negro employment in the South. Volume 3. *State and local governments.* Washington, D.C.: U.S. Department of Labor.

Rytina, Joan Huber, William H. Form, and John Pease. 1970. Income and stratification ideology: Beliefs about the American opportunity structure. *American Journal of Sociology* **75:**703–717.

Sasaki, Yuzuru, and George De Vos. 1967. A traditional urban outcaste community. In *Japan's invisible race,* edited by George De Vos and Hiroshi Wagatsuma. Berkeley: Univ. of California Press. Pp. 130–136.

Schermer, George. 1965. Effectiveness of equal opportunity legislation. In *The Negro and employment opportunity,* edited by Herbert N. Northrup and Richard L. Rowan. Ann Arbor: Univ. of Michigan Press. Pp. 67–107.

Schild, E. O. 1973. On the meaning of military service in Israel. In *Israel: Social structure and change,* edited by Michael Curtis and Mordecai Chertoff. New Brunswick, N.J.: Transaction Book. Pp. 419–432.

Schmidt, Fred H. 1970. *Spanish surnamed American employment in the Southwest: A study prepared for the Colorado Civil Rights Commission under the auspices of the Equal Employment Opportunity Commission.* Washington, D.C.: U.S. Government Printing Office.

Schulz, David A. 1969. *Coming up black: Patterns of ghetto socialization.* Englewood Cliffs, N.J.: Prentice Hall.

Schwimmer, Erik, ed. 1968. *The Maori people in the nineteen-sixties.* New York: Humanities Press.

Sears, Jesse B., John C. Almack, Percy E. Davidson, Walter H. Brown, Neils P. Neilson, Nancy Bayley, and David C. Green. 1938. *Stockton school survey.* Stockton: Board of Education, Stockton, California.

Segall, M. H., M. J. Herskovits, and D. T. Campbell. 1966. *The influence of culture on visual perception.* Indianapolis, Ind.: Bobbs Merrill.

Senior, Clarence. 1972. Puerto Ricans on the mainland. In *The Puerto Rican community and its children on the mainland: A source book for teachers, social workers, and other professionals,* edited by Francesco Cordasco and Eugene Bucchiono. Metuchen, N.J.: Scarecrow Press. Pp. 182–195.

Sexton, Patricia Cayo. 1961. *Education and income: Inequalities in our public schools.* New York: Viking.

———. 1968. City schools. In *Negroes and jobs: A book of readings,* edited by Louis A. Ferman, Joyce L. Kornbluh, and J. A. Miller. Ann Arbor: Univ. of Michigan Press. Pp. 222–236.

———. 1972. Schools: Broken ladder to success. In *The Puerto Rican community and its children on the mainland: A source book for teachers, social workers, and other professionals,* edited by Francesco Cordasco and Eugene Bucchiono. Metuchen, N.J.: Scarecrow Press.

Shack, William A. 1970. On black American values in white America: Some perspectives on the cultural aspects of learning behavior and compensatory education. Paper prepared for the Social Science Research Council: Sub-Committee on Values and Compensatory Education, 1970–71.

Shibutani, Tamotsu, and Kian M. Kwan. 1966. *Ethnic stratification: A comparative approach.* New York: Macmillan.

Shuey, A. M. 1966. *The testing of Negro intelligence.* New York: Social Science Press.

Shukla, Snehlata. 1974. Achievements of Indian children in mother tongue (Hindi) and science. *Comparative Education Review* **18:**237–247.

Siegel, Paul M. 1969. On the cost of being a Negro. In *Race, and poverty: The economics of discrimination,* edited by John F. Kain. Englewood Cliffs, N.J.: Prentice-Hall. Pp. 60–67.

Similansky, Moshe, and Sarah Similansky. 1967. Intellectual advancement of culturally disadvantaged children: An Israeli approach for research and action. *International Review of Education* **13:**410–429.

Similansky, Sarah. 1964. *Progress report on a program to demonstrate ways of using a year of kindergarten to promote cognitive abilities, etc.* Jerusalem, Israel: Henrietta Szold Institute.

Singh, K. K. 1967. *Patterns of caste tension: A study of intercaste tension and conflict.* London: Asian Publishing House.

Sivertsen, Dafinn. 1963. *When caste barriers fall: A study of social and economic change in a South Indian village.* New York: Humanities Press.

Smith, Thomas C. 1967. "Merit" as ideology in the Tokugawa period. In *Aspects of social change in modern Japan,* edited by R. P. Dore. Princeton, N.J.: Princeton Univ. Press. Pp. 71–90.

Southall, A. W., ed. 1961. Introduction. In *Social change in modern Africa,* edited by A. W. Southall. New York: Oxford Univ. Press.

South Stockton Parish. 1967. A statistical study of South and East Stockton. Mimeo.

Southern School News. 1956. Under survey. **3**(1):2.

——. 1957a. Types of major legislation adopted before 1957. **3**(4):2.

——1957b. Academic achievement and standards. **3**(12):13.

Sowell, Thomas. 1973. Arthur Jensen and his critics: The great I.Q. controversy. *Change* **5**:33–37.

Spear, Allen H. 1967. *Black Chicago: The making of a Negro ghetto, 1890–1920.* Chicago: Univ. of Chicago Press.

Spicer, Edward H. 1962. *Cycles of conquest: The impact of Spain, Mexico, and the United States on the Indians of the Southwest, 1533–1960.* Tuscon: Univ. of Arizona Press.

Spiro, Melford E. 1958. *Children of the Kibbutz: A study in child training and personality.* Cambridge, Mass.: Harvard Univ. Press.

Spradley, James P. 1972. The cultural experience. In *The cultural experience: Ethnography in complex society,* edited by James P. Spradley and David W. McCurdy. Chicago: SRA. Pp. 1–20.

Squibb, P. G. 1975. Education and class. In *The sociology of education: A sourcebook* (3rd ed.), edited by Holger R. Stub. Homewood, Ill.: Dorsey Press. Pp. 142–163.

Srinivas, Mysore N. 1962. *Caste in modern India and other essays.* New York: Asian Publishing House.

Stanley, Julian C., ed. 1973. *Compensatory education for children, ages 2 to 8: Recent studies of educational intervention.* Baltimore: Johns Hopkins Univ. Press.

Stein, Annie. 1971. Strategies for failure. *Harvard Educational Review* **41,**2:158–204.

Stewart, William. 1968. Continuity and change in American Negro dialects. *Florida Foreign Language Reporter* **6,**1.

——. 1970. Toward a history of American Negro dialect, In *Language and poverty: Perspectives on a theme,* edited by Frederick Williams. Chicago: Markham. Pp. 351–379.

Stockton Unified School District (SUSD). 1967. *Annual Report.* Washington Elementary School. Unpublished Manuscript.

——. 1968. *Annual Report.* Edision Senior High School. Unpublished Manuscript.

——. 1969. *Annual Report.* John Marshall Junior High School. Unpublished Manuscript.

Stockton Unified School District (SUSD), Minutes, Board of Education. 1968a. Feb. 27: Mrs. Fields asked about policy on teachers that demean Negro children. Pp. 4211–4212.

——. 1968b. May 14: Superintendent's reactions and recommendations to black unity council. Pp. 4251–4255.

——. 1968c. Nov. 26: Resolutions from Mexican-Americans united for action. P. 4422.

——. 1968d. Dec. 26: Response to Mexican-Americans united for action. Pp. 4428–4430.

———. 1969a. March 25: New courses approved for 1969–70. P. 4497.

———. 1969b. July 8: Report to the council for the Spanish-speaking and needs of Mexican-Americans. P. 4623.

Stoddard, Ellwyn. R. 1973. *Mexican Americans.* New York: Random House.

Stodolsky, Susan, and Gerald Lesser. 1971. Learning patterns in the disadvantaged. *Harvard Educational Review, Reprint Series,* No. 5, 22–69.

Stone, Chuck. 1972. The psychology of whiteness vs. the politics of blackness: An educational struggle. *Educational Researcher* **1,**1:4–6.

Strauss, George, and Sidney, Ingerman. 1968. Public policy and discrimination in apprenticeship. In *Negroes and jobs,* edited by Louis A. Ferman, Joyce L. Kornbluh and J. A. Miller. Ann Arbor: Univ. of Michigan Press. Pp. 298–322.

Strong, Alice C. Three hundred fifty white and colored children measured by the Binet-Simon scale of intelligence. *Pedagogical Seminar* **20:**485–515.

Sung, B. L. 1971. *The story of the Chinese in America.* New York: Collier.

Sutherland, I. L. G. 1947. Maori and Pakeha. In *New Zealand,* edited by H. Belshaw. Los Angeles: Univ. of California Press. Pp. 48–72.

Szasz, Margaret. 1974. *Education and the American Indian: The road to self-determination, 1928–73.* Albuquerque: Univ. of New Mexico Press.

Taeuber, Karl E. 1969. The Negro population and housing: Demographic aspects of a social accounting scheme. In *Race and the social sciences: A survey from the perspectives of social psychology, education, political science, demography, economics, and sociology,* edited by Irwin Katz and Patricia Gurin. New York: Basic Books.

Taeuber, Karl E., and Alma F. Taeuber. 1965. *Theory and processes of history.* Los Angeles: Univ. of California Press.

Thernstrom, Stephan. 1973. *The other Bostonians: Poverty and progress in the American metropolis, 1880–1970.* Cambridge, Mass.: Harvard Univ. Press.

Toledano, Henry. 1973. Time to stir the melting pot. In *Israel: Social structure and change,* edited by Michael Curtis and Mordecai Chertoff. New Brunswick, N.J.: Dutton. Pp. 33–48.

Totten, George O., and Hiroshi Wagatsuma. 1967. Emancipation: Growth and transformation of a political movement. In *Japan's invisible race,* edited by George De Vos and Hiroshi Wagatsuma. Berkeley: Univ. of California Press.

Truman, A. Roy. 1965. School. In *Colour in Britain,* edited by Richard Hooper. London: British Broadcasting Corporation. Pp. 98–103.

Turner, Ralph H. 1961. Modes of social ascent through education: Sponsored and contest mobility. In *Education, economy, and society: A reader in the sociology of education,* edited by A. H. Halsey, Jean Floud, and C. Arnold Anderson. New York: Free Press.

U.S. Bureau of Census. 1962. *U.S. census of population and housing: 1960. Census tract final report.* PHC(1)-153. Washington, D.C.: U.S. Government Printing Office.

———. 1972. *U.S. census of population and housing: 1970. Census tracts: Stockton, California, PHC(11)-208.* Washington, D.C.: U.S. Government Printing Office.

U.S. Commission on Civil Rights. 1967. *Racial isolation in the public schools: A report,* Vol. 1. Washington, D.C.: U.S. Government Printing Office.

U.S. Commission on Civil Rights. 1968. *Mobility in the Negro community: Guidelines for research on social and economic progress.* Clearinghouse Publication, No. 11. Washington, D.C.: U.S. Government Printing Office.

———. 1971a. *Report I: Ethnic isolation of Mexican Americans in the public schools of the Southwest: Mexican-American study project.* Washington, D.C.: U.S. Government Printing Office.

————. 1971b. Report II: The unfinished education: Mexican-American study project. Washington, D.C.: U.S. Government Printing Office.

————. 1972a. The excluded student: Educational practices affecting Mexican-Americans in the Southwest: Report III,: Mexican-American study project. Washington, D.C.: U.S. Government Printing Office.

————. 1972b. Report IV: Mexican-American Education in Texas: A function of wealth: Mexican-American education study. Washington, D.C.: U.S. Government Printing Office.

————. 1973a. Teachers and students: Report V: Mexican-American education study, differences in teacher interaction with Mexican-American and Anglo students. Washington, D.C.: U.S. Government Printing Office.

————. 1973b. The federal civil rights enforcement efforts—a reassessment. Washington, D.C.: U.S. Government Printing Office.

————. 1974a. Bilingual/bicultural education: A privilege or a right? A Report of the Illinois State Advisory Committee to the United States Commission on Civil Rights. Washington, D.C.: U.S. Government Printing Office.

————. 1974b. Toward quality education for Mexican-Americans: Report VI: Mexican-American education study. Washington: D.C.: U.S. Government Printing Office.

U.S. Department of Commerce, Bureau of the Census. 1972. Characteristics of the low-income population 1972. Series P-60, No. 91.

U.S. Department of Health, Education, and Welfare. 1970. Urban school crisis: The problem and solutions. A report of the HEW Urban Education Task Force. Washington, D.C.: Editors of Education, U.S.A.

U.S. Department of Interior. 1974. Statistics concerning Indian education. Washington, D.C.: Office of Indian Education Program, Bureau of Indian Affairs.

U.S. Department of Labor. 1971. The social and economic status of Negroes in the United States, 1969. BLS Report No. 375. Current Population Reports, Series P-23, No. 29.

————. 1973. Negro employment in the South: Vol. 3: State and local governments. Washington, D.C.: U.S. Government Printing Office.

U.S. Equal Employment Opportunities Commission. 1972. A unique competence: A survey of employment opportunity in the Bell System. Congressional Record, Feb. 17. Pp. E-1260–E-1261.

U.S. Government, Manpower Administration. 1973. A study of black male professionals in industry. Washington, D.C.: U.S. Government Printing Office.

U.S. National Advisory Commission on Civil Disorders. 1968. Report. Washington, D.C.: U.S. Government Printing Office.

U.S. Office of Education. 1972. Educational performance contracting. Washington, D.C.: U.S. Government Printing Office.

U.S. Senate, Select Committee. 1970a. Hearing before the Select Committee on Equal Educational Opportunity, Part 4—Mexican-American education. Washington, D.C.: U.S. Government Printing Office.

————. 1970b. Hearing before the Select Committee on Equal Educational Opportunity, Part 8: Equal educational opportunity for Puerto Rican children. Washington, D.C.: U.S. Government Printing Office.

————. 1971. Equality of educational opportunity: Report, Part 17: Delivery systems for federal aid to disadvantaged children. Washington, D.C.: U.S. Government Printing Office.

————. 1972. Report: Toward equal educational opportunity. Washington, D.C.: U.S. Government Printing Office.

U.S. White House Conference on Children. 1970. Profiles of children. Washington, D.C.: U.S. Government Printing Office.

Valentine, Charles A. 1968. *Culture and poverty: Critique and counter proposals.* Chicago: Univ. of Chicago Press.

———. 1971. Deficit, difference, and bicultural models of Afro-American Behavior. *Harvard Educational Review* **41**:137–157.

Vandenberg, Steven G. 1971. What do we know today about inheritance of intelligence and how do we know it? In *Intelligence: Genetic and environmental influences,* edited by Robert Cancro. New York: Grune and Stratton. Pp. 182–218.

van den Berghe, Pierre. 1967. *Race and racism: A comparative perspective.* New York: Wiley.

Van Zeyl, Cornelis J. 1974. *Ambition and social structure: Educational structure and mobility orientation in the Netherlands and the United States.* Lexington, Mass.: D.C. Heath.

Vernon, P. E. 1965a. Environmental handicaps and intellectual development. *British Journal of Educational Psychology* **35**:9–20, 117–126.

———. 1965b. Ability factors and environmental influences. *American Psychologist* **20**:723–733.

———. 1969. *Intelligence and cultural environment.* London: Methuen.

Vogel, Ezra F. 1967a. Kinship structure, migration to the city, and modernization. In *Aspects of social change in modern Japan,* edited by R. P. Dore. Princeton, N.J.: Princeton Univ. Press. Pp. 91–111.

Wagatsuma, Hiroshi. 1967a. Nonpolitical approaches: The influence of religion and education. In *Japan's invisible race,* edited by George De Vos and Hiroshi Wagatsuma. Berkeley: Univ. of California Press. Pp. 88–109.

———. 1967b. The pariah caste in Japan: History and present self-image. In *Caste and race: Comparative approaches,* edited by Anthony de Reuck and Julie Knight. London: J. & A. Churchill. Pp. 118–140.

———. 1967c. Postwar political militance. In *Japan's Invisible Race,* edited by George De Vos and Hiroshi Wagatsuma. Berkeley: Univ. of California. Pp. 68–87.

Wagatsuma, Hiroshi, and George De Vos. 1967. The ecology of special Buraku. In *Japan's invisible race,* edited by George De Vos and Hiroshi Wagatsuma. Berkeley: Univ. of California Press.

Wallace, Phyllis A. 1973. Employment discrimination: Some policy considerations. In *Discrimination in labor markets,* edited by Orley Ashenfelter and Albert Rees. Princeton, N.J.: Princeton Univ. Press.

Warner, W. Lloyd. 1965. Introduction: Deep South—a social anthropological study of caste and class. In *Deep South: A social anthropological study of caste and class,* edited by Allison Davis, Burleigh B. Gardner and Mary R. Gardner. Chicago: Univ. of Chicago Press. Pp. 3–14.

———. 1970. A methodological note. In *Black metropolis: A study of Negro life in a northern city,* Vol. 2, edited by St. Clair Drake and Horace R. Cayton. New York: Harcourt. Pp. 769–782.

Washington State Advisory Committee on Civil Rights. 1974. *Report on Indian education: State of Washington.* Washington, D.C.: U.S. Government Printing Office.

Wax, Murray L., and Robert W. Buchanan, eds. 1975. *Solving "The Indian problem": The white man's burdensome business.* New York: New York Times Book.

Wax, Murray L., Stanley Diamond, and Fred Gearing, eds. 1971. *Anthropological perspectives on education.* New York: Basic Books.

Wax, Rosalie H. 1967. The Warrior dropouts. *Transaction* **IV**:40–46.

Weaver, Robert C. 1946. *Negro labor: A national problem.* New York: Harcourt.

———. 1948. *The Negro ghetto.* New York: Harcourt.

Weaver, S. J. 1963. Interim report: Psycholinguistic abilities of culturally deprived children. George Peabody College for Teachers, mimeo.

Webster, Staten W. 1974. *The education of black Americans.* New York: John Day.

Weinberg, M. 1970. Desegregation research: An appraisal. (2nd ed.) *Phi Delta Kappa,* Bloomington, Indiana.

Weingrod, Alex. 1966. *Reluctant pioneers: Village development in Israel.* Ithaca, N.Y.: Cornell Univ. Press.

Wheeler, L. R. 1942. A comparative study of the intelligence of East Tennessee mountain children, *Journal of Educational Psychology,* **33:**321–334.

Whipple, G. 1967. The culturally and socially deprived reader. In *Education of the disadvantaged,* edited by A. Harry Passow et al. New York: Teachers College Press. Pp. 398–406.

White, Sheldon H. 1970. The national impact study of Head Start. In *Compensatory education: A national debate,* edited by Jerome Hellmuth. *Disadvantaged Child* **3:**163–184.

Whiteman, M., and M. Deutsch. 1968. Social disadvantage as related to intellectual and language development. In *Social class, race and psychological development,* edited by Martin Deutsch, Irwin Katz, and Arthur R. Jensen. New York: Holt.

Whiting, Beatrice B., ed. 1963. *Six cultures: Studies of child rearing.* New York: Wiley.

Wilkerson, Doxey A. 1970. Compensatory education: Defining the Issues. In *Disadvantaged child,* Vol. 3, *Compensatory Education: A national debate,* edited by Jerome Hellmuth. New York: Brunner/Mazel. Pp. 24–35.

Willhelm, Sydney M. 1971. *Who needs the Negro?* New York: Anchor Books.

Williams, John Smith. 1960. *Maori achievement motivation: Victoria University of Wellington Publications in Psychology No. 13.* Wellington: Department of Psychology, Victoria Univ.

Wilson, Alan B. 1969. *The consequences of segregation: Academic achievement in a Northern community.* Berkeley: The Glendenssary Press.

Wilson, H. Clyde. 1972. On the evolution of education. In *Learning and culture: Proceedings of the American Ethnological Society,* edited by Solon T. Kimball and Jacquetta Hill-Burnett. Seattle: University of Washington Press. Pp. 211–241.

Wise, Arthur E. 1972. *Rich schools, poor schools: The promise of equal educational opportunity.* Chicago: Univ. of Chicago Press.

Witkin, H. A., H. B. Lewis, M. Hertzman, K. Machover, P. B. Meissner, and S. Wapner. 1954. *Personality through perception.* New York: Harper.

Witkin, H. A., H. F. Paterson, D. R. Goodenough, and S. A. Karp. 1962. *Psychological differentiation.* New York: Wiley.

Woodard, C. Vann. 1968. *The burden of Southern history.* New York: Mento Books.

Woodson, Carter G. 1915. *The education of the Negro prior to 1861.* New York: Putnam.

Work, Monroe N., ed. *Negro year book: An annual encyclopedia of the Negro, 1931–1932.* Tuskegee, Alabama: Tuskegee Institute, The Negro Year Book Publishing Company.

Yinger, J. Milton. 1965. *A minority group in American society.* New York: McGraw-Hill.

Index

B
C 8
D 9
E 0
F 1
G 2
H 3
I 4
J 5